To Al

Congratulations on the Michigan Defenders of Liberty Award. It is obvious that the members of the party greatly appreciate all your efforts.

Keep up the fight for Liberty!

Autographed especially for our readers

LAISSEZ FAIRE BOOKS

FREEDOM IN CHAINS

ALSO BY JAMES BOVARD

The Farm Fiasco (1989)

The Fair Trade Fraud (1991)

Lost Rights: The Destruction of American Liberty (1994)

Shakedown (1995)

FREEDOM IN CHAINS

THE RISE OF THE STATE
AND THE DEMISE OF THE CITIZEN

James Bovard

St. Martin's Press
New York

Quotation in chapter 4 from Gordon Wood, "The Success of the American Revolution,"
reprinted by kind permission of Gordon Wood.

ISBN 0-312-21441-3

Library of Congress Cataloging-in-Publication Data

Bovard, James.
    Freedom in chains: the rise of the state and the demise of the
citizen / James Bovard
        p. cm.
    Includes bibliographical references and index.
    ISBN 0-312-21441-3
    1. Civil rights--United States. 2. Government, Resistance, to-
-United States. 3. Liberty. 4. State, The. I. Title.
JC599.U5B596 1999
320.1'0973--dc21   98-38006
                                                    CIP

First edition: February, 1999
10 9 8 7 6 5 4 3 2 1

CONTENTS

FREEDOM IN CHAINS

ONE

INTRODUCTION

The history of political thought is the history of the moral evaluation of political power.
—Hans Morgenthau, 1945[1]

PERVASIVE CONFUSION OVER THE NATURE OF GOVERNMENT AND FREEDOM has opened the gates to perhaps the greatest, most widespread increase in political power in history. If we are to regain and safeguard our liberty, we must re-examine the tenets of modern political thinking. We must reconsider the moral presumptions and prerogatives that have allowed some people to vastly expand their power over other people.

The State has been by far the largest recipient of intellectual charity in the twentieth century. The issue of government coercion has been taken off the radar screen of politically correct thought. The more government power has grown, the more unfashionable it becomes to discuss or recognize government abuses—as if it were bad form to count the dead from government interventions. There seems to be a gentleman's agreement among some contemporary political philosophers to pretend that government is something loftier than it actually is—to practice noblesse oblige and to wear white gloves when discussing the nature of the State.

The great political issue of our times is not liberalism versus conservatism, or capitalism versus socialism, but Statism—the belief that government is inherently superior to the citizenry, that progress consists of extending the realm of compulsion, that vesting arbitrary power in government officials will make the people happy—eventually. What type of entity is the State? Is it a highly efficient, purring engine, like a hovercraft sailing deftly above the lives of ordinary citizens? Or is it a lumbering giant bulldozer that rips open the soil and ends up clear-cutting the lives of people it was created to help?

The effort to find a political mechanism to force government to serve the people is the modern search for the Holy Grail. Though no such mechanism has been found, government power has been relentlessly expanded anyhow. Yet, to base political philosophy on the assumption that government is inherently benevolent makes as much sense as basing geography on the assumption that the earth is flat. Too many political thinkers treat government like some wizard of Oz, ordaining great things, enunciating high ideals, and symbolizing all that is good in society. However, for political philosophy to have any value, it must begin by pulling back the curtain to bare the nature of the State.

For many politicians and political commentators, government is not the problem; instead, the problem is people who don't appreciate government or who are insufficiently docile to its commands. President Bill Clinton declared in January 1997 that people can "make [America] better if we will suspend our cynicism" about government and politicians.[2] This is the Peter Pan theory of good government: government would be wonderful if only people would believe that it has magical powers.

Trusting contemporary governments means dividing humanity into two classes: those who can be trusted with power to run other people's lives, and those who cannot even be trusted to run their own lives. Modern Leviathans give some people the power to play God with other people's lives, property, and domestic tranquility. Modern political thinking presumes that restraints are bad for the government but good for the people. The first duty of the citizen is to assume the best of the government, while government officials assume the worst of him. Congressmen are far more fretful about private gun ownership than about the Federal Bureau of Investigation (FBI) using 54-ton tanks to gas the children of gun owners.

The history of the rise of the idealistic conception of the State is inevitably also the history of the decline of liberty. We cannot put the State on a pedestal without putting the people under the heel of the politician and bureaucrat. To glorify the State is to glorify coercion—the subjugation of some people to other people's wills and dictates.

The notion of the citizen's inviolable right to liberty—the underlying principle of the Declaration of Independence—has vanished from the American political landscape. Attorney General Janet Reno, in a 1995 speech vindicating federal actions at Waco, informed a group of federal law enforcement officers, "You are part of a government that has given its people more freedom . . . than any other government in the history of the world."[3] If freedom is a gift from the government to the people, then government can take freedom away at its pleasure.

Reno's comment epitomizes the shift in American political thinking away from the individual and towards the State as the fount of all good and all rights.

Welfare State freedom is based on the illusion that government can financially strip mine the citizens' lives without undermining people's ability to stand on their own two feet. Citizens are assured that dependence on government is the same as self-reliance, only better. Today's citizen is obliged to find his freedom only in the narrow ruts pre-approved by his bureaucratic overlords. In the name of "freedom," the citizen is obliged to lower the drawbridges around his own life to any government employee who thinks he knows better.

The Supreme Court declared in a 1988 decision "Servitude means 'a condition in which a person lacks liberty especially to determine one's course of action or way of life.'"[4] Yet, despite the vast increase in the number of government decrees restricting people's "course of action or way of life," there is little recognition of the growing servitude of the American people to the federal government. Lives are made up of choices. Insofar as government confiscates, nullifies, or decimates the choices that people can make, it effectively confiscates part of their lives.

DEMOCRACY AS PSEUDO-SAVIOR

Nowadays, "democracy" serves mainly as a sheepskin for Leviathan, as a label to delude people into thinking that government's big teeth will never bite them. Voting has changed from a process by which the citizen controls the government to a process that consecrates the government's control of the people. Elections have become largely futile exercises to reveal comparative popular contempt for competing professional politicians. The question of who nominally holds the leash has become far more important than whether government is actually leashed.

The ability to push a lever and register a protest once every few years is supposedly all the protection citizens' liberties need—or deserve. Americans are implicitly taught in government schools that they will be able to control their government, regardless of how large it becomes. But the bigger government grows, the more irrelevant the individual voter becomes. The current theory of democracy is a relic of an era when government was a tiny fraction of its current size. The illusion of majority rule is now the great sanctifier of government abuses—and perhaps the single greatest barrier to people understanding the nature of government. No amount of patriotic appeals can hide the growing imbalance between the citizen's power to bind the government and the government's power to bind the citizen. Does the appearance of someone's name on a ballot for political office automatically entitle that person to dispose of 38 percent of any voter's income?

Rather than "government by the people," we now have Attention Deficit Democracy. Less than half of the voters show up at the polls; less than half of the voters who do show up understand the issues; and politicians themselves are often unaware of what lurks in the bills they vote for. The larger government becomes, the less democratic it will tend to be, simply because people become less able to comprehend and judge the actions of their rulers. The great issue for modern democracy is whether politicians can fool enough of the people enough of the time to continue expanding their power over everyone.

Modern democracy is now largely an overglorified choice of caretakers and cage keepers. Are citizens still free after they vote to make themselves wards of the State? Supposedly, as long as citizens are permitted to push the first domino, they are still self-governing—regardless of how many other government dominos subsequently fall on their heads. Democracy is further corrupted by a demagogy that portrays a right to vote as a license to steal.

NIGHTSTICK ETHICS

Faith in the redemptive powers of government permeates contemporary political thinking. In 1993, Food and Drug Administration (FDA) Commissioner David Kessler, a regulatory hero among modern Statists, declared, "This morality, this moral glue that binds us together . . . to a great degree comes from the governments that we choose to conduct our affairs. The morality that the best of governments has to offer is what defines us as a nation, what makes us different, for better or for worse, from our neighbors on this planet."[5] (Kessler resigned a few years later after news reports and controversy over alleged expense account overstatements.[6]) Equating government with righteousness removes all the moral restraints to expanding political power.

"Fairness" has become a bewitching word, to lull people to sleep before politicians attach the latest "shackle-of-the-month." The more activities are criminalized, the fairer society supposedly becomes. The tighter the regulatory thumbscrews are twisted, the higher citizens' souls presumably rise.

Private citizens have become the moral underclass in the modern State. The values of politicians and bureaucrats are presumably so inherently superior that they have a right to coercively impose them on others, the same way that imperialists in the 1800s forcibly "saved" the backward natives in Africa and Asia. But now, instead of the "White Man's Burden," we have the "Bureaucrat's burden"—consisting of endless *Federal Register* notices, entrapment schemes, and abusive prosecutions. In practice, "justice" has become whatever serves the political or bureaucratic needs of the government. Every new definition of fairness becomes another trump card that politicians and bureaucrats play against private citizens. Public policy disputes routinely degenerate into morality plays in which the government is almost always the "good guy."

THE MIRAGE OF PATERNALISM

In the nineteenth century, socialists openly ridiculed the notion of a Night Watchman State—a government limited to protecting the rights and safety of citizens. The Night Watchman State has long since been junk heaped, replaced by governments zealous to reengineer society, control the economy, and save individuals from themselves. Unfortunately, rather than a triumph of idealism, we now have Highway Robber States—governments in which no asset, no contract, no domain is safe from the fleeting whim of a bevy of politicians. Public policy today is a vast maze of payoffs and kickbacks, tangling everything that the State touches in political intrigue and bureaucratic dependence. Modern societies are increasingly dominated by political money laundering—by politicians commandeering scores of billions of dollars from one group to foist on another group, from one generation to another, or from the general populace to specific occupational groups (such as farmers). And when government defaults on its promises to the citizenry, it is not robbery, but merely sovereign immunity.

Like Tom Sawyer persuading his boyhood friends to pay him for the privilege of painting his aunt's fence, modern politicians expect people to be grateful for the chance to pay for the fetters that government attaches to them. Former congressman James Byrnes warned in 1949 that "an individual will soon be an economic slave pulling an oar in the galley of the State."[7] Even though the average family now pays more in taxes than it spends for housing, clothing, transportation, and food combined,[8] tax burdens are not an issue for the vast majority of American political thinkers.

It was a common saying before the Civil War: "That government is best which governs least." Nowadays, the rule appears to be "that government is best that penalizes most." Salvation through increased State power means maximizing the number of Damocles swords hanging over each citizen's head—maximizing the number of individual lives that can be destroyed by political edicts, the number of people who can be locked away for possessing prohibited substances, whose homes and cars and wallets can be seized without proof of wrongdoing, whose children can be taken away from their parents, who can be barred from using their own land, and whom the government has pretexts to forcibly disarm.

The Welfare State offers an "under my thumb" recipe for happiness. Paternalism presumes that the path to the citizen's happiness consists in increasing the number of government restrictions imposed on him and the number of government employees above him. The more power government actuaries, the more the State becomes a symbol of the superiority of some people over other people. Every expansion of government budgets and statute books is another step towards the nationalization of the pursuit of happiness. While earlier types of government coerced people to keep them in their place, the Welfare State uses coercion to make them happy—in their place. But the success of the Welfare State cannot be measured by the number of citizens who rattle their tin cups when politicians pass by.

The issue is not whether government should or can be abolished; instead, the issue is whether the use of force should be minimized. In the American colonies from the early 1700s onwards, fierce disputes raged between prerogative parties and anti-prerogative parties—between those that favored an expansive interpretation of the king of England's power and those that sought to restrain or roll back the monarch's authority over colonists. In the future, the grand division in American politics will be between those who champion increased government power and those who demand that government power be slashed.

The notion that governments are inherently entitled to obedience is the most costly entitlement program of them all. Seventeenth-century English philosopher John Locke, who inspired the Founding Fathers, declared, "Tyranny is the exercise of Power beyond Right."[9] Locke recognized that governments that oppress citizens destroy their own legitimacy. Yet, there now seems to be an irrefutable presumption of legitimacy for any exercise of government power not involving genocide or racial discrimination.

To govern means to control. The question of the proper scope of government power is: "How many activities and behaviors should politicians be permitted to punish?"

Government is force, and we must consider the rightful limits and the moral sanction of that force. Government power is little more than political will enforced by bureaucratic aggression. What does the citizen owe the State? Or, more accurately, what does the citizen owe the politicians and bureaucrats who claim to represent and embody the State? By what metaphysical process does the government become superior to the governed? Does the creation of political machinery automatically void all prior restraints on the interference of one person with another person's life?

Modern political philosophy largely consists of glorifying poorly functioning political machinery—the threats, bribes, and legislative cattle prods by which some people are made to submit to other people. It is a delusion to think of the State as something loftier than all the edicts, penalties, prison sentences, and taxes that it imposes. This book will take an uncompromising look at the mechanics of political salvation.

Each person has a natural right not to be made a government pawn—a right to sovereignty over his own body, his own life, and his own peaceful actions. As Etienne de la Boetie, a sixteenth-century French thinker, observed, "It is fruitless to argue whether or not liberty is natural, since none can be held in slavery without being wronged."[10] The challenge is to calculate how far the sovereignty of each person over his own life must be abridged in order to preserve civil peace.

We will begin by seeking a clearer understanding of the nature of the State and of the meaning of freedom. We will then examine how the glorification of government leads to swollen democracies that crash and burn; consider how exalting government corrupts conceptions of justice, fairness, and equity; ask where government's right to command originates, and how far it extends; and conclude by considering the forgotten blessings of liberty.

Have we transferred to government the rights that we previously condemned in slaveowners? We cannot understand the current system of government without examining the premises upon which it is built and the principles upon which it acts.

THE GREAT PRETENDING: THE STATE, IDEAL & REAL

*Government power expands under cover of the beliefs enter-
tained about it.*
—Bertrand de Jouvenel, 1948[1]

*The State is only an obscure clerk hidden in some corner of a
governmental bureau.*
—William Graham Sumner, 1879[2]

MARK TWAIN, after enduring numerous marathon concert performances in Germany in the 1880s, concluded that "Wagner is better than he sounds." Similarly, political philosophers and political scientists have long assured Americans that government is more competent, more trustworthy, and more benevolent than it seems.

The more people that have died at the hands of the State this century, the louder some philosophers have preached that citizens need little or no defense against their rulers. From the First World War's trenches, to the slaughter of the Armenians, to the Soviet Gulag and the terror-famine in the Ukraine, to the Nazi Holocaust, to Mao's death camps, to Khmer Rouge experiments in urban renewal, the higher the body counts have risen, the more detached from reality some political observers have become. Amazingly, the State has retained its good name.

We shall review the development of the concept of the State in modern times to gain insight into current thinking about government. While few contemporary commentators explicitly invoke Rousseau or Hegel, the residue of their political and moral doctrines burdens hundreds of millions of people to this day. The idealist concept of government paved the way for a vast expansion of government power. While Statist ideas may have lost some of their panache, their legacy lives on in Leviathans around the world. To better understand how modern idealism became what it is—a philosophy far more inclined to idealize government force than individual choice—we need to retrace the origin of the concept of the State.

HOW THE STATE BECAME IMMACULATE

The Founding Fathers took a dim view of claims of the unlimited beneficence of government. George Washington declared, "Government is not reason, it is not eloquence—it is force."[3] John Adams wrote in 1772: "There is danger from all men. The only maxim of a free government ought to be to trust no man living with power to endanger the public liberty." Thomas Jefferson wrote in 1799, "Free government is founded in jealousy, not confidence. It is jealousy and not confidence which prescribes limited constitutions, to bind those we are obliged to trust with power. . . . In questions of power, then, let no more be heard of confidence in men, but bind him down from mischief by the chains of the Constitutions."[4] James Madison bluntly warned: "The nation which reposes on the pillow of political confidence will sooner or later end its political existence in a deadly lethargy."[5]

The Founding Fathers' views on government power were shaped by the fact that that power was held by an increasingly hostile foreign nation; thus, they had few incentives to delude themselves about the inherent goodness of government. Besides, they had seen government operate in Rhode Island—and that was all they needed to know about the potential degeneration of political institutions.[6] (Madison wrote of Rhode Island: "Nothing can exceed the wickedness and folly which continue to reign there. All sense of Character as well as of Right is obliterated.")[7]

However, a different intellectual tide was rising in continental Europe. As political scientist Carl Friedrich observed in 1939, "In a slow process that lasted several generations, the modern concept of the State was . . . forged by political theorists as a tool of propaganda for absolute monarchs. They wished to give the king's government a corporate halo roughly equivalent to that of the Church."[8] Thomas Hobbes, writing in 1651, labeled the State Leviathan "our mortal God."[9]

Jean Jacques Rousseau, with his 1762 book, *The Social Contract,* effectively made self-delusion about the nature of government into the highest political virtue. British political philosopher Harold Laski later noted, "Rousseau's theory of the general will made him . . . the modern founder of the idealist school of politics."[10] Rousseau's "idealistic" method was rarely more clearly stated than in the opening of his book, *Discourse on Inequality:* "Let us begin by laying facts aside, as they do not affect the question."[11] Rousseau propagated faith in absolute power at the same time he appeared to be preaching democracy: "The sovereign, being formed wholly of the individuals who compose it, neither has nor can have any interest contrary to theirs; and consequently the sovereign power need give no guarantee to its subjects, because it is impossible for the body to wish to hurt all its members. . . . The Sovereign, merely by virtue of what it is, is always what it should be."[12] Rousseau's doctrine of the General Will also created the perfect pretext to pretend that government is not coercive: the people were willing whatever government did to them. Rousseau recommended that a lawgiver "ought to feel himself capable . . . of changing human nature, of transforming each individual . . . into part of a greater whole from which he in a manner receives his life and being."[13]

While Rousseau's romantic glorification of democracy is well-known, his passion for unlimited government power is less recognized. In a short essay entitled "On Public Happiness," Rousseau declared in 1767, "Give man entirely to the State or leave him entirely to himself."[14] And Rousseau clearly believed that men could not be left to themselves. Rousseau also foresaw the need for the government to nullify private property. In an essay on a proposed constitution for Corsica, Rousseau declared, "In a word, I want the property of the state to be as great and powerful, and that of the citizens as small and weak, as possible. . . . With private property being so weak and so dependent, the Government will need to use very little force, and will lead the people, so to speak, with a movement of the finger."[15]

In *The Social Contract,* Rousseau declared, "The citizen is no longer the judge of the dangers to which the law desires him to expose himself; and when the prince says to him: 'It is expedient for the State that you should die,' he ought to die, because it is only on that condition that he has been living in security up to the present, and because his life is no longer a mere bounty of nature, but a gift made conditionally by the State."[16] Rousseau implied that people should be grateful that the government had not yet killed them. Thus, Rousseau vested in the State more power over the lives of the citizens than many southern states in the United States vested in slaveowners. (It was a crime for a slaveowner to wrongfully kill one his slaves, though such killings were not often punished.) Rousseau based his political philosophy on his own peculiar version of the "social contract": "The State, in relation to its members, is master of all their goods by the social contract, which, within the State, is the basis of all rights."[17] But Rousseau never explained why people would voluntarily put their heads on a political chopping block.

Rousseau's consecration of government power had vast influence on subsequent philosophers. German philosophers zeroed in on some of Rousseau's more absurd ideas and refined them into sufficiently obscure language that they commanded respect among academics for generations to follow.

Johann Gottlieb Fichte declared in 1809 in his "Addresses to the German Nation": "The State is the superior power, ultimate and beyond appeal, absolutely independent." Fichte had earlier advocated sharply limiting government power. But, as German humiliation grew over Napoleon's conquest and occupation of the German states, Fichte deified the State in order to give it the power to drive the French out of the German lands—and to purify the German people so that they would never again be conquered. Fichte wrote, "The end of the State is none other than that of the human species itself: namely that all its [humanity's] relations should be ordered according to the laws of Reason." And since the government alone was able to know what Reason dictated, that meant that it must have unlimited power to "rationalize" the citizenry. Fichte lifted the State above traditional moral standards: "It is the necessary tendency of every civilized State to expand in every direction. . . . Always, without exception, the most civilized State is the most aggressive."[18] Thus, the fact that a State successfully attacked its neighbors proved its moral superiority over its victims.

G. W. F. Hegel, renowned as the "Royal Prussian Court Philosopher" at the University of Berlin, matched Fichte and raised the ante of glorified servitude. According to Hegel, "The State is the Divine Idea as it exists on earth."[19] Hegel praised the State as the "realization of the ethical idea" and asserted that "all the worth which the human being possesses—all spiritual reality, he possesses only through the State."[20] Hegel revealed that the State is "the shape which the perfect embodiment of Spirit assumes."[21] Hegel opposed any limits on government power: "The State is the self-certain absolute mind which recognizes no authority but its own, which acknowledges no abstract rules of good and bad, shameful and mean, cunning and deceit."[22] Hegel also declared that "the State is . . . the ultimate end which has the highest right against the individual, whose highest duty is to be a member of the State."[23] Hegel stressed the benefits of war, and stated that "sacrificing oneself for the individuality of the State is . . . a general duty."[24]Hegel was also an early advocate of positive thinking: "In considering the idea of the State, one must not think of particular states, nor of particular institutions, but one must contemplate the idea, this actual God, by itself."[25]

Hegel was followed at the University of Berlin by Friar J. Stahl, who revealed that the State is "a moral and intellectual domain . . . a moral authority and power exalted and majestic, to which the subjects must submit."[26] Historian Heinrich von Treitschke, who became famous for his advocacy of Realpolitik, wrote that "if the State may not enclose and repress like an egg-shell, neither can it protect" and stressed that "the moral benefits for which we are indebted to the State are above all price."[27] Historian F. S. C. Northrup noted in his book *The Meeting of East and West*, "The development of German thought and culture following Kant clearly shows the individual person becomes swallowed up in the Absolute."[28]

Hegel's work increasingly dominated nineteenth- and early twentieth-century thinking about the State. German philosopher Ernst Cassirer observed in 1945, "No other philosophical system has exerted such a strong and enduring influence upon political life as the metaphysics of Hegel. . . . There has hardly been a single great political system that has resisted its influence."[29] Cassirer noted that Hegel's system "is an entirely new type of absolutism."[30]

Hegel's deified State doctrine found vigorous proponents in Britain. According to Oxford professor T. H. Green, "It is not supreme coercive power, simply as such, but supreme coercive power exercised in a certain way and for certain ends, that makes a State; viz. exercised according to law, written or customary, and for the maintenance of rights."[31] Thus, a true State could never violate a citizen's rights; thus, a State is automatically trustworthy—or else it would not be a State. Oxford Professor David Ritchie wrote in 1891, "The State has, as its end, the realization of the best life by the individual. The best life can only be realized in an organized society—i.e., in the State; so that the State is not a mere means to individual welfare; in a way, the State is an end to itself."[32] Oxford professor Bernard Bosanquet in 1912 urged readers to recognize that "the State is a name for a special form of self-transcendence, in which individuality strongly anticipates the character of its perfection."[33] Bosanquet wrote, "It is such a 'real' or rational will that thinkers after Rousseau have identified with the State. . . . The idea is that in [the State], or by its help, we find at once discipline and expansion, the transfiguration of partial impulses, and something to do and to care for, such as the nature of a human self demands."[34] In other words, subservience to politicians and bureaucratic regimes is necessary for the fulfillment of man's inner self. As Harvard University historian Adam Ulam noted in 1951, "Modern idealism in its most representative modern spokesman becomes . . . worship of the state. The church of the Middle Ages reappears in a new guise and the modern State is endowed with powers and significance in consequence of man's fallen status."[35]

Even the carnage of the First World War did not oust the State from its intellectual pedestal. German philosopher Ernst Troeltsch, writing in 1916, praised the "state mysticism" which "has created all that is great in the past German century."[36] University of London professor L. T. Hobhouse observed in 1918, "As a fashionable academic philosophy, genuine Hegelianism . . . the doctrine of the State as an incarnation of the Absolute, a super-personality which absorbs the real living personality of men and women, has in many quarters achieved the position of an academic orthodoxy."[37] British professor A. R. Wadia, writing in a 1921 article entitled "The State Under a Shadow," argued that the citizen has a duty to perceive the State—or, rather, to *imagine* the State—in the best possible light and always to presume that the State is innocent, regardless of how many million people it has killed.[38] Even two decades after the start of the First World War—and after the collapse of democracies across central and eastern Europe—Harold Laski considered the "idealist theory of the state" to be "the most widely accepted [theory of the State] at the present time."[39]

The cult of the State helped pave the way for the triumph of fascism. Guido de Ruggiero, author of the 1927 book *History of European Liberalism,* proclaimed that "the State, organ of compulsion par excellence, has become the highest expression of freedom."[40] The ultimate result of idealizing the State was to vest vast power in the hands of idealists like Mussolini and Hitler. Political scientist Carl J. Friedrich, writing in 1939, noted that the idea of "The 'State' as some kind of neutral god charged with looking after the national interest is . . . central in all dictatorial ideologies" spreading across Europe. Italian dictator Benito Mussolini declared in 1932, "The foundation of Fascism is the conception of the State, its character, its duty and its aim. Fascism conceives of the State as an absolute, in comparison with which all individuals or groups are relative, only to be conceived of in their relation to the State."[41] Professor Carmen Haider, writing in 1933, noted, "The Fascists draw their right of government control from the theory of the superiority of the State. . . . From it flow the principles of authority, hierarchy, discipline and control."[42] The State became portrayed as the equivalent of Nietzsche's Superman, exempt from traditional rules of good and evil. Yet, this was a parody of Nietzsche, who saved his sharpest contempt for the State, declaring that "whatever it says it lies; and whatever it has it has stolen. . . . It even bites with stolen teeth."[43]

Academics, politicians, and others habitually ignored or understated the coerciveness of government throughout the twentieth century. John Maynard Keynes hailed the Soviet Union in a 1936 radio interview as "engaged in a vast administrative task of making a completely new set of social and economic institutions work smoothly and successfully."[44] American churchman Sherwood Eddy wrote in 1934 that in Russia, "All life is . . . directed to a single high end and energized by such powerful and glowing motivation. . . . It releases a flood of joyous and strenuous activity."[45] American philosopher John Dewey visited the Soviet Union and proclaimed upon his return, "The people go about as if some mighty, oppressive load had been removed, as if they were newly awakened to the consciousness of released energies."[46]

While Western intellectuals painted the Soviet Union as a utopia, some communists had fewer illusions. In 1928 Grigori Pyatakov, one of six Soviet leaders personally named in Lenin's last testament, proudly declared, "According to Lenin the Communist Party is based on the principle of coercion which doesn't recognize any limitations or inhibitions. And the central idea of this principle of boundless coercion is not coercion by itself by but the absence of any limitation whatsoever—moral, political, and even physical. Such a Party is capable of achieving miracles. . . . "[47] Pyatakov was one of the stars of the 1937 Moscow show trials, confessing to ludicrous charges of sabotaging mines in Siberia, and was executed shortly thereafter.[48] Professor Virgil Michel, writing in 1939, noted, "Up to the very recent Russian developments, bolshevistic communism was by some liberals openly championed as the only source of hope for liberalism in the modern world."[49]

After 1945, the Soviet Union brutally suppressed any resistance in the Eastern European nations that its armies had overrun. Yet, as Ulam noted in his biography of Stalin, "Truman in his 1948 campaign said that he liked Uncle Joe, but alas, that Stalin was a prisoner of the Politburo."[50] Jean-Paul Sartre, France's most respected postwar philosopher, declared, "Soviet citizens criticize their government much more and more effectively than we do. There is total freedom of criticism in the U.S.S.R."[51] Members of the American Political Science Association in 1978 voted to cancel contracts for their annual conference in Chicago the following year to protest the fact that Illinois had not ratified the Equal Rights Amendment—at the same time they voted in favor of sending delegates to an International Political Science Association meeting in Moscow.[52] After controversy erupted in France in 1997 over a book on how communist regimes had killed up to 100 million of their own citizens, a French Communist Party spokesman sought to differentiate Stalin and other communist leaders from Hitler: "Agreed, both Nazis and communists killed. But while the Nazis killed from hatred of humanity, the communists killed from love."[53]

The idealist concept of the State initially faced rough sledding in the United States because it clashed with American experience. Mark Twain bragged that American legislators brought the highest prices of any legislators in the world. Though government employees began agitating for special pensions near the turn of the century, a congressional committee report noted that their effort got nowhere because many Americans were convinced "public service was a refuge for unemployables."[54] In a 1921 speech, James Reed, a Republican senator from Utah, denigrated people who came to Washington to become federal employees: "Examine in 99 cases out of 100 and you will find that they are failures and could not make a living at home."[55]

However, in the same period, the State was being championed as the great hope for American redemption. "The Best Shall Serve the State" was the motto of the Massachusetts Civil Service Reform Association.[56] Philosopher William James, in his 1910 essay entitled "The Moral Equivalent of War," proclaimed his belief in the "gradual advent of some sort of a socialistic equilibrium" and declaimed that moral progress could come from government de facto ownership of the citizens: "We should be owned, as soldiers are by the army, and our pride would rise accordingly. . . . All the qualities of a man acquire dignity when he knows that the service of the collectivity that *owns* him needs them."[57] (James, like many intellectuals glorifying the State in the late 1800s and early 1900s, avoided military service during the Civil War.) Herbert Croly, a Progressive author who heavily influenced Theodore Roosevelt, had boundless faith in government: "While it is true that an active state can make serious and perhaps enduring mistakes, inaction and irresponsibility are more costly and dangerous than intelligent and responsible interference." Croly proclaimed in 1909 that national life should be a "school," and that "the exigencies of such schooling frequently demand severe coercive measures, but what schooling does not?" Croly also informed his fellow citizens that "a people are saved many costly perversions" if "the official schoolmasters are wise, and the pupils neither truant nor insubordinate."[58] President Wilson declared that Americans should "marry our interests to the State."[59] Prof. Charles Haines argued that, rather than limit government power, "the American people should establish governments on a theory of trust in men in public affairs."[60] Haines surveyed American history and essentially concluded that damage control should be disregarded in designing political institutions. John Dewey stressed in 1916, "No ends are accomplished without the use of force. It is consequently no presumption against a measure, political, international, jural, economic, that it involves a use of force."[61] Dewey, who had boundless faith in government power, declared that "squeamishness about [the use of] force is the mark not of idealistic but of moonstruck morals."[62] Dewey enunciated a standard that would be widely used in subsequent decades to justify the expansion of government power: "Force becomes rational when it is an organized factor in an activity instead of operating in an isolated way or on its own hook."[63] Thus, as long as government officials claim to be well organized, force must be presumed to be rational, and thus superior to the "anarchy" of individual freedom. Yale law professor Thurman Arnold, later appointed by Franklin Roosevelt to be the nation's chief antitrust enforcer, declared that Americans needed "a religion of government."[64]

During the 1920s and early 1930s, the U.S. government provided huge loans to foreign nations whose exports were subsequently blocked by high U.S. tariffs, artificially held down interest rates and flooded the nation with cheap credit, and championed cartel operations by private businesses.[65] Economic historian Robert Skidelsky recently attributed the start of the Great Depression to the collapse in world grain prices[66]—a collapse directly tied to the disastrous attempt to corner the world wheat markets by the Hoover Administration's Federal Farm Board.[67] The federal government also severely reduced the currency supply from 1929 through 1932—thereby aggravating the economic slowdown.[68] After the stock market crash, politicians were quick to place the blame on laissez faire economic policies. President Franklin D. Roosevelt denounced the economic system of the 1920s as an "economic tyranny" and declared that "the collapse of 1929 showed up the despotism for what it was."[69] The selling of the Great Depression as proof of the failure of free markets was one of the greatest intellectual cons in history.

President Roosevelt declared in his first inaugural address: "We now realize . . . that if we are to go forward, we must move as a trained and loyal army willing to sacrifice for the good of a common discipline, because without such discipline no progress is made, no leadership can become effective."[70] The military metaphors, which practically called for the entire populace to march in lockstep, were similar to rhetoric used by European dictators at the time. Roosevelt had assured listeners in 1932, "The day of enlightened administration has come."[71]

FDR perennially glorified government power as the great liberator of the common man. In a 1936 message to Congress, he denounced his critics: "They realize that in 34 months we have built up new instruments of public power. In the hands of a people's government this power is wholesome and proper. But in the hands of political puppets of an economic autocracy such power would provide shackles for the liberties of the people."[72] Because FDR proclaimed that the federal government was a "people's government," good citizens had no excuse for fearing an increase in government power. The question of liberty became totally divorced from the amount of government power—and instead depended solely on politicians' intent toward the governed. The mere fact that the power was in the hands of benevolent politicians was the only safeguard needed.

Roosevelt sometimes practically portrayed the State as a god. In his 1936 acceptance speech at the Democratic National Convention, he declared, "In the place of the palace of privilege we seek to build a temple out of faith and hope and charity."[73] In 1937, he praised the members of political parties for respecting "as *sacred* all branches of their government."[74] In the same speech, Roosevelt assured listeners, in practically Orwellian terms, "Your government knows your mind, and you know your government's mind."[75] For Roosevelt, faith in the State was simply faith in his own wisdom and benevolence. Roosevelt's concept of the State is important because he radically expanded the federal government— and most of the programs he created survive to this day.

The members of Roosevelt's Brain Trust were confident of their ability to forcibly improve other Americans' lives. Assistant Secretary of Agriculture Rexford Tugwell, in a 1934 book that praised the Soviet Union's economic management, captured the spirit of the New Deal: "We have developed efficiency and science in the art of government. Our administrative, executive, and judicial bodies have proved competent to handle the most difficult matters."[76] Tugwell informed America: "We must now supply a real and visible guiding hand to do the task which that mythical, non-existent invisible agency was supposed to perform, but never did."[77] The Roosevelt administration's "guiding hand" paid farmers in 1933 to slaughter 6 million baby pigs (at a time of widespread hunger) and plow up 10 million acres of cotton fields (at a time when millions were wearing rags). The Agriculture Department was ridiculed for "solving the paradox of want amidst the plenty by doing away with the plenty."[78] Tugwell did concede that a major impediment to government planning in the United States was the "unreasoning, almost hysterical attachment of certain Americans to the Constitution."[79]

The more powerful the federal government became, the more avidly some politicians exalted government. Adlai Stevenson, the governor of Illinois and later a two-time Democratic Party presidential candidate, declared in 1948 "Government is more than the sum of all the interests; it is the paramount interest, the public interest."[80] Passion for the use of government force was hailed as the distinguishing trait of progressive thinking. Senator Joseph Clark of Pennsylvania wrote in 1953 that "a liberal is here defined as one who believes in utilizing the full force of government for the advancement of social, political, and economic justice at the municipal, state, national, and international levels."[81] President John F. Kennedy declared in 1963: "The Federal Government is the people and the budget is a reflection of their need."[82] Thus, the fact that politicians wanted to increase government revenue and expand their own power automatically proved that the American people had unmet needs—especially the need to pay more taxes. Liberals were not alone in putting government on a pedestal; Russell Kirk, one of the most respected conservative writers of the 1950s, declared, "Government is . . . a device of Divine wisdom to supply human wants."[83] Kirk's comment should be considered blasphemy by any religious enthusiast who imagines a deity possessing fewer character defects than the average congressman.

During the New Frontier in the early 1960s, Kennedy and his experts promoted the idea of government as an all-wise problem solver, the natural home of the "best and the brightest." President Lyndon Johnson declared in 1964: "I believe there is always a national answer to each national problem, and, believing this, I do not believe that there are necessarily two sides to every question."[84]

Hubert Humphrey, Johnson's Vice President and a three-time presidential candidate, denounced critics of government: "Candidates who make an attack on Washington are making an attack on government programs, on the poor, on blacks, on minorities, on the cities. It's a disguised form of racism, a disguised new form of conservatism."[85] Thus, anyone who did not support Big Government was practically the moral equivalent of a Klansman.

Today President Bill Clinton is devoting his presidency to persuading the American people that government is far more wonderful than they suspect. In a speech to the Democratic National Committee on January 21, 1997, he listed as one of the top achievements of his first term: "We ended the notion that government is the problem. . . . Make no mistake, our view prevailed. And you should be proud of it."[86] Clinton also sought to change the public perception of the presidency: "I think that it is my job to lead, challenge and take care of the country. And I suppose the older I get, the more it becomes the role of a father figure instead of an older brother."[87]

President Clinton does not have a monopoly of redemption aspirations in his family. Shortly after the president appointed her chief of the Task Force on National Health Care, Hillary Clinton declared that Americans suffer "from a sleeping sickness of the soul . . . we lack at some core level meaning in our individual lives, and meaning collectively, that sense that our lives are part of some greater effort, that we are connected to one another."[88] Ms. Clinton, echoing Rousseau, exhorted her audience: "Let us be willing to remold society by redefining what it means to be a human being." And naturally, increased government power is the only way to wake up people's souls. (Federal judge Royce Lamberth ruled in December 1997 that the Health Care Task Force violated federal law by refusing to publicly disclose the names of its members. He condemned high-ranking Clinton administration officials for being "dishonest with the court. . . . This type of conduct is reprehensible, and the government must be held accountable for it."[89])

GOVERNMENT = FORCE

Occasionally throughout the twentieth century, commentators have clearly recognized the coercive nature of government. British political scientist Harold Laski wrote in 1935, "At any critical moment in the history of a State the fact that its authority depends upon the power to coerce the opponents of the government, to break their wills, to compel them to submission, emerges as the central fact of its nature."[90] Political scientist Theodore Lowi, author of the 1969 book *The End of Liberalism,* observed, "Government is obviously the most efficacious way of achieving good purposes in our age. But alas, it is efficacious

SIDEBAR: STATISM AND THE CORRUPTION OF ECONOMICS

Blind faith in the State profoundly influenced the development of modern economics. French economist Frederic Bastiat labeled the State in 1847 as "the great fictitious entity by which everyone seeks to live at the expense of everyone else." But the view of another French thinker—socialist Etienne Cabet—seems to have had more influence on subsequent economic thought: "Nothing is impossible for a government that wants the good of its citizens."[91] The rising faith in the State contributed to the enthusiasm among economists and other professionals for increasing government power. Nobel laureate economist George Stigler noted in 1963, that, for the preceding century, "No economist deemed it necessary to document his belief that the State could effectively discharge the new duties he proposed to give it."[92] Stigler also observed: "The economic role of the state has managed to hold the attention of scholars for over two centuries without arousing their curiosity."[93] Instead, many economists based their policy prescriptions on the implicit assumption that government was full of wise Platonic guardians who automatically recognized the failures of the market and instinctively knew the remedies for all such problems.

The triumph of the Idealist concept of the State paved the way for schools of economics that portrayed government intervention as inherently redemptive. Keynesian economics is practically based on the notion that government officials are in possession of magic beans, and that regardless of how wasteful a government policy appears to be, the existence of the magic beans will cause the policy to increase society's wealth, or at least government revenue. The actual keys to the Keynesian policies were, naturally, not referred to as "magic beans;" instead, they were referred to as "multipliers." And government policies that, under traditional economic thinking, would have been seen as squandering capital and undermining living standards were "proven" to actually produce prosperity because of the existence of the magic beans/multipliers. Keynesianism championed the notion that politicians could spend taxpayers rich—or at least that the government could spend itself rich, which is even better than making the taxpayers rich. As political analyst Frank Chodorov observed, "The oft-used statement that 'we owe it to ourselves' is indicative of the tendency to obliterate from our consciousness the line of demarcation between governed and governors."[94] Keynes became so popular not because his theory was innovative, but because he provided a pretext that politicians gleefully seized upon to justify increasing their own power and buying reelection with tax dollars to be collected in the distant (post-election) future. By portraying government spending as the key to economic growth, Keynes' doctrines were invoked to sanction a vast expansion of government. A

1998 study for Congress's Joint Economic Committee noted that government expenditures of advanced industrial nations increased from 27 percent of Gross Domestic Product (GDP) in 1960 to 48 percent of GDP in 1996.[95] In a preface he wrote to the 1936 German edition of his *General Theory of Employment, Interest, and Money,* Keynes stated that his economic theory "is much more easily adapted to the conditions of a totalitarian state" than to "conditions of free competition and a large measure of laissez-faire."[96] Keynes' popularity was also due in part because of his implicit whitewashing of governments of any responsibility for inflation.[97]

because it is involuntary . . . modern policymakers . . . pretend . . . that the unsentimental business of coercion need not be involved and that the unsentimental decisions about how to employ coercion need not really be made at all."[98] Former British prime minister David Lloyd George put it bluntly in his 1933 memoirs: "What is a Government for except to dictate! If it does not dictate, then it is not a government."[99] As a 1940 federal court decision noted, "The 'State,' as used in political science, means the coercive force of government."[100]

What matters is not the rhetoric in politicians' speeches but the power in prosecutors' and enforcement agents' hands. Governments rest upon the statute book. The essence of a law is the threat of government force to compel obedience to a legislative or regulatory edict. The Supreme Court observed in a 1909 decision, "'Law' is a statement of circumstances in which public force will be brought to bear on men through the courts."[101] A 1996 Justice Department report observed, "The feature distinguishing police from all other groups in society is their authority to apply coercive force. . . . "[102] Throughout history, the mere acquisition of government uniforms has often been all that is required to legitimize coercion. As Carmen Haidar noted in 1933, "Once in power, the Fascists legalized their violence by employing it in the name of the State. . . . This step from illegal violence to state police methods is natural."[103]

The first question is not whether government is good or evil, but whether government is coercive—whether government relies on force to fill its coffers, enforce its commands, and impose its will. To get a clear understanding of the pervasive use and threat of force in daily government actions is the first step towards political realism.

Few issues make the nature of the State clearer than taxation. The average American worked until May 10 in 1998 simply to pay his taxes, according to the Tax Foundation.[104] The average family with two earners paid nearly as much in taxes in 1998 as their total nominal earnings in 1980.[105] Taxation permeates the lives of modern Americans. Taxes account, on average, for 31 percent of the price of a loaf of bread, 30 percent of the price of a hotel room, and 43 percent of the price of a bottle of beer.[106]

Taxation is not a mere technicality to be relegated to the footnotes of political science and public administration. Taxation goes to the heart of the relation of the citizen to the State: the higher the taxation, the greater the subjugation—the more that politicians are preempting individuals from building their own lives. Every increase in taxation is a proclamation that government knows best, and thus that politicians are entitled to commandeer more of the individual's paycheck and save him from himself.

American politicians and the Internal Revenue Service perennially proclaim the voluntary nature of income taxes. The IRS's 1992 Annual Report declared, "Our system of taxation is based on the willingness of citizens to assess and pay their taxes voluntarily."[107] Unfortunately, this is a doctrine that exists largely in the imaginations of politicians and the IRS public relations staff.[108] The U.S. General Accounting Office, in a 1995 report, noted, "In order to . . . encourage voluntary compliance with the Internal Revenue Code, IRS is authorized to seize and sell the assets of delinquent taxpayers and those who violate internal revenue laws. . . . "[109] IRS Commissioner Charles Rossotti told a Senate Committee in April 1998 that the IRS's Criminal Investigation Division's "primary mission is to foster voluntary compliance with our tax laws."[110] Author Daniel Pilla observed, "Virtually all of the constitutional rights regarding search and seizure, due process, and jury trial simply do not apply to the IRS. Its investigative powers are enormous; the IRS has more enforcement agents than the EPA, the OSHA, and the DEA combined."[111]

The U.S. Treasury Department defines a tax as "a compulsory payment for which no specific benefit is received in return."[112] No matter how many taxes a person pays or what politicians promise, the taxpayer is not irrevocably entitled to a single benefit from government. The fact that some people benefit from how their tax dollars are spent does not make the process of taxation any less coercive.

Assume that an individual is raising money for some worthy charity. He asks his neighbor for a contribution and the neighbor refuses. The individual then forcibly seizes the neighbor's paycheck, cashes it, and deposits the money into the worthy charity's account. Did the individual use coercion against his neighbor? Certainly. The question of whether the action was coercive is not determined by which bank account the neighbor's check is finally deposited into, but by how the paycheck was seized.

Or, to refine the analogy, if a mugger were sufficiently demented that, upon tearing wallets and purses out of people's hands, he rushed to the Treasury

Department and donated the loot to the general revenue fund of the United States of America, would that make his action any less coercive to his victims? What difference, then, would it make if the same guy were given an IRS badge and a government-issue semiautomatic pistol? The issue is not the purported purpose for which a government official knocked the citizen in the head or grabbed his paycheck. Instead, it is simply this: Was there a threat of eventual government force if the citizen did not surrender his money? One measure of the "voluntariness" of taxes is the tiny number of citizens who respond to the IRS's annual appeal, contained in its Form 1040 booklets, for voluntary contributions to reduce the national debt. In 1993, taxpayers bestowed a total of $1.8 million in gifts for this cause.[113] Americans paid $641,333 in Federal taxes under threat of legal penalty in 1993 for each dollar they voluntarily contributed to the IRS.

Laws are structured so that government agents rarely need to soil their hands with citizens' blood. For instance, IRS rules and regulations allow IRS agents to confiscate a citizen's bank account without a court order, without any proof of the citizen's wrongdoing, based merely on the IRS agent's unsubstantiated allegation that the citizen owes taxes. This power is exercised over three million times a year (six times more often than in 1979);[114] the IRS wrongfully seizes tens of thousands of bank accounts and paychecks each year, according to the General Accounting Office.[115] Such seizures are often accomplished by an IRS agent sending an official notice to a bank and some timid bank clerk kowtowing to the government's demand. The IRS routinely does not even officially notify citizens when it confiscates their savings and checking accounts; the only "notice" a person deserves, according to the IRS, is a notation on their monthly bank records informing them of their loss.[116]

Confusion and false representations over the nature of taxes permeate American political rhetoric. In December 1994, House majority leader Richard Gephardt denounced congressional Republicans as "trickle-down terrorists" because of their proposal to reduce federal income tax rates.[117] This phrase captures the contemporary enlightened attitude towards taxation: the terrorist is not the politician who strips the citizens of the fruits of their labor, or seizes almost half of their income for political purposes. Instead, the terrorist is that person who suggests that politicians confiscate less of the citizen's property. Government confiscation of a citizen's paycheck is a passive nonevent—but any proposal to reduce the amount of confiscation is equivalent to blowing up a federal office building.[118] When the Senate Finance Committee announced plans for a week of oversight hearings on IRS abuses in April 1998, Democratic senators hotly protested, fearing dire results if people perceived the extent of IRS heavy-handedness.[119] Instead, the Democrats sought to portray the agency as a victim of tax-dodging citizens, and to persuade people that the IRS is simply another federal agency—sort of like the National Park Service but with higher fees. President Clinton morally inverted the issue of taxation in November 1997 when, campaigning for a pro-tax Democratic candidate, he denounced Virginians who wanted a cut in taxes as "selfish." Clinton condescended to voters: "And think how you felt every time in your life you were tempted to do something that was selfish and you didn't do it, and the next day you felt wonderful."[120] Politicians' greed for additional revenue is the great moral non-event of the twentieth century.

Government coercion and penalties influence Americans' daily lives far more often than most Americans realize. One example of "death by regulation" is the Corporate Average Fuel Economy (CAFE) mandate. These regulations dictate that each automakers' total fleet of cars must achieve at least 27.5 miles per gallon on average. CAFE was mandated in 1975, in the midst of the panic over the Arab oil embargo; Congress decided to solve the nation's energy problems by forcing manufacturers to build cars that got better gas mileage. As Competitive Enterprise Institute lawyer Sam Kazman observes, CAFE "is an important factor in product design, manufacturing and marketing decisions, and even in plant locations."[121] Federal CAFE regulations are simply a government command to build smaller, lighter cars.

The regulations have done little or nothing to conserve gasoline, but have provided economic relief for funeral homes. A 1989 study by Robert Crandall of the Brookings Institute and John Graham of the Harvard School of Public Health concluded that CAFE regulations resulted in auto manufacturers building cars that weighed 500 pounds less on average than they otherwise would have weighed.[122] The lighter cars resulted in an increase of between 14 and 27 percent in auto traffic fatalities, an additional 2200 to 3900 deaths and up to 20,000 serious injuries over the ten-year lifetime of 1989 model cars. The *New York Times* noted in an editorial in 1991 that "CAFE has meant more fatalities and serious injuries as manufacturers have been forced to sell smaller cars to meet the standards."[123] A federal appeals court declared in 1992, "By making it harder for consumers to buy large cars, the 27.5 mpg standard will increase traffic fatalities."[124]

Government regulations are not mere expressions of codified benevolence. To regulate means to use or threaten force to subordinate private behavior to government commands. For instance, in New York City, building owners face a gauntlet of potential penalties. As author Jim Powell noted in the *Wall Street Journal*, owners face fines of up to $1,000 for illegally watering a lawn or flushing a sidewalk, up to $5,000 for failure to post a floor-numbering sign, up to $1,000 and a year in jail for recklessly or purposely failing to post a waste-collection sign, up to $1,000 for failure to post a sign about employee benefits, and up to $10,000 for failure to post a sign informing employees that the employer has no legal right to require them to take a lie detector test.[125] The hundreds of potential penalties turn government housing inspectors into petty czars, since almost every building will be in violation of at least one of the edicts.

Some citizens learn about the punitive nature of government after committing petty offenses. The District of Columbia government, after the heaviest snows in 70 years in the winter of 1996, failed to plow many residential streets. Yet, at the same time the government claimed it could not afford to clear its own roads, it launched its Solid Waste Education and Enforcement Program (SWEEP)—hiring 25 new inspectors to search for private homes and businesses with unraked leaves or other violations of city regulations.[126] Many residents received $25 tickets for not raking leaves in the two-foot area between the sidewalk and the street in front of their residences. The *Washington Post* noted, "Some residents said the District is 'fixated' on the public space between the sidewalk and the curb while the streets are filled with potholes and trash."[127] Some angry residents declared that they would not pay the fines. But the *Post* reported that Leslie Hotaling, a high-ranking official in the D.C. Public Works Department, "said it would be unwise for residents not to pay the fines because the city could put liens on their properties."[128] Thus, because of a few unraked leaves and a refusal to kowtow, a person could lose the title to his house. (At the same time the city government was cracking down on leaf hooligans, it had accumulated over 2,000 unsolved murders on its books from the previous decade—equal to almost one-half of one percent of the city population.[129])

Some politicians openly brag about the power that zoning regulations give them. In Chicago in August 1996, just before the Democratic National Convention opened, city inspectors arm-twisted many businesses near the convention site to erect fancy black wrought-iron fences around their sites, even though city regulations did not require such lavish decorations. The targeted area was on the dilapidated side, and many business owners saw no reason to spend thousands of extra dollars. Peg Kane, who owns a truck-leasing firm, said the government's action cost her $8,500 and that "they didn't need to come in here like the Gestapo." Mayor Richard Daley Jr. told the *Chicago Tribune:* "I've been hard all over the city. I kicked butt, in other words . . . I asked them to put up instead of a wire fence a wrought-iron fence. That's for me, the mayor."[130]

Chicago does not have a monopoly on visionary zoning dictates. Professor Gideon Kanner noted in 1998 that "the city of Norwalk [California] told an Indian Sikh congregation that its temple could not look like a proper Indian temple, but had to be disguised as an ersatz Spanish mission. How invading the Sikhs' religious freedom and forcing them to worship their God in a building that looks like a Spanish Catholic church advances any legitimate government policy has gone without explanation."[131]

The Montgomery County, Maryland, government sought to soften its image in 1995 by dropping the word "government" from the county seal, from government workers' business cards, and even from the sides of county government automobiles. County executive Douglas Duncan justified the change by saying that the word government was "arrogant" and "off-putting" and "didn't present the image of public service."[132] Duncan concluded that the word "government" sent the message: "We're in charge, and you'll do whatever we say." A memo to county government department heads explained that the word "government" was being removed because it "still screams 'bureaucracy' to many of our citizens."[133] But, at the same time that it pretended not to be a government, "Montgomery County" continued its efforts to compulsively micromanage the lives of local residents. These efforts included rigid racial quotas on schools (which prevented the transfer of half-Asian children from assigned schools)[134] and development restrictions that were intended to concentrate new business in a narrow corridor already strangled with traffic jams (to preserve "open space" elsewhere in the county).[135] Duncan admitted in a speech to a chamber of commerce that dealing with the county government was a "bureaucratic nightmare."[136]

Some academics seek to transcend the unpleasantries of day-to-day government action by stressing the benefits of intervention. Cass Sunstein, a highly respected law professor at the University of Chicago, recently argued: "Government regulation prevents coercion or chaos, and thus promotes liberty by making it easier for people to do or to get what they want. For example, the rules of the road . . . do not interfere with freedom, rightly understood."[137] If enforcing general rules that apply equally to everyone were all that police did, traffic laws would indeed be minimally coercive. But the "rules of the road" have been replaced by endless commands by government employees. Gerard Arenberg, executive director of the National Association of Chiefs of Police, observed, "We have so damn many laws, you can't drive the streets without breaking the law. I could write you a hundred tickets depending on what you said to me when I stopped you—the book is full of them."[138] Across the nation, governments are not merely enforcing general rules; they are setting up checkpoints to search cars and drivers for drugs, guns, alcohol, and other contraband, as well as to check drivers for signs of alcohol consumption, unfastened seatbelts, or other offenses.[139] Many local and state governments actively target and confiscate cars of drivers who violate one of a rapidly multiplying list of offenses. In 1996, Chicago suburbs enacted ordinances to authorize seizure of automobiles if a car radio is too noisy, or if the cars are being driven by teenagers out past 11:00

P.M.[140] Detroit officials seized 3,000 cars in 1995 from drivers who allegedly used their vehicles for trysts with prostitutes. They even seized the cars of innocent owners who had no involvement or knowledge of the crime.[141] District of Columbia police seized so many cars from "johns" that they lost count; many of the confiscated cars were destroyed by vandals who plundered police impoundment lots.[142] Perhaps Statists believe there is little difference between general, abstract rules governing the side of a street a person must drive on and the seizure of a specific person's car by a government agent. Supposedly, because government is needed to enforce some general rules to preserve a minimum of order, there is little or no need to minimize coercion. This is like saying that because there will always be some people who die of contagious diseases, there should be no effort to control a plague.

Asset forfeiture laws symbolize unlimited government power. Nowadays, a person has a right to his property, unless and until some government employee makes an accusation against him; then the government can take the title. Federal agents can seize a person's house, car, wallet, boat, or other property by invoking over a hundred different federal statutes, covering, for example, alleged offenses involving narcotics, wildlife, making large withdrawals from or cash deposits to a bank account, playing poker for cash with friends and relatives in one's home, or having too much cash in a wallet or luggage.[143] Since 1979, federal seizures of property under forfeiture laws have increased 25-fold; over $5 billion in property has been confiscated from accused private citizens and businesses.[144] Hearsay evidence is all that is required: A mere rumor or scrap of gossip can justify government seizure of a person's most valuable belongings.[145] Justice Department lawyer Irving Gornstein, arguing a forfeiture case for the Clinton administration before the Supreme Court in November 1997, claimed that the federal government had a right to confiscate practically any property involved in a violation of law. When pressed on this issue, Gornstein conceded to the Court: "I would except that one small category of cases where perhaps the property is involved in what might be a minor infraction such as a parking offense."[146] Thus, in the view of the U.S. Justice Department, Americans now stand in the same relation to government as English peasants stood to the king prior to Magna Carta, when the king's agents could automatically confiscate all the property of almost anyone convicted of any crime.

The threat of government punishment increasingly permeates everyday life. Law enforcement agencies arrested over 15 million Americans in 1996, according to the Federal Bureau of Investigation—almost 6 percent of the population.[147] Since 1973, the number of people confined in American prisons has increased by over 500 percent.[148] Almost 10 percent of all American males will end up in prison at some point in their lives, according to an estimate based on current trends in a 1997 Justice Department report, and almost one-third of black males will end up in prison during their lives.[149] Every week, 200,000 Americans have their bank accounts seized by the IRS, or have IRS liens put on their houses or land, or endure a tax audit, or receive notice of penalties and demands for additional taxes.[150] The number of different penalties the IRS imposes on taxpayers has increased more than tenfold since 1954. The number of federal crimes has increased from 3 in 1789 to over 3000 today. Police issue between 25 and 30 million traffic tickets per year, many the result of unnecessarily low speed limits, according to the National Motorist Association.[151]

Politicians often talk of how they wish to benefit, protect, or help the citizenry. But the tools of the State are limited. The State can impose new prohibitions and restrictions, create new penalties, or impose taxes in order to finance benefits. It is misleading to conceive of politicians offering both carrots and sticks: Government must first use a stick to commandeer the money to pay for the carrot. Every increase in the size of government means an increase in coercion—either an increase in the amount of a person's paycheck that government seizes or an increase in the number of types of behavior for which a government can jail, imprison, or fine a citizen. Every increase in government spending means an increase in political power—and a new pretext to seize private paychecks. Coercion is the essence of government in the same way that profit is the essence of private businesses. In the same way that businesses occasionally finance social projects in order to polish their public image, government occasionally engages in noncoercive activities. But, for both institutions, these are sideshows.

THE NEW PECULIAR INSTITUTION

Thanks to Supreme Court rulings in recent decades, it is now the law of the land that mandating a 60-second silent period in public school classrooms during which pupils might pray is coercive. However, prohibiting a person from getting almost any use of their own land is neither coercive nor foul play. Asking a suspect about a murder he may have committed without reading him his Miranda rights is coercive, while evicting a person from their own house is simply an issue of aesthetics. Terminating the employment of a political appointee after his party loses an election can be coercive, while throwing hundreds of thousands of low-skilled individuals out of work by raising the minimum wage is neither coercive nor a violation of any right those people possess. Requiring a 24-hour waiting period before getting an abortion is coercive, while forcing a person to spend three or more years and hundreds of thousands of dollars because of the delaying tactics of a federal agency is simply due process. Placing a crèche on a courthouse lawn during the holiday season involves psychological coercion against non-Christians, while sending policemen wearing guns into a closed bus and pressuring passengers to submit to searches and frisks is not coercive.

In order to understand the contemporary concept of the State, it is important to recognize the radical changes in the concept of coercion that have occurred in this century in federal courts, the halls of Congress, and elsewhere. The common use of the word "slavery" in the disputes of the Revolutionary period captured colonists' hatred of the arbitrary coercive power vested in British government officials and Parliament members. Even if that power was not used by every British colonial official on a daily basis, the mere fact that power existed in the statute books fatally compromised the colonists' freedom. In the mid-1800s, Southerners' habit of referring to slavery as "the peculiar institution" indicated their squeamishness about admitting the degree of coercive power that that institution required.

In modern times, we have a new "peculiar institution": government coercion. Many political thinkers' fixation on government benevolence obscures the reality of the growing subjugation of American citizens to government employees. Federal agencies have been able to seize far more power over citizens in part because judges and others have redefined many forms of government coercion out of existence.

The word "coercion" is not mentioned in the U.S. Constitution. However, the Bill of Rights is a compact to restrict the amount of force that the government can use against the citizenry. As one Pennsylvania writer observed in 1776, a constitution "*describes* the portions of power with which the people invest the legislative and executive bodies, and the portions which they *retain* for themselves."[152] A 1937 Senate report aptly declared that "the Constitution . . . is the people's charter of the powers granted those who govern them."[153] The Bill of Rights recognized the rights of American citizens—it did not bestow those rights on a conquered populace. Americans of the Revolutionary Era would only permit a national government to come into existence if the leaders of that government would solemnly pledge to limit their power in perpetuity. The Bill of Rights has never provided perfect protection, but it is an invaluable standard by which to judge the legitimacy of any law or government policy.

The word "coercion" was used in 378 Supreme Court decisions between 1960 and 1998. Many, if not most, of these cases involved convicted criminals who claimed that their confessions had not been fully voluntary or prayer in school and other issues involving religion. Supreme Court Justice William Douglas observed in 1957 that "it was obvious that coercion might be the product of subtlety as well as of violence."[154] In a 1991 case, the Court observed, "Our cases have made clear that a finding of coercion need not depend upon actual violence by a government agent; a credible threat is sufficient. . . . Coercion can be mental as well as physical, and . . . the blood of the accused is not the only hallmark of an unconstitutional inquisition."[155] The Court's action on police procedures has had a salutary effect in reducing the tyranny of law enforcement. (Unfortunately, some court decisions have gone overboard in sifting for supposed evidence that confessions were not completely voluntary.) But, while the Supreme Court and other federal courts were creating one new intricate rule after another on police questioning, the Court stuck its head in the ground regarding government agencies' abuse of peaceful citizens.

In the early 1900s, the Supreme Court often vigorously protected citizens' property and contracts (if not always their free speech) against the power grabs of legislatures and government agencies. But, after Roosevelt's threat to pack the Court in 1937, the Supreme Court wrote one blank check after another to federal agencies in the late 1930s and early 1940s—checks upon which the agencies are still drawing. In the 1938 case *U.S. v. Carolene Products Co.,* the Court upheld a 1923 federal law enacted to benefit dairy producers by banning the interstate shipment of evaporated milk mixed with coconut oil.[156] Geoffrey Miller, the associate dean of the University of Chicago Law School, observed: "The statute upheld in the case was an utterly unprincipled example of special interest legislation. The purported 'public interest' justifications . . . were patently bogus. . . . The consequences of the decision were to expropriate the property of a lawful and beneficial industry; to deprive working and poor people of a healthful, nutritious, and low-cost food; and to impair the health of the nation's children. . . ."[157] Canned milk mixed with coconut oil (so-called filled milk) was much cheaper than canned whole milk because coconut oil was much cheaper than butterfat. Filled milk was also healthier than fresh whole milk, because filled milk was sterilized at high temperatures while the fresh whole milk of that period often transmitted typhoid fever and tuberculosis. But the dairy industry hated the product because butterfat was the primary source of dairy farmers' profit. (The lobbying campaign against filled milk included racist depictions of Asians who did not consume as much whole milk as Americans[158]).

The Court swallowed Congress's assertion that filled milk encouraged consumer fraud, although the main evidence offered was that recent immigrants who could not read English might buy the product by mistake. Congress also claimed that filled milk "threatened the public health," but the only "threat" occurred because filled milk lacked the vitamin A that butterfat contained. There was no evidence that drinking filled milk deterred people from consuming vitamin A from other sources. By this same standard, Congress could have banned the vast majority of items sold in American groceries. Besides, for many consumers, it was not a choice of filled milk or whole milk, but of filled milk or no milk at all. Justice Harlan Stone wrote, "Regulatory legislation affecting ordinary commercial transactions is not to be pronounced unconstitutional unless . . . it is of such a character as to preclude the assumption that it rests upon some rational basis within the knowledge and experience of the legislators."[159] And how much evidence was necessary to presume a "rational basis" for legislation? "Any state of facts either known or which could reasonably be assumed" would suffice, Stone announced. Thus, as long as government only destroyed people's freedom to contract, or their freedom to work, or their freedom to use their own land, or their freedom to buy and sell, such coercion was unworthy of judges' notice.

Carolene Products enshrined the notion that the edicts of politicians have far more credibility than the voluntary decisions of private persons—that politicians are more trustworthy when seizing power over citizens' property than citizens are when using their own property. Federal judge Douglas Ginsburg in 1995 labeled the portions of the Constitution that safeguard property rights as "the Constitution-in-exile . . . banished for standing in opposition to unlimited government."[160]

One of the most important decisions for sanctifying increased government coercion occurred in 1942 in *Wickard v. Filburn.* The Supreme Court went hip-deep into one of the administrative law regimes created in the 1930s—and the justices basically made fools of themselves through their lack of understanding of federal policies. Their ruling led to the de facto takeover of every wheat farm.

From 1933 on, the Roosevelt administration used every means possible to drive up crop prices. But, by promising to pay farmers far more than the market value of their crops, the New Deal signaled farmers to grow far more than could be sold at inflated prices. Politicians encouraged farmers to overproduce, and then cited crop surpluses as proof of the need for political control of agriculture. Beginning in 1938, the Agriculture Department dictated how much wheat each of America's 1.5 million wheat farmers could produce. Government administrators could seize the title to a farmer's entire wheat harvest if he planted a single acre more wheat than federal farm bureaucrats permitted. When this policy was challenged by an Ohio farmer, the Roosevelt administration warned in its brief to the Supreme Court that it must have a free hand to "suppress . . . a public evil [crop surpluses]."[161] But the "evil" had been directly caused by lavish government subsidies. The court observed,

> The wheat industry has been a problem industry for some years. Largely as a result of increased foreign production and import restrictions, annual exports of wheat and flour from the United States during the ten-year period ending in 1940 averaged less than 10 per cent of total production, while during the

1920's they averaged more than 25 per cent. The decline in the export trade has left a large surplus in production which, in connection with an abnormally large supply of wheat and other grains in recent years, caused congestion in a number of markets. . . . [162]

But, the Court failed to mention that the Roosevelt administration had intentionally sabotaged wheat exports in order to isolate American farmers from world market prices and give politicians unlimited control over domestic prices. Federal agricultural policy drove domestic wheat prices to almost triple the level of world market prices in 1941; not surprisingly, few foreigners wanted to buy American wheat at exorbitant prices.[163] The Roosevelt administration first murdered the wheat exports, and then threw itself on the Court's mercy on the grounds that wheat farmers were orphans. The court further noted, "It is of the essence of regulation that it lays a restraining hand on the self-interest of the regulated and that advantages from the regulation commonly fall to others. . . . It is hardly lack of due process for the government to regulate that which it subsidizes."[164] The Court concluded that the government was justified even in restricting "the amount of wheat . . . to which one may forestall resort to the market by producing for his own needs."[165] The government's intent to benefit some wheat farmers gave government officials a right to absolutely control all wheat farmers, even those who were not selling their wheat.

A dozen years later, in *Berman v. Parker,* the Supreme Court blessed confiscation in the name of beautification. In 1954, the Supreme Court heard a challenge to a federal urban renewal program operating in the District of Columbia. The previous year, a federal district court had struck down the program, observing, "There is no more subtle means of transforming the basic concepts of our government, or shifting from the preeminence of individual rights, to the preeminence of government wishes, than is afforded by redefinition of 'general welfare,' as that term is used to define the Government's power of seizures."[166] But the Supreme Court overturned the lower-court decision and gave government officials almost unlimited power to confiscate and redistribute land.

Justice William Douglas, writing for the Court, declared, "The concept of the public welfare is broad and inclusive. The values it represents are *spiritual* as well as physical, aesthetic as well as monetary. It is within the power of the legislature to determine that the community should be *beautiful* as well as healthy, spacious as well as clean, well-balanced as well as carefully patrolled."[167] Douglas concluded, "Once the object is within the authority of Congress, the right to realize it through the exercise of eminent domain is clear." Professor Dennis Coyle characterized this decision: "The implicit message of the Court . . . was that in land use regulation, the king can do no wrong."[168] The resulting waves of urban destruction did long-term damage to the health of American cities; a 1998 *Washington Post* report cited the massive slum destruction campaigns of the 1950s and 1960s and the resulting dislocations as a major cause of the skyrocketing homicide rates in subsequent decades.[169] Law Professor John Nivala noted, "Cities and villages, townships and boroughs, have acquired an almost unreviewable authority to impose aesthetic standards on single-family housing—standards which . . . create 'a condition of conformity that makes it impossible to differentiate one locale from another.'"[170]

Douglas also declared in that decision, "When the legislature has spoken, the public interest has been declared in terms well-nigh conclusive." Almost 30 years later, in *Chevron v. Natural Resources Defense Council*, the Court awarded sweeping discretion to federal agencies to interpret federal laws as they chose—and thus, in many cases, to decree the limits of their own power.[171] Lawyer Michael Greve, the director of the Center for Individual Rights, observed that the Supreme Court now relies on an "insanity test—if an agency's interpretation of a federal statute is not clinically insane, then it stands."[172] The combination of the Court's acceptance of legislatures' definition of the public interest and its deference toward government agencies' interpretations of laws creates an overwhelming bias against citizens seeking relief from government oppression. Law professor E. P. Krauss observed that "judicial review is played out like a cynical shell game, in which the government always wins and the institutional checks and balances of administrative power are proven to be ineffectual."[173]

Since the 1930s, Supreme Court decisions have routinely rested on a blanket assumption that whatever any legislature does is "to promote the general welfare." As historian James Ely noted, "Since 1937 the Supreme Court has not overruled any economic or social legislation on due process grounds."[174] In a 1955 case upholding an Oklahoma law that severely restricted the practice of opticians, Justice Douglas declared: "It is enough that there is an evil at hand for correction, and that it might be thought that the particular legislative measure was a rational way to correct it."[175] Thus, the mere existence of alleged private evil is all that is required to sanctify almost any political seizure of power. (The Court does not show such naivete towards politicians' motives in First Amendment legislation).

In the twentieth century, the Supreme Court has "defined down" coercion by rewriting the "state action" doctrine to allow politicians and judges to pretend, in more and more cases, that government force or threats were not used. The Supreme Court's creativity in not discovering coercion reached new heights in its 1979 decision in *United Steel Workers of America v. Weber*.[176] In 1974, Kaiser Aluminum, which supplied materials to the Defense Department, came under severe pressure from the Office of Federal Contract Compliance to institute a training quota program to increase the number of blacks promoted to more skilled positions. (The name of the agency was later changed to Office of Federal Contract Compliance Programs—OFCCP.) Kaiser, with the cooperation of the steelworkers union, imposed a racial quota for a training program for carpenters, electricians, machinists, and other crafts, mandating that 39 percent of all people admitted to the program must be black. (This number was chosen because it equaled the percentage of blacks in the local area, without regard to how many had the experience and ability necessary to enter the training program.) Brian Weber, a white steelworker, was denied entry into the training program even though he had higher scores on the admission test than did several blacks who were accepted. Weber sued, claiming that the racial preferences violated his civil rights.

The case turned on whether the racial hiring targets imposed on federal contractors were mandatory. If a company fails to satisfy the OFCCP, it can be debarred from receiving any federal contracts. For many businesses, this is equivalent to a death penalty. Assistant Secretary of Labor Bernard Anderson later described the federal power of contract debarment as "a kind of nuclear bomb."[177] The fact that a corporation or university has a single federal contract of over $50,000 automatically gives federal regulators veto power over many of its personnel policies. (Over 25 million people work for private companies, universities, and other groups under OFCCP jurisdiction.)

Even though the 1964 Civil Rights Act made racial discrimination in hiring or promotions a violation of federal law, the Supreme Court denied that Weber's rights had been violated. Justice William Brennan stressed the Court's concern to "avoid undue federal regulation of private business"—even though the racial quota was implemented in response to federal threats. The Court ruled that a company may "trammel the interests of the white employees" in favor of black employees in order to eliminate "racial imbalance"—even though any such trammeling of black employees for any reason would have been illegal. The Court repeatedly insisted that the Kaiser quota was "voluntary," contradicting a decision by a federal appeals court. Justice Brennan also justified the plan because it was temporary—even though it would take 30 years to reach the racial targets the company set.[178]

Chief Justice Warren Burger condemned the ruling as "intellectually dishonest." Justice William Rehnquist compared the majority's tortured rationale in the decision to George Orwell's novel *1984* and noted, "The OFCC employs the 'power of the purse' to coerce acceptance of its affirmative action plans. . . . The Court's frequent references to the 'voluntary' nature of Kaiser's racially discriminatory admission quota bear no relationship to the facts of this case."[179] Herman Belz, author of *Equality Transformed,* observed, "*Weber* transformed Title VII [of the Civil Rights Act of 1964] from a law to protect individual employees irrespective of race into a law for the protection of employers who were forced to adopt racial hiring practices."[180] As long as politicians and bureaucrats evoked "goals and timetables," the resulting de facto quotas were assumed to be noncoercive, regardless of how large the hammer waiting to fall on any company that missed a goal or schedule. By legitimizing coercive racial quotas, the Weber decision helped sow the seeds for renewed racial animosity.

Further insight into the disappearance of the concept of government coercion can be gained from an examination of how congressmen use—and don't use—the word "coercion." "Coercion" was a term commonly used by the Founding Fathers to describe the abuses of British colonial rulers. However, nowadays, one could read thousands of pages of the *Congressional Record* and never realize that the federal government coerces any citizen.

During the 104th Congress (January 1995 through October 1996), the word "coercion" appeared in 176 entries of the *Congressional Record*. Considering that the *Record* for those years totaled 65,162 small-print pages, the word "coercion" was conspicuous by its absence.

A cursory examination of the *Record* shows that congressmen are far more concerned to prevent the coercion of foreigners and foreign governments than of American citizens. Coercion was mentioned 32 times in reference to coercion of foreigners by foreign governments, including concerns about coercion of the East Timorese by the Indonesians and concern about Russian coercion of the Ukraine.

The single example of coercion that most concerned congressmen involved U.S. government contributions to the United Nations Population Fund, which was accused of financing forced abortions in communist China. This issue was raised 18 times in the 104th Congress—more than 10 percent of all references to coercion.

The word "coercion" was mentioned 16 times in relation to the official definition of terrorism in proposed antiterrorist legislation. However, the final act was concerned solely with coercion of governments, not citizens.[181]

Federal policies that allegedly coerced local and state governments were mentioned 8 times, including comments about prison construction mandates and the effect of welfare reform on state governments.

Congressmen used the word "coercion" 24 times in condemning or warning against allegedly abusive private behavior, including several references to companies that fired workers after they walked out during strikes and coercion by drug dealers and pornographers.

Nine congressmen spoke of their fears of private HMOs coercing Medicare patients with higher fees or terminations as a result of Medicare reform. Sen. Chris Dodd, a Connecticut Democrat, complained that the Republican plan to reform Medicare would result in "financial coercion" of Medicare patients: "Seniors choosing to remain in the fee-per-service part of Medicare would face more than $1,000 a year or more in added premiums, co-payments and deductibles."[182] There were no comments made in the 104th Congress about the coercion suffered by young people heavily taxed to finance Medicare benefits for affluent senior citizens.

There were 4 mentions of coercion of either Congress or the president as a result of the passage of the Line Item Veto Act and 2 mentions of coercion regarding the budget impasse in late 1995 and early 1996. On November 13, 1995, Senate Minority Leader Tom Daschle bewailed, "This is the Republican effort to coerce the President to sign legislation that otherwise he would veto; to sign legislation that he philosophically finds at fault. . . . "[183] (Republicans rejected President Clinton's demands for higher federal deficit spending.)[184] Any legislative action that prevents politicians from continuing to spend more money than government collects is presumed coercive.

Congressmen referred to the coercion of private citizens by the federal government or by federal laws only 15 times—less than 10 percent of all mentions of the word "coercion." There were three references to coercive federal labor laws, and 1 reference each to the coercive burden of taxes, plans for national ID cards, federal racial preferences, the television V-chip, economically targeted investments, imprisonment for civil contempt of court, new FDA rules on teen smoking, the public debt, the Supreme Court's rulings on religion, police interrogations, and citizens' right to own firearms.

Coercion by federal agencies or by federal laws was mentioned an average of once every 4000 pages of the *Congressional Record*. Of course, not all references by congressmen to abusive federal agencies or policies would be captured by the word "coercion." But the fact that coercion was commonly used to refer to the actions of foreign governments makes it a fair measure of congressmen's concerns about the actions of the United States government.

In the classic theory of republican government, one of the representatives' highest duties was to protect voters from the abuses of executive agencies. Edmund Burke declared that Parliament "was not instituted to be a control *upon the* people. . . . It was designed as a control *for* the people."[185] Charles Carroll of Maryland, one of the signers of the Declaration of Independence, declared that it was the task of elected representatives "to examine severely, and judge impartially the conduct and the measures of those employed in the administration, to represent the grievances, and watch over the liberties and the properties of the people of this nation." Unfortunately, such mundane duties fail to hold the attention of today's congressmen.

CURRENT STATISM OF AMERICA

Some people may think that Statism is only a hobgoblin threat of reactionary thinkers. While America is praised as "the land of the free," the type of prerogatives and policies established in recent decades grant practically unlimited power to government in many areas.

One example of the Statist mentality in contemporary America consists of the federally subsidized Drug Abuse Resistance Education (DARE) program, taught to 25 million American children each year. The core of DARE consists of police in the classroom as role models and trusted confidants. As a result, some children have concluded from this training that becoming a government informant is the apex of virtue. One lesson that police give students in kindergarten through fourth grade stresses DARE's "Three R's": "Recognize, Resist, and Report."[186] The official "DARE Officer's Guide for Grades K-4" contains a worksheet that instructs children to "Circle the names of the people you could tell if . . . a friend finds some pills"; "Police" are listed along with "Mother or Father," "Teacher," and "Friend." The next exercise instructs children to check boxes for whom they should inform if they "are asked to keep a secret"—"Police" are again listed as an option. Apparently, the idea that anyone should keep a secret from the proper authorities is inconceivable—as if people have a duty to report to the government everything they hear. A federal Bureau of Justice Assistance report noted that DARE "students have an opportunity to become acquainted with the [police] officer as a trusted friend who is interested in their happiness and welfare. Students occasionally tell the officer about . . . relatives who use drugs."[187] As a result of children turning informant, parents have been jailed, jobs have been lost, and families have been destroyed.[188] A federal judge, in a 1997 case brought by a Searsport, Maine student, ruled that the alleged actions of the DARE officer of "lying to and threatening of an 11-year-old girl . . . in order to force her to incriminate her parents is contemptible and exceeds all notions of fair play and decency" and "strikes at the basic fabric of all parent-child relationships: love, trust and faith."[189] A DARE America spokesman sought to intimidate the *American Journal of Public Health* in 1994 to prevent them from publishing an excerpt from a federally funded report that criticized DARE's effectiveness.[190] Academics who criticize DARE have faced reprisals; as *New Times Los Angeles* reported in 1997, "Many scientists—even those lauded by their peers and published in prestigious academic journals—had found themselves ostracized for reporting research critical of DARE."[191]

The proliferation of Special Weapons Assault Teams (SWAT) is another symbol of the changed relation between government and citizens. Prof. Peter Kraska estimated that the use of police SWAT teams has "increased by 538%" since 1980, leading to the "militarization" of civilian police.[192] Ninety percent of police departments responding to a 1995 survey by Kraska reported having an active paramilitary unit. The *Boston Globe* reported, "Cities such as Fresno, Calif., and Indianapolis routinely send officers into communities to patrol in full battle dress, giving these communities all the ambience of the West Bank."[193] The *Washington Post* noted in 1997, "The explosive growth and expanding mission of SWAT teams has, in turn, led to complaints that an occupying army is marching through America's streets—that they are too aggressive, too heavily armed, too scary."[194] Kraska observed: "We have never seen this kind of policing, where SWAT teams routinely break through a door, subdue all the occupants and search the premises for drugs, cash, and weapons."[195]

One of the clearest measures of Statism is what a government believes it can get away with. Few episodes epitomize contemporary Statism better than the federal actions at Waco, Texas in early 1993 and the subsequent cover-up.

On February 28, 1993, 76 Bureau of Alcohol, Tobacco and Firearms (ATF) agents roared up to the Branch Davidians' residence in two large cattle trailers—reportedly shouting as if they were going into war. The ATF had secured a search warrant based on allegations that the Davidians possessed automatic weapons for which they had no federal license. A 1996 congressional investigation concluded that "ATF's investigation [of the Davidians] . . . was grossly incompetent," that "the affidavit filed in support of the warrants contained an incredible number of false statements," and that "[i]f the false statement in the affidavits . . . were made with knowledge of their falsity, criminal charges should be brought" against federal officials.[196]

According to the ATF master plan for the raid, after its agents completed a no-knock raid—smashing in windows, ransacking and searching the entire building, and handcuffing and dragging out the parents in front of TV cameras—the ATF agents intended to prove they cared. The ATF's Bill Buford later testified that the agents planned to bring Happy Meals from McDonald's "for all of the children once we got them outside of the compound" (i.e., once the government took the children away from their parents).[197]

The raid went awry; after the shooting stopped, 4 ATF agents were dead, 16 were wounded, and several Branch Davidians were also dead. Four ATF agents later told the Texas Rangers that they believed federal agents fired the first shots.[198] After the ATF botched the initial assault, the FBI's Hostage Rescue Team took charge. On April 19, the FBI sent Abrams tanks smashing into the walls of the Davidians' home. The tanks pumped CS, a potentially lethal, flammable gas, into the residence for six hours. Around noon, fires broke out that quickly burnt the compound to the ground; 76 bodies were found in the rubble. After the fire, ATF agents proudly planted their flag over the embers where scores had died a few hours before. CS gas can kill: United Nations officials estimated that the use of CS gas resulted in 44 fatalities in the Gaza Strip in 1988, as well as over 1200 injuries and numerous miscarriages.[199] Rep. Steven Schiff of New Mexico declared that "no rational person can conclude that the use of CS gas under any circumstances against children, would do anything other than cause extreme physical problems and possibly death. . . . I believe the deaths of dozens of men, women and children can be directly and indirectly attributable to the use of this gas in the way it was injected by the FBI."[200] Rep. John Mica of Florida observed that even if the children didn't die directly from the CS gas, "We sure as hell tortured them for six hours before they died."[201]

Snap polls just after the Waco fire showed that the American people overwhelmingly supported the action of the FBI. Rep. Jack Brooks, chairman of the House Judiciary Committee, commented that the Davidians were "horrible people. Despicable people. Burning to death was too good for them."[202] A few days later, the opening of a Senate Appropriations Committee hearing had to be delayed so senators could have their pictures taken with Attorney General Janet Reno, who became a national hero for announcing that she authorized the final attack on the Davidians.[203]

At the trial of the Davidian survivors, federal prosecutors compared David Koresh to Hitler and Stalin and declared that the 11 defendants were "as much religious terrorists as the people who blew up the barracks in Lebanon, the people who blew up the World Trade Center in New York and Pan Am 103."[204] The jury rejected murder charges, instead finding 7 of the 11 defendants guilty of manslaughter—a much lighter charge. The jury verdict was characterized by the *New York Times* as a "stunning defeat" for the federal government.[205] The defendants received relatively light sentences—until the Justice Department arm-twisted the judge to reinstate charges that had originally been dismissed.[206]

Waco quickly became canonized as a law enforcement triumph. In October 1993, FBI Director Louis Freeh lavishly praised FBI agents for demonstrating "great excellence" during the confrontation: "I am quite satisfied with the operational aspects, planning aspects, chain-of-command aspects and leadership aspects of that operation." Congress looked at Waco and concluded that the government needed more; the size of the Hostage Rescue Team was sharply expanded.[207] When a journalist on a television talk show shortly after the April 19, 1995, bombing of the federal building in Oklahoma City stated that he considered the 1993 FBI attack on Waco a terrorist act, Labor Secretary Robert Reich hastened to distinguish Waco from the bombing at Oklahoma City: "We are talking about acts of violence that are not sanctioned by the government—that are not official."[208] Attorney General Janet Reno told a group of federal law enforcement officers on May 5, 1995: "There is much to be angry about when we talk about Waco—and the government's conduct is not the reason. David Koresh is the reason. . . ."[209]

The House of Representatives avoided conducting substantive oversight hearings on Waco for over two years, until after the Republicans captured control of Congress. The FBI's Larry Potts, though demoted from the number two position in the agency on suspicion of obstruction of justice only a few days before the hearing, presented the FBI's official statement on Waco: "I am immensely proud of all the FBI personnel who worked so conscientiously for so long to bring peace and justice to Waco."[210] Attorney General Reno, in her testimony, revealed that the tanks that smashed through the Davidian residence should not be considered military vehicles—instead, they were "like a good rent-a-car."[211] This comment reflected the Clinton administration's view that Waco was a routine law enforcement effort, except for the number of toe tags needed afterwards. (Respectable opinion continues pretending that the Waco debacle never occurred. The Women's Bar Association of the District of Columbia created a special award to honor the nation's first female attorney general: the Janet Reno Torchbearer Award. The first recipient, in 1997, was Supreme Court justice Sandra Day O'Connor; the award was presented by justice Ruth Bader Ginsburg.[212])

Politicians frequently lecture citizens on their duty to trust government. But, regarding Waco, which government version of events must conscientious citizens believe? Are citizens obliged to trust the ATF when they said they launched the military-style raid because they feared the Davidians might commit suicide; or to trust FBI spokesmen when they promised that the tanks the FBI brought in would never be used to assault the Davidians' home; or to trust Janet Reno when she initially said that the final assault on the home's residents was launched because of reports of child abuse; or to trust Reno when she later said that the assault was necessary because the FBI agents surrounding the Davidians were getting fatigued; or to trust Reno in May 1995 when she said the number one reason for the assault was that federal agents feared being attacked from behind by antigovernment vigilantes? Or should they believe FBI special agent Eugene Glenn, who told the Senate in 1995 that the Justice Department "investigation" of federal actions at Waco was recognized by FBI agents as a "whitewash"?[213]

Perhaps nothing evinces more clearly the Statism of contemporary America than the number of new laws and regulations promulgated each year. At this writing, federal agencies are in the process of finalizing over 4,000 new regulations.[214] Since Reagan won the presidency in 1980 and launched a supposed era of conservative deregulation, over 1 million pages of new regulations, proposed regulations, notices, and rulings have appeared in the *Federal Register*. And the *Federal Register* shows only the surface of federal commands. Federal Trade Commission economist Robert Rogowsky, in an essay entitled "Sub Rosa Regulation: The Iceberg Beneath the Surface," observed:

> An impressive underground regulatory infrastructure thrives on investigations, inquiries, threatened legal actions, and negotiated settlements. Without having to "break cover," as one career regulator termed it, savvy bureaucrats can fulfill an agenda of intervention without resorting to rulemaking or other formal mechanisms. Threats of regulation or litigation and the skillful use of public opprobrium can be very effective instruments of a command and control economy.[215]

One example: after the liquor industry announced an end to its voluntary ban on television advertising for its products, Federal Communications Commission chairman Reed Hundt warned the industry to abstain from such ads, even though no statutory authority existed to ban such ads. Hundt reminded the liquor and broadcasting industries: "Many steps can be taken, the government has many options, but it is not necessary that these options be explored if broadcasters say no to airing the liquor ads."[216]

People have been encouraged to continually look to the government for their own deliverance. English constitutional scholar A. V. Dicey observed in 1905:

> Every law or rule of conduct must . . . lay down or rest upon some general principle, and must therefore, if it succeeds in attaining its end, commend this principle to public attention or imitation, and thus affect legislative opinion. Nor is the success of a law necessary for the production of this effect. A principle derives prestige from its mere recognition by Parliament, and if a law fails in attaining its object the argument lies ready to hand that the failure was due to the law not going far enough, i.e., to its not carrying out the principle on which it is founded to its full logical consequences. . . . The true importance, indeed, of laws lies far less in their direct result than in their effect upon the sentiment or convictions of the public.[217]

Each new law, each new proscribed behavior further encourages citizens to rely on politicians for their deliverance, to cede more of their judgment in daily life to their political and bureaucratic overlords. Each additional law vesting new power in government agencies, or creating new penalties for private conduct, further preempts and politicizes the citizen's life. Each new law authorizing new

penalties reinforces the principle that the State is superior to the individual—
that social uplift must come from the bureaucrat's memo and citation book, not
from the efforts of free citizens.

STATIC VERSUS DYNAMIC
CONCEPTS OF POLITICAL/GOVERNMENT POWER

The prevailing conception of government power today is practically the mirror
image of the view held by the Founding Fathers. The two views can be
characterized as the static and the dynamic view of government.

The Founding Fathers took up arms against the British government largely
because of what the British government was becoming, not merely because of
what it already was. The British were confounded by the Americans' hostility
because the British were not oppressing the Americans any worse than they were
the Irish or other colonists. In contrast, Americans looked at the precedents being
established by British rulers—the suspension of colonial legislatures, the dra-
gooning of Americans into the British navy, the suppression of the right to trial
by a jury of one's peers—and saw their cherished "ancient liberties" rapidly
vanishing. John Dickinson, a prominent colonial pamphleteer, wrote in 1768
that "the crucial question in the colonists' minds is 'not, what evil *has actually
attended* particular measures—but, what evil, in the nature of things, *is likely to
attend them.*'"[218] Edmund Randolph, George Washington's first attorney general
and governor of Virginia, declared that the American Revolution was a
revolution "without an immediate oppression, without a cause depending so
much on hasty feeling as theoretic reasoning."[219]

The inexorable tendency of government power to expand haunted many of
the Founding Fathers. Thomas Jefferson declared: "One precedent in favor of
power is stronger than an hundred against it."[220] The Founding Fathers
presumed that government power would continue expanding unless citizens
vigilantly defended their rights and liberties. In contrast, some contemporary
political thinkers exult over how much power government has already acquired.
University of Chicago professor Stephen Holmes gushed in his 1995 book,
Passions and Constraint: On the Theory of Liberal Democracy: "It now seems
obvious that [contemporary Statist] liberalism can occasionally eclipse authoritarianism as a technique for accumulating political power. . . . Liberalism is not
allergic to political power. . . . For good or ill, liberalism is one of the most
effective philosophies of state building ever contrived."[221] Prof. Cass Sunstein
called for "enthusiasm about the use of national governmental power to promote
economic productivity and to help the disadvantaged" and urged Americans to
abandon "anachronistic conceptions of the relationship between the citizen and

the State."[222] Some Establishment members imply that only government can prevent mass blindness: Susan Berresford, president of the Ford Foundation, informed Congress in 1997 that "Government sets standards, protects the weak, provides services, and projects a vision for us all."[223]

The American revolutionaries were concerned about the potential for unlimited power inherent in British laws and policies. The initial conflicts at Lexington and Concord occurred because British regiments were marching out to confiscate the colonists' arms caches. The British assumed that seizing the weapons would quell resistance to the expansion of their power. George Mason, the father of the Bill of Rights, later declared that the British decided that "to disarm the people . . . was the best and most effectual way to enslave them."[224] If the colonists reasoned like some contemporary Americans, they would have interpreted the British troops' attempt to seize their guns as proof of how much they cared about the colonists.

The colonists recognized that each new precedent for expanding government power would eventually affect far more people than the initial incident did. The Americans of that era scrutinized each new claim to power, each principle asserted in acts of Parliament, recognizing that once tolerated, the power would grow year by year. From the Founding Fathers' perspective, the more power British rulers sought, the less trustworthy they became. In contrast, according to some contemporary experts, the more power government officials acquire, the more legally untouchable they should become. Stanford University law professor Kathleen Sullivan argued that President Clinton should be exempt from being sued during his time in office for his alleged personal wrongdoing because "he's the only person who works alone for us 24 hours a day."[225]

While the Founding Fathers perceived the dangers of concentrated power, contemporary Statists instinctively blame all problems on insufficient political-bureaucratic power. Economist Robert Kuttner declaimed in 1996, "For nearly a century, the Russians were deprived of freedom by an overarching state. Now, they are suffering the loss of freedom that comes from too weak a state."[226] But a shortage of good government is no proof of a shortage of government power. The political class in Russia continues to have far too much power for the good of the Russian people. Nobel laureate Aleksandr Solzhenitsyn complained in 1997, "During the last 10 years, the bureaucracy has doubled and tripled in size, all of it supported at the expense of a nation that is being reduced to beggary."[227] The Russian economy remains hobbled by an incurably inept collective farm system because communist legislators have refused to allow the sale of land; the few private farmers are also hog-tied because the government prohibits using land as a collateral for borrowing, thus making it very difficult for farmers to modernize their operations.[228] Much of the pervasive corruption in contemporary Russia is the result of excessive government power—and the necessity to bribe numerous officials to get anything done.

As government has become more powerful and interventionist, it has become fashionable to look beyond the coercion and to focus on the proclaimed goals. When the Clinton administration was seeking public support in February 1998 for bombing Iraq, Secretary of State Madeline Albright told a student audience, "We are talking about using military force, but we are not talking about a war. That is an important distinction."[229] This is a distinction that may have been lost on survivors of the 1941 Japanese attack on Pearl Harbor. Albright clarified her thinking a few days later: "If we have to use force, it is because we are America. We are the indispensable nation. We stand tall. We see further into the future."[230] Politicians' intentions and definitions are thus presumed more powerful than actual bombs. Or, at a certain point, America's moral superiority means that its bombs didn't count—or at least that its bombs have a different meaning than bombs dropped by a morally inferior nation.

Americans of the Revolutionary Era recognized that the passage of a law does not signal the end of a legislative onslaught. Instead, it is merely the starting point for a push to further extend government in the same direction—to pursue the "logic" of a new act to further political power. As James Madison wrote in 1787, "The sober people of America . . . have seen that one legislative interference is but the first link of a long chain of repetitions, every subsequent interference being naturally produced by the effects of the preceding."[231] Unfortunately, most contemporary Americans are complacent or naive about politicians planting their flag on new turf.

The war on drugs exemplifies how government power, from humble beginnings, can spread like a computer virus through the statute book. The American war on drugs began in 1914 with the Harrison Act, which imposed taxes and controls on the sale of certain narcotics. Supreme Court decisions in the first years after the act's enactment effectively made it a crime for doctors to prescribe controlled drugs in most cases and made possession of listed drugs without a prescription a federal crime. Presidents Nixon, Reagan, Bush, and Clinton have expanded government power to suppress and punish any activity remotely connected to illicit drugs. Because some people sell and consume illicit drugs, government now must have the power to search everyone's pockets (the Supreme Court's endorsement of the "plain feel" doctrine) and everyone's cars; to institute mandatory urine tests for school children; to treat anyone engaged in indoor gardening like a marijuana kingpin; to spray marijuana with toxic substances intended to poison users; to prohibit the sale of clean hypodermic needles, thus leading to tens of thousands of additional deaths from AIDS among heroin addicts; and to ban selling oregano in plastic bags on the street. Yet, in spite of such valiant efforts, illicit drugs continue to be available throughout the country—in part because government restrictions make their sale so profitable. Politicians respond not by admitting the futility of attempts to micromanage what every citizen ingests, but by calling for the suspension of the Bill of Rights, proposing laws to arrest teenagers for possessing beepers and to permit the Coast Guard to shoot down civilian airplanes suspected of carrying drugs.[232] Once government's right and duty to control a certain behavior is accepted, the "problem" becomes not any specific abuse in pursuit of that end, but any limitation on government power.

Another example of this dynamic of government power is historic preservation. In 1949, Congress chartered the National Trust for Historic Preservation, which became a cheerleader for preservation efforts. Preservation efforts initially concentrated on designating highly respected specific land-marks; however, the momentum of the preservation movement led to government controls over hundreds of thousands of mundane, aging homes, businesses, and churches. While early preservationists spoke glowingly about the need to protect the old Post Office building in Washington, contemporary preservation laws set the "history police" loose on stacks of pumpkins in front of hardware stores on Long Island, pet cemeteries in Maryland, and run-down McDonald's restaurants in California.[233] Over 2,000 cities, towns, and counties have historic preservation ordinances; in over 300 locales, the power of the preservation police extends *inside* private buildings. A 1995 *Wall Street Journal* article on Seattle noted, "Just about anything more than 25 years old can qualify as a historical landmark here. City rules require only that a structure meet certain broad criteria, such as 'prominence of spatial location.' Or it must be 'an easily identifiable visual feature of a neighborhood.'"[234] The National Trust for Historic Preservation in 1993 placed the entire state of Vermont on its official "11 Most Endangered Historic Places" list. The trust did not specify whether it favored arresting any farmer who herded his cows away from a scenic highway.[235]

The history of federal highway subsidies also illustrates how government power mushrooms. Congressman James Beck, in his 1932 book, *Our Wonderland of Bureaucracy*, declared of highway subsidies: "No other subsidy law had gone so far as to offer a bribe to the States to amend their Constitutions in conformity with the ideas of the Federal bureaucracy."[236] Federal subsidies and the accompanying mandates have multiplied in subsequent decades. The taxes that finance federal highway construction are exacted from drivers in each state in gas taxes and supposedly deposited into a special "trust fund"; yet congressmen perennially impose new restrictions and mandates on how state governments spend the money that Congress returns to them. Congress added new dictates to the receipt of subsidies in 1965 (banning billboards along almost all interstate highways, which harmed rural states such as South Dakota that depended on snaring passing tourists),[237] 1974 (imposing a nationwide 55-mile-per-hour speed limit on interstate highways, thereby putting much of the western United States into a time warp), 1984 (requiring state governments to raise the drinking age to 21, thereby turning millions of 18 to 20-year-old citizens into criminals), 1990 (requiring states to comply with draconian Clean Air Act mandates), 1992 (requiring state governments to revoke the driver's license of anyone caught in possession of marijuana or other illicit substances, thereby helping many potheads become unemployed), 1993 (requiring state governments to make it a crime for any front-seat car occupant to not wear a seat belt), and 1995 (requiring state governments to penalize as drunk any driver under the age of 21 who had consumed a single beer).[238]

To better comprehend how government power perennially expands, consider the laws that Congress enacted in a single year—1996:

- **The Personal Responsibility and Work Opportunity Reconciliation Act** created the most intrusive "citizen locating and tracking measure" in U.S. history; all employers are required to report to the government within 20 days the name, address, and Social Security numbers of all newly hired employees. This provision was justified as a means to track down "deadbeat dads," but the information gathered will be available to the Justice Department, the IRS, and other federal agencies.[239]
- The **Health Insurance Portability and Accountability Act** (known as the Kennedy-Kassebaum Act) imposed new federal mandates that boosted insurance rates by up to 600 percent for some individuals and could require that people receiving subsidized health insurance continue receiving government benefits even after their income exceeds program eligibility limits.[240] The bill mandated five-year prison sentences for doctors who fail to turn over patients' records promptly to law enforcement officials and ten-year sentences for health plan administrators who intentionally "misapply" any asset of the health care plan by providing a specific service to a patient deemed "medically unnecessary" by federal investigators. The law also mandated that every American be assigned a "unique health identifier"—a "computer code that could be used to create a national database that would track every citizen's medical history from cradle to grave," as the *New York Times* noted.[241] But there was no provision for any privacy protection in the new federal databank.

- The **Immigration Act** empowered low-level INS officials to make "on-the-spot expulsions" of foreigners, banning them from the United States for five years, based on the flimsiest of pretexts. The act effectively gave low-level INS employees more powers than were previously held by federal judges.[242] The act also contained a provision mandating federal criteria for all state drivers' licenses. Many critics believe that this is the first step towards a national identification card and the creation of a comprehensive database for law enforcement.[243]

- The **Telecommunications Act** made it a felony for 17-year old teenagers to exchange by e-mail the same type of zesty love letters that teenagers have sent each other since at least the time of Romeo and Juliet. Anyone who sends or places on the Internet material that could be considered "patently offensive" to children under 18 could face five years in prison. Even transmitting information "over computers about drugs and other medical paraphernalia needed to perform abortions" was prohibited[244] (The Supreme Court struck down those provisions as unconstitutional in June 1997, but Congress in 1998 enacted another law to punish the same behavior.)

  The Telecommunications Act also mandated that all new TVs sold in the United States must contain a "V-chip" to jam receipt of programs that a government-mandated rating system classified as having violent or other offensive content. (The chip could add up to $20 to the price of a new television.)[245] In 1997, the FCC followed up by demanding that most new computers also include a V-chip.

- The so-called **Lautenberg Domestic Violence Prevention Act** made it a felony, punishable by ten years in prison and a $250,000 fine, for anyone who has ever been convicted of a misdemeanor of domestic use or attempted use of force against a spouse or child to possess a firearm or a single bullet. (Some states consider even verbal threats to be a "domestic assault.") Experts estimated that the law created 1 million new felons overnight, in part because few people are aware of the bill's retroactive sweep—its requirement for people with such misdemeanors to surrender their firearms.[246]

- The **Gun Free Schools Act** created more than 100,000 federal gun ban zones across the country. The estimated 5 million Americans who routinely carry guns with them in their cars or on hunting trips can now be stopped and arrested if they pass within a thousand feet of any school. (Congress enacted this law even though the Supreme Court had struck down an almost identical law in 1995 as unconstitutional.)

To be fair, not all the legislation passed in 1996 stretched the power of government. Public Law 104-128, enacted on April 9, 1996, eliminated the Board of Tea Experts of the Commerce Department.

The issue is not a new law's intent; the issue is how much additional power over the people a law conveys to the government—how many additional prerogatives it creates to trammel, shackle, and punish. Every law with new penalties increases the power of some government employees over some citizens. The momentum of increasing government power is more important than the words presidents or congressmen utter at the time a law is enacted.

Proponents of the static view of government pretend that the only power that is worth noticing is the power that government is currently using. But trying to understand government from a snapshot of coercion exercised at any given moment is like trying to understand the power of a diesel engine merely by looking at a photograph of a train parked on a side track. The issue is not how much power the government is exercising this hour, this week, or even this month. The issue is how much power government has accumulated and how much power government can potentially exercise over any citizen it decides to bring down. It is not a question of what politicians do this year, but what politicians have done the last 70 years. If a law is still on the books, power is still within the politician's grasp. Territory does not revert back to the private sector or the individual's domain merely because politicians neglect giving speeches about it for a few months. Each law enacted in a momentary panic is the equivalent of a permanent conquest of new territory for the State.

The extent of government force cannot be gauged by how much violence government uses. Even the Central Intelligence Agency eschews the iron fist. In a how-to-torture manual the agency supplied to its Latin American friends during the 1980s, the CIA cautioned against "direct physical brutality" that "creates only resentment, hostility and further defiance." But, the agency noted, "if a subject refuses to comply once a threat has been made, it must be carried out."[247] (The manual offered helpful hints on administering electric shocks.) A 1985 addendum to the manual stressed pragmatic reasons for limiting coercion: "If [interrogators] break the subject's jaw, he will not be able to answer questions."[248]

The increase in government power is like a political arms-buildup against the citizenry—a vast expansion of the pretexts that the governing class has to attack the governed. A massive military buildup by one government can often subdue its foreign enemies without a fight. Similarly, contemporary statute books convey sufficient punitive power that citizens surrender without a fight in most potential conflicts with the government. As former IRS Commissioner Sheldon Cohen observed, "Power is not having to exercise power."[249]

Few governments in history have violently assaulted a majority of their subjects simultaneously; instead, high-profile "examples" are made of selected citizens or groups. After watching one of their neighbors or townsmen be destroyed, few people are willing to stand up to government authority. The lack of violent government coercion is often a measure of how many citizens' wills have already been broken.[250] The issue is not the private casualty counts, but the size of the legal arsenal politicians and bureaucrats possess. The fact that most people surrender without a fight does not make government action nonaggressive. By this standard—to take an extreme example from a darker time—the roundup of European Jews bound for Nazi concentration camps appeared largely nonaggressive prior to the 1943 Warsaw ghetto uprising.

Thinking of government power as an abstraction blurs the relation of the citizen to the State—and thus invites far more subjugation. Ignoring the amount of coercion that government uses greatly understates the cost of political action. Simply because the impact of coercion is not registered in the official statistics of the GDP does not mean that its victims' lives are any less thwarted.

Some Americans may believe that Big Government has already been leashed, or at least that the tide against government abuses has been finally turned. Politicians seek to quell citizen resistance by assuring them that "the era of Big Government is over" at the same time that they propose dozens of expansions of government power.[251] But, on this issue, consider the Soviet experience. Khrushchev and Brezhnev governed with less overt brutality than did Stalin, in part because Soviet power was already established and people's resistance had long since been broken. In the same way, American politicians need not lavishly praise the power of government because they already have vast power in their hands. The extent of government power is rarely an issue in respectable circles—not because the government does not have more power now than ever before, or because the government is not more invasive than ever before—but because most people have become accustomed to government supremacy in scores of areas of their lives.

CONCLUSION

In many prosecutions, the question arises as to whether the defendant has shown a pattern of or proclivity towards criminal behavior. Yet, in judging the character and nature of the State, such a question is considered inadmissible. Despite the recidivist ways of politicians around the world, the State still gets respect.

The idealist theory of the State has been replaced by the antiseptic theory of the State. Experts concede that the State is no longer some transcendent entity, yet there appears to be a continued resolve to pretend that government does little or no harm. Government has not been tamed merely because political scientists have redefined its bites out of existence.

The State is specific officials, specific penalties, and specific jails and prisons. The coercive power is the reality and the political rhetoric is the illusion. No number of speeches by politicians can counterweigh the vast expansion of the federal statute book. There is no rhetorical or metaphysical trick by which government can transcend its coercive nature.

Citizens first must recognize that government is coercive; second, recognize how pervasive the coercion and threat of coercion is; and finally, recognize the meaning of that coercion—for the life of the individual and for the nature of the polity. While the notion that government is coercive may seem self-evident, it is a truism that rarely permeates the consciousness of political reformers. To recognize the inherent coercive nature of government and government action is necessarily to limit all pretensions of using the State to uplift, purify, redeem, or otherwise transubstantiate citizens.

THREE

THE MIRAGE OF WELFARE STATE FREEDOM

The more powerful the State, the more freedom.
—Tito[1]

To accept a benefit is to sell one's liberty.
—Publilius Syrus[2]

IN THE MIDDLE AGES, priests encouraged peasants to come to the monastery and pledge themselves to be the serf of a church. Why? Because the serf would thereby gain true freedom. As historian Marc Bloch noted, "In this world he would share in the immunities of a privileged corporation, and in the next be guaranteed 'the eternal freedom which is in Christ.'"[3]

Unfortunately, much of the twentieth century's debates over the meaning of liberty appear to be a throwback to the Middle Ages, with one political party after another promising people true freedom if only they submit to increased government power. Freedom has long since transcended mere individuals, and now resides at loftier levels, in collectives, in absolutes, in States, and in the abstruse texts of tenured professors. Welfare State freedom is based on government's superior wisdom, superior goodness, and superior claim to as much of the citizen's rights and property as it demands. Around the world, politicians have generously preshrunk the individual's liberty so that it will better fit him.

The definitions of liberty devised in ivory towers and elsewhere have a profound impact on the thinking of lawmakers and others. Though liberty may be an inherently murky concept, and while no single concept of liberty will satisfy everyone, the pursuit of different visions of liberty produce radically different results in the real world. Regardless of how wrongheaded some concepts of liberty prevalent earlier in this century may now appear, law after law was enacted based on those ideas. And those laws continue binding today's citizens to the intellectual follies of previous generations of thinkers and reformers.

FREEDOM DURING THE REVOLUTIONARY ERA

The Founding Fathers' concept of liberty was forged by decades of abuses by British colonial rulers. "The Restraint of Government is the True Liberty and Freedom of the People" was a common American saying in the eighteenth century.[4] Historian Forrest McDonald wrote that "political discourse [in Revolutionary Era America] was an ongoing public forum on the meaning of Liberty."[5] John Phillip Reid, in his classic study *The Concept of Liberty in the Age of the American Revolution,* explained:

> It is apparent that people in the eighteenth century did not distinguish between what today is termed "positive liberty" and "negative liberty.". . . Very few writers identified liberty with a freedom to do what one wished to do without restraint. . . . Rather, liberty in the eighteenth century was thought of much more in relation to "negative liberty," that is, freedom from, not freedom to, freedom from a number of social and political evils, including arbitrary government. . . .
>
> The test of law's "goodness" in the eighteenth century was the degree to which it freed the individual from government direction, the very test that Blackstone set for "civil liberty." Put another way, the less a law restrained the citizen, and the more it restrained government, the better the law. Stated positively, the rule was that the "Society whose laws least restrain the words and actions of its members, is most free."[6]

The Founding Fathers' concepts of freedom fit into the classical British tradition. In 1721, John Trenchard and Thomas Gordon defined liberty as "the power which every man has over his own actions, and his right to enjoy the fruit of his labor, art, and industry, as far as by it he hurts not the society, or any members of it, by taking from any member, or by hindering him from enjoying what he himself enjoys."[7] Adam Smith, in his *Wealth of Nations,* advocated a system of liberty whereby "every man, as long as he does not violate the laws of justice, is left perfectly free to pursue his own interest in his own way."[8]

However, changing political circumstances and shifting intellectual tides would eventually help to obscure American thinking.

REDEFINING LIBERTY:
LIBERATION VIA LEVIATHAN

Jean Jacques Rousseau, writing in 1762, declared, "The individuals see the good they reject; the public wills the good it does not see. All stand equally in need of guidance. The former must be compelled to bring their wills into conformity with their reason; the latter must be taught to know what it wills."[9] And, naturally, the State is the only power sufficiently wise to provide "guidance." Rousseau wrote that the social contract required that "whoever refuses to obey the general will shall be compelled to do so by the whole body. This means nothing less than that he will be *forced to be free....* "[10]

C. E. Vaughan, in a 1915 study of Rousseau's work, observed that in the *Social Contract,* "freedom is no longer conceived as the independence of the individual. It is rather to be sought in his total surrender to the service of the State...."[11] London School of Economics professor Maurice Cranston observed:

> Throughout the *Social Contract* it is clear that Rousseau never sees institutions as a threat to freedom. The image of a king or prince in Rousseau's eyes is the image of a master, and he sees such monarchs as enemies of liberty. But the image of the State touches him quite differently.... He says that things should be so arranged that every citizen is perfectly independent from all his fellow citizens and "excessively dependent on the republic." The word "excessive" is significant ... because he thinks such dependence can never be too great: because dependence on the State guarantees men against all dependence on men, against "toute dependance personnel."[12]

Rousseau's equation of dependence on government with true freedom helped pave the way for socialism and a revival of the cult of the State.

Some of Rousseau's ideas were adapted and mutated by German idealists. Philosopher Johann Gottlieb Fichte proclaimed in 1808 that, in the perfect, rational State, freedom would be achieved because "the *individuality* of all is dissolved in the *species* of all...."[13] Fichte declared that "true freedom only occurs by means of passing through the highest obedience to law" and denounced "that slack in the reins of State which in foreign terms is called humanity, liberality, and popularity, but which in the German language is ... devoid of dignity."[14] Thus, freedom is the product of government flagellation of the citizenry: the harsher the government, the more liberated the citizens.[15]

Hegel followed in Fichte's footsteps, trumpeting the doctrine that the more the citizen is forced to obey, the freer he becomes. Hegel asserted that "in duty the individual finds his liberation . . . duty is not a restriction of freedom, but only on freedom in the abstract, i.e., on unfreedom. Duty is the attainment of our essence, the winning of positive freedom."[16] According to Hegel, "only that will which obeys law, is free," for in obeying law—"the objective, universal, and rational will of the State"—"it obeys itself."[17] Hegel asserted that "the State is that in which Freedom obtains objectivity, and lives in the enjoyment of this objectivity."[18] Hegel derided the notion of freedom as people doing what they wanted to do as "uneducated superficiality."[19] Hegel's notion of freedom was a deduction from his notion of the State: since the State was divine, then permitting individuals to live as they please was a heresy.

Hegel's thoughts still heavily influence American academia and political thinking; a search of major law journals showed over 900 references to Hegel in recent decades. From Hegel onwards, many philosophers presumed that the State can conjure and awake the spirits of its subjects, that there is some magical power in the State. Throughout history, the more political philosophers talk about people's "spirit," the more serene they are about real people getting racked by real government officials.

The Hegelian concept of freedom entered mainstream British thought in the 1870s with the work of Oxford philosopher T. H. Green.[20] Green made government coercion irrelevant to freedom: "the mere removal of compulsion, thereby merely enabling a man to do as he likes, is itself no contribution to true freedom."[21] Green wrote that the ability to make the best of oneself is "what I call freedom in the positive sense."[22] Green also defined freedom as "the development and exercise on the whole of those powers of contributing to a social good with which we believe the members of society to be endowed. . . ."[23] Thus, compulsion to work for the social good became equated with a higher freedom. Green's work abounded with references to the "cosmic spirit"—which perhaps left him less time to notice how government actually operates. As an *American Political Science Review* article noted in 1962, "Instead of renouncing liberty as the great end in politics, the positive liberals [beginning with Green] found it convenient to enlarge and adapt the notion of liberty."[24]

Other writers quickly followed in Green's footsteps. Oxford professor F. C. Montague, in a book aptly named *The Limits of Individual Liberty,* announced that "what is important is not liberty to do as we like—his is not real freedom; rightly conceived, freedom is the release from instinct and thoughtless desire."[25] Thus, increased government power to liberate people from their thoughtless desires became the catapult to freedom. Oxford professor David Ritchie, author of *The Principles of State Interference,* observed in 1891: "Liberty in its positive sense may therefore mean the sovereignty of law, as distinct from the sovereignty of individuals."[26] Ritchie defined "real freedom" as "growing up intelligent, useful citizens"[27] and stressed "the positive side of subjection to good laws."[28]

Professor Bernard Bosanquet jumped on the bandwagon in 1897, defining freedom as "the passage of a being or content beyond itself"—as the characteristic of "a world which reshapes itself in virtue of its nature and that of its contents, and, in doing so, extends its borders, and absorbs and stamps itself upon something that before seemed alien."[29] Bosanquet argued that the empirical person must be shackled by the State in order for the higher, idealistic person buried inside to blossom. Bosanquet, defending government restrictions, declared, "The fetters of the bad self are the symbol of freedom."[30] Bosanquet explained: "The claim to obey only yourself is a claim essential to humanity; and the further significance of it rests upon what you mean by 'yourself.' . . . When man is in any degree civilized, in order to obey yourself as you want to be, you must obey something very different from yourself as you are. . . . Conversely we feel like a free man compared with a slave when we *conquer the alien will within us.* . . ."[31] Bosanquet offered a theory of liberty that elevated bureaucrats into priests of self-actualization. For each notch the philosophers raised the concept of freedom, governments were permitted to attach another shackle to the legs of the citizenry. To free a people's individuality and spontaneity, government must wage a quasi-theological war against all the evil purportedly lurking in their souls.

In America, few academics did more than John Dewey to exalt government power in the name of a new liberty. Dewey, probably the most respected philosopher in early-twentieth-century America, declared in 1935 that "organized society must use its power to establish the conditions under which the mass of individuals can possess actual as distinct from merely legal liberty."[32] Dewey perceived the "problem of freedom" as the "problem of establishing an entire social order, possessed of a spiritual authority that would nurture and direct the inner as well as the outer life of individuals."[33]

Dewey called for a reversal of values regarding liberty and government: "The idea that liberalism cannot maintain its end and at the same time reverse its conception of the means by which they are to be attained is false. The ends can now be achieved *only* by reversal of the means to which early liberalism was committed."[34] In a 1916 essay entitled "Force and Coercion," Dewey revealed: "The question of the limits of individual powers, or liberties, or rights, is finally a question of the most efficient use of means for ends . . . it is as an efficiency factor that [liberty's] value must ultimately be assessed . . . older and coarser forms of liberty may be obstructive; efficiency may then require the use of coercive power to abrogate their exercise."[35] Thus, as long as government officials believed that expanding their own power would be more "efficient" than allowing people to make their own choices, more government power was justified.

Dewey declared in 1935: "Today, liberty signifies liberation from material insecurity and from the coercion and repressions that prevent multitudes from participation in the vast cultural resources that are at hand."[36] In other words, as long as the government guarantees people free food and subsidized opera, they are free—regardless of what else the government does to them or takes from them. Dewey in 1922 referred to people as "political animals" and argued that people should get their "freedom" from the government the same way that an ox got his "freedom" from his master: "The ox accepts in fact not the yoke but the stall and the hay to which the yoke is a necessary incident. But if the ox foresees the consequences of the use of the yoke, if he anticipates the possibility of harvest and identifies himself not with the yoke but with the realization of its possibilities, he acts freely, voluntarily."[37] According to Dewey's interpretation, the fact that the farmer gave the ox hay at the end of the day essentially made the ox a free animal. Thus, the citizen should find his "freedom" by accepting the yoke of his political rulers, by becoming harnessed to the latest five-year plan. Yet, if oxen truly accepted yokes voluntarily, farmers would not need to keep them penned in. As Alan Ryan, author of *John Dewey and the High Tide of American Liberalism,* observed, "Dewey's detestation of the capitalist order had a semireligious quality, and so, therefore, did his vision of socialism."[38]

Alexander Meiklejohn, a professor whose writings have been cited in a dozen Supreme Court decisions, especially in major free speech cases, also helped "spiritualize" American thinking about liberty. Meiklejohn, in a 1935 book entitled *What Does America Mean?,* began with a laborious distinction between "spirit" and "matter," and then revealed that freedom was for spirits, not physical beings: "Freedom has no clear meaning except as we separate 'inner' from 'outer' action . . . the freedom which men demand when they know their own minds is the freedom of the spirit."[39] Meiklejohn declared, "On the one hand, Religion, Speech, the Press, Assemblage, Protest—these the Federal Congress may not touch. On the other hand, Life, Liberty, and Property—these are to be regulated and restrained by Congress; they may even be taken away provided that the action by which this is done is justly and properly performed."[40] (Meiklejohn also asserted that government should be allowed to take from citizens and corporations "whatever part of their annual income" government deems "just and necessary."[41]) Meiklejohn endowed the government with daunting spiritual responsibilities in the name of freedom:

> The major problem of any social order, as seen in external, political terms, is that
> of so constructing and controlling our institutions that they shall serve the

purposes of the inner life. I am not saying that the outer should be ignored. Rather it must be the servant of the inner and to this end it must be whipped into such shape and behavior that its service will be adequate and dependable."[42]

In other words, Meiklejohn believed that achieving inner freedom required vesting in politicians the power to *whip* external life into shapes that would supposedly serve the inner life.

Meiklejohn sounded a call to holy war: "We cannot allow whims and caprices and ambitions to run riot. These have no right to freedom. And we, who care for spiritual values, must bring them under control. We must take the social order into our hands and set it right. . . . And it is for the doing of this task that we demand, and must have, spiritual freedom."[43] Meiklejohn's glorification of freedom of speech, combined with his derision of freedom of action in everyday life, was adopted by the Supreme Court in the 1930s and afterwards. Regrettably, Meiklejohn did not explain how whipping for spiritual liberation differed from whipping for oppression: Does it depend on the grip the master used on the whip? Or does it depend on the pattern of the whip marks on the back of the victim? Or does it depend solely on the intent of the whipmaster?

FDR AND THE OFFICIAL
REDEFINITION OF AMERICAN FREEDOM

The clearest turning point in the American understanding of freedom came during the presidency of Franklin Roosevelt. Roosevelt often invoked freedom, but almost always as a pretext to increase government power. FDR proclaimed in 1933: "We have all suffered in the past from individualism run wild." Naturally, the corrective was to allow government to run wild.

Roosevelt declared in a 1934 fireside chat: "I am not for a return of that definition of liberty under which for many years a free people were being gradually regimented into the service of the privileged few."[44] Politicians like FDR began by telling people that control of their own lives was a mirage; thus, they lost nothing when government took over. In his renomination acceptance speech at the 1936 Democratic Party convention, Roosevelt declared that "the privileged princes of these new economic dynasties . . . created a new despotism. . . . The hours men and women worked, the wages they received, the conditions of their labor—these had passed beyond the control of the people, and were imposed by this new industrial dictatorship."[45] But if wages were completely dictated by the "industrial dictatorship"—why were pay rates higher in the United States than anywhere else in the world, and why had pay rates increased rapidly in the decades before 1929? FDR never considered limiting government intervention to safeguarding individual choice; instead, he favored multiplying power to impose "government-knows-best" dictates on work hours, wages, and contracts.

On January 6, 1941, Roosevelt gave his famous "Four Freedoms" speech, promising citizens freedom of speech, freedom of worship—and then he got creative: "The third [freedom] is freedom from want . . . everywhere in the world. The fourth is freedom from fear . . . anywhere in the world."[46] Proclaiming a goal of freedom from fear meant that the government henceforth must fill the role in daily life previously filled by God and religion. (For further analysis of this concept, see later in this chapter.) FDR's list was clearly intended as a "replacement set" of freedoms, since otherwise there would have been no reason to mention freedom of speech and worship, already guaranteed by the First Amendment.

Roosevelt's new freedoms liberated government while making a pretense of liberating the citizen. FDR's list offered citizens no security from the State, since it completely ignored the rights guaranteed by the Second Amendment (to keep and bear firearms),[47] the Fourth Amendment (freedom from unreasonable search and seizure), the Fifth Amendment (due process, property rights, the right against self-incrimination), the Sixth Amendment (the right to a speedy and public trial by an impartial jury), the Eighth Amendment (protection against excessive bail, excessive fines, and cruel and unusual punishments). Roosevelt's revised freedoms also ignored the Ninth Amendment, which specifies that the listing of "certain rights, shall not be construed to deny or disparage others retained by the people," as well as the Tenth Amendment, which specified that "powers not delegated" to the federal government are reserved to the states or to the people.[48]

And, even though Roosevelt included freedom of speech in his new, improved list of progressive freedoms, he added:

> A free nation has the right to expect full cooperation from all groups. . . . We must especially beware of that small group of selfish men who would clip the wings of the American eagle in order to feather their own nests. . . . The best way of dealing with the few slackers or trouble makers in our midst is, first, to shame them by patriotic example, and, if that fails, to use the sovereignty of government to save government.[49]

Thus, the "new freedom" required that government have power to suppress any group not actively supporting the government's goals. (The United States was still at peace at the time of FDR's speech.) The expansions of freedoms in the list were promised to the whole world—primarily people who did not vote in U.S. elections—while the implicit contractions of previously sanctified freedoms would affect only Americans.

FDR's Four Freedoms doctrine was swallowed whole by most of the political establishment and has since become enshrined, by Norman Rockwell and others, in American political mythology. President George Bush, speaking on the fiftieth anniversary of the Four Freedoms speech, called FDR "our greatest American political pragmatist" and praised him for having "brilliantly enunciated the 20th-century vision of our Founding Fathers' commitment to individual liberty."[50] President Clinton declared in October 1996, "In Franklin Roosevelt's view, government should be the perfect public system for fostering and protecting the 'Four Freedoms' . . . Roosevelt . . . enumerated these freedoms not as abstract ideals but as goals toward which Americans—and caring people everywhere—could direct their most strenuous public efforts."[51]

Roosevelt elaborated his concept of freedom in his 1944 State of the Union address. He declared that the original Bill of Rights had "proved inadequate to assure us equality in the pursuit of happiness."[52] Roosevelt called for a "Second Bill of Rights," and asserted that: "True individual freedom can't exist without economic security." And security, according to FDR, included "the right to a useful and remunerative job," "decent home," "good health," and "good education."[53] Thus, if a government school did not teach all fifth graders to read, the nonreaders would be considered oppressed. Or, if someone was in bad health, then that person would be considered as having been deprived of his freedom, and somehow it would be seen as the government's fault. Roosevelt also declared that liberty requires "the right of every farmer to raise and sell his products at a return which will give him and his family a decent living"—a nonsensical concept that would require setting food prices high enough to keep the nation's least efficient farmer behind his mule and plow.[54]

Roosevelt clarified the necessary underpinnings of his new freedom when, in the same speech, he called for Congress to enact a "national service law—which for the duration of the war . . . will make available for war production or for any other essential services every able-bodied adult in this Nation."[55] Roosevelt promised that this proposal, described in his official papers as a Universal Conscription Act,[56] would be a "unifying moral force" and "a means by which every man and woman can find that inner satisfaction which comes from making the fullest possible contribution to victory."[57] Presumably, the less freedom people had, the more satisfaction they would enjoy.

Commenting on foreign policy, Roosevelt praised Soviet Russia as one of the "freedom-loving Nations" and stressed that Marshal Stalin was "thoroughly conversant with the provisions of our Constitution." Roosevelt's concept of freedom required people to blindly trust their leaders—a trust he greatly abused. Roosevelt also denounced those Americans with "suspicious souls" who feared that he had "made 'commitments' for the future which might pledge this Nation to secret treaties" at the summit of Allied leaders in Tehran the previous month.[58] But, at that summit, Roosevelt secretly agreed to allow Stalin to move the Soviet border far to the West—thus consigning millions of Poles to life under direct Soviet rule.[59] (Roosevelt and Stalin used roughly the same dividing line that Hitler and Stalin used in 1939 to divide Poland into Nazi and Soviet spheres.)

Subsequent politicians have further muddled Americans' understanding of freedom. President Clinton, in an April 19, 1994 television interview, maligned traditional American notions of freedom and constitutional rights:

> When we got organized as a country and we wrote a fairly radical Constitution with a radical Bill of Rights, giving a radical amount of individual freedom to Americans, it was assumed that the Americans who had that freedom would use it responsibly. . . . But it assumed that people would basically be raised in coherent families, in coherent communities, and they would work for the common good, as well as for the individual welfare.
>
> What's happened in America today is, too many people live in areas where there's no family structure, no community structure, and no work structure. And so there's a lot of irresponsibility. And so a lot of people say there's too much personal freedom. When personal freedom's being abused, you have to move to limit it.[60]

The Bill of Rights did not give freedom to individual Americans; instead, the Bill of Rights was a solemn pledge by the government that it recognized and would not violate certain pre-existing rights of the people. The Bill of Rights was not "radical" according to the beliefs of Americans of that era; instead, it codified rights both long recognized in English common law and purchased in blood during the Revolution. The Constitution was almost rejected because many people believed it vested too much power in the federal government.

And it is laughable for Clinton, a former professor of constitutional law, to say that the Founding Fathers presumed that men would "work for the common good." As Madison wrote, "If men were angels, no government would be necessary."[61] Clinton implied that because some people abuse freedom, government must reduce everyone's freedom. But that is why even free societies have jails—because some people commit violent acts against others. Clinton also implied that because some people do not live in traditional families and do not have jobs, government needs more power over everyone. This is an ironic pretext to justify reducing freedom, since government welfare programs have been the major cause of the skyrocketing of out-of-wedlock births and the breakup of families.[62]

POSITIVE FREEDOM: FREEDOM AS GOVERNMENT-PROVIDED AUTHENTICITY

In recent decades, many analyses have contrasted "negative liberty" and "positive liberty." Unfortunately, this dichotomy probably sows more confusion than it alleviates. Positive freedom, which is presumably created by government intervention, is routinely contrasted with negative freedom— freedom as being left alone. However, the simple contrast of two types of freedom does little to help one get a grip on the contemporary use and abuse of the word "liberty."

Positive liberty is a jumble of notions, including freedom to achieve authenticity, autonomy, and freedom from want. We shall examine these abstract concepts and their concrete results.

Positive freedom presumes that not only does the government know what is good for the people, but government officials also somehow know what people want subconsciously.

The doctrine of freedom as authenticity has produced some edifying examples from academics. For instance, Oxford professor George Crowder explained in 1988:

> Although it cannot be said that positive liberty, in most of its forms, can strictly speaking be forced on the individual, it may still be argued that much can be done by others to push the individual in the direction of freedom thus understood.
>
> Consider this example. I am on a long train journey. The authentic part of my personality would have me read an improving work of literature, but is opposed by the crudely appetitive element in me which would rather I looked at a glossy magazine. The authentic, literary side of my character would have a better chance of gaining ascendancy if all temptation to look at the magazine were removed—if it were stolen, perhaps, or taken from me by literature police. This obstruction of my empirical self could effectively force me *toward* authenticity.... Authentic action can be assisted but not guaranteed by external intervention.[63]

But how are the literature police to know the authentic needs of each train traveler? And if the literature police are to maximize the citizen's authentic freedom, why not prohibit him from reading *Lady's Chatterly's Lover* and instead foist the *Critique of Pure Reason* in his hands, and then prohibit him from exiting the train until he can render an adequate account of Kant's categorical imperative? In this example, the average person's "authentic freedom" is based on a presumption that literature police on a train will be practically omniscient and omnibenevolent. However, if a person were that bright, he would probably not be working as a train inspector.

Charles Taylor, another British professor and defender of positive freedom, declared in 1979 that "one is free only to the extent that one has effectively determined oneself and the shape of one's life. The concept of freedom here is an exercise-concept. . . . You are not free if you are motivated, through fear, *inauthentically internalized standards, or false consciousness, to thwart your self-realization.*"[64] (emphasis added) Taylor offered the following example of the meaning of positive freedom: "Say the fear of public speaking is preventing me from taking up a career that I should find very fulfilling, and that I should be quite good at, if I could just get over this 'hang-up.'"[65] Taylor thus implied that he could not be considered free as long as he was afraid of public speaking. Taylor did not explain what remedy, such as paying for a membership for him in a Toastmasters Club, government must provide to bequeath real freedom. Taylor concluded by redefining freedom to mean "the absence of internal or external obstacles to what I truly or authentically want."[66]

The same notion of Government as psychological miracle worker permeated the Great Society programs. President Lyndon Johnson declared on June 26, 1964: "For the first time in world history we have the abundance and the ability to free every man from hopeless want and to free every person to find fulfillment in the works of his mind or the labor of his hands."[67] In 1965, Johnson declared that the goal of his Great Society programs was "to give the individual identity and self-esteem—not to impose upon him any oppressive paternalism."[68] Johnson's Great Society sought to promote individual identity with arts subsidies, job training programs that failed to provide real skills,[69] community organizing programs which were often blamed for subsequent riots,[70] as well as providing all-expense-paid trips to bomb Hanoi. The Great Society maximized individual identity by multiplying dependence on government and political control over the private sector. LBJ's vision practically assumed that government bureaucrats had somehow monopolized the secret of how to achieve internal authenticity, as if they were psychological Brahmins, and thus uniquely suited to be psychological mid-wives.

Regrettably, Johnson never explained the mechanics of mass production of individual identity. Did LBJ assume that individual authenticity is so undifferentiated that the same government policies can automatically authenticate every individual? Or did he concede that government intervention must recognize different degrees of potential authenticity—perhaps rated the same as civil service pay scales, ranging from GS-2 to GS-16? (Johnson's expectations ignored the natural instincts of bureaucrats; as de Tocqueville observed, "Every central government worships uniformity: uniformity relieves it from inquiry into an infinity of details, which must be attended to if rules have to be adapted to different men, instead of indiscriminately subjecting all men to the same rule."[71])

Prof. Cass Sunstein discussed the meaning of freedom in his 1990 book, *After the Rights Revolution: Reconceiving the Regulatory State.* Sunstein begins by equating freedom with autonomy, and then shows why government must sometimes disregard people's values and preferences in order to impose freedom on them:

> The satisfaction of private preferences, whatever their content, is an utterly implausible conception of liberty or autonomy. The notion of autonomy should be taken to refer instead to decisions reached with a full and vivid awareness of available opportunities, with all relevant information, or, most generally, without illegitimate constraints on the process of preference formation. When those conditions are not met, decisions might be regarded as unfree or nonautonomous.[72]

Who is to say whether someone's awareness of his opportunities is "full and vivid," or merely semivivid? If the citizen's eyes do not sparkle when he considers his chances in life, can a bureaucrat conclude the citizen lacks "vivid awareness"? Apparently, any time any government official thinks he knows more than private citizens (who do not possess "all relevant information"), he would be justified in forcibly trumping people's preference. Sunstein's standard makes the citizen's freedom totally dependent on the self-restraint and intellectual modesty of government officials. (President Clinton issued a statement on the night of his 1996 reelection victory praising his advisers and assorted preachers: "I thank them all for bringing me closer to God and to the eternal wisdom without which a President cannot serve."[73] Clinton did not specify how close he considered himself to be to "eternal wisdom.")

Sunstein offers examples of the types of private decisions that require government intervention to liberate the individual, including "a decision of a woman to adopt a traditional gender role because of the social stigma of refusing to do so" and "a decision not to purchase cars equipped with seatbelts or to wear motorcycle helmets because of the social pressures imposed by one's peer group." Sunstein concludes, "In all of these cases, the interest in liberty or autonomy does not call for governmental inaction, even if that were an intelligible category. Indeed, in all of these cases *regulation removes a kind of coercion.*"[74]

Is there any evidence that buying a car with a seatbelt resulted in anyone being ostracized prior to the federal government making seatbelts mandatory in the 1960s? And as for "social stigma" and gender roles, there are probably now more women who feel a social stigma from not having a career than from working outside the home. Does that mean that government should forcibly drive a certain number of women out of the work force (as it did in the 1930s) in order to redeem the self-concepts of those who don't have jobs?

Positive freedom presumes that bureaucratic decrees are more authentic than individual choices. Sunstein, in the name of freedom, essentially calls for more government handcuffs and jail cells to counteract the "coercion" of private frowns and smirks. The doctrine of positive freedom rests on a glorification of government coercion—measuring a person's freedom by the number of benevolent shoves he receives from government officials.

Sunstein declared that "people should not face unjustifiable constraints on the free development of their preferences and belief." Sunstein labeled as a "failure of autonomy, and a reason for collective response . . . the case of people who are indifferent to high quality broadcasting because they have experienced only banal situation comedies and dehumanizing, violence-ridden police dramas."[75] Government subsidies liberate citizens to savor such Public Broadcasting Service (PBS) specials as "Woof!" (which taught viewers how to communicate with their dog)[76] instead of chortling at David Letterman's Top Ten lists. The higher taxes necessary to pay for government broadcasting subsidies preempt some individuals from being able to afford cable television, and thereby to choose to watch the Arts and Entertainment, Bravo, Disney, or Playboy channels.

Another authenticity champion is philosopher Robert Goodin, who, in his 1988 book *Reasons for Welfare,* declared: "Even if we are willing to respect people's tastes in general, we should draw the line at respecting tastes for risks. People are notoriously bad at assessing the probabilities in 'low probability, high risk ventures.'"[77] Goodin observed that "it has been argued that 'passive restraints' such as automobile air bags . . . deprive passengers of the freedom to risk a crash unprotected. . . . I simply cannot see this as a serious infringement of the freedom of the ordinary passenger, who may have failed to belt up out of carelessness or haste but not out of a considered preference for death over life." Joan Claybrook, the chief of the National Highway Traffic Safety Agency (NHTSA) at the time the government issued its first air bag mandate, similarly declared that the bags "really work beautifully and they work automatically and I think that that gives you more freedom and liberty than being . . . forced to wear a seatbelt."[78] In reality, air bags (actually, explosive devices built into car dashboards) symbolize the bogus paternalism that increasingly blights Americans' lives. Federal safety czars have been more concerned about preserving consumer confidence than about killing consumers. Over 90 children and short female adults have been killed by the bags, and over 300,000 people are injured by the bags each year, according to the federal Department of Transportation.[79] A Harvard University study concluded that there was no proof that air bags had saved the life of a single child.[80] The Department of Transportation was informed in the late 1970s that the devices could pose severe safety risks for some passengers. But the information was suppressed because, as a confidential 1991 NHTSA memorandum noted, "bad press [on air bag deaths] could cause a lot of harm to the public's positive perception" of air bags.[81] Once scandal erupted over the rising number of dead babies, federal safety officials denounced parents because children had not been sitting in the back seats. Yet, years earlier, federal officials promised that the bags posed no threat to children in the front seat. Federal bureaucrats responded to public outrage over air bag killings by demanding a new law to criminalize parents who permitted children to sit in the front seat.[82]

The Food and Drug Administration provides Americans with "authentic freedom" by suppressing freedom of speech. FDA commissioner David Kessler invoked this concept of freedom to justify FDA restrictions on information citizens see on bottles of nutritional supplements: "Freedom of choice means little unless consumers have meaningful and accurate information on safety and effectiveness in deciding whether to purchase these products."[83] Kessler has repeatedly derided "freedom of choice" as an illusion unless people are presented with only government-approved choices. Vitamin makers are prohibited from claiming any health benefits for their products unless the FDA gives prior approval to the claim, which is given only when a health claim meets FDA's standard of "significant scientific agreement." But the agency has refused to define this standard, and instead has repeatedly rejected the findings of other federal agencies and highly respected research publications on the benefits of supplements. [84] Studies published in medical journals and elsewhere have established the health benefits of vitamin C, vitamin E, folic acid, and numerous other supplements.[85] But, if vitamin producers quote an article from the *New England Journal of Medicine* on their product labels, the FDA could claim they have committed a criminal act and seek to confiscate and destroy all of their vitamins. The FDA even considers it to be a federal crime for a vitamin producer to quote a report issued by the National Institutes for Health on a bottle label.

The FDA "liberates" people by shielding them from information that might save their lives.

Some advocates of positive freedom seem entranced by the idea of government itself. They seem to view a typical government intervention as the equivalent of Jesus touching Lazarus and raising him from the dead, as the equivalent of a divine burst of light striking Saul on the road to Damascus and suddenly awakening him to his true mission in life, as a voice from the clouds above commanding, "Thou Shalt Wear a Motorcycle Helmet!" But, rather than God, the divine awakening light is administered by government bureaucrats. And instead of the light of divine truth, the bureaucrats have a hefty rule book with some picayune regulation that the citizen has violated.

"THREE HOTS AND A COT": THE HIGH COST OF POLITICAL GENEROSITY

"Freedom from want" is another frequently invoked version of positive freedom. "The most fundamental question of politics is: 'How shall we provide daily bread for our people?'" declared Adolph Hitler in a speech in 1927,[86] at a time when the concept of freedom was shifting from leaving people alone to promising to fill their bellies.

Sidney and Beatrice Webb, two of the founders of British socialism and authors of *The Soviet Union: A New Civilization?*, declared in 1936: "Personal freedom means, in effect, the power of the individual to buy sufficient food, shelter and clothing."[87] The Webbs, writing during Stalin's bloodiest decade, also asserted that, for government economic planning to succeed, "any public expression of doubt . . . is an act of disloyalty and even treachery."[88] Thus, to liberate people with food and clothing, government must have authority to execute anyone who criticized the Five Year Plan for agriculture and textiles. After visiting the Ukraine, the Webbs endorsed Stalin's war on the kulaks (the least impoverished peasants), commenting that "it must be recognized that the liquidation of the individual capitalist in agriculture had necessarily to be faced if the required increase of output was to be obtained."[89] (Output plummeted.) The Webbs did not specify how many millions of people government should be permitted to kill in the name of "freedom from want."

Equating liberty with satisfactory living standards became far more common as the twentieth century went on. "Real freedom means good wages, short hours, security in employment, good homes, opportunity for leisure and recreation with family and friends," wrote Sir Oswald Mosley, the most prominent British supporter of Nazi Germany, in his 1936 book, *Fascism*.[90] James Gregor noted in his book *The Ideology of Fascism* that fascism aimed at "restraints which foster the increased *effective* freedom of the individual."[91] President Roosevelt noted in 1937 that "even some of our own people may wonder whether democracy can match dictatorship in giving this generation the things it wants from government."[92] University of Chicago professor Leslie Pape noted in 1941 that "democracies readily admit the claims of totalitarian states to great achievements in the cause of positive freedom."[93]

British historian E. H. Carr, writing in 1951, observed that, for the modern era, "freedom from the economic constraint of want was clearly just as important as freedom from the political constraint of kings and tyrants."[94] Carr justified the array of economic controls in post-war Britain:

> When we consider the paraphernalia of controls and rationing and taxation necessary to the organization of freedom from want for all, and the restrictions which these involve on the cherished liberties of some, it is not unnatural that some feel like the new freedoms are not an extension of their old freedoms, but their negations. . . . The price of liberty is the restriction of liberty. The price of some liberty for all is the restriction of the greater liberty of some.[95]

However, with this standard, there is no limit to the amount of freedom that government can destroy in the name of creating "greater liberty for some." The British Labour government that Carr championed advanced freedom by conscripting labor for the coal mines and empowering the Ministry of Labour to direct workers to whatever employment it considered in the national interest—empowering over 10,000 government officials to carry out searches (including private homes) without a warrant—prohibiting restaurants from serving customers meals costing more than 5 shillings (less than $2 in 1947)—fining farmers who refused to plant the specific crops government demanded—and even prohibiting any homeowner from "decorating his own house without getting a license, if the cost of raw materials plus the estimated cost of his own labour comes to more than 10 pound Sterling."[96] (As John Jewkes noted in his 1948 classic, *Ordeal by Planning,* "Strong protests forced the government to exclude the cost of labour but not to drop the control."[97]) The government also "nationalized all potential land uses in the United Kingdom, permitting only continuation of existing ones and requiring 'planning permission' for any others," as law professor Gideon Kanner noted.[98] The Labour government offered freedom via the solidarity of standing in the same rationing line—liberation via deprivation. (A 1998 *New York Times* article cited the postwar food rationing, which continued into the 1950s, by the Labour government as a contributing factor to the long-term decline of British cuisine.[99])

The more politicians promise to give, the more they entitle themselves to take. Carr, serving in 1945 as chairman of the UNESCO Committee on the Principles of the Rights of Man, declared that "no society can guarantee the enjoyment of such rights [to government handouts] unless it in turn has the right to call upon and direct the productive capacities of the individuals enjoying them."[100] Thus, the price of government benefits is unlimited political control over people's paychecks and work lives. To finance government handouts, British income tax rates approached 100 percent, inspiring the Beatles song "Taxman."

Once freedom is equated with a certain material standard of living, confiscation becomes the path to liberation. Thus, the more avidly a politician raises taxes, the greater his apparent love for liberty. In the name of providing "freedom from want," the politician acquires a pretext to destroy the basis of private citizens' independence. "Freedom from want" becomes a license for politicians, rather than a declaration of rights of citizens.

Anyone who does not have certain possessions is assumed not to be free—and in need of political rescue. President Johnson, justifying a vast expansion of government social programs, declared in 1965, "Negroes are trapped—as many whites are trapped—in inherited, gateless poverty. . . . Public and private poverty combine to cripple their capacities."[101] Vice President Hubert Humphrey defined a poor person as "the man who for reasons beyond his control cannot help himself." This perspective on poverty and self-help mocks all of American history. This implies that any individual who earns less than $7,890 a year (the official poverty line cutoff for a single person) is incapable of any discipline or resolution.

The new concept of poverty justified a federal war against self-reliance—a massive effort to re-educate the American people about the virtues of government dependency. Professor Nathan Glazer wrote in 1971 that the Community Action Agencies created by the War of Poverty sent out "100,000 recruiters for welfare. . . . One of the major tasks of this legion was to tell poor people about welfare, accompany them to welfare agencies, argue for them, organize them in sit-ins, distribute simplified accounts of the rules governing welfare and the benefits available."[102] After Congress mandated an outreach program for food stamps, an Agriculture Department magazine reported that food stamp workers could often overcome people's pride by saying, "'This is for your children' . . . the problem is not with welfare recipients but with low-income workers: It is this group which recoils when anything even remotely resembling welfare is suggested. . . . With careful explanations . . . coupled with intensive outreach efforts, resistance from the 'too prouds' is bending."[103] But according to USDA dietary surveys, most of the poor did not need federal aid to have an adequate diet. And, after a 30-fold increase in federal food aid spending, the intake of key nutrients by low-income Americans actually declined.[104]

While advocates of positive freedom insist that government must intervene so that each person "can be all that they can be," government aid programs are notorious for rewarding people for making the least of themselves. President Roosevelt warned in 1935 that "continued dependence on relief induces a spiritual and moral disintegration fundamentally destructive to the national fiber."[105] President Clinton declared in 1996: "For decades now, welfare has too often been a trap, consigning generation after generation to a cycle of dependency. The children of welfare are more likely to drop out of school, to run afoul of the law, to become teen parents, to raise their own children on welfare."[106] A rising tide no longer lifts all boats when the government rewards people for scuttling their own ships.

How does the federal government liberate handout recipients? By giving people more money than many could earn working. Government welfare spending is now almost ten times higher (in constant dollars) than it was in 1964.[107] As a result, low-income Americans' work efforts have plummeted. A 1995 Heritage Foundation study reported: "In 1960, among the lowest income quintile of population, nearly two-thirds of households were headed by persons who worked. By 1991 this figure had fallen to around one-third, and only 11 percent were headed by persons who worked full-time throughout the year."[108] A 1998 report by the Milton S. Eisenhower Foundation found that "for the first time in the twentieth century most adults in many inner-city neighborhoods are not working in a typical week."[109] A 1995 Cato Institute analysis found that in 40 states, welfare pays more than an $8-an-hour job, in 17 states, more than a $10-an-hour job. The report declared, "In nine states, welfare pays more than the average first year salary for a teacher, and in 29 states more than the average starting salary for a secretary. . . . In the six most generous states, benefits exceed the entry-level salary for a computer programmer."[110] The higher the benefits, the less work recipients perform. Economist June O'Neill, currently director of the Congressional Budget Office, found, in a federally funded study, that "a 50 percent increase in monthly AFDC and Food Stamp benefit levels was found to lead to a 75 percent increase both in the number of women enrolling in AFDC and in the number of years spent on AFDC."[111] And even though Congress and President Clinton ballyhooed a welfare reform law enacted in 1996, total welfare spending is still expected to increase from $412 billion in 1997 to $532 billion by the year 2002.[112]

Faith in positive freedom depends on a political myopia that focuses on only one side of the ledger of government action. This is measuring freedom according to how much government does *for* people, and totally disregarding what government does *to* people. Government provides freedom for the welfare recipient by imposing tax servitude on the worker. Federal, state, and local governments will collect an average of $26,434 in taxes for every household in the country, or an average of $9,881 for every U.S. resident in 1998, according to the Tax Foundation.[113] In an age of unprecedented prosperity, government tax policies have turned the average citizen's life into a financial struggle and ensured that he will likely become a ward of the state in his last decades.

Some Statists insist that taxation is irrelevant to freedom. One former career IRS lawyer informed a congressional committee in 1997: "Although no one likes to pay taxes, all reasonable people know that our taxes are the price we pay for our liberty!"[114] Taxation is sometimes portrayed practically as an "act of God"— or, more accurately, an "act of a political God"—and thus above reproach. According to Robert Goodin,

> If what the rich man loses when his property is redistributed is described as a loss of freedom, then the gain to the poor must similarly be described as a gain of freedom. . . . No net loss of freedom for society as a whole, as distinct from individuals within it, is involved in redistributive taxation. Thus, there is no basis in terms of freedom . . . for objecting to it.[115]

What does Goodin mean by "freedom for society as a whole"? By this standard, slavery would not reduce a society's freedom, since the slave's loss of freedom would be equaled by the slaveowner's gain. Nor is there any difference, vis-à-vis freedom between permitting people to retain their earnings and spend them as they choose, and government confiscating their money to use to hire more regulators and inspectors and informants to better repress the citizenry.

What are the practical results of modern "freedom from want?" Economist Edgar Browning, writing in 1993, examined the marginal cost of redistribution—defined as "the ratio of the aggregate loss to the top four quintiles of households to the aggregate gain to the bottom quintile of households."[116] Browning estimated that the "marginal cost" to the most affluent 80 percent of households of increasing the income of the poorest 20 percent of households was $7.82 for each $1 increase in cash income over the course of the lifetimes of both low-income and more affluent citizens.[117] The marginal costs of redistribution are much larger than people might presume because of reduced incentives to work, both among the taxpayers and recipients. Also, as Browning noted, "marginal tax rates must be increased very sharply relative to the amount of income that is redistributed." Combining Browning's analysis and Goodin's definition, confiscatory redistribution destroys almost eight times as much "freedom" as it creates.

Once the notion of "freedom from want" is accepted as the preeminent freedom, it becomes a wish list justifying endless political forays deeper and deeper into people's lives. Princeton professor Amy Gutmann, in her 1982 book *Liberal Equality,* declared: "Liberal egalitarians want to say that freedom of choice is not very meaningful without a right to those goods necessary to life itself."[118] Gutmann's elaboration of "necessary goods" reveals how government would be obliged to control almost everything: "Supplying the poorest with more primary goods will be insufficient if their sense of self-worth or their very desire to pursue their conceptions of the good is undercut by self-doubt."[119] By this standard, freedom is violated when people suffer self-doubt, and the government is obliged to forcibly intervene to guarantee that all people think well of themselves.

Political scientist Alan Wolfe, a self-described "welfare liberal," asserted in 1995 that "people need a modicum of security and income maintenance, underwritten by government, in order to fulfill the ideal of negative liberty, which is self-sufficiency."[120] Government dependency is the new, improved form of self-reliance: dependency on government doesn't count because government is a better friend to you than you are yourself. But the more dependent people become on government, the more susceptible they are to political and bureaucratic abuse. Freedom from want is conceivable only so long as people are allowed to want only what the government thinks they should have.

Freedom from want requires that politicians and bureaucrats decree who will be subjugated to meet other people's needs. Every increase in government handouts requires a corresponding decrease in people's right to retain their own paychecks. "Positive freedom" is based on a general political confiscation and redistribution of opportunity. But after private opportunity is confiscated and run through the ringer of the State, it is no longer opportunity, but merely the privilege to live off of someone else's labor without their consent.

Freedom from want supposedly results from government taking away what a person owns so that it can give him back what it thinks he deserves. The Welfare State is either a way to force people to finance their own benefits via political-bureaucratic bagmen, or it is a way to force some people to labor for other people's benefit. In the first case, government sacrifices the person's freedom to the fraud that government must tax him to subsidize him; in the second, government sacrifices the person's freedom in order to "liberate" someone else—often someone who chooses not to work. If someone pays the taxes that finance the government benefits he receives, he is less free than he would otherwise have been.

Government handouts, rather than the key to positive freedom, are merely a rebate on political serfdom. The Office of Management and Budget (OMB) estimated in 1994 that males born between 1980 and 1992 will have to surrender over half of their lifetime earnings to tax collectors. The average male born in 1952 will be forced to pay $171,000 more in taxes than he receives from the government, and the average male born in 1967 will pay in over $200,000 more than he receives, according to OMB.[121] And these estimates are based on the cheery assumption that the Social Security system will not crash and burn. As the federal government has repeatedly asserted in briefs to the Supreme Court, Social Security is a welfare system—not a system of contractual, earned rights.[122] A person is entitled to a Social Security benefit; but that entitlement exists only until Congress chooses to reduce or abolish benefits. And then the person is entitled to write a letter to his congressman.

Some apologists for the Welfare State imply that the so-called tax burden is an illusion because whatever title anyone has to own something came originally from government. Cass Sunstein, for instance, stresses that "a system of private property is a construct of the state" and "governmental rules are implicated in, indeed constitute, the distribution of wealth and entitlement in the first instance. . . ."[123] Thus, government can presumably effectively revoke the rights to property without violating people's rights. Anything the government does not confiscate from the citizen becomes practically a government benefit. This presumes that government is the equivalent of some pagan Earth Mother from whom all things come . . . and thus who has a right to take all things back. The only way to justify ignoring tax burdens as morally irrelevant is to assume that government owns all the labor of all the citizens in the society. An edifice of freedom cannot be built on a foundation of slave ethics. It is absurd to pretend that the government bequeathed the sweat of the brow of the carpenter who built a house that he sold, that government created the muscle by which a laborer dug a ditch, that government begot the idea that the software writer used to revolutionize computer use around the world, or that government forged the courage of a businessman who staked his life savings on a new product that made life easier for millions.

Some "freedom from want" advocates imply that government is a great benefactor when it promises citizens "three hots and a cot"—the old-time recruiting slogan of the Marine Corps. But trading freedom for a full belly is a worse bargain now than ever before. As Nobel Laureate economist Friedrich Hayek observed, "As the result of the growth of free markets, the reward of manual labor has during the past hundred and fifty years experienced an increase unknown in any earlier period in history."[124] The average worker in industrialized countries can purchase the bare necessities of life with fewer hours of labor than ever before. Economist Julian Simon found, comparing current wages and prices with those of 1800, that the average American worker needs to work less than one-tenth of the time now than his predecessors did two centuries ago to earn enough to purchase a bushel of wheat.[125] While the real price of food has plummeted (in spite of government farm policies), the "real price" of political servitude has not diminished.

It is understandable that some well-intentioned people would assume that "freedom from want" is the most important freedom. It is difficult for many people to conceive of enjoying anything (much less their freedom) if they lack food, clothing, or shelter. However, freedom is no guarantee of prosperity for every citizen; the fact that some people have meager incomes does not prove that they are shackled. It is a cardinal error to confuse freedom with the things that free individuals can achieve or produce, and then to sacrifice the reality of freedom in a deluded shortcut to the bounty of freedom. Freedom is not measured by how much a person possesses, but by the restrictions and shackles under which he lives.

The question is not whether a starving person can savor a sense of personal freedom. Obviously, there is some point of deprivation at which most people would trade their birthright of freedom for a mess of pottage. But government control of the economy—in the name of "freedom from want" or any other cause—is far more likely to produce poverty than affluence. According to the United Nations Development Program, the citizenries of 70 nations were, on average, poorer in 1997 than they were in 1980.[126] Almost all of those nations pursued central economic planning or were characterized by pervasive violations of property rights. By contrast, citizens in Hong Kong, Singapore, and Taiwan have had among the most economic freedom of any nations in the world for the last four decades, and per capita income in those countries has increased almost tenfold or more in constant dollars.[127]

Throughout history, politicians have used other people's property to buy themselves power. That is the primary achievement of the Welfare State. The danger of government handouts to freedom was clear to some political writers hundreds of years ago. The French writer Etienne de la Boetie, in his 1577 *Discourse of Voluntary Servitude,* noted of ancient Rome: "Tyrants would distribute largess, a bushel of wheat, a gallon of wine . . . and then everybody would shamelessly cry, 'Long live the King!' The fools did not realize that they were merely recovering a portion of their own property, and that their ruler could not have given them what they were receiving without having first taken it from them."[128]

We will now proceed to examine specific government policies created in the name of advancing freedom, and see how every "positive freedom" policy requires an increase in government coercion and arbitrary power.

FREEDOM VIA REDISTRIBUTING RENT

Government rental subsidies exemplify how politicians provide selected beneficiaries with "freedom." Section 8, the largest rental subsidy program, currently gives $9 billion a year in rental subsidies to 3 million families. The Clinton administration 1996 budget proposal declared: "Current residents of public housing and the privately owned assisted housing projects will get certificates and the *freedom* to use them to help pay rent in the private market."[129] William Shaw, HUD's chief coordinator for the state of Indiana, asserted in 1995 that "freedom of choice" is one of the "basic expectations of anyone HUD's programs serve."[130] But the only people today who have such "freedom" are those who have HUD vouchers that force other taxpayers to cover all or most of their rent.

Section 8 recipients are technically required to pay 30% of their income towards rent (though this is often not enforced), and the government pays the difference between the tenant's contribution and the apartment rent. Section 8 seeks to end the stigma of welfare by treating welfare recipients like a privileged class. HUD will pay up to $1802 a month for welfare recipients to live on the island of Nantucket, Massachusetts; $1584 a month in Stamford, Connecticut; and $1611 a month in Westchester County, New York.[131]

HUD finally admitted in 1997 that its subsidized rents are often far above that of surrounding unsubsidized housing.[132] In Buffalo, NY, Section 8 was paying triple the so-called fair market value for some rental apartments; in Rock Island, Illinois, HUD was paying above fair market values for every subsidized apartment in town. In Washington, D.C., Section 8 rents averaged almost 50 percent higher than the rent of similar unsubsidized apartments. [133] HUD Secretary Andrew Cuomo proclaimed, "To be subsidizing rents which are higher than market rates is inexcusable."[134] However, HUD trumpeted the high rents not as a sign that its program is incurably mismanaged, but instead as a ploy to garner a multibillion dollar bailout from Congress to renew subsidized rental contracts.

HUD's "freedom" awards to some low-income people make life more difficult for other citizens. As Bertha Conger of Davenport, Iowa, complained to HUD, "Ordinary people may have a hard time finding a place to rent because some landlord will only rent to subsidized people because they can get twice the rent from them."[135] The *Baltimore Sun* noted in 1996, "In an area where many houses ordinarily could be leased for under $350, the poor families' $600 a month housing vouchers have made renting to Section 8 tenants so profitable many speculators are no longer interested in ordinary working-class renters."[136] One HUD study concluded that Section 8's lavish subsidies could be inflating rents for unsubsidized tenants.[137]

Any family or person with less than 80 percent of the median income for their area is eligible for Section 8—a total of tens of millions of Americans. A family of five with an annual income of $52,250 in Westchester County, New York, is eligible for Section 8, as is a family of four with an income of $60,000 in Nantucket County, Massachusetts.[138] (Some local governments have an even more expansive concept of neediness; the Battery Park City Authority of New York announced in 1998 that it would provide rental subsidies to selected families with incomes as high as $108,000,[139] and in Aspen, Colorado, families with two children and incomes of up to $118,000 a year are eligible for subsidized housing.[140]) Once people initially qualify for Section 8, some housing authorities make little or no effort to check their income in subsequent years—thus encouraging people to stay permanently on the dole.[141]

Not only do Section 8 recipients receive a large financial windfall, but HUD forces landlords to treat Section 8 renters better than renters who pay their own bills. HUD decreed that landlords can require only a $50 security deposit from Section 8 renters instead of the usual full month's rent deposit required for unsubsidized renters. It would be difficult to concoct a rule better designed to maximize the irresponsibility of a privileged class of renters.[142] Howard Husock of Harvard's Kennedy School of Government observed, "The Chicago Housing Authority has faced objections by black developers who assert that public housing tenants [who were given Section 8 certificates] placed in mixed-income buildings have vandalized the premises and alienated non-subsidized neighbors through their behavior."[143] And such problems are not limited to Chicago: the *Kansas City Star* noted that "in some neighborhoods, a single Section 8 house can significantly drag down property values."[144] Apartment owners can supposedly get reimbursement from local HUD bureaucrats for damage done by Section 8 renters, but the bureaucrats routinely make it extremely difficult to collect.

Section 8 vivifies how "positive freedom" rests on the discretionary power of bureaucrats. The budget for housing subsidies is limited, and far more people are eligible than actually receive benefits. In the District of Columbia between 1990 and early 1994, 98 percent of all the Section 8 certificates were awarded as a result of bribes or kickbacks.[145] On October 3, 1996 a former administrator of the Detroit Housing Administration was convicted of 49 counts of conspiracy to solicit bribes, using false documents, and receiving bribes for charging people to move their names up on the Section 8 waiting list.[146] On September 26, 1996, a former employee of the Pomona Housing Authority in California was indicted for accepting bribes to process applications for Section 8 for people who were not eligible for the program.[147]

FREEDOM VIA DISABILITIES

President Clinton declared on July 26, 1994, "The Americans with Disabilities Act (ADA) is a national monument to freedom. Contained within its broad pillars of independence, inclusion, and empowerment is the core ideal of equality that has defined this country since its beginnings."[148] In reality, the ADA symbolizes a "freedom" based on maximizing the number of legal clubs that politically favored groups can use against everyone else.

The Equal Employment Opportunity Commission (EEOC), in its official regulations implementing the 1990 law, declared: "The ADA is intended to enable disabled persons to compete in the workplace based on the same performance standards and requirements that employers expect of persons who are not disabled."[149] And how is this laudable goal to be achieved? In many cases, by forcing the employer to make expensive "accommodations" for the disabled worker and by lowering performance standards. Some police departments have lowered their strength requirements for new hires to comply with the ADA.[150] The EEOC announced, "Providing personal assistants [at the business's expense], such as a page turner for an employee with no hands . . . may also be a reasonable accommodation."[151] The EEOC ruled in 1997 that even if individuals formally apply for government disability benefits, they will still be eligible to sue an employer who would not hire or promote them because the employer perceived them to be disabled.[152]

The ADA advances the disabled's freedom by suppressing employers' freedom of speech. Employers are now prohibited from directly asking job applicants any questions about mental illness—and once a person is hired, the person becomes "entitled to extra support and accommodation."[153] The EEOC issued an official "Enforcement Guidance on Pre-Employment Disability-Related Inquiries" in 1994. Allegedly, recovering alcoholics are covered by the ADA. The EEOC declared that it is legal to ask, "Do you drink alcohol?" but illegal to ask, "How much alcohol do you drink per week?" Regarding vision-impaired people, the EEOC decreed that it is legal to ask, "Do you have 20/20 corrected vision?" but illegal to ask, "What is your corrected vision?"[154] If an employer asks too directly about a disability during a job interview, the employer is presumed to be discriminating against the handicapped person and can be forced to pay large settlements to avoid a lawsuit.

"Freedom to arrive at work late" is one of the EEOC's latest creations. According to rules issued by the agency in March 1997, employers may now be obliged to accommodate workers taking antidepressants by letting them arrive later in the morning, or provide time off ("reasonable accommodation") for workers who announce they are "depressed and stressed," or to provide "job coaches" to people acting hostile and abusive to co-workers or customers.[155] Considering the "protections" the EEOC demands for the so-called mentally disabled, surliness could become the shortcut to job tenure. Psychiatrist Michael Reznicek observed, "With the EEOC's help, unmotivated employees will soon learn to protect their jobs by taking their health-insurance cards to the nearest mental-health clinic, where they will find psychiatrists with every incentive to make the diagnosis of depression."[156]

The ADA also provides "freedom" to the handicapped by sacrificing other people's safety. In March 1997, the EEOC sued the United Parcel Service for refusing to hire one-eyed drivers for its big trucks. EEOC lawyer Bill Tamayo told *Traffic World,* "If they [UPS] feel that these people cannot do the job, then let them prove it. Don't assume that people with one eye cannot drive."[157] Yet, the National Transportation Safety Board prohibits one-eyed drivers from driving any truck above 10,000 pounds. "Fairness" apparently obliges people to let themselves get killed by truck drivers with little or no depth perception.

ADA supporters pretend that freedom is the product of giving some people the right to command other people to provide them with special treatment. Politicians wanted the disabled to receive more aid, but did not have the courage to directly appropriate additional subsidies for them—they also wanted to pretend that there was no "charity" in the law's operation. The result of this political cowardice and dishonesty is a law that is far more intrusive than is necessary to achieve the goal of helping the handicapped. Kathi Wolfe, a vision-impaired writer, commented in the *Washington Post:* "A huge number of frivolous complaints brought under the ADA in recent years has contributed to the widespread impression that hiring disabled people is an invitation to trouble. . . . The ADA is becoming a nightmare."[158]

CABLE RACKETEERING IN THE NAME OF FREEDOM

The doctrine of "positive liberty" is being invoked in other ways to reduce freedom of speech. In 1992, Congress enacted the Cable Television Consumer Protection and Competition Act. Unfortunately, the primary means of protecting consumers and promoting competition in the act consisted of increasing political control over cable systems. Congress refused to challenge the local cable monopolies that have, with its blessing, been granted throughout the country—often in sweetheart deals with local politicians. (There is no technological reason why cable systems need monopolies; cable rates are much lower in locales with two or more competing cable systems.) The 1992 act forced cable systems both to transmit local broadcast television stations' signals (a "must-carry" provision) and to pay them for the honor. The "must-carry" provisions of the 1992 act also required the FCC to rule on which stations are in the public interest. Given the finite number of cable channels, a requirement to carry some stations effectively knocks other stations off the cable. The FCC ruled in 1993 that more than 100 home shopping stations were programming in the public interest and thereby compelled cable systems to carry them.[159] As a result of "must-carry," C-SPAN, the public-affairs network that broadcasts the proceedings of the House and Senate, was dropped by many cable systems; C-SPAN lost an estimated 7 million potential viewers.[160]

Cable companies challenged the act, but a 1994 Supreme Court decision upheld most of its provisions. Justice Anthony Kennedy, writing for the majority, announced that "assuring that the public has access to a multiplicity of information sources is a *governmental* purpose of the highest order, for it promotes values central to the First Amendment."[161] Kennedy concluded: "The First Amendment's command that government not impede the freedom of speech does not disable the government from taking steps to ensure that private interests not restrict, through physical control of a critical pathway of communication, the free flow of information and ideas." As Matthew Bunker and Charles Davis noted in a 1996 article in the *Journal of Broadcasting and Electronic Media,* "Rather than seeing the First Amendment as a restraint on government intervention, the new vision makes government an intervening agent responsible for furthering societal norms such as diversity of opinion and community participation in mass communication."[162] It would have been far more effective to solve the problem by announcing that government-mandated local cable television monopolies are as unconstitutional as government-decreed local newspaper monopolies.

FREEDOM FROM FEAR:
OR, MODERN POWER WORSHIP

Few phrases better symbolize the confusion of current debates over liberty than "freedom from fear." In the past decade, "freedom from fear" has become one of the most widely invoked promises in American politics.

President George Bush told the National Baptist Convention on September 8, 1989: "Today freedom from fear . . . means freedom from drugs."[163] A few days earlier, Bush informed the American Legion: "Today I want to focus on one of those freedoms: freedom from fear—the fear of war abroad, the fear of drugs and crime at home. To win that freedom, to build a better and safer life, will require the bravery and sacrifice that Americans have shown before and must again."[164] Naturally, foremost among the sacrifices that Bush demanded was that of traditional liberties. Bush's 1990 crime bill would have allowed the use of illegally seized evidence against defendants in criminal trials and would have elevated government employees into a special class by making the penalties for killing government workers much harsher than those for killing private citizens.[165] (The Democratic congressional majority altered Bush's bill, and he vetoed the final version because it was insufficiently tough on criminals.) The Bush administration also expanded government's power to compel people to seize people's property without a criminal conviction and approved a vast expansion of the use of the U.S. military for domestic law enforcement.[166] Bush, in a 1992 speech dedicating a new Drug Enforcement Agency office building, declared, "I am delighted to be here to salute the greatest freedom fighters any nation could have, people who provide freedom from violence and freedom from drugs and freedom from fear."[167] But people are killing each other over drugs not because of the drugs themselves but because of the illegal nature of the drug business: prohibition generates excessive profits that make violence worthwhile, as Nobel laureate economist Milton Friedman has courageously argued for decades.[168] Bush's drug czar, William Bennett, clarified how "freedom from fear" could be achieved when he endorsed the public beheading of drug dealers.[169]

The Fourth Amendment was enacted by the Founding Fathers to give Americans freedom from government agents rampaging through their homes and lives. However, contemporary politicians prefer a loftier concept of freedom. In 1993, the Chicago Housing Authority (CHA) began a series of warrantless sweep searches of residents' apartments to confiscate firearms. (Other cities, such as Baltimore and Philadelphia, also used warrantless mass sweeps of public housing apartments to seize guns and other items.)[170] Law professor Tracey Maclin observed, "During these sweeps, officers would rifle cabinets and dresser drawers, look inside refrigerators, overturn mattresses and sofa cushions, and inspect private papers and closed boxes."[171] In early 1994, the CHA proposed beginning routine no-knock raid sweeps.[172] On April 7, 1994, federal judge Wayne Andersen ruled that the dragnet searches were unconstitutional, warning: "The erosion of the rights of people on the other side of town will ultimately undermine the rights of each of us."[173]

President Clinton was outraged that a judge limited the power of the police, and announced, "I'm so worried that all the progress that's been made will be undermined by this court decision."[174] Two months later, Clinton visited the Chicago housing projects, again endorsed the searches, and declared, "The most important freedom we have in this country is the freedom from fear. And if people aren't free from fear, they are not free."[175] In Clinton's view, public housing residents apparently had no reason to fear the housing police storming into their apartments. Yet, court testimony showed that the warrantless searches—none of which occurred within 48 hours of actual shooting incidents[176]—were ineffective at reducing crime. Harvey Grossman of the American Civil Liberties Union observed: "Instead of meeting their obligations to provide real safety, Chicago officials perpetrated a hoax by convincing many residents that warrantless sweep searches of all apartments would enhance their safety."[177]

Clinton also sought to provide public housing residents with "freedom from fear" by urging public housing authorities nationwide to prohibit any tenant from possessing firearms.[178] Clinton effectively sought to force people to forfeit their Second Amendment rights when living in government housing. Had Clinton's proposal been widely accepted, it may have been only a question of time until Clinton or subsequent politicians proposed expanding the ban to include anyone living in housing purchased with a government-backed mortgage. Clinton used similar rhetoric to push other gun control proposals, declaring on May 12, 1994: "Freedom from violence and freedom from fear are essential to maintaining not only personal freedom but a sense of community in this country."[179] (The Clinton administration, in its official 1995 budget, proposed to ban all semiautomatic weapons[180]—which could have meant confiscating 35 millions rifles and handguns produced since 1890.) But crippling citizens' right to defend themselves has far more impact on poor people than on rich people. Public housing projects, for instance, have crime rates as high as 20 times the national average.[181] Gun bans in response to high crime rates mean closing the barn door after the horse has escaped. The essence of Clinton's "freedom from fear" is forcing people to depend on the State even when the police cannot or will not defend them; public housing residents apparently should be honored to die martyrs to "freedom from fear."

Clinton invoked the same theme in his push for the federal government to seize control over health care: "For individuals, health security means freedom from fear and the freedom to prosper and the freedom to make choices that now are becoming narrower and narrower for most Americans in health care."[182] Yet Clinton's health care legislative proposal would have created over 170 new statutory federal crimes. Among other achievements, as Grace-Marie Arnett noted in a *Washington Post* article entitled "Cops and Doctors," his proposal would have compelled all American citizens not specifically exempted to register with a government-certified health alliance; created an "All-Payer Health Care Fraud and Abuse Control Program" run by federal authorities and financed solely by fines and property forfeitures; imposed 5-year prison sentences on anyone who "knowingly creates or uses any documents that contain false statements" regarding health care; imposed 10-year prison sentences on anyone who acquired health care services under false pretenses; imposed 15-year prison sentences on patients who gave and doctors who accepted "anything of value" from patients to be their advocates with a health alliance; imposed $10,000 fines on doctors who failed to submit data on "clinical encounters" in the form required by the Quality Management Council; and empowered state governments to dictate fees to doctors—and to withhold payments to doctors if a health care alliance was facing a budgetary squeeze.[183] Many small businesses feared that the Clinton proposal, by saddling them with huge new expenses, would bankrupt them; private experts estimated that the original plan would destroy more than 3 million jobs.[184] First Lady Hillary Clinton sneered at job loss fears when she was asked about the impact of the plan on small business: "I can't go out and save every undercapitalized entrepreneur in America."[185] Apparently, people have no right to fear losing their jobs when political leaders are busy inflicting freedom from fear upon them.

In early 1996, Clinton, adding conservative stripes for his reelection campaign, endorsed forcing children to wear uniforms at public schools. Clinton justified this fashion dictate: "Every one of us has an obligation to work together, to give our children freedom from fear and the freedom to learn."[186] But, if mandatory uniforms were the secret to ending violence, Postal Service employees would have a lower homicide rate.[187] New York City school board president William Thompson imposed mandatory uniform policies in March 1998 for a half-million school children, declaring that the "policy is important to diminish peer pressure."[188] And, naturally, the surest way to decrease peer pressure is to increase government pressure on children and their parents.

Almost every proposal for freedom from fear is based on the sacrifice of traditional freedoms for an illusory higher freedom. Sen. Bob Dole, the 1996 Republican presidential nominee, repeatedly promised voters "freedom from fear" by means of new anti-crime measures. How did Dole intend to provide "freedom from fear"? By proclaiming that "we must . . . untie the hands of the police."[189]

Politicians' promises of "freedom from fear" imply that freedom properly understood is a risk-free, worry-free condition. "Freedom from fear" is the sort of promise that a mother would make to a young child. The fact that the promise is now routinely made by politicians symbolizes the infantilizing of the American people.

The phrase "freedom from fear" epitomizes how freedom is now seen as the antithesis of self-reliance, as something that exists only in the womb of government paternalism. "Freedom from fear" is to be achieved by the citizen becoming a psychological ward of the State, accepting everything that politicians say, and surrendering everything that politicians demand. "Freedom from fear" means security via mass delusions about the nature of political power. As French philosopher Bertrand de Jouvenel wrote, "The timid run to cover and support; so that the degree of their subjection will give the almost exact measure of their fears."[190]

If government must provide "freedom from fear," then any citizen's fear is sufficient pretext to increase government power. Giving government more power based on people's fears is like giving firemen pay raises based on how many false alarms are reported. The Environmental Protection Agency (EPA), for instance, in the last 15 years has repeatedly alarmed the public by greatly exaggerating the risk from radon, global warming, dioxin, and industrial waste sites.[191] The more frightened the public becomes, the more power the EPA commandeers.[192]

The premise underlying every "freedom from fear" scheme is that the fewer inviolable rights the citizen has, the better the government will treat him. The fewer liberties a person has, the fewer dangers he will face—except from the power that took away his liberty. As John Locke observed 300 years ago, "I have no reason to suppose, that he, who would take away my Liberty, would not when he had me in his Power, take away every thing else."[193]

THE "FREEDOM UNDER THE LAW" ANACHRONISM

Montesquieu, the author of *The Spirit of the Laws,* declared in 1748: "Liberty is the right to do whatever the law permits."[194] Yet, even in Montesquieu's time, that was an absurd definition. While an affluent aristocrat like Montesquieu had many legal immunities from the law (such as being exempt from taxation), "law" was a mockery for the masses of downtrodden Frenchmen. In the mid-1700s, the French government was severely restricting internal trade (resulting in recurrent famines in some parts of France while other parts had grain surpluses),[195] executing tradesmen for charging "excessive" prices, jailing anyone who criticized the king, having hangmen burn controversial new books, and sending tax collectors out to violently pillage the peasantry. In some parts of Europe, *droit du seigneur* was the "law," and young maidens became "free" by submitting to being deflowered by the nearest loutish aristocrat. "Law" was effectively whatever the king said it was, since France had not had a viable parliament for over a hundred years at that point and the courts lacked power to overrule what the king declared.

Not surprisingly, the doctrine of freedom under the law has long been popular with politicians. William McKinley declared in a July 4, 1894 speech: "Liberty is responsibility, and responsibility is duty, and that duty is to preserve the exceptional liberty we enjoy within the law and for the law and by the law." McKinley's statement was a peculiar spin on Lincoln—as if the law were an end in itself and obedience Americans' highest glory. (As President, McKinley liberated Americans by requiring them to pay tariff taxes of up to 289 percent on the value of wool clothing they bought.[196]) President John F. Kennedy declared on September 30, 1962: "Our nation is founded on the principle that observance of the law is the eternal safeguard of liberty and defiance of the law is the surest road to tyranny."[197] (Kennedy, according to subsequent revelations, apparently exempted the FBI, IRS, and CIA from the duty of observing the law. And, before imposing a trade embargo on Cuba in 1962, he made sure that a stock of over a thousand Cuban cigars was purchased for his personal use.[198])

"Freedom under the law," in its contemporary incarnation, is one of the great "let's pretend" games of intellectual history. If we pretend that the law is what it should be, and if we pretend that those in power do not desire to unnecessarily subjugate or plunder the citizenry, then people become free by obeying the laws that the good government enacts. The fact that neither the laws nor the rulers are actually "good" are mere technicalities that cannot tarnish the majesty of "freedom under the law."

Faith in "freedom under the law" derives from a time when the law was based on rules of conduct that were "known from time immemorial"—rules of just conduct by which people had lived for generations. As Professor John Phillip Reid observed, "It is sometimes assumed by legal scholars that law was command during the era of the American Revolution, but that is an error. To a remarkable extent law even in the eighteenth century was still thought of as it had been in medieval times, as the *sovereign* and not as the command emanating from the sovereign."[199] When the law respects freedom, freedom under the law is a viable ideal. As Blackstone, the English legal philosopher, wrote in 1766, "The public good is in nothing more essentially interested, than in the protection of every individual's private rights."[200] With a Blackstonian concept of the "public good," "liberty under the law" makes sense, since government could not then legitimately infringe upon the individual's rights.

However, today, laws themselves are far and away the largest violators of individual rights. Nowadays, "freedom under the law" makes as much sense as "freedom under the lash." The doctrine of "freedom under the law" is one of the most dangerous political relics of our age. "Freedom under the law" now means freedom to kowtow, to curtsy, to grovel before any government employee with a memo or a ticket book; freedom to admit and accept one's legally inferior status; freedom to accept as many burdens as politicians and bureaucrats deign to impose.

To idealize the law is to delude oneself about the nature of contemporary political power. "Law" cannot miraculously transcend the politicians who make it. Contemporary law retains far more respect than it deserves. Laws are simply political edicts, with little or no resemblance to traditional, accepted principles of justice. Coercion and expropriation have become tools in politician's reelection campaigns: whenever increased coercion garners votes or campaign contributions, new laws are promulgated and government agents sent out to inflict politicians' will. When law itself is the means by which the citizen is stripped of the fruits of his labor, confined to ever narrower portions of his own existence, and subjugated to a thousand insect authorities—then "freedom under the law" means simply freedom by submitting to your worst enemy. Nowadays, to obey every law is to accept a life sentence as a political pawn. When the laws are a travesty of decency—when the lawmakers are more intent on pillaging than on protecting rights—then obeying every law means signing the death warrant on one's own freedom.

In the classical concept of "freedom under the law," law was a leash on both the government and the governed. But nowadays, law is something government imposes, not something that government obeys. This is clear in environmental law (the federal government is by far the biggest violator of environmental statutes), tax law (the General Accounting Office has repeatedly reported that the IRS is unable to account for much of its revenue and expenditures), labor relations law (which Congress exempted itself from), and smoking bans (from which Congress continues to exempt itself).

According to John Locke, "The Reason why men enter into society . . . is, that there may be laws made, and Rules set as guards and fences to the properties of all the members of the Society, to limit the Power, and moderate the Dominion of every part and member of the society.[201] Locke defined "properties" much more broadly than current usage of the term, including a person's "Life, Liberty, and Estate," as well as "the Labour of his Body, and the Work of his hands." Laws, insofar as they mark boundaries between private citizens and between the citizen and the State, can safeguard freedom. By sacrificing a sliver of freedom, laws can provide greater security to the large amount of remaining freedom. By protecting private domains, law—ideally—maximizes each person's chance to run his own life.

Some laws have advanced and better protected individual freedom and individual rights, such as laws permitting women and blacks to own property and make contracts on an equal legal basis to white males. But such laws did not "create liberty"; instead, they merely razed previously erected legal barriers against a particular group. Laws that deter private violence—such as restrictions on mob violence—safeguard freedom. Another example of a government rule that promotes freedom is the Thirteenth Amendment, enacted in 1866, which states: "Neither slavery nor involuntary servitude, except as a punishment for crime whereof the party shall have been duly convicted, shall exist within the United States." This amendment was interpreted by the Supreme Court in the late nineteenth century to outlaw a variety of types of labor contracts that resembled peonage, thereby curbing the power of an employer over an employee. State laws enacted in the 1960s and afterwards refining the procedures and rules of evidence for investigating and prosecuting rapists have safeguarded women's freedom. (Many police departments had been criminally negligent in their attitude towards any rapist who did not cross racial lines.) Such laws did not create new legal rights so much as they sought to correct gross inadequacies in enforcing existing rights. Laws holding individuals liable for the environmental damage they inflict on other people's property are safeguards of freedom, since no individual has the right to poison his neighbors.

"Few laws are necessary to preserve property; a multitude are required for transferring it," Senator John Taylor wrote in 1822.[202] A small number of laws can be invaluable as a buttress to individual liberty, but the vast majority of laws necessary to safeguard freedom have been on the statute books for decades, if not centuries. What has been added, almost uniformly, are laws subversive of freedom and destructive of individual rights—laws explicitly intended to multiply the pretexts for which government employees can punish private citizens.

PROPERTY AND LIBERTY

Property is "the guardian of all other rights," as Arthur Lee of Virginia wrote in 1775.[203] The Supreme Court declared in 1897: "In a free government almost all other rights would become worthless if the government possessed power over the private fortune of every citizen."[204] Unfortunately, legislators, judges, and political philosophers in the twentieth century have perennially disparaged property's value to freedom.

Without private property, there is no escape from State power. Property rights are the border guards around an individual's life that deter political invasions. Those who disparage property often oppose any meaningful limits on government power. John Dewey, for instance, derided "the sanctity of private property" for providing "freedom from social control."[205] Socialist regimes despise property because it limits the power of the State to regiment the lives of the people. A 1975 study, *The Soviet Image of Utopia,* observed, "The closely knit communities of communism will be able to locate the anti-social individual without difficulty because he will not be able to 'shut the door of his apartment' and retreat to an area of his life that is 'strictly private.'"[206] Hungarian economist Janos Kornai observed: "The further elimination of private ownership is taken, the more consistently can full subjection be imposed."[207]

Oxford professor John Gray asserted in 1990 that "very extensive State intervention in the economy has nowhere resulted in the extinction of basic personal and political liberties."[208] One wonders which freedoms Bulgarian and Romanian citizens enjoyed under communism that Gray neglects to mention. Gray's view is valid only for a wonderland in which politicians desire only to serve, not to control. Perpetual shortages of almost all goods characterized East Bloc economies; politicians and bureaucrats maximized both their power and people's subjugation through discretionary doling out of goods. Shortages created new pretexts to demand further submission: the worse the economic system functioned, the more power government acquired—until the people rose up and destroyed the governments.[209]

Government cannot control the economy without controlling the lives of everyone who must rely on that economy to earn their sustenance. There is more to life than wealth. But the more wealth government seizes from people, the more likely that government will be able to control all the other good things in life. Once government domineers the economy, it becomes far more difficult to resist the extension of government power further and further into the recesses of each person's life.

Property rights are not concerned merely with the sanctity of the estates of the rich. The property rights that each citizen has in himself are the foundation of a free society. As James Madison observed, "Government is instituted to protect property of every sort; as well that which lies in the various rights of individuals, as that which the term particularly expresses."[210] The property that each citizen has in his rights is the foundation of his ability to control his own life and strive to shape his own destiny.

Some contemporary liberals argue that government ownership is the ultimate safeguard of freedom. According to Alan Wolfe, "No one would be able to enjoy the negative liberty of walking alone in the wilderness if it were not for the regulatory capacity of government to protect the wilderness against development."[211] Wolfe implies that if the government did not own much of the nation's land, private citizens would ravage the landscape from coast to coast. However, private landowners have a better record of safeguarding the environmental quality of their land than does the federal government.[212] The Army Corps of Engineers has destroyed far more of the natural river beauty in this country than has any private malefactor, and the Federal Emergency Management Agency's lavish subsidies for "flood insurance" have made possible vast numbers of buildings on ecologically fragile coastlines.[213] Wolfe also implies that no private forest owner would permit anyone else to walk on his land. However, the proliferation of contracts for hunting on private land show that, with a sound incentive system, access to private land can easily be negotiated. Citizens have different values, and many citizens prefer to keep their land in semi-pristine condition. Besides, even if all citizens wanted to sell their land to developers, only a small percentage of such land would be developed—simply because there is no economic rationale for developing much of rural America.

The sanctity of private property is the most important bulwark of privacy. University of Chicago law professor Richard Epstein wrote that "private property gives the right to exclude others *without* the need for any justification. Indeed, it is the ability to act at will and without need for justification within some domain which is the essence of freedom, be it of speech or of property."[214] Unfortunately, federal law enforcement agents and prosecutors are making private property much less private. In 1984, the Supreme Court ruled in *Oliver v. United States*—a case involving Kentucky law enforcement agents who ignored several "No Trespassing" signs, climbed over a fence, tramped a mile and a half onto a person's land, and found marijuana plants—that "open fields do not provide the setting for those intimate activities that the [Fourth] Amendment is intended to shelter from government interference or surveillance."[215] (The Founding Fathers apparently forgot to include a parenthesis in the original Fourth Amendment specifying that it applied only to "intimate activities.") And the Court made it clear that it was not referring only to open fields, adding: "A thickly wooded area nonetheless may be an open field as that term is used in construing the Fourth Amendment."[216] Justice Thurgood Marshall dissented: "Many landowners like to take solitary walks on their property, confident that they will not be confronted in their rambles by strangers or policemen."[217] Even prior to this ruling, it was easy for law enforcement agents to secure warrants to search private land merely by concocting an imaginary confidential informant who told police about some malfeasance.[218]

The core of the "open fields" decision is that the government cannot wrongfully invade a person's land because government agents have a right to go wherever they damn well please. After this decision, any "field" not surrounded by a 20 foot-high concrete fence is considered to be "open" to inspection by government agents. (And for those areas that are sufficiently fenced in, the Supreme Court has blessed low-level helicopter flights to search for any illicit plants on the ground.)[219] The Supreme Court's decision, which has been cited in over 600 subsequent federal and state court decisions, nullified hundreds of years of common law precedents limiting the power of government agents. The ruling was a green light for warrantless raids by federal immigration agents; the *New York Times* reported in late 1997 cases of upstate New York farmers complaining that "immigration agents plowed into fields and barged into packing sheds like gang busters, handcuffing all workers who might be Hispanic and asking questions later . . . doors were knocked down, and workers were wrestled to the ground."[220] In a raid outside of Elba, New York, at least one INS agent opened fire on fleeing farm workers.[221] Many farms' harvests subsequently rotted in the fields because of the shortage of farm workers.

The "open fields" doctrine provides an acid test of conflicting views on freedom. Are people more or less free when government agents can roam their land? Are they more or less free when they can be accosted by government agents any time they step past the shadow of their front door? Is freedom the result of government intrusions—or of restrictions on intruders? The scant controversy the 1984 decision evoked is itself a sign of how Statist contemporary American thinking has become.

Few government policies better symbolize the contempt for property rights than the rising number of no-knock raids. "A man's home is his castle" was an accepted rule of English common law since the early 1600s. It required law enforcement officials to knock on the door and announce themselves before entering a private home. But this standard has increasingly been rejected in favor of another ancient rule—"the king's keys unlock all doors."[222] A *New York Times* article observed in 1998 that "[I]nterviews with police officials, prosecutors, judges and lawyers paint a picture of a system in which police officers feel pressured to conduct more raids, tips from confidential informers are increasingly difficult to verify and judges spend less time examining the increasing number of applications for search warrants before signing them."[223] The *Times* noted that "the word of a single criminal, who is often paid for his information, can be enough to send armed police officers to break down doors and invade the homes of innocent people."[224] No-knock raids have become so common that thieves in some places routinely kick down doors and claim to be policemen.[225]

The Clinton administration, in a 1997 brief to the Supreme Court, declared that "it is ordinarily reasonable for police officers to dispense with a pre-entry knock and announcement."[226] Many law enforcement agencies are paranoid that the slightest delay in barging into someone's home could allow residents to flush small amounts of drugs down the toilet. In a 1995 brief to the Supreme Court, the Clinton administration stressed that "various indoor plumbing facilities . . . did not exist" at the time the common law "knock-and-announce" rule was adopted.[227] Making a grand concession to civil liberties, the administration admitted that "if the officers knew that . . . the premises contain no plumbing facilities . . . then invocation of the destruction-of-evidence justification for an unannounced entry would be unreasonable."[228] Thus, the more advanced a nation's plumbing becomes, the more repressive police must be permitted to act. The Supreme Court has not imposed effective restraints on the police's prerogative to carry out no-knock raids. Professor Craig Hemmens observed that the Court's "recent decisions involving the knock and announce rule, essentially gutted the rule, reducing it to little more than a 'form of words.'"[229]

It is as much a violation of property rights and liberty when government agents storm into the shabbiest of rental apartments as when they invade the richest mansion. The sanctity acquired by renters to a private domain illustrates how the exchange of private property can give someone vested rights—rights within which they can build and live their own lives. Local and state governments, however, routinely treat renters as second-class citizens; many localities have mandatory inspection policies for all rental units that permit government officials to search private dwellings without a warrant or any pretext. In 1994, Park Forest, Illinois, enacted an ordinance that authorizes warrantless searches of every single-family rental home by a city inspector and police officer, who are authorized to invade rental units "at all reasonable times." No limit was placed on the power of the inspectors to search through people's homes, and tenants were prohibited from denying entry to government agents. The Institute for Justice, a private legal foundation, challenged the law.[230] Federal judge Joan Gottschall struck down the searches as unconstitutional in February 1998, but her decision will have little or no effect on the numerous other localities that authorize similar invasions of privacy.[231]

Some socialists have argued that private property is a bane of freedom because inequality of wealth is equivalent to political tyranny. According to historian R. H. Tawney, "Oppression . . . is not less oppressive when its strength is derived from superior wealth, than when it relies on a preponderance of physical force."[232] But regardless of how much wealth a person owns, he has no legal right to coerce other citizens. The possession of great wealth makes it easier for a person to persuade other people to serve him by making them better offers than they receive elsewhere, but this is unlike holding a gun to someone's head. As philosopher Ayn Rand declared, "Economic power is exercised by means of a positive, by offering men a reward, an incentive, a payment, a value; political power is exercised by means of a negative, by the threat of punishment, injury, imprisonment, destruction."

To understand the difference between economic wealth and political power, consider the difference between the power of a boss and that of a government agent. Any power that a boss or company has over a person is based on that person's contracting with that boss or company; the power of the boss or company is limited to the work and time contracted for. (Contracts for lifetime labor are illegal in the United States.) A boss's power is conditional, dependent on an employee's choosing to continue to receive a paycheck. In contrast, the government agent's power is often close to absolute: for example, citizens who refuse to pull over for a traffic cop who flashes his lights can face jail time, regardless of whether the cop had a legitimate reason to stop them. Market economies allow people a choice of whom to deal with, while government dictates that citizens must submit to its orders. As Nobel laureate James Buchanan observed, "As individuals become increasingly dependent on 'the market,' they become correspondingly less dependent on any identifiable person or group. In political action, by contrast, increasing dependence necessarily becomes increasing subjection to the authority of others."[233] Markets limit the power of some people to dictate to other people because both parties can seek other bidders. Markets provide venues for people to voluntarily agree with other people. Markets are symbolic of voluntary activities in the same way that jails are symbolic of coercion.

A viable concept of freedom must consist of more than psychological wish fulfillment—more than a fantasy world in which every citizen can buy low and sell high, in which every citizen gets the wages he demands and pays the prices he pleases. It is crucial to distinguish between the "compulsion" of economic aspirations and the compulsion of government coercion. Feeling a compulsive need to impress neighbors by buying a swimming pool is not the same as facing arrest for planting grass seed in your yard and allegedly disturbing a federally designated wetland. The compulsion to buy a suit of the latest fashion is not the same compulsion as experienced during an IRS audit, especially if the agent decides to employ a notorious "lifestyle audit," which forces citizens to detail and justify how much cash they had on hand at any one time a year or two before, whether they have a safe deposit box and what it contains, how much they spend on groceries, where they eat out, what toys they buy for their children, and what books or jewelry they purchase.[234] The compulsion to buy a new car is different than the compulsion you feel when police pull you over, announce that your appearance matches that of a "drug courier profile," and proceed to rummage through your trunk, glove compartment, tire hubs, and pockets, and to ask a bevy of hopefully incriminating questions about your personal life.[235] The fact that a person spends himself deeply into debt, and thus feels obliged to keep working at a job he despises, is not coercive because no one compelled the person to become a mindless consumer.

Property is the basis of freedom of contract, which is simply liberty in action. Without freedom to exchange, government places all exchanges at the discretion of the political-bureaucratic ruling class. As new forms of property and wealth have developed in the last two hundred years, it is now much clearer how vital property is to the freedom of all citizens, not merely that of landowners. By holding title to certain resources (including themselves and their own labor), they can make exchanges with others that allow them to raise themselves, to better provide for their families, to pursue their own values. Freedom is more than the right to own property or the right to buy and sell. But once the citizen loses the right to own—even if he previously owned nothing—he loses the ability to control his own life. If the citizen is denied the right to own or control his own computer disks, or the clothes on his back, he has little chance of being able to shape his own future.

An inability to find a satisfactory job or satisfactory career path is not a violation of liberty—unless government or private action forcibly blocks or restrains people. A person is not "oppressed" by his own lack of marketable job skills: every former art history major who did not find a good job after college is not a victim of some sinister force.

One of the clearest violations of freedom of contract involves government licensing laws, which prohibit millions of Americans from practicing the occupation of their choice. Over 800 professions—from barbers to masseuses to interior designers to phrenologists to tattooists to talent agents—now require a government license to practice. Licensing laws are usually engineered by professional associations that want to "protect" the public from competitors who might charge them lower prices.[236] Licensing laws kept many blacks out of the skilled professions until the Civil Rights era. The Federal Trade Commission perennially reports on the anticompetitive aspects of state government licensing boards.[237] For many professions, private accreditation systems—many of which have already been developed—would provide a much more reliable guide than do politically controlled certification systems.

Property rights and market economies are vital stepping stones to political freedom. Private property gives people a place to stand if they must resist the government. Market economies and private property allow citizens to build up sufficient wealth to resist government pressure.

It is important to have freedom to buy and sell, to invest, to innovate, to choose one's risks and reap one's profits, but it is not enough. It is also vital that police not be able to break people's heads, or entrap them on bogus charges, or intercept their e-mail at a whim, or target them because of their race, ethnicity, or political ideas. Unfortunately, some advocates of economic freedom seem nonchalant about practically any use of government power that does not interfere with profit making.

THE REAL MEANING OF LIBERTY

Various laws and court decisions in American history have offered clear visions of the meaning of freedom. The Civil Rights Act of 1866 declared that all citizens of the United States "shall have the same right, in every State and Territory, to make and enforce contracts, to sue, to be parties, to give evidence, to inherit, purchase, lease, sell, hold and convey real and personal property, and to the full and equal benefit of all laws and proceedings for the security of person and property, as is enjoyed by white citizens."[238] (Unfortunately, courts, state legislatures, and the federal government often ignored the law.) In 1886, a Supreme Court decision eloquently described the prevailing American concept of freedom: "The very idea that one man may be compelled to hold his life, or the means of living, or any material right essential to the enjoyment of life, at the mere will of another, seems intolerable in any country where freedom prevails, as being the essence of slavery itself."[239] Supreme Court justice David Brewer declared in 1892: "The utmost possible liberty to the individual, and the fullest possible protection to him and his property, is both the limitation and the duty of government."[240] A 1923 Supreme Court decision, which struck down a state law that prohibited the teaching of any modern language other than English to children, declared:

> The term [liberty] has received much consideration. Without doubt, it denotes not merely freedom from bodily restraint but also the right of the individual to contract, to engage in any of the common occupations of life, to acquire useful knowledge, to marry, to establish a home and bring up children, to worship God according to the dictates of his own conscience, and generally to enjoy those privileges long recognized at common law as essential to the orderly pursuit of happiness by free men.[241]

Being left alone, uncoerced, is the true meaning of freedom. Freedom means being able to take to the open road without being stopped and searched by every second policeman. People value freedom so highly because freedom symbolizes life without a master—a life of minimal subjugation and shackles. Freedom means being able to make choices and contracts. Freedom means not having one's place in life assigned to one by one's superiors. (One of the most burdensome elements of East European socialism was the compulsory assignment of careers to young people by political and bureaucratic overlords.) Freedom means being able to take risks and suffer the consequences. Freedom means individuals having rights and having their own domains—if only within themselves. Freedom means limits on government's—and everyone else's—power to invade other's private lives.

Liberty is a result of the *minimization* of coercion—both governmental and private. The less coercion, the more liberty. A small amount of coercion—enough to secure respect of other people's rights and safety—is necessary to minimize coercion. The fact that some government coercion occurs does not mean that the citizen has no freedom. Even though perfect freedom is an unattainable ideal, it is invaluable as a measuring rod to judge government policy and political proposals.

This concept of freedom is sometimes referred to as "negative liberty"—an unfortunate phrase. "Negative liberty" makes as much sense as "negative rape"—as if to imply that not getting shafted by the government is somehow a negative condition—as if not being a vassal is a negative condition, as if not being a member of a political chain gang is something negative. The term "negative liberty" implies that something is missing if the State does not intervene—almost like an apology that liberty does not give more.

The nature of government action is the crux of the disagreement between advocates of "positive" and real liberty. Advocates of positive liberty routinely take political promises and government interventions at their face value. Positive liberty is premised on denying the negative character of government action. Government is the great Naysayer. The only things government can do are regulate and redistribute, prohibit and penalize, confiscate and command. Are these the things that liberty is made of? Somebody else's money and an endless list of Thou Shalt Nots?

In concepts of positive freedom, the fact that government may be imprisoning and punishing more people now than ever before is irrelevant, because government is bestowing more benefits than ever before. It is as if any benefit automatically outweighs any shackle, and therefore nullifies the existence of the shackle. By shifting the meaning of liberty away from absence of coercion, twentieth-century political philosophers paved the way for a vast increase in coercion.

Some critics of liberty as the absence of coercion deride such liberty for not providing everything that a person supposedly needs. According to Robert Goodin, "Notional negative liberties—opportunities without the means of making use of them—are worthless."[242] Goodin sees the State as a giant factory designed to produce opportunity—and the larger the State becomes, the more opportunity it can produce. Goodin presumes that there is a finite amount of opportunity that can be counted, measured, packaged, sliced, diced, and redistributed. He assumes that everyone is obliged to make sure that everyone else makes the most of themselves—that is that every person must maximize their meddling in everyone else's lives. This view is equivalent to pretending that a door is not really open unless the government carries a person through it. But, as Francis Bacon observed, "A wise man will make more opportunity than he finds."[243]

The critics of so-called negative liberty presume that the absence of tyranny is not enough, that government also has an affirmative obligation to make many flowers bloom in each person's life. But this assumes that the government is a better gardener of each person's life than is that person himself.

Freedom depends upon each citizen's willingness to respect others' rights and to refrain from forcibly intruding into others' lives. It depends on each person's willingness to mind his own business and to tolerate the oddities, stupidities, and vulgarities of other people. Freedom is also based on each person taking responsibility for his own actions. Regardless of what any law says or omits, no citizen has a right to rob, rape, kill, or defraud any other citizen. Civil law cannot repeal the obligations that every citizen owes to others by the mere fact of their being human.

There has long been confusion between freedom in the sense of a person mastering his own will—and freedom in the sense of a person living his own life without being shackled by others. Much of the contemporary confusion over the meaning of liberty is the result of a shift in political thinking away from history to psychology—from notions of external freedom derived from past experience, to notions supposedly deduced from inner longings. There are different types of freedom: a person may have *political* freedom but still be a slave to his vices and passions. Conversely, a person may lack *political* freedom but still have achieved mastery over his own will. Unfortunately, much of modern thought, from Rousseau onwards, has favored political structures contrived to allow government to forcibly intervene in the individual's own psyche and liberate him from himself.[244] Yet, as Kant observed, "Any one may be free, although his freedom is entirely indifferent to me, or even if I wished in my heart to infringe it, so long as I do not actually violate that freedom by *my external action.*"[245]

Liberty alone is not sufficient for a good life. There is no substitute for individual character. If people make foolish choices that undercut their personal freedom—such as having children out of wedlock at an early age—that is regrettable but not a lack of freedom. The fact that some people lack self-control does not justify giving politicians and bureaucrats more control over everyone. Freedom necessarily includes freedom to screw-up one's life. The fact that some people mangle their lives does not prove they are not free; instead, it proves they are fallible.

CONCLUSION

Once government action is recognized as inherently coercive, then any concept of liberty based on government "liberating" the citizen from himself becomes a contradiction in terms. Welfare State freedom is preeminently freedom through submission to one's superiors: the fact that someone holds a government job is sufficient proof that he has both the right and the competence to command other citizens.

Welfare State freedom is freedom to do what politicians and bureaucrats want you to do. Empowering the State to liberate the individual makes sense only if the State has no incentive to exploit, abuse, or shackle the individual for its own profit.

"Positive freedom" offers freedom from inauthenticity, courtesy of your local sheriff. The individual's control over his own life thus becomes the biggest threat to his own freedom, and the government must intervene to forcibly drag him off the low road and onto the high road. The less the individual wants to be reformed by government officials, the more certain it is that his own values are a betrayal of his higher self.

"Positive freedom" liberates the citizen by liberating his rulers to treat him however they please. Almost all the contemporary notions of positive freedom rest on a blind trust in government—on an assumption that the government would not want to exploit or unnecessarily subjugate the citizen.

"Freedom from fear" and "freedom from want" are not possible unless the government is allowed to control all things people fear and want. Americans must beware of Trojan horse definitions of freedom—definitions that, once accepted, allow bureaucrats to clamor out and take over everyone's lives. Government handouts insinuate political power into the deepest recesses of a person's life. And when the time is ripe, politicians take command where they previously lavished their gifts.

Welfare State freedom is based on making everyone responsible for everyone else's mistakes, and allowing politicians and bureaucrats to decree how much burden each citizen must bear. Most importantly, Welfare State freedom is based on forcing citizens to carry a government swollen by endless false political promises, swollen by taking on tasks for which it has no competence, swollen by its own arrogance and eternal meddling.

FOUR

CAGEKEEPERS AND CARETAKERS: MODERN DEMOCRACY

The people are the bosses in this country and it's time they stopped blaming everybody else for what they don't know.
—President Bill Clinton, November 2, 1994[1]

A man is none the less a slave because he is allowed to choose a new master once in a term of years. . . . What makes them slaves is the fact that they now are, and are always hereafter to be, in the hands of men whose power over them is, and always is to be, absolute and irresponsible.
—Lysander Spooner, 1867[2]

Democracy: two wolves and one lamb voting on what to eat for dinner.
—Common unpatriotic saying, 1990s

IF A FOREIGN POWER TOOK OVER THE UNITED STATES and dictated that American citizens surrender 40 percent of their income to foreign agents, required them to submit to tens of thousands of different commands (many of which were effectively kept secret from them), prohibited many of them from using their land, and denied many of them the chance to find work, there would be little dispute that the people were being tyrannized. Yet, the main difference between the current reality and the foreign invasion scenario is the democratic forms by which government power is now sanctified.

We saw in the second chapter that coercion is the distinguishing trait of government. Now we must examine whether democratic institutions allow governments to transcend their coercive nature. The issue of who nominally holds the leash on a government has become far more important than whether government is actually leashed. As Hayek observed in a 1976 speech, "The magic word democracy has become so all-powerful that all the inherited limitations on government power are breaking down before it. . . . It is unlimited democracy, not just democracy, which is the problem today."[3]

Do politicians have the right to control what they do not own? This is the fundamental question about modern government—especially democracy—that is rarely asked. How much power does the voting booth confer upon people whose names are on the ballot? How much power over himself does a citizen necessarily cede by pushing a few levers on a voting machine? Is an election the delegation of power over specific issues, or an automatic grant of near-absolute power over all persons and property? Do elections choose representatives or czars?

The issue is not whether democracy is good or evil; that question can only be answered by comparing it to other forms of government, and to the alternative of allowing people to run their own lives. This essay is not an argument against democracy; rather, it is an argument against excessive expectations about democracy.

OTIS'S QUESTION AND
ROUSSEAU'S CURSE: THE ROAD NOT TAKEN

To understand contemporary American democracy, we need to understand two great controversies of the mid-1700s. The first involved ideological clashes between the Americans and British over the doctrine of representation. The second concerned the radical redefinition of democracy by Jean-Jacques Rousseau—a change that helped turn the French Revolution into a bloodbath.

Conflicts between the American colonists and British rulers reached a fever pitch in the 1760s. The Sugar Act of 1764 resulted in British officials confiscating hundreds of American ships, based on mere allegations that the shipowners or captains were involved in smuggling; Americans were obliged, in order to retain their ships, to somehow prove that they had never been involved in smuggling—a near-impossible burden.[4] The Stamp Act of 1765 obliged Americans to purchase British stamps to be used on all legal papers, newspapers, cards, dice, advertisements, and even on academic degrees. After violent protests throughout the colonies, the Parliament rescinded the Stamp Act but passed the

Declaratory Act, which announced that Parliament "had, hath, and of right ought to have, full power and authority to make laws and statutes of sufficient force and validity to bind the colonies and people of America, subjects of the crown of Great Britain, in all cases whatsoever."[5] The Declaratory Act meant that Parliament could never do an injustice to the Americans, since Parliament had the right to use and abuse the colonists as it chose.

Many American colonists believed that, for them, British representative government was a fraud. The "Declaration of the Causes and Necessity of Taking Up Arms," issued by the Second Continental Congress on July 6, 1775, a few weeks after the Battle of Bunker Hill, highlighted the crimes of the British Parliament. (The Declaration of Independence, issued almost a year later, concentrated on King George III as the personification of British abuses.) The Declaration, written by John Dickinson and Thomas Jefferson, complained that "the legislature of Great-Britain, stimulated by an inordinate passion for power . . . attempted to effect their cruel and impolitic purpose of enslaving these colonies by violence. . . . "[6] The Continental Congress demanded to know: "What is to defend us against so enormous, so unlimited a power? Not a single man of those who assume it, is chosen by us; or is subject to our control or influence. . . . "[7]

Americans and British profoundly disagreed on the source of their freedom. Many British believed that freedom depended on vesting unlimited power in the Parliament, since they believed the only threat to their freedom came from the king and his lackeys. Sir William Meredith praised the British constitution in 1769 because it was the privilege of the Englishman alone "to choose those delegates to whose Charge is committed the Disposal of his Property, his Liberty, his Life."[8] In 1768, the Speaker of the House of Commons announced, "The freedom of this house is the freedom of this country. . . ."[9] As Professor John Phillip Reid observed in 1988, "This new or 'radical' constitutional theory was a departure from the British tradition of defining liberty without having its preservation depend on specific institutions, presaging the nineteenth century and the general British acceptance of what in the eighteenth century had been constitutional heresy—that liberty and arbitrary power are not incompatible, if the power that is arbitrary is 'representative.'"[10]

Because Parliament supposedly automatically had the concerns of the entire British Empire at heart, Americans were told they had "virtual representation," regardless of the fact that they could not vote for any member of Parliament. The British claimed that the Americans were free because they were permitted to petition members of Parliament with their grievances, even though their petitions were routinely not accepted or read.[11]

"Slavery by Parliament" was the phrase commonly used to denounce British legislative power grabs.[12] Americans believed that the power of representatives was strictly limited by the rights of the governed, a doctrine later enshrined in the Bill of Rights. Pamphleteer John Cartwright in 1776 derided "that poor consolatory word, *representation,* with the mere sound of which we have so long contented ourselves."[13] James Otis, an influential Massachusetts lawyer, asked, "Will any man's calling himself my agent, representative, or trustee make him so in fact? At this rate a House of Commons in one of the colonies have but to conceive an opinion that they represent all the common people of Great Britain, and . . . they would in *fact* represent them."[14] One New York critic declared in 1775 that it was inconceivable that Americans' liberty should depend "upon nothing more permanent or established than the vague, rapacious, or interested inclination of a majority of five hundred and fifty-eight men, open to the insidious attacks of a weak or designing Prince, and his ministers."[15]

At the same time that the Americans were fighting a revolution against the fraud of representation, continental Europe was entranced by contrary doctrines. From the 1600s onwards, the abuses of monarchs made representative government increasingly attractive. Unfortunately, at a time when most continental Europeans had scant political experience, the doctrines of Rousseau swept the intellectual field. As Harvard professor Irving Babbitt noted in 1924, "The commanding position of Rousseau in the democratic movement is at all events beyond question."[16] Rousseau unleashed the genie of absolute power in the name of popular sovereignty.

Rousseau's 1762 book, *Social Contract,* merged contemporary romanticism and mysticism with eighteenth-century political thought. Rousseau thereby gave people an engraved invitation to delude themselves about the nature of majorities, government, and freedom. Rousseau asserted that representative governments are based on the "general will," which, naturally, could be different from the conscious will of the people themselves:

> It follows from what has gone before that the general will is always right and tends to the public advantage; but it does not follow that the deliberations of the people are always equally correct. Our will is always for our own good, but we do not always see what that is; the people is never corrupted, but it is often deceived, and on such occasions only does it seem to will what is bad.[17]

Regrettably, Rousseau provided few hints on how either rulers or ruled could recognize the general will. The fact that people opposed surrendering more power to government simply proved that people did not know their own will. Rousseau waved a philosophic magic wand over representative government and pretended that his doctrine of the general will had solved all its problems. As historian William Dunning noted in 1920, "The common interest and the general will assumed, through [Rousseau's] manipulation, a greater definiteness and importance than philosophy had hitherto ascribed to them. They became the central features of almost every theory of the State."[18] Rousseau's doctrine of the general will became the invocation of rulers seeking unlimited power; Hitler's *Volk* was the Teutonic rendition of Rousseau's doctrine. J. L. Talmon, author of *The Origins of Totalitarian Democracy*, concluded that Rousseau "was unaware that total and highly emotional absorption in the collective political endeavor is calculated to kill all privacy . . . and the extension of the scope of politics to all spheres of human interest and endeavor . . . was the shortest way to totalitarianism."[19]

In contrast to Rousseau, the Founding Fathers were keenly aware of the potential abuses of popular government. The American Revolution was based on cynicism about the fraud of representation in the British Parliament; the French Revolution, following Rousseau's doctrine, was based on the delusion that the People are infallible and that democratic government automatically pursues the common good. One revolution was based on distrust of government, the other on messianic expectations from a change in form of a government. While John Adams naively declared in 1775 that "a democratical despotism is a contradiction in terms,"[20] few Americans held that belief by the mid-1780s. Judge Alexander Hanson declared in 1784, "The acts of almost every legislature have uniformly tended to disgust its citizens and to annihilate its credit."[21] One commentator in the 1780s, noting the early dashed hopes of democratic governments, declared that the usurpation of "40 tyrants at our doors, exceeds that of one at 3,000 miles."[22] Gordon Wood, author of *The Creation of the American Republic*, noted, "Throughout the years of the war and after, Americans in almost all the states mounted increasing attacks on the tendencies of the American representational system. . . . "[23] James Madison wrote in the *Federalist Papers*, "Complaints are everywhere heard . . . that [government] measures are too often decided, not according to the rules of justice and the rights of the minor party, but by the superior force of an interested and overbearing majority."[24]

Unfortunately, the doctrines of Rousseau have had far more influence on subsequent thinking about democracy than the insights of Madison and other Founding Fathers. Throughout American history, more attention has been paid to the rhetoric and ideals of democracy than to its substance. Lysander Spooner, a Massachusetts abolitionist, ridiculed President Lincoln's claim that the Civil War was fought to preserve a "government by consent." Spooner observed, "The only idea . . . ever manifested as to what is a government of consent, is this—that it is one to which everybody must consent, or be shot."[25]

THE ETERNAL SCAPEGOATS

Democracy is a system of government under which the people are automatically liable for whatever the government does to them.

In 1798, President John Adams pushed through Congress the Alien and Sedition Acts, which empowered Adams to suppress free speech and imprison without trial any critic of the federal government. When the citizens of Westmoreland County, Virginia, petitioned Adams in 1798 complaining of the acts, President Adams responded by denouncing the citizens: "The declaration that Our People are hostile to a government made by themselves, for themselves, and conducted by themselves, is an insult."[26] Adams's response to the people of Westmoreland County—few of whom had voted for Adams—was the classic trick of a would-be democratic tyrant: declaiming to people that they were obliged to submit to oppression because the chief executive had been duly elected by other voters. (Kentucky and Virginia enacted resolutions declaring the sedition act null and void; the Kentucky resolution observed that the doctrine "that the general government is the exclusive judge of the extent of the powers delegated to it [is] nothing short of despotism; since the discretion of those who administer the government, and not the Constitution, would be the measure of their powers."[27])

Many of the most deadly errors of contemporary political thinking stem from the notion that in a democracy the government is the people and vice versa, so there is scant reason to distinguish between the two—or to worry about protecting citizens from the government.

President Woodrow Wilson declared in 1919: "In the last analysis, my fellow countrymen, as we in America would be the first to claim, a people are responsible for the acts of their government."[28] Wilson had campaigned for reelection three years earlier bragging that he had kept the country out of World War I; then, shortly after he started his second term, he submitted to Congress a declaration of war against Germany. Were the people responsible for President Wilson's 1916 peace promises or his 1917 declaration of war? How can they be responsible for both? Wilson campaigned for the presidency in 1912 as a progressive. Shortly after he took office, mass firings of black federal employees occurred. The chief federal revenue collector in Georgia announced: "There are no Government positions for Negroes in the South. A Negro's place is in the cornfield."[29] How were voters who opposed Jim Crow laws responsible for Wilson's unexpected racist purge?

President Franklin Roosevelt declared in 1938, "Let us never forget that government is *ourselves* and not an alien power over us. The ultimate rulers of our democracy are not a President and senators and congressmen and government officials, but the voters of this country."[30] When Roosevelt ran for reelection in 1936, he never mentioned his plan (revealed in early 1937) to pack the nation's highest court with new appointees to rubber-stamp his decrees. Yet, because he won in 1936, he effectively implied that the citizenry were somehow bound to accept all of his power grabs as if they themselves had willed them.

President Bill Clinton declared on October 7, 1996, "The Government is just the people, acting together—just the people acting together."[31] But, was it "the people" who invited wealthy businessmen to give $50,000 to the Democratic National Committee to come to White House coffee klatches? Was it "the people" who approved a plan to rent out the Lincoln bedroom for $100,000 a night? Was it "the people" who ordered FBI agents to illegally deliver over 900 confidential files on Republicans to the White House?

The "people = government" doctrine is equivalent to political infantilism—an agreement to pretend that the citizen's wishes animate each restriction or exaction inflicted upon him. This doctrine essentially makes masochism the driving force of political life—assuming that if government is beating the citizens, they must want to be beaten, and thus they have no right to complain.

The notion that "the people are the government" is one of the biggest slanders that the average citizen will endure in his lifetime. To presume that any specific private citizen must be held responsible for all the cabals and conspiracies engaged in by all the bureaucrats and politicians is absurd. This is the political version of the doctrine of original sin; it assumes that a person is born politically damned with the weight of all of the past and future sins of his government upon his head. The notion that "you are the government" is simply a way to shift the guilt for every crime by the government onto every victim of government. This makes as little sense as holding each "widow and orphan" owner of a single share of a company's stock fully liable for crimes secretly committed by the corporate management and holding the actual corporate directors blameless, since they merely followed the unspoken will of individual shareholders.

RUBE GOLDBERG,
PATRON SAINT OF MODERN DEMOCRACY

President Ronald Reagan, in his January 11, 1989 farewell address, declared, "'We the People' tell the government what to do, it doesn't tell us. 'We the people' are the driver—the government is the car. And we decide where it should go, and by what route, and how fast."[32] However, democratic mechanisms do not provide the perfect power steering Reagan claimed.

Archimedes said long ago, "Give me a long enough lever and I can move the world." Nowadays, switches in voting booths are portrayed as

Archimedean levers by which average citizens can magically control Leviathan-sized governments.

We are brought face to face with the divine miracle of democratic engineering. The federal government is like a vast machine purportedly controlled by the 200,000,000 levers at one far end of the contraption. The machine has tens of thousands of different functions and moving parts, lathes, threshers, shredders, graders, post-hole diggers, etcetera. Merely by pushing a few levers in a voting booth every other year, the individual is somehow able to direct all the functioning of that machine—to automatically force the machine to follow the person's will, even on the vast majority of issues on which he has no opinion.

But regardless of which levers he pushes, the machine is almost guaranteed to eventually shove, yank, shackle, pickpocket, blindfold, or gag the voter. The machine has vastly more opportunity to tyrannize the voter than the voter has to direct the machine. While the voting lever the citizen flips can be counteracted by a hundred different sources, from other voters to political agreements to judge's edicts to outright fraud, government employees have such "levers" over the voter as seizing his bank account, destroying his job, or evicting him from his home.

And no matter how unhappy a person becomes with the machine, he is told that, since he had a chance to push a few levers in a voting booth, he has no right to resist the machine's workings. He is told that he has only himself to blame for the machine's defects, since he had a chance to push a lever—even if it was a lever attached to nothing. The mere existence of the voting lever supposedly creates an unlimited obligation on the part of the voter to do whatever the masters of the machine command.

Citizens are told that an infinitesimal voice in choosing one's rulers automatically protects them against the massive force of the State. The fact that the citizen can push a few levers every other year supposedly automatically protects him against 107,000 tax collectors, 126,000 federal regulators, and legions of federal law enforcement officers.[33]

In the 1992 presidential elections, 44,909,326 Americans voted for Bill Clinton for president.[34] In the subsequent four years, the Clinton administration issued over 260,000 pages of proposed and final new regulations, rulings, and notices; made more than 10 million administrative rulings; confiscated over $2 billion worth of property from private citizens, most of whom were never convicted of any crime; and effectively seized control of over 8 million acres through new regulations and presidential proclamations. Yet, even though few of his subsequent actions were promised or forewarned in his 1992 presidential campaign, the people that voted for him (not to mention those who opposed him) were somehow fully represented by, and fully liable, for his actions.

THE GREATEST
IGNORANCE OF THE GREATEST NUMBER

The specter of an ignorant populace has long haunted democracy. Montesquieu wrote in 1748: "The tyranny of a principal in an oligarchy is not so dangerous to the public welfare as the apathy of a citizen in a democracy." James Madison warned: "A popular Government, without popular information, or the means of acquiring it, is but a Prologue to a Farce or a Tragedy; or, perhaps both."[35] President John F. Kennedy declared in 1963, "The ignorance of one voter in a democracy impairs the security of all."[36] But, despite numerous eloquent warnings, political ignorance has mushroomed as government power has multiplied.

If citizen comprehension of government and public affairs is the currency of democracy, America is long since bankrupt. Philip Converse observed in 1975 in his *Handbook of Political Science:* "The most familiar fact to arise from sample surveys is that popular levels of information about public affairs are, from the point of view of the informed observed, astonishingly low."[37] A 1989 survey found that less than 20 percent of respondents knew what the Superfund program was, even though it had been the most controversial environmental program of the 1980s.[38] A May 1997 poll by the Pew Research Center for the People and the Press found that only 8 percent of the public could identify the name of Louis Freeh, the FBI director who has presided over the most scandal-racked period of the nation's premier law enforcement agency.[39] Columnist George Will, commenting on opinion polls showing support for expanding NATO membership in 1998, observed that "not one American in 100 can say which nations (Poland, Hungary, the Czech Republic) are to be brought into NATO. Not one in 100,000 knows that five more—Estonia, Latvia, Lithuania, Slovenia and Romania—have been invited to apply for membership next year."[40]

A January 1995 ABC News–*Washington Post* poll found that, two months after the midterm congressional elections, only 39 percent of the public were aware of the "Contract with America," even though it was the hottest ideological issue in congressional elections in recent decades.[41] A *Washington Post*–Harvard University 1996 study revealed: "Four in 10 Americans don't know that the Republicans control Congress; and half either think the Democratic Party is more conservative politically than the GOP or don't feel they know enough to offer a guess."[42] The survey also found that "only 26% percent knew the 6-year term of office of a U.S. senator" and less than half the public knows that a member of the House of Representative is elected to a two-year term.[43] Professor Stephen Earl Bennett, in a 1988 article entitled, "'Know-Nothings' Revisited: The Meaning of Political Ignorance Today," observed, "Very few Americans do well on tests of political knowledge; beyond recognizing presidential figures, the public is just as hazy about things political as it was five decades ago . . . 74% did not know the name and party of even one local congressional candidate."[44]

Political scientist Michael Delli Carpini, after analyzing thousands of voter surveys, told the *Washington Post* that there was "virtually no relationship" between the political issues that low-knowledge voters said "matter most to them and the positions of the candidates they voted for on those issues. It was as if their vote was random."[45] The *Post* estimated that roughly 36 percent of voters were "low knowledge"—a far larger percentage than the deciding margins in almost all contested congressional and presidential elections. Thirty percent were classified as "high knowledge."[46]

Most surveys implicitly exaggerate the citizen's understanding of government. Government policies are not generic. It takes a mental effort to understand each specific government policy: there is no Rosetta stone with which to decode the myriad actions of government. Most surveys focus on whether someone is "aware of" a certain policy or a certain law, or whether they know the name of certain elected representatives. But, knowing the name of one's congressmen does not assure that a citizen will know that Congress in 1997 gave away to television stations a windfall of digital airwave rights worth billions of dollars.[47] Knowing the name of the vice president does not mean the citizen will automatically comprehend the hidden $668 billion annual cost of government regulation, which imposes over $6,000 in hidden taxes on the average American family each year.[48] Knowing the name of the secretary of agriculture does not mean the citizen will recognize the billions of dollars of surcharges in higher sugar, dairy, and peanut prices caused by federal farm policy.[49] Assuming that knowing the names of a few political candidates provides sufficient knowledge for democracy is like assuming that owning a box of tools enables a person to rebuild his car engine.

Overall, the *Post*-Harvard survey found that more than half of all Americans agreed with the following statement: "Politics and government are so complicated that a person like me can't really understand what's going on."[50] If someone declared that traffic laws are so complicated that he couldn't figure out which side of the road to drive on, most people would support yanking that person's driver's license. Yet, no amount of ignorance can disqualify a voter from a role in choosing representatives and presidents.

Many Americans are also profoundly ignorant of their legal rights. A 1979 Gallup poll found that 70 percent of respondents did not know what the First Amendment was or what it dealt with.[51] A 1991 poll commissioned by the American Bar Association found that only 33 percent of Americans surveyed knew what the Bill of Rights was.[52] A 1987 survey found that 45 percent of adult respondents believed that Karl Marx's communist principle "from each according to his abilities, to each according to his needs" was in the U.S. Constitution.[53] Most Americans do not understand the doctrine of the separation of powers; a 1977 poll found that only 33 percent of respondents knew that governors did not have the power to veto state court rulings.[54] If a citizen is unaware of his rights, then, for all practical purposes in disputes with government officials, he does not have them.

Citizens' ignorance of their own tax burdens also vivifies their failure to understand their relation to government. A 1995 survey by Grassroots Research, an independent polling firm, found that 83 percent of the respondents underestimated the tax burden faced by the average family.[55] The survey showed that the tax burden on a family earning $35,000 is actually 54 percent higher than most people think. A 1998 report by Congress's Joint Tax Committee concluded that "hidden taxes force more than 33 million Americans into higher tax brackets" than they are aware of; House Ways and Means Committee chairman Bill Archer of Texas declared that such covert tax increases are "akin to false advertising by the government."[56] If people do not even notice how much government confiscates from them every paycheck, how likely are they to pay attention to political events that have less immediate impact on their lives?

Citizens' ignorance may be increasing as fast as politicians' spending. Assume that the average citizen devotes the same amount of time studying politics and current affairs today that voters did in 1947. This may be optimistic: newspaper readership has plummeted in recent decades, though average years of education have risen.[57] In 1947, 77 percent of high school graduates knew which political party controlled the House of Representatives; in 1996, only 54 percent could answer that question.[58] Total government spending has increased from $61.9 billion in 1950, or $410 per person, to $2.257 billion in 1994, or $8,681 per person.[59] In inflation-adjusted terms, this is an increase in spending of more than 700 percent. The annual *Federal Register* has gone from 7,417 pages in 1947 to 69,364 in 1996. The Code of Federal Regulations is now 14 times larger than it was in 1950.[60] The Republican Party Platform was 14 times longer in 1996 than it was in 1948.[61] While the amount of citizens' knowledge about government and politics appears stagnant, the amount of government spending, laws, and regulations has soared.

Thus, even if citizens understood government policies a half century ago, they and their progeny likely comprehend only a small fraction of such policies now. The growth of government is like the spread of a dense jungle, and the average citizen is able to mentally hack his way through less and less of that jungle every year. The larger the government, the more the average citizen and average voter is at the intellectual mercy of his rulers. And the more ignorant the voters, the easier it becomes for politicians to treat people like Pavlovian dogs, simply throwing out some phrase after which the citizen, reflexively, runs to vote more power to the politicians.

The only way to presume that citizen's ignorance of government is irrelevant to democracy is to presume that government is so inherently benevolent that people do not even need to know what it is doing. People can ignore the details of government policies—since they are essentially making a choice between two competing political caregivers—in the same way that an infirm person might choose between two nurses competing for hire, with no understanding of the drugs the nurses planned to inject him with.

The issue of citizen ignorance is rarely raised in discussions over whether citizens consented to some expansion of government power. However, citizen ignorance is the rallying cry of the political establishment and judges determined to nullify limitations on how long politicians can hold power over other people. As Rep. Pat Williams of Montana concluded regarding popular support for congressional term limits, "Sometimes the American people are just wrong."[62]

On October 7, 1997, a federal appeals court struck down the 1990 initiative enacted by California voters to restrict the number of terms that politicians could serve in the state assembly and senate. Judge Stephen Reinhardt, writing for the majority, noted that "a number of voters who do not fall within the classification 'average' . . . may . . . have failed to understand that a lifetime ban was contemplated" on the number of terms state legislators could serve. (The phrase "banned for life" was used nine times in the primary ballot literature on the referendum.) Reinhardt's response to the existence of voters of below "average" intelligence was to treat all voters like Dred Scott, prohibiting them from running away from their political masters. (An *en banc* ruling of the court of appeals overturned Reinhardt's verdict, holding that "[L]ong-term entrenched legislators may obtain excessive power which in turn may discourage other qualified candidates from running for office, or may provide the incumbent with an unfair advantage.")[63]

The average citizen's negligence towards civic affairs should come as no surprise. Political economist Joseph Schumpeter, writing in 1942, observed:

> Normally the great political questions take their place in the psychic economy of the typical citizen with those leisure-hour interests that have not attained the rank of hobbies, and with the subjects of irresponsible conversation. These things seem so far off; they are not at all like a business proposition; dangers may not materialize at all and if they should they may not prove so very serious; one feels oneself to be moving in a fictitious world. . . . Without the initiative that comes from immediate responsibility, ignorance will persist in the faces

of masses of information however complete and correct. Thus the typical citizen drops down to a lower level of mental performance as soon as he enters the political field. He argues and analyzes in a way which he would readily recognize as infantile within the sphere of his real interests.[64]

The anemic reasoning of many citizens on political issues is not a factor of a lack of intelligence; rather, citizens lack a strong, pressing incentive to do the mental heavy lifting necessary to grasp political issues.[65] Also, considering how many people fail to concentrate on their own affairs (such as financial planning or balancing their checkbooks), how likely are they to function at a higher level in considering government taxation or budget controversies?

The issue is not whether a viable democracy can survive an unlimited level of government complexity. Obviously, at some point, there will be so much on the public-agenda plate that even conscientious citizens are overwhelmed. The question is, has America reached that point yet? Or, perhaps more importantly, has America already reached that point for sufficient numbers of voters that elections are turned into mere contests of demagoguery and bathos?

Some people believe that a nation can still enjoy a type of democracy even if many or most people know little or nothing of government policy. One commentator in 1934 offered a vision of "ennobled democracy . . . in which the people gives a few men the right to command, but on the other hand reserves the right to criticize these few men on general lines. This right is exercised in the elections." However, regardless of whether this definition captures the reality for many voters, it would be distasteful for most Americans to accept their concept of democracy from Nazi propaganda minister Joseph Goebbels.[66]

THE NEAR-OMNISCIENCE
OF LEGISLATORS

Harvard professor John Rawls built his book *A Theory of Justice* around the concept of a "veil of ignorance" that people would stand behind before agreeing to the ground rules of a social contract.[67] Today's congressmen are so idealistic that they stand behind a veil of ignorance every chance they get—as if the fewer congressmen who peak past a bill's cover page, the fairer its contents must be.

Representative government depends not only on well-informed voters but on competent legislators. Yet, in contemporary Washington, many people are too important to read. According to a 1977 survey of House members by the House Administration Committee, the average congressman spends only 11 minutes a day reading at work.[68] The results of that survey were so embarrassing that no follow-up has been done in subsequent decades. However, according to several congressional aides interviewed for this study, there is no evidence that today's representatives are more devoted bookworms than their 11-minute-a-day predecessors. (Contemporary congressmen are upholding a vaunted tradition; Will Rogers suggested in the 1920s that elected representatives adopt the slogan "Why sleep at home when you can sleep in Congress?")[69] Congressmen apparently rarely read the reports they command federal agencies to produce; federal agencies routinely fail to submit reports demanded by Congress—or turn in reports 10 or 20 years after a deadline set in federal law—and suffer little or no retribution.[70]

Congressmen routinely confess that they have not read important bills on which they vote. The larger a congressional bill becomes, the more likely that congressmen are ignorant of what it contains. For instance, on the night of November 27, 1991, a massive highway bill was rammed through the House of Representatives. As author Eric Felten observed,

> Members [of Congress] may not have been given a chance to see the bill after the conferees were done with it, but they didn't care. Each member knew there would be some road, bridge, tunnel, sidewalk, bus or subway earmarked for his home district. . . . Around 2 a.m. Nov. 27, the bill was taken up by the House Rules Committee, which sets the ground rules for debate on legislation before it is sent to the floor, specifying what amendments can be considered and in what order. At 4 a.m., debate began—though no one had yet seen the bill. Not until nearly 5 a.m., halfway through the debate, was one copy of the document plunked down on the Speaker's table on the House floor. There it sat until 6 a.m., when the vote was taken. 372 for, 47 against—not a single member had read it.[71]

The 1994 crime bill was another such unread wonder. On August 14, 1994, President Clinton revealed that it was God's will that Congress enact the bill and make the nation "as safe as we possibly can."[72] However, Clinton's Democratic allies in Congress made sure that the Republican minority in Congress only received the 972-page bill a few hours before being allowed to vote on it.[73] Perhaps Clinton assumed that the less that congressmen know about a bill, the more likely they were to follow God's will.

The Republican-controlled 104th Congress continued this hallowed tradition. On September 30, 1996, Congress passed a 2,000-page, 17-pound bill appropriating almost $400 billion and adding several new criminal offenses to the federal statute books. Sen. Robert Byrd of West Virginia complained, "I dare say no staff person has had the time to carefully review the thousands of programs funded in this resolution, or to read and comprehend the many nonappropriations, legislative matters contained in this resolution."[74] (Byrd's statement implied that reading is a task long since delegated to underlings.) Sen. Jim Inhofe of Oklahoma said, "I would suggest there is not one Member of this body who has read this [2000-plus-page bill]. But we go through that quite often and quite often we vote on things that we have not read in their entirety."[75]

Congress in recent years has repeatedly heaped vast amounts of legislation and appropriations into a single bill. Sen. David Boren of Oklahoma observed in 1991 that congressional "bills are five times longer on the average than they were just as recently as 1970, with a far greater tendency to micromanage every area of government."[76] The *Washington Post* editorialized on the eve of a 1998 congressional vote on a massive appropriations bill: "Most members will have only the vaguest idea of what the bill contains. Nor will they have more than a fleeting opportunity to amend the measure. The future: Are you for it or against it? You have 15 minutes to decide."[77] Each time such a mega-bill passes, the months afterwards are filled with the caterwauling of congressmen who are shocked to learn what they actually voted for. Ignorance of the law is an excuse only for the congressmen who voted for the law.

Is the average congressman, voting on the average bill, more or less ignorant than the average voter making his choice between two congressional candidates? Comparing a congressional election with the average congressional vote on a hefty legislative package, the percentage of voters who have examined the candidates and issues is probably higher than the percent of congressmen who have actually read and comprehended the bill. The voters only have to vote for congressional candidates once every two years, while congressmen near the end of the legislative session may have to vote 20 times or more a day. The citizens' vote is practically a will-o'-the-wisp, while congressmen blithely vote in favor of permanently increasing government power. Besides, the citizen is not being paid to be a competent voter, while congressmen have awarded themselves a salary of $133,600 a year for the privilege of dictating rules to other Americans.

The U.S. Congress does not have a monopoly on sub-omniscient legislators. The *New York Times* reported on July 2, 1996, that some state "lawmakers wandered about the Capitol [in Albany], frustrated, befuddled and outraged that they will soon be asked to vote on a slew of complex bills, some they have not even read, in a fevered dash to end the legislative session by the Fourth of July."[78] (The legislators, who receive a $57,500 annual salary plus $89 per diem, were late for their traditional long summer vacation.) The *Times* reported 11 days later: "Individual lawmakers are passing all sorts of bills wily-nilly, without the benefit of committee meetings and sometimes before the staff has had time to print enough copies of bills for every member to read."[79]

Some of the legislature's procedures are not ideally suited to allow New Yorkers the benefit of their representatives' wisdom. A *New York Times* 1996 editorial noted: "In the Assembly, [budget] votes will be taken by an instant roll-call system that automatically registers every legislator as voting 'aye' unless he or she makes a deliberate effort to vote 'no.'"[80] This is a Book-of-the-Month Club formula for big government—counting a politician as supporting any new law or new program that he does not specifically vote against. The *Times* suggested that the "State legislature could curb the passage of half-digested special-interest legislation simply by ending the practices that allow legislators to vote automatically without actually being at their desks."[81] It is ironic that the first step to good government consists of actually requiring legislators to physically appear to push a button on their desk—with no requirement that they have grasped what they are voting on. The challenge of getting "better-read" legislators brings to mind Dorothy Parker's quip on the word "horticulture": you can lead a whore to culture, but you can't make her think. Similarly, you can put a bill in front of a legislator, but you can't make him read or understand it.[82] (Regrettably, despite the *Times'* heroic efforts, the legislators in 1997 did not repent; a *Times* editorial noted that "in the final days of its sessions, the New York state legislature passed . . . a series of major changes in regulation of insurance and banking that virtually no one had read."[83])

Legislators in other states are often equally well informed. The Georgia legislature meets for only 40 days each year, and, as a 1997 *Wall Street Journal* article noted, "With so many lawmakers holding down full-time jobs, and juggling families and constituent service along the way, most say they have only a weak familiarity with the policies they put into law."[84] The legislature passed a bill in 1996 to simplify the process for applying for a driver's license. But, after the bill was signed into law, many legislators were stunned to learn that it also required any applicant for a driver's license to be fingerprinted—a provision that ignited a public outrage. Georgia state representative Tim Perry observed, "I didn't have a clue [the fingerprinting requirement] was in that bill, and 99% of the legislators didn't know about it."[85] Perry concluded, "Our state is being run more and more by the bureaucrats because we don't have the time to watch over them. They're there 365 days, and we're there 40."[86] California state senator H. L. Richardson observed, "Legislators consistently vote on legislation without understanding what is in it, especially when the final vote is taken. Every legislator has his own system for judging how he will vote, but reading the bill usually isn't part of the procedure."[87]

Congressmen and other legislators will object that it is unreasonable or unfair to expect a politician to read or understand everything that he votes on. But, if congressmen cannot be expected to know what they are doing, that proves that they are doing too much, that their political power exceeds their mental grasp. Once congressmen are routinely voting on things that they have not read and do not understand, we are left with a blind trust in their good characters, or in the good intentions of whoever is pulling the strings behind the scenes or whichever lobby is actually writing the bill language.

Sometimes congressional staffers vindicate the public interest by writing laws themselves. The *Washington Post* in 1997 reported a controversy over a provision in an appropriations bill written by Jason Alderman, a staffer for Rep. Sidney Yates of Illinois.[88] Alderman had been frolicking in Meridian Hill Park in Washington, D.C., with his dog when a U.S. Park Service policeman informed him and other dog owners that they had to have their pets on a leash. Alderman became outraged and demanded the policeman's name and badge number. As the *Post* noted, Alderman "got language added to a House appropriations bill ordering the National Park Service to build a dog run at Meridian Hill Park 'as expeditiously as possible.' Park Service officials began, reluctantly, to design a fenced area where dogs could roam without a leash." Rep. Yates was not aware of the dog-run mandate his aide had inserted into the law until after a Jack Anderson column sparked a flurry of protests to Yates's office.

DELIBERATING TO UTOPIA

In recent years, German theorist Jurgen Habermas and a host of American followers have promoted "deliberative democracy" as the solution to many of the problems of representative government. According to this theory, if citizens can meet and use "public reason" to dissect, deliberate, and resolve the major issues of the day, government policies will achieve new legitimacy and the citizenry's distrust of their rulers will dissipate.

In their 1996 book, *Democracy and Disagreement: Why Moral Conflict Cannot Be Avoided in Politics, and What Should Be Done about It,* Princeton professor Amy Gutmann and Harvard professor Dennis Thompson argued that the core of modern democracy consists of potentially grandiose debates about issues such as whether abortion should be legal, whether welfare should be provided, or whether racial hiring quotas should be imposed. According to Gutmann and Thompson, "Of the challenges that American democracy faces today, none is more formidable than the problem of moral disagreement."[89] Discussion is the great panacea: "Deliberation is not only a means to an end, but also a means for deciding what means are morally required to pursue our common ends."[90]

If government were simply a matter of paperwork, or of moral calisthenics, then mere deliberations might solve political problems. However, the opportunity to whine at public meetings is scant consolation for the financial devastation and wrecked lives produced by government policies. It is absurd to assume that discussions will resolve differences between people who wish to live as they please and others who demand power to bring them to their knees. The town meetings of early 1800s New England, chronicled by de Tocqueville and others, were effective means of governance largely because the sphere of government was narrow. The wider the swath of government action, the more fruitless deliberations become between aggressors and victims.

Gutmann, writing in 1993, declared, "Deliberative democracy legitimates the collective judgment resulting from deliberative procedures."[91] Faith in "deliberative democracy" presumes that if the right forums could be designed and attended, then democracy could transcend day-to-day political conniving and arrive at some type of collective nirvana. But what citizen-legislator summits could debate and decree, as federal bureaucrats currently do, the number of pounds of raisins that California farmers will be permitted to sell this year;[92] the number of pairs of Indonesian panties and bathrobes American consumers will be permitted to buy;[93] the number of acres of land Uncle Sam will pay farmers to leave idle;[94] the types of garments, if any, women will be allowed to sew in their own homes;[95] and the price differentials between whole milk and cheddar cheese the federal government will impose in the federally designated milk marketing order encompassing southwestern Idaho and eastern Oregon?[96]

Government is currently so intrusive that neither representatives nor voters have any idea of many, if not most, government edicts. In a typical week in 1997—March 3 through March 7—the *Federal Register* contained over 800 different rulings, notices, and new and proposed regulations. What sort of moral deliberations could citizens have regarding the following?

- The Commerce Department's preliminary ruling on alleged dumping of polyethylene terephthalate film, sheet, and strip from South Korea.[97]
- The arcane provisions of new subsidized loans to rural utilities, as authorized by the 1996 Federal Agriculture Improvement Act of 1996.[98]
- The Treasury Department's latest guidelines for confiscating assets allegedly involved in narcotics trafficking.[99]
- The Department of Education's "List of Approved 'Ability-to-Benefit' Tests and Passing Scores."[100]
- The Agriculture Marketing Service's proposed amendments to the "Honey Research, Promotion, and Consumer Information Order."[101]
- The National Labor Relation Board's revisions of procedures.[102]
- The National Marine Fisheries Service's announcement of the commercial quota of summer flounder that Delaware fishermen could harvest in 1997.[103]

- The Department of the Interior's amendments to "Gas Valuation Regulations for Indian Reservations."[104]
- The Agriculture Department's announcement of the assessment [tax] rate for onions grown in South Texas.[105]
- The Department of Transportation's ruling on whether CSX Inc. would be permitted to reduce rail service in Harrison County, West Virginia.[106]
- The Immigration and Naturalization Service's new rules for "expedited removal of aliens."[107]
- The Federal Communications Commission's ruling on radio broadcasting services in Nikiski, Arkansas.[108]

"Deliberative democracy" is also a delusory ideal because most government interventions have nothing to do with moral principle. Instead, they are the result of political finagling and counter-finagling. Regardless of how many meetings occur, or how many citizens vent their views, the federal government will still be meddling in and miring people's lives in a thousand different ways on a hundred different pretexts.

DEMOCRACY AND
THE NATURE OF POLITICS

President Wilson declared in a January 6, 1916, speech: "Politics I conceive to be nothing more than the science of the ordered progress of society along the lines of the greatest usefulness and convenience to itself."[109] President Richard Nixon declared on April 30, 1973, the day his top White House aides resigned over their role in the Watergate scandal, "I reject the cynical view that politics is inevitably, or even usually, a dirty business."[110]

In reality, a successful politician is often merely someone who caged more votes than the other liar running for office. James Madison, in his 1787 essay "Vices of the Political System of the United States," observed:

Representative appointments are sought from 3 motives: 1. Ambition. 2. Personal interest. 3. Public good. Unhappily, the two first are proved by experience to be most prevalent. Hence, the candidates who feel them, particularly the second, are most industrious and most successful in pursuing their objects; and forming often a majority in the legislative Councils, with interest viewed, contrary to the interest and vices of their constituents, join in a perfidious sacrifice of the latter to the former. . . . How easily are base and selfish measures masked by pretexts of public good and apparent expediency?[111]

Defenders of modern democracy presume that voters will choose representatives who will dutifully see that government serves the people. But it is a
delusion to think that congressmen can control the government when they often
cannot even control themselves. One episode highlighting their moral fortitude
occurred at the 1991 annual House of Representatives golf tournament, held at
Andrews Air Force Base in the Washington suburbs. As a *Wall Street Journal*
editorial noted,

> The 70 members who participated were each instructed to round up corporate
> "sponsors" in their districts who would donate prizes. Presumably businesses
> that refused knew it would be harder to get their phone calls returned. After a
> day on the links and dinners, literally hundreds of prizes were handed out. As
> the hour grew late, the MC dropped any pretense that the prizes recognized
> achievement and invited Members to take home anything they wanted. One
> Member called the ensuing scene a "feeding frenzy," as Members stuffed
> everything from crystal to CD players into their "donated" $400 golf bags and
> high-tailed it home.[112]

Organized looting rarely occurs in such a visible forum; however, the same
mentality can permeate the writing of a legislative bill. Sometimes Congress
appears to be more of a kleptocracy—government of thieves—than a democracy.
In 1992, at Sen. John "Jay" Rockefeller IV of West Virginia's behest, Congress
decreed that any company, or corporate successor of a company, that had hired
any member of the United Mine Workers (UMW) for even a single day since
1950 must pay into a health and pension fund for UMW retirees. The companies
that had hired UMW members decades before had made no contractual
agreement to pay for the employees' and their dependents' and descendants'
health care costs until the year 2043. Davis H. Elliott Co., an electrical contractor
of Roanoke, Virginia, was hit with a 50-year, $2200 per year quasi-tax assessment
because it had employed a UMW member for the single day of September 11,
1951.[113] Alan Law, president of the Mountain Laurel Resources Co. of Mount
Hope, West Virginia, was forced into bankruptcy by the law. At the time he
bought the company in 1987, it had only six employees, none of whom were
miners, and was developing recreational sites in West Virginia. In 1993, Law
was informed that the federal government assigned the health care costs of over
2,000 miners and dependents to his company and demanded over $5 million a
year in payments. Law's company's annual revenue was only $1 million a year,
so he folded.[114] The IRS went through the Appalachian states threatening
companies with $100-a-day fines for each assigned beneficiary until the
company bowed to the government's unjust demands. Sam Richardson, a

lobbyist critical of the provision, observed in 1995, "It's like taxing me for something my grandfather did 40 years ago."[115] Sen. Thad Cochran observed, "Congress harmed all of these Reachbacks [companies targeted for retroactive assessments], devastated many and ruined others. The tax has caused perhaps irreparable damage to many small and family-owned businesses."[116] For a business, there is little practical difference between IRS agents collecting the UMW health care assessments and a mob of union workers carrying baseball bats—except that a businessman has a chance of hiring security guards and standing up to a mob, but is hopelessly outnumbered by the government. (The Supreme Court, by a 5-4 margin, struck down the retroactive tax scheme in a June 1998 decision.[117])

Bertrand Russell wrote in 1938, "In a social system in which power is open to all, the posts which confer power will, as a rule, be occupied by men who differ from the average in being exceptionally power-loving."[118] According to the ancient Romans, that person who was least interested in political power was the person who would be the most trustworthy in office. Nowadays, the lust for power is perhaps the single most important determinant of who gets the job. As long as a candidate claims to have benevolent motives, power lust is treated practically as a virtue, or, in the vast majority of cases, never raised as an issue. Alan Ehrenhalt, editor of *Governing* magazine and the author of *The United States of Ambition*, wrote:

> What matters most [to the outcome of elections] is individual ambition and the corresponding willingness to do whatever it takes to win office in America. . . . For most [contemporary political leaders] the commitment to a political life has been accompanied by a positive attitude toward government itself as an instrument for doing valuable work in American society. . . . [119]

The more a candidate favors government power, the more sacrifices he will make to seize that power. This causes a Gresham's law to operate in politics: government-loving candidates squeeze out candidates who support individual liberty and low taxes. (Some individuals first elected to Congress in 1994 claimed to be above such vulgar motives; as Rep. Zach Wamp of Tennessee announced in 1995, he and his 72 Republican freshmen colleagues were "the purest, most worthy group of leaders elected to this body in my lifetime."[120] However, many members of that class are now busily seeking to perpetuate their power by claiming credit for highway projects and other boondoggles.)

The larger government grows, the more irrelevant the individual voter becomes. The power of government agencies dwarfs the influence of the individual voter; congressmen become fixated more on getting favors from federal agencies than on respecting the values of the individual voter. As a result, congressmen kowtow to government agencies that voters send them to Washington to leash. HUD Inspector General Charles Dempsey explained the HUD scandals that occurred during the 1980s: "Congress was more interested in getting favors from HUD than in overseeing its operations."[121]

POLITICAL MENDACITY
AND ITS MEANING

Election results cannot be more sacred than candidates' electioneering methods. Economist John Burnheim, in his 1985 book, *Is Democracy Possible?*, observed of electoral campaigns: "Overwhelming pressures to lie, to pretend, to conceal, to denigrate or sanctify are always present when the object to be sold is intangible and its properties unverifiable until long after the time when the decision to buy can be reversed."[122] Dishonesty is practically the distinguishing trait of the political class. Thomas Jefferson observed in 1820, "Whenever a man casts a longing eye on offices, a rottenness begins in his conduct."[123] Soviet premier Nikita Khrushchev observed, "Politicians are the same all over. They promise to build a bridge even where there is no river." One carpetbagger Reconstruction-era Louisiana governor declared, "I don't pretend to be honest. I only pretend to be as honest as anybody in politics."[124] Clinton administration communications director George Stephanopolous, responding to questions about Clinton's integrity, deftly explained in early 1996 that "the President has kept the promises he meant to keep."[125] Political masquerades were so stark at the 1996 Republican and Democratic national conventions that commentators labeled the month of the conventions as the "season of political cross-dressing."

In 1964, President Lyndon Johnson campaigned for election by warning that if his Republican opponent, Barry Goldwater, were elected, the United States would end up in a major war in South Vietnam. Johnson won and promptly sent half a million troops to fight in Vietnam. Were the citizens who voted for Johnson personally responsible for his decision to go to war in Vietnam, despite his promise not to get so heavily involved?

In 1988, George Bush ran for president with a centerpiece pledge of "No New Taxes." Two years into office, Bush betrayed the voters and raised taxes. In 1992, running for reelection, Bush offered the same promise but found fewer takers. (One comic suggested that Bush's reelection campaign slogan should have been: "This time I am not lying!")

The nation's capital offers inspiring examples of representative government at work. In 1978, when Marion Barry first ran for mayor of the District of Columbia, he declared that elected officials have a "moral responsibility" to send their kids to public schools.[126] Late in his second mayoral term, Barry sent his six-year old son to a private school. When he was challenged at a public debate about his inconsistency, Barry announced that his earlier statement "was a tactical direction of mine in 1978" and that he did "not really" believe what he said at that time—"just tactics on that one." The *Washington Post* reported shortly before the 1986 mayoral election, "Asked yesterday if he were making any 'tactical' statements in this year's campaign that he did not really believe, Barry quipped, 'I'll tell you November 5,' the day after Tuesday's general election."[127] (Barry won a third term and, after a brief intermission in federal prison on cocaine charges, a fourth term.)

Not surprisingly, some Americans doubt politicians' integrity:

- A 1992 poll showed that 73 percent of all Americans agreed "the entire political system is broken. It's run by insiders who don't listen to working people and are incapable of solving our problems."[128]
- A 1995 survey by the *Washington Post,* Harvard, and the Kaiser Foundation found that 89 percent of respondents agreed with the statement that "politicians tell voters what they want to hear, not what they will actually try to do if elected"; only 10 percent disagreed.[129]
- A 1994 survey found that 80 percent agreed that "those we elect to Congress in Washington lose touch with the people pretty quickly."[130] The same survey found that 49 percent of respondents felt Congress was more corrupt than it was 20 years ago, while only 7 percent believed it was less corrupt.(In response to public hostility, some congressmen ceased holding town meetings in their home districts.[131])
- A 1996 *Washington Post* poll found that 97 percent of people interviewed trusted their spouses, 87 percent trusted teachers, 71 percent trusted the "average person," but only 14 percent trusted politicians.[132]
- A 1994 poll found that only 3 percent of those surveyed had a "high" opinion of politicians.[133] Burns Roper, the director of the Roper poll, observed, "Those in government-related occupations are at the very bottom of the list of occupational groups thought well of."[134]

Scorning such poll results, President Clinton has sought to make any American who does not idealize politicians feel guilty. In a 1997 speech at a California fund-raiser, he declared, "Contrary to what you may read or feel, the overwhelming majority of people I have known of both parties and all philosophies have been scrupulously honest people who worked hard and made less money than they could have made doing nearly anything else with people of their talent and energy and ability, who wanted to make this a better country."[135] (Actually, over

90 percent of members of Congress first elected in 1994 earned more money in their new government jobs than they had in their previous jobs.[136]) Clinton also revealed that people who criticized the character of politicians are trying to "keep the American people in a bad frame of mind because they just can't bear to think that somebody is happy and successful somewhere."[137]

In the 1996 presidential election, an exit poll conducted by CBS News found that more than 5 million people who voted for Clinton did not believe he was honest and trustworthy.[138] On the other hand, a CBS News–*New York Times* October 1996 poll found that 65 percent of respondents stated that they believed that "Bill Clinton cares about the needs and problems of people like you"[139]— a trait that only 49 percent believed Bob Dole to possess.[140] Similarly, an NBC News–*Wall Street Journal* poll taken just before the election found that, by a margin of 51 to 25 percent, respondents believed that Clinton was "stronger" than Dole "when it comes to caring about average people."[141] The fact that Clinton appeared to "care" was more important in many voters' minds than the impression that he was dishonest. (*Time* noted that Clinton's campaign team recognized early on that "Clinton did well with intuitive types and emotion-based people rather than fact-based people.")[142] Since Clinton was, compared to Dole, the Big Government candidate of 1996, the paradoxical result of the polls and the election was: "Clinton may be a liar, but he cares, so I want him to have more power over my own life"—as if it was inconceivable that Clinton was also lying about caring.[143]

People's expectations of politicians have plummeted at the same time that politicians' power has multiplied. A 1997 CNN–*USA TODAY*–Gallup poll asked, "Is Clinton honest and trustworthy?"; 44 percent of respondents said yes and 51 percent said no. Yet, when asked, "Is Clinton honest/trustworthy enough to be president?" 55 percent said yes and 41 percent said no.[144] Apparently, the more power a person acquires, the more irrelevant his character becomes. Someone who is not scrupulous enough to sell used cars somehow becomes sufficiently honest to wield coercive power over everyone else. It is almost as if people presumed that the power a president receives somehow compensates for his moral depravity.

If politicians are honest, then presumably everything they say about their political opponents is correct, which means that politicians as a class are contemptible. Alternatively, if we assume that politicians are lying about the character of their opponents, then why should anyone believe that they are telling the truth when they proclaim that they themselves are benevolent? There is no way that politicians as a class can both be honest and morally respectable.

Legitimacy in contemporary democracy often consists merely of lying to get a license to steal. Candidates have almost unlimited prerogative to deceive the voters as long as they do not directly use force or violence during election campaigns. And once they capture office, they can use government power against those they deceived. The sanction of legitimacy a government wins from an electoral victory is like a nuclear reactor core meltdown—almost impossible to retrieve.

VOTING AS BARKING AT THE MOON

What does a vote mean? Whatever a winning politician says it means. The larger the government, the more that voting levers confer blank checks upon rulers. Voting becomes a process by which voters consecrate the loss of their rights and freedoms, rather than actively control the government.

The doubtful meaning of election results is illustrated by voters' tendency simultaneously to offer very low opinions of state legislators and to reelect almost all incumbents. A 1988 study found that, between 1978 and 1986, state legislator incumbents won reelection at the rate of 96 percent (Rhode Island and Kentucky houses), 97 percent (Pennsylvania and California houses), and 99 percent (Michigan and Missouri Senates).[145] Political scientists Malcolm Jewell and David Breaux concluded, "At the state level, it is possible that challengers have literally vanished, that more and more incumbents are winning elections without opposition."[146] One frustrated *Buffalo News* columnist observed in 1997 of New York politics: "Unless a state legislator gets thrown in jail or opens a district office in Orlando [Florida], he gets re-elected."[147] (Ninety-eight percent of New York state legislators were reelected in 1996.)

A *Time*–CNN poll in November 1996 revealed that only 14 percent of voters in the presidential election agreed with President Clinton's policy positions.[148] Voters in general are poorly informed about the positions of candidates, and many of those who "agreed" with the president's positions did not know those positions. Since respondents faced only a "yes" or "no" choice of whether they agreed with his positions, that poll likely overstated the number of people who agreed with Clinton's specific positions.[149]

Thus, perhaps only 10 percent of voters who knew Clinton's positions saw their vote as a ratification of Clinton's policies. America has a president with discretion over hundreds of agencies and policies whose own positions—at least on some issues—are opposed, or at least not supported, by 90 percent of the voters.

A *New York Times* story on the eve of the 1996 presidential election quoted one voter who succinctly captured the reality of modern democracy: "It's a question of who can hurt us the least. I don't think Mr. Clinton is going to hurt us, because he's got too many other things to worry about" (referring to the president's legal problems regarding Whitewater, Paula Jones, etcetera).[150] Rather than a means to direct government, voting is now an unreliable Kevlar jacket against political and bureaucratic attacks—simply an often futile way to limit the number of wounds a citizen receives from "his" government.

The sanction of elections based on the choice of lesser evils is paltry compared to that of elections won by a candidate who stands for the ideas and principles held by a majority of voters. What moral sanction can politicians now claim from a victory in an election in which most government policies are not mentioned, or, at a minimum, rarely understood by the vast majority of voters? What grounds exist for taking an election victory as a license to run the lives of everyone who voted or could have voted?

The notion of a "political contract" between voters and elected representatives underlies citizens' purported control over the government. But, nowadays, going into a voting booth is akin to a "contract" in which the seller has an unlimited right to deceive and defraud the buyer. ("The more you promise, the less you will have to deliver" is an old-time American political maxim.) The "political contract" essentially gives elected representatives the prerogative to abuse voters for a set period of time—two, four, or six years—like a temporary license to molest someone or pilfer his bank account. (When controversy erupted in Maryland in 1998 over blatant conflicts of interest among state legislators, Baltimore delegate Clarence Mitchell IV dismissed the clamor: "The public has the opportunity every four years to express its concern.")[151] And after the elections are over, who judges whether politicians have upheld their side of the contract? Politicians and political appointees.

Voting for a politician can be like hiring someone to landscape your front lawn, paying him, and then being forcibly restrained after he shows up with a bulldozer and instead razes your house, afterwards handing you a bill to cover the additional expense of his civic beautification project. This is the situation in which thousands of voters in Detroit, Denver, Atlantic City, and elsewhere have found themselves. Citizens voted for candidates for local government, and then watched in horror as those politicians announced some urban renewal scheme, evicted them, and sent in wrecking balls to destroy their homes—often simply to give their land to some politically influential corporation or business. And, according to Gideon Kanner, the nation's leading expert on eminent domain, governments usually pay citizens less than fair value for their condemned homes and displaced businesses; tens of thousands of people see their property condemned each year.[152]

The lethargic preferences of voters are no match for political and bureaucratic aggrandizement. In 1980, over six times as many people believed that the federal government was too powerful, compared to the number who believed it needed additional power.[153] Political scientists Linda and Stephen Earl Bennett observed that "1964 may have been the last time when Americans saying that Washington had *not* gotten too strong outnumbered those who believed that it had."[154] Yet, even after 1980, government power continually increased, year by year, edict by edict, hundred billion dollars by hundred billion dollars.

Political dishonesty mixed with voter ignorance is a recipe for Leviathan. Almost anyone who favors increasing government power profits from voter ignorance. A *Washington Post* 1996 survey concluded, "The more people know, the less confidence they had in government."[155] Every apathetic voter or nonvoter is a victory for Statism because much of the modern State has been built on the ignorance and deception of the citizenry. Since voters distrust government and politicians, the less they comprehend proposals for additional government power, the less vigorously they will oppose the power grabs.

The great paradox of contemporary American democracy is that people do not trust politicians, and a majority of citizens believes that government is too complex for them to understand, yet people acquiesce or actively support politicians who expand their power over them. Even though people believe that politicians are profoundly untrustworthy and that, according to a 1996 CBS poll, the federal government wastes 49 cents out of every dollar it spends, people continue to tolerate government running their lives and confiscating the lion's share of their paychecks.[156] (In the same poll, 56 percent of respondents said they believed that "more tax money" could "solve problems.") It is almost as if the more that politicians are presumed to be knaves or thieves, the more money they deserve to receive for safekeeping and spending.

At one level, complaints about political mendacity are moth-eaten platitudes. Yet much of the American public and the political establishment fastidiously avoid the obvious lessons from the conduct of their rulers. Each lie told by a politician is another reason for the citizen to presume that government deceives him in order to wrong him. Every lie by a politician is further evidence that government is more abusive, exploitative, and wasteful than government portrays itself to be. Politicians do not lie to cover up evidence of their good deeds. A false promise by a politician is not merely another gust of hot air wafting over people's heads; instead, it is an invitation for the citizen to lower his guard to his rights and liberties. There are no innocent false promises by would-be rulers.

Obviously, at some point, government officials and politicians will be telling so many lies, and making it so difficult for citizens to discover the truth, that any semblance of democracy will be subverted. The question is, how can we determine that point—and have we reached it yet?

SIDEBAR: THE FED'S VOTER FRAUD MANDATE

Further insight into the meaning of legitimacy in American democracy comes from the National Voter Registration Act of 1993. When President Clinton signed the bill, known as the Motor-Voter Act, he proclaimed, "This bill in its enactment is a sign of a new vibrancy in our democracy."[157] Clinton also bragged that, because of the new law, "Every year from now on, we're going to have more registered voters and more people voting." (Voter turnout fell sharply in the following presidential election.) The Justice Department in 1998 settled a case against Pennsylvania that will require the state to expand voter registration efforts at county mental health and mental retardation agencies. At Illinois mental institutions, a *Chicago Sun-Times* editorial noted, "Voter registration drives . . . turned up poor souls who tore off their clothes to get attention. One patient hee-hawed like a donkey when the Democrats were mentioned. Others only stared blankly into space."[158] The new law also effectively made it a federal crime for state and local governments to be vigilant against voter fraud. Brent Thompson, executive director of the Fair Government Foundation, observed after the November 1996 election, "The Motor Voter law did away with a panoply of anti-fraud mechanisms long relied on by the states to police and deter fraudulent voting." Congressmen presumed that any increase in voter turnout meant increased legitimacy, regardless of how fraudulent the votes or how illegitimate the voters were. Though a 1996 immigration act made it a felony for noncitizens to vote, the Immigration and Naturalization Service refuses to aid local governments in comparing voting registration lists with INS records.[159] Columnist Paul Craig Roberts observed, "The Democrats have passed a bill consciously designed to give the vote to illegals, because, as the Welfare State party and self-designated champion of minorities, the Democrats expect the illegals to vote for them."[160] The act required state governments to set up voter registration booths in every welfare office and food stamp office in the country, as well as in driver's registration offices. Congressmen concluded that American democracy would be more legitimate if more welfare recipients cast ballots ratifying the government's confiscation of other people's paychecks. The Justice Department is compelling the government of Texas to allow welfare recipients to register to vote even after they admitted to being noncitizens, and thus ineligible to vote.[161] Politicians presumed that any increase in the number of voters would further sanctify their own power—regardless of how much corruption resulted from subverting state and local governments' anti-fraud efforts.

THE CAPSIZING OF AMERICAN DEMOCRACY

American democracy is capsizing as a result of the vast increase in the number of government dependents and employees—a voting bloc that overwhelms every other potential force. H. L. Mencken quipped in the 1930s that the New Deal divided America into "those who work for a living and those who vote for a living"—a division more true now than ever before.

Political dependence is growing as fast as federal spending. Forty million adults are receiving Social Security payments.[162] (Social Security retirees now receive up to four times as much back in benefits as they paid in, including inflation and interest.[163]) Five million Americans are receiving Supplemental Security Income payments. Eight million people, including over two million adults, are receiving "Temporary Assistance to Needy Families." Twenty million people, including roughly ten million adults, are receiving food stamps. Over five million families receive federal subsidies for their heating and air conditioning. Twenty-six million kids receive federally subsidized school lunches each day, and seven million kids receive subsidized school breakfasts. More than 30 million low-income people received subsidized medical treatment under Medicaid. More than 10 million Americans benefit from federal housing subsidies or public housing. Twenty million households receive $26 billion a year in benefits from the falsely labeled Earned Income Tax Credit program, one of the fastest-growing welfare programs. The number of government transfer recipients is further swollen by the 2.5 million Americans receiving veterans benefits, the 1.7 million people receiving federal civil service retirement benefits, the 1.1 million receiving military pensions, and the 3 million receiving state and local government pensions. No one knows the precise number of handout recipients, in part because of the profusion of overlapping programs—the federal government alone runs 77 welfare programs.[164]

In addition to income transfer recipients, there are also almost 20 million government employees in the United States—more than the total number of Americans employed in manufacturing. Not only has the number of government employees multiplied in recent decades, but the rise of government unions further stacks the political odds against private citizens.[165] Thirty-seven percent of government workers now belong to unions; government worker membership in unions has skyrocketed while private sector membership has plummeted.

Unfortunately, few Americans recognize how some government employees are becoming an organized conspiracy against private citizens. *Forbes* nicknamed the National Education Association the "National Extortion Association" because of its obsession with squeezing more money out of school boards and local governments.[166] Harvard professor Caroline Hoxby found that "a reduction in the power of teachers' unions lowered per-pupil spending while raising indicators of student performance."[167] The *Washington Monthly* observed in 1992, "Once teachers get those licenses [and are hired], you can only hope that the semi-literate ones also have a predilection for pedophilia; little else will get them dismissed."[168]

Postal unions exemplify how government workers can commandeer public policy. When Rep. Bill Clay of Missouri was chairman of the House Post Office Committee, he explained what guided postal policy on Capitol Hill: "Anything the postal unions want, I want."[169] The unions have torpedoed proposals to permit Americans to escape from the federal monopoly over first-class mail delivery, and have persuaded congressmen to block the Postal Service from saving billions of dollars a year by contracting out more postal work. A clause in the American Postal Workers Union contract illustrates how government unions define workers' rights by the degree of contempt that can be shown for customers: the rule prohibits postal supervisors from pitching in to help customers aging in long lines in post offices. Unions hold the reins on some of the same congressmen who determine Postal Service appropriations. As a result, the agencies kowtow to union demands in order to avoid the wrath of Capitol Hill.

The political power of some unions creates a license for tyranny. The Mollen Commission, created to investigate the corruption in the New York Police Department, concluded in 1994 that the Patrolmen's Benevolent Association, the union representing 29,000 New York City cops, "often acts as a shelter for and protector of the corrupt cop."[170] The New York State Senate passed a bill in 1997 that, as the *New York Times* reported, "would eliminate the New York City Police Commissioner's ability to fire corrupt or brutal officers." The *Times* sneered: "History demonstrates that rank-and-file Assembly members will vote in favor of any bill sought by the city police unions, no matter how idiotic."[171] Law professor Peter Davis observed, "The union contract is so strong in Bridgeport, Connecticut that an officer who pleaded guilty to police brutality not only remained on the force, but was promoted."[172] Davis noted that, in other localities, "even when a police brutality victim wins a civil suit against the officer or the department, it is rare for the officer to lose as much as one day of work, much less his job." Joe McNamara, former police chief of San Jose and currently a Hoover Institution fellow, observed, "The worst part is that in this time of great public fear of crime, mayors and other politicians want those police union endorsements. That often translates into an order from city hall to the chief not to antagonize the union."[173] As a result, internal affairs corruption investigations may be sidelined or undermined.

Unions are in a far better position to extort favors and preferential treatment from politicians than are citizens, in part because of their political contributions and their organized voting strength. For instance, in 1993 the Clinton administration ruled that federal employee members of the American Federation of Government Employees could lobby Congress for higher pay for themselves during their "official time" work hours.[174] Rep. Dan Miller of Florida proposed the Workplace Integrity Act of 1997 to curb this abuse, declaring: "Those who are hired to work for the taxpayer should spend a minimum of 50 percent of their time actually doing their jobs."[175] (Actually, this punitive standard could adversely effect many federal employees not dallying on union-related activities.)

At least 90 million Americans are either directly dependent on government handouts or on government jobs. There are approximately 82 million full-time private employees in the United States, according to the Bureau of Labor Statistics. (There are also approximately 12 million part-time private workers, though most of them make less than $140 a week and some of them also receive government handouts.) Thus, each full-time private worker must support not only himself and his family, but also effectively carry some government dependent or employee on his shoulders at the same time.

The power of the government dependents–government employee bloc has radically changed the nature of American government. Federal, state, and local government transfer payments amounted to more than $1.1 trillion dollars in 1998—equal to roughly one-third of the total of all pre-tax private employee compensation.[176] On top of this, government employees received over $680 billion in total compensation. Over 50 percent of all tax payments now go directly to the benefit of government workers and government dependents.

Politicians have divided America into two blocs of voters officially labeled "more deserving to other's paychecks," and "less deserving to their own paycheck." Between 1986 and 1996, government transfer payments per capita rose at a rate six times faster than pretax compensation per private worker, according to economist Erich Heinemann.[177] The income of the elderly has risen nine times faster than the income for average Americans since 1971 largely because Social Security benefits have increased far faster than average wages.[178] Compensation expert Wendell Cox, publisher of the *Public Purpose,* estimated that pay for local and state government employees has risen more than five times faster than private sector pay since 1980.[179] Cox also found that federal employees receive roughly 50 percent more total compensation than do private employees performing similar jobs. Private sector workers have struggled in recent decades largely because of the bigger tax bite: between 1982 and 1992, combined state and federal taxes increased roughly twice as fast as personal income, and more than 50 percent faster than inflation.[180]

Further proof of the clout of the "tax eaters" bloc comes from the unwillingness of Congress and the president to correct the exaggerated cost-of-living adjustments (COLAs) to federal salaries and entitlement programs. A 1996 report by a panel of respected economists for the Senate Finance Committee estimated that official calculations, based on the Consumer Price Index (CPI), exaggerate inflation by about 1 percent each year.[181] The federal government uses those calculations to boost over $400 billion in benefits and salaries each year. The cumulative effect of exaggerating inflation means that government dependents are unjustifiably receiving tens of billions of dollars in windfall benefits each year. In the bipartisan budget agreement reached in the summer of 1997, the CPI calculations were left almost untouched, guaranteeing that government dependents will receive far more in undeserved benefit increases in coming years than the average taxpayer will receive in tax "cuts" (which equaled about 1 percent of the worker's tax obligation over the next five years).

Anything that increases dependency on government undermines liberty. "Self-government" becomes a farce when the citizen looks to the government three times a day for his next meal, while the government curtsies to the citizen only once every couple of years after often meaningless elections. How can a citizen help steer the ship of State at the same time that he has his hand out for another government benefit?[182] Once a person becomes a government dependent, his moral standing to resist the expansion of government power is fatally compromised. Every increase in the number of government dependents means an increase in political power. Each increase in the number of government dependents means another person who sees limits on government power as a threat to his own personal well-being. (Senior citizen lobbies have been among the most vociferous opponents of a proposed constitutional amendment to require a balanced federal budget.) Clinton's and the Democratic Party's 1996 "Mediscare" campaign exemplified how politicians exploit dependency. The *Chicago Tribune* described one of the key television advertisements used by the 1996 Clinton campaign as showing "a steadily beeping EKG machine monitoring a patient's heartbeat. After a voice described how the GOP wanted to raise Medicare premiums and cut benefits, the machine stopped beeping and went into a monotone. Everyone who watches 'ER' knew what that meant—someone had died."[183]

Not surprisingly, the Welfare State is a full-employment program for demagogues. When the government is perceived primarily as a source of alms, the personality at the helm becomes crucial. The supreme issue for the largest bloc of voters becomes not what a candidate believes, but whether he seems to "care" enough to keep giving them their checks. The desperation of tens of millions of voters over any purported threat to their government handouts helps emotionalize politics.

The sheer number of government employees and welfare recipients effectively transforms the purpose of government from maintaining order to confiscating as much as possible from vulnerable taxpayers. Elections nowadays, instead of a vote on what government should do, are largely referendums on how much it should take. The more government dependents, the more likely that democracy will become a conspiracy against self-reliance. (Not all government workers, or all retirees, or all handout recipients will vote for candidates championing Big Government. However, politicians' ability to frighten and mobilize much of this huge voter base is often sufficient to turn elections into routs.)

The danger of excessive dependency to democracy has been obvious for nearly two thousand years. Plutarch observed of the dying days of the Roman Republic, "The people were at that time extremely corrupted by the gifts of those who sought office, and most made a constant trade of selling their voices."[184] Montesquieu wrote, "It is impossible to make great largesses to the people without great extortion: and to compass this, the state must be subverted. The greater the advantages they seem to derive from their liberty [of voting], the nearer they approach towards the critical moment of losing it."[185]

DEMOCRACY VERSUS LIBERTY

People have long been encouraged to confuse self-government of their own lives with "self-government" via majority rule over everyone. Because abusive rule by foreigners or a king personified oppression, many people presumed that rule by people of one's own nationality meant freedom. Boston pastor Benjamin Church proclaimed in 1773 that liberty was "the happiness of living under laws of our own making. Therefore, the liberty of the people is exactly proportioned to the share the body of the people have in the legislature. . . ."[186] However, the rampages of state and local majorities during and after the American Revolution debunked this faith.

But as time passed, enthusiasm for government power returned and, new doctrines arose to again vindicate unleashing the majority. Progressive Herbert Croly declared in 1909, "Individual freedom is important, but more important still is the freedom of a whole people to dispose of its own destiny."[187] However, in practice, this means the "freedom of the whole people" to dispose of the individuals' rights, property, and lives.

Some theoreticians and politicians have reconciled democracy and liberty by redefining liberty as submission to whatever the majority ordains. J. Allen Smith, author of *The Spirit of American Government,* wrote in 1907: "True liberty consists not in divesting the government of effective power, but in making it an instrument for the unhampered expression and prompt enforcement of public opinion."[188] Thus individual freedom is whatever the majority deigns to permit—or whatever politicians and bureaucrats claim the majority dictates—or would dictate, if it was as smart as government workers. More recently, British Labour Party leader Hugh Scanlon declared, "Liberty, in my view, is conforming to majority opinion."[189]

Hans Kelsen, one of the most respected political and legal theorists of the twentieth century, wrote in 1957: "Democracy, by its very nature, means freedom."[190] In his 1945 *General Theory of Law and State,* Kelsen declared that "a subject is politically free insofar as his individual will is in harmony with the 'collective' (or 'general') will expressed in the social order"; for Kelsen, "freedom under the social order" meant "self-determination of the individual by participating in the creation of the social order."[191] But most "subjects" have little or no effective means of "participating in the creation of the social order," as far as determining the edicts that government imposes upon them. As long as the citizen has a vote, he is presumed to be a free man—no matter how little the vote means, how meaningless the choice at the election booth is, or how much power politicians have to scorn, punish, or plunder voters after the election.

Vesting unchecked power in elected representatives is sometimes equated with liberty. Former federal judge and Supreme Court nominee Robert Bork in 1996 called for "a constitutional amendment making any federal or state court decision subject to being overruled by a majority vote of each House of Congress."[192] Bork appealed to "our most precious freedom, the freedom to govern ourselves democratically."[193] According to this view, the greatest danger to freedom is having frustrated legislators. Bork presumed that there was little or nothing to fear from elected politicians: "This is a civilized nation; there is no reason to suppose that the citizens of some benighted town would suddenly become fascists and return to a regime of racial segregation."[194] But the likely problem from omnipotent legislators is not fascism, but garden-variety exploitation and oppression by the type of laws that judges routinely strike down as unconstitutional. Bork's faith that there is no danger of a revival of racial segregation is puzzling, since it was primarily judges who sheared the legal fetters that legislators had imposed on blacks. Federal judges have an abysmal record of mandating expanded government power in some areas, such as forced busing, prison operation, and education financing. There is no reason for blind faith in the former lawyers appointed to the Supreme Court or other judicial posts. But the majority of Supreme Court rulings of unconstitutionality have curbed government power. The primary problem is not the Court's power but the fact that justices are too often lap dogs of legislators.

What are the mechanics by which majority-mandated shackles liberate the individual? How does a shackle supported by 51 percent of the populace affect an individual differently than one endorsed by a mere 49 percent? Is the secret to democracy some law of inverse political gravity—so that the more people who support imposing a shackle, the less a shackle weighs? Are citizens obliged to pretend that any restriction favored by the majority is not a restraint, but instead a badge of freedom? Shackles are shackles are shackles, regardless of what rhetorical holy water they are blessed with.

Some of those who portray democracy as the incarnation of freedom have little respect for individual freedom; rather, they see freedom as an attribute of collectives, groups, certified majorities—something that individuals are allowed to share upon condition of abandoning themselves to the majority's whims. And why is "collective liberty" liberty? Simply because the majority says so—or at least said so at the last election. This presumes that there can be no objective political reality apart from the most recently registered whims of a majority.

The fiction of majority rule has become a license to impose nearly unlimited controls on the majority and everybody else. The doctrine of "majority rule equals freedom" is custom made to turn mobs of voters into spoiled children with a divine right to plunder the candy store. The only way to equate submission to majority-sanctioned decrees with individual freedom is to assume that individuals have no right to live in any way that displeases the majority.

Political charlatans tell people they are ruling themselves when the government commands obedience to its dictates. But, is a citizen governing herself when she is arrested for possessing a handgun in her own home for self-defense in a crime-ridden District of Columbia neighborhood where police long since ceased providing minimum protection? Is a citizen governing himself when he is arrested for converting a garage into a playroom for his children without a permit from the local zoning board? Is a 20-year old citizen governing himself when he is arrested in his own home by police for drinking a beer? The fact that a majority—or, more likely, a majority of the minority who bothered to vote— may have sanctioned such laws and government powers has nothing to do with the self-government by each citizen of his own life.

The policies of government schools epitomize how democracy sacrifices liberty. As John Chubb and Terry Moe observed in a 1990 Brookings Institution book on education policy, "Democracy is essentially coercive. The winners get to use public authority to impose their policies on the losers."[195] Whether it is a question of distributing free condoms to 12-year-old kids, or teaching the Biblical version of human history, or promoting alternative sexual lifestyles, or jamming bilingual education down the throats of Hispanic American parents, public schools have become a behemoth that routinely scorns the values and

preferences of children and their parents. New York City Schools Chancellor
Rudy Crew prohibited parents at one Greenwich Village school from voluntarily
raising money to pay the salary of one esteemed fourth-grade school teacher
targeted for a transfer. He claimed that such an act would "adversely affect the
opportunity for equity" in New York public schools.[196] Thus, "equity" is
supposedly the result of allowing government school bureaucrats to have
unlimited control over who may teach parents' children. Under court orders,
the Texas legislature decreed that no school district could spent more than
$4,200 per student for education, which forced schools in wealthy areas to slash
their school expenditures by more than half.[197] A 1983 federal report entitled *A
Nation at Risk: The Imperative for Educational Reform* observed, "If an unfriendly
foreign power had attempted to impose on America the mediocre educational
performance that exists today, we might well have viewed it as an act of war."[198]
But, many parents probably have as much chance of influencing a foreign
dictator as they have of influencing a big-city school board. The citizen's rights
end as soon as his tax dollar reaches the public treasury. When parents pay for
schooling indirectly, they become beggars instead of buyers. Nor does the
opportunity to vote in school board elections vindicate the average citizen's
rights, since those elections in many urban areas are dominated by teacher unions
and their cronies.[199]

Would the essence of slavery change if the rules at a slave auction permitted
a slave to choose between the two highest bidders for himself? Could the fact that
he made such a choice be interpreted as his sanction for his chains? How can it be
argued that the citizen is free in a democracy when he has the choice of two
candidates if neither candidate is willing to recognize his right to freedom? A
convict given the choice of wearing a suit with horizontal stripes or vertical stripes
may appreciate that choice, but it doesn't make him free. Is a person to be
considered free because he has a choice between one presidential candidate who
wants to send the National Guard storming across his back yard in search of
cannabis and another candidate who wants to send the cigarette police storming
into his lifestyle? Is a voter free if he is forced to choose between a political party
that would raise his taxes by 10 percent and a party that would raise his taxes by
20 percent; or between two parties, both of whom pledge to destroy free speech
on the Internet? (Republican presidential nominee Bob Dole, in a 1996 presidential debate with President Clinton, declared, "The president wants to increase
spending 20% over the next six years. I want to increase spending 14%. That's
how simple it is. . . . We're talking about six points over six years."[200])

Historian Gordon Wood, in a 1996 speech on the French and American
revolutions, beautifully contrasted the effects of a fixation on political participation and a devotion to restraining government power:

The English and French had very different views of . . . positive liberty . . . that is, the freedom of people to participate in politics and government in a classic sense. The French, having little experience with popular government, naturally followed Rousseau in emphasizing this sort of positive liberty. The English, on the other hand, while never scorning positive liberty, more or less took it for granted. . . . But they regarded representative institutions, their positive liberty, largely as means to an end which they took even greater pride in—the people's individual rights that were free from violation by the king's government. In fact, unlike the French revolutionaries, it is doubtful that Englishmen, including the American colonists, ever much cared about classical political participation, or their positive liberty, except insofar as it protected their individual negative liberties. . . .

Ultimately it was their preoccupation with their individual rights and liberties, their negative liberty, even at the expense of their positive liberty, that enabled the American Revolutionaries to succeed in creating such a liberal regime without the great violence and bloodshed and failure of other revolutions. . . . Americans came to understand that there could be no general will, no embodiment of a single public good, because there was no democratic way of discovering that general will and promoting that public good. There was no majority or series of majorities that could ever speak for the American people; all there were clamoring multitudes of interests. Under such chaotic and licentious circumstances all that government was capable of deciphering and promoting were individual rights and liberties; anything else that government tried to do would be diffused, dissipated and individualized by the clashing and jostling interests of this unusually democratic society. There could be no reign of terror and no despotism where there was no state authority to exert its will. The American Revolution succeeded in avoiding the tyranny and dictatorship of the French Revolution because the democracy it unleashed virtually destroyed all semblance of traditional state power.[201]

MAJORITY MANIFEST
DESTINY VERSUS INDIVIDUAL RIGHTS

The problem with democracy is not only that government routinely scorns citizens' values; it is also that government imposes majority preferences that have no legitimacy.

Majorities are routinely the ephemeral creations of political promises to confiscate one group's property and render it to someone else. What virtue does a majority of tenants have when the one policy they demand is the looting of all apartment owners via rent control? There is no virtue in a citizen voting for a politician who promises him something for nothing. Multiplying that by tens of millions increases the amount of the graft, but not the sum of the virtue.

There is nothing sacrosanct in a majority. In the South after the Civil War, "The barriers of racial discrimination mounted in direct ratio with the tide of political democracy among whites."[202] As long as the remnants of the old Southern aristocracy retained some grip on power, the worst excesses of Jim Crow repression did not occur.[203] In Germany in 1934, a majority of Germans ratified Hitler's dictatorship. (Hitler was not elected into the chancellorship but took office in early 1933 after a deal with some dimwitted aristocratic political hacks; Hitler had received only 32 percent of the vote in an election six months earlier.) In Serbia in 1995, a majority of voters cast their lot with Slobodan Milosevic, even though his dictatorial tendencies had long been clear. As *Foreign Affairs* editor Fareed Zakaria wrote in 1997, "From Peru to the Palestinian Authority, from Sierra Leone to Slovakia, from Pakistan to the Philippines, we see the rise of . . . illiberal democracy."[204]

Can a swing in votes of 1 percent automatically nullify the rights of 49 percent of the populace? Do rights have no existence in themselves, but only in comparative herd counts? Is the purpose of voting merely to allow citizens to decide which pack of politicians they will be milked by? For the *reductio ad absurdum* of democracy, consider the experience of Liberia. Charles Taylor won the presidency in July 1997 with 75 percent of the popular vote in an election judged "free and fair" by international observers, despite the fact that he had ignited a civil war that left 200,000 people dead and "more than half of the population of 3 million driven from their homes," according to the *Washington Post*.[205] Taylor's political party, capitalizing on his supporters' long record of atrocities, adopted the campaign slogan: "The devil you know is better than the angel you do not." Taylor supporters chanted:

> He killed my ma,
> He killed my pa,
> And I will vote for him!

The *Post* noted, "Taylor had the money to give them something tangible for their vote—like the bags of rice people hoped for."

Legitimacy is not a question of head counts, but of rights. Majority rule cannot sanctify any action that would be immoral if done by an individual. It is far more important to determine the extent of the rights of individuals than the preferences of a majority. Since individual rights are not created by levers in voting booths, voting levers cannot nullify individual rights.

To say that the majority's rights are unlimited is to say that the individual's rights are nonexistent. Yet, if the individual has no rights, then of what does the right of the majority consist? If the individual is a zero, how can a multiplication of zeroes equal more than a single zero? If the majority scorns the rights of the individual, what obligation does the individual have to respect the majority's preferences? If sheer power is the only source of legitimacy in a democracy, any individual or group of individuals who can muster more power is entitled to subdue the majority.

PROPER SCOPE OF DEMOCRACY

Many of those who glorified democracy in the past presumed that universal suffrage would lead to the creation of a new and higher form of humanity. President Franklin Pierce proclaimed in 1855 that government abuses "disappear before the intelligence and patriotism of the people, exerting through the ballot box their peaceful and silent irresistible power."[206] Professor Alexander Meiklejohn proclaimed in 1935 that women's suffrage "in its hoped-for effect upon the quality of women's living, the spiritual gain may be, in time, tremendous."[207] Democracy was supposed to lead average people to begin examining and questioning the great questions of national policy, and thereby raise their minds. Some proponents of democracy even believed that its triumph would awake people to their common interest with humanity and lead to benefits such as the end of war and the abolition of trade barriers.

But, rather than broadening people's minds, the exercise of voting too often merely debases their character. Politicians scapegoat whatever group is least popular at the moment (such as immigrants), encourage the elderly to maximize their greed, use race-baiting tactics, and foment private distrust in order to maximize people's reliance on politicians. When people have no sense of responsibility and respect for the rights of other citizens, going into the polling booth is about as morally uplifting as receiving a one-day license to shoplift in a fancy department store. When voting is exercised primarily as a ticket to plunder, voting will not be any more edifying than other types of larceny.

Democracy allows the peaceful transition of political power; but it is often a transition from one abusive, corrupt party to another inept, corrupt party. The issue is not whether democratic processes are the best means to choose rulers. Obviously, if some people are to have coercive power over other people, it is preferable that the coerced have at least some nominal voice in expressing a preference for their coercers. How much trust or faith should be placed in rulers merely because they took office through elections?

The fact that some politicians seem to be honorable people cannot vindicate the honor of politicians as a class. There is perhaps the same percentage of upright characters in contemporary politics as there were wise benevolent kings in European history. But the existence of good kings in the distant past is irrelevant to the question of how much power to vest in the hands of contemporary rulers. The question is not whether democracy is good; but rather, what is it good for?

"Whenever majority rule is unnecessarily substituted for individual choice, democracy is in conflict with individual freedom," wrote Italian professor Bruno Leoni in his 1961 book, *Freedom and the Law.*[208] Majority rule is a means, not an end. There is nothing superior in majorities running (or thinking they run) a government compared to an individual running his own life. Collective rule will always be inferior to the self-rule of a citizen in his own life.

The solution to most of the problems of contemporary democracy is not rule by the elite, or authoritarianism, or dictatorship, but simply a smaller government. Such problems illustrate why government power should be minimized, regardless of how the rulers are chosen. The more power government acquires in the name of the people, the easier it becomes to ignore and oppress the people. In his *First Treatise of Government,* John Locke skewered absolutist Robert Filmer for pretending that it was self-evident who should be the divinely anointed ruler.[209] Similarly, contemporary pro-government theoreticians refuse to admit or to recognize how unreliable elections are as a means of selecting wise rulers. Every known method of choosing political rulers has profound flaws. Since there is no sure-fire method of choosing good rulers, the amount of power available to any ruler, good or bad, must be minimized. The defects in any system of choosing and anointing rulers outweigh the risks of letting people run their own lives.

Democracy is a valuable tool to peacefully resolve differences. But the more often that a majority forcibly imposes its will, the less viable majority rule becomes. The proliferation of majority-sanctioned dictates will eventually cause the minority to deny the legitimacy of the entire political system. And the use of power is addictive, both to politicians and majorities. As author Frank Chodorov noted, "The more power the politician wields, the greater his self-esteem—and the more readily does he justify a widening of his area of power."[210] Pervasive government intervention undercuts people's incentives to reach voluntary agreements among themselves. Instead, each side in a dispute will seek to capture the machinery of government to jam their preferences down the other side's throat. Efforts that could have been directed towards reaching peaceful accommodations are instead spent pursuing political power.

Democracy can be more noble for what it prevents than for what it achieves. Democracy is valuable largely as an insurance policy against tyranny. Yet, as with other insurance schemes, there is a moral hazard. The fact that people believe they have a democracy leads them to neglect the precautions against political oppression that many would take under other forms of government. Democracy encourages people to lower their guards precisely when government has the most momentum for expansion.

The scope of majority rule should be limited to those issues and areas in which common standards must prevail to preserve public peace. Democracy is a relatively good method for reaching agreement on a system of roads, but is a lousy method for dictating where each citizen must go. Democracy can be a good method for reaching agreement on standards of weights and measurements used in commerce, but is a poor method for dictating wages and prices. Democratic rule is a satisfactory method for reaching concurrence on issues for which uniformity is necessary to avoid total chaos. But natural diversity is preferable to compulsory uniformity in any area in which such diversity can exist without dire consequences. Democracy should be a system of government based on common agreement on issues that must be agreed upon, and tolerance— however grudging—on all other differences.

Freedom to vote is valuable primarily as a way to defend other freedoms. King Charles I of England, writing shortly before he was beheaded in 1649, declared that the people's "liberty and freedom consisted in having the govern- ment of those laws by which their life and their goods may be most their own; 'tis not for having share in government that is nothing pertaining to them."[211] The king's comments are ironic, since he had worked unceasingly for decades to achieve unlimited power over his subjects: levying illegal taxes that he intended to use to build a standing army to impose his edicts; greatly expanding the power of the Star Chamber which, as Macaulay wrote, allowed the government "to fine, imprison, pillory, and mutilate without restraint;"[212] seeking to violently suppress the Presbyterian Church; and betraying every promise he made to accept limits on his power.

Without political involvement—without active monitoring of the actions of politicians and bureaucrats, and without vigorous resistance to government overreaching—people have few means to safeguard their lives and property. Freedom to vote is valuable as a means to avoid being trampled by the government, rather than as a means to participate in collective stampedes.

The most important issue is not whether the government rules in the name of the majority, but how the government rules—whether its power is limited or unlimited. Any form of government, when granted effectively unlimited power, will become corrupt and destructive of its subjects. There are plenty of automobiles that handle adequately at 60 miles per hour but fall apart and crash at 130 miles per hour. The fact that the Supreme Court exercises scant oversight over legislation attacking property and contract rights, for instance, is the equivalent of the removal of the brakes from a racing car. And the fact that many congressmen feel entitled to intervene on any issue that strikes their fancy is like an accelerator stuck to the floor. The more power government acquires, the more likely democracy will self-destruct.[213]

Criticism of the abuses of existing democracies in no way tarnishes the heroism of those people around the world who are fighting oppressive governments. Voting, especially in nations that did not previously have democratic traditions, gives a person the opportunity to stand up bravely to their government and, at the least, slap it around a bit. Nicaraguans demonstrated their spunk in 1990 when they ignored government intimidation and voted out the Ortega communist regime. To see people scorn the wrath of a corrupt government and march resolutely to polling booths despite government attempts to cow them into submission is a triumph of character and courage that should inspire oppressed people and indolent citizens of democracies everywhere.

CONCLUSION

The pretenses of many modern democracies to "represent the people" are as hollow as that of bygone monarchies to "serve the people." The Revolutionary War was fought on the principle that a facade of representation is not enough to make a people free. Now, 220 years later, we must recognize that political representation is once again largely a sham—an impossibility as a result of all the things over which government has seized power. We must, as the founding Fathers did, denounce the frauds of representation by which government lulls people into submission.

Governments and citizens blend together only in the imaginations of political theorists. Government is, and always will be, an alien power over private citizens. There is no magic in a ballot box that makes government any less coercive.

Rather than "government by the people," we now have "government by numbers." In a government by the people, the bulk of the citizenry would be politically informed, would follow public policy debates, and would make sure that their legislators know their views. In a government by numbers, in contrast, masses of voters are frightened or bribed into voting for certain candidates with little or no idea of what those candidates stand for and have stood for. In government by the people, most citizens would understand legal processes and be capable of standing up for their rights against aggrandizing bureaucracies. In government by numbers, people technically have legal and constitutional rights, but most are overawed by petty government officials in their daily lives. In government by the people, the citizenry would understand legislative practices and could not be easily deceived by political sleight of hand. In government by numbers, politicians preserve the rites of democracy to avoid triggering popular discontent in the same way that the early Roman emperors preserved the Roman Senate as a hollow formality.

It is a pipe dream to expect government to transcend the character of its leaders. There is no reorganization of bureaucratic departments or change in campaign finance laws or election procedures that can validate contemporary democracy. As long as the scope of government vastly exceeds the limits of citizen's understanding, "democracy" will simply be a ruse invoked by the political-bureaucratic ruling class to keep people in their places, paying and obeying.

Voting symbolizes the equality of people, premised on the fact that no person has an inherent right to exercise coercive power over other people. But voting is not enough. The more that voting is glorified as a panacea, the more lackadaisical people are about knowing or defending their rights as citizens. The point is not to abolish elections, but to recognize that elections are a dubious means to safeguard people's rights, liberties, and vital interests.

Election results are more likely the voice of fraud than the voice of God. It is good to have a representative government, but it is naive to expect much from it. A democratic government will still be a government—which is more important than it being a democracy.

Freedom consists of more than a mere choice of political masters. Once it becomes stark that "the people" cannot control Big Government, then the democratic sheen of Leviathan is gone and all that is left is . . . Leviathan. If we are to have a real democracy, government must be limited to a size that the average voter can understand. The solution is not to abolish voting, but to reduce the size of the government in order to maximize the relative power of each individual voting lever. The amount of power that politicians receive should be limited to the degree of citizens' trust in the politicians' characters.

This essay is not a plea to distrust democracy; rather, it is a plea to distrust the pretensions and false claims of any government, regardless of its purported sanction. It is not a call to reject democracy; rather, it is a call to protect democracy against those who would destroy it by driving it over the cliff of unlimited power. Idealizing any form of government is one of the worst mistakes a free people can make. The idealizing of American democracy is one of the worst threats to the future of American liberty.

FIVE

THE MORAL GLORIFICATION OF LEVIATHAN

People dream of making the virtuous powerful, so they can depend on them. Since they cannot do that, people choose to make the powerful virtuous, glorifying in becoming victimized by them.
—Thomas Szasz[1]

The majesty of the State is due not to its command of an unlimited force, but to its ethical nature, its supreme necessity as an indispensable instrument for the growth of the spiritual nature of man.
—A.R. Wadia[2]

THE WORD "FAIRNESS" sometimes has the same mesmerizing effect upon people's critical faculties that the phrase "divine right" had a few centuries ago. Modern morality is based on "push-button fairness": the government announces a new regulation, enforcers twist arms, and—voila!—fairness triumphs. The vast expansion of government power in recent decades has stemmed in part from the presumed moral superiority of the government over the private sector; the presumed moral superiority of government commands over private voluntary agreements; and the presumed moral superiority of politicians and bureaucrats over private citizens. Moral assumptions and pretenses have played a much larger role in the expansion of government power than most Americans realize. And the cloud of moral rectitude that surrounds political and bureaucratic action undermines citizens' will to resist further intrusions into their lives.

It is in the abstruse details of government policies that the moral character of the State can best be divined. We shall examine some areas in which the moral pretensions of the Welfare State have been greatest.

THE NEW DEAL AND
THE NATIONALIZATION OF FAIRNESS

The New Deal established much of the moral framework of contemporary political life. Though some of the programs and policies of that era have been terminated, the moral heritage of the New Deal continues to permeate American government and American political thinking. No American president has rivaled Franklin Roosevelt in his denunciation of "economic royalists." Roosevelt declared in 1936, "I should like to have it said of my first Administration that in it the forces of selfishness and of lust for power met their match. . . . I should like to have it said of my second Administration that in it these forces met their master."[3] Roosevelt sought to "master" the "forces of selfishness" by making government master of every person's private financial destiny.

We will examine two of the New Deal's most controversial policies: the seizure of citizens' gold and the imposition of fair-practice codes via the National Industrial Recovery Act.

Roosevelt announced on March 8, 1933, a few days after taking office, that the gold standard was safe. But, three days later, Roosevelt issued an executive order forbidding gold payments by banks; Treasury Secretary Henry Morgenthau announced on March 11 that "the provision is aimed at those who continue to retain quantities of gold and thereby hinder the Government's plans for a restoration of public confidence."[4] Ogden Mills, who had served as President Hoover's treasury secretary, observed that "it was not the maintenance of the gold standard that caused the banking panic of 1933 and the outflow of gold. . . . [I]t was the definite and growing fear that the new administration meant to do what they ultimately did—that is abandon the gold standard."[5]

Fear of devaluation spurred a panic, which Roosevelt invoked to justify seizing people's gold. On April 5, 1933, Roosevelt commanded all citizens to relinquish their gold to the government. No citizen was permitted to own more than $100 in gold coins, except for rare coins with special value for collectors. Treasury Secretary Morgenthau announced on the same day that "gold held in private hoards serves no useful purpose under present circumstances."[6] Gold was thus turned into the same type of contraband substance that rum had been during Prohibition. Roosevelt announced, "Many persons throughout the U.S. have hastened to turn in gold in their possession as an expression of their faith in the Government and as a result of their desire to be helpful in the emergency. There are others, however, who have waited for the Government to issue a formal order for the return of gold in their possession."[7] To speak of the "return of gold" implied that government was the rightful owner of all the gold in the nation, and thus that no citizen had a right to possess the most respected source of value in history. Roosevelt assured the country that the "order is limited to the period of the emergency." But the order stayed on the books until 1974.

Roosevelt labeled anyone who did not surrender their gold a "hoarder." Roosevelt's executive order defined "hoarding" as "the withdrawal and *withholding* of gold coin, gold bullion or gold certificates from the recognized and customary channels of trade."[8] Actually, Roosevelt was not concerned with the gold being in the "customary channels of trade"; instead, he wanted government to possess all the gold. And the notion that someone was "withholding" their gold merely because they did not rush to the nearest Federal Reserve bank to relinquish it was political logic at its best. Roosevelt, in a later note to his *Public Papers,* justified the order because it "served to prevent the accumulation of private gold hoards in the U.S."[9] Roosevelt used the same "hoarding" rhetoric against anyone who owned gold that Stalin used against Ukrainian peasants who sought to retain part of their wheat harvest to feed their families. But, while Stalin sent execution squads to kill peasants who had a few bushels of grain hidden in their hovels, Roosevelt was kinder and gentler, seeking only ten-year prison sentences for any citizen who retained more than five Double Eagle gold coins.

Citizens who distrusted the government's currency management or the government's integrity were branded as social enemies. Shortly after Roosevelt banned private ownership of gold, he announced a devaluation of 59 percent in the gold value of the dollar. In other words, after Roosevelt seized the citizenry's gold, he proclaimed that the gold would henceforth be of much greater value in terms of the dollar. Citizens who had desired to hold gold as a hedge against government policies were completely vindicated. FDR's administration subsequently did everything possible to inflate prices, foolishly confident that a mere change in numerical prices would produce prosperity. Citizens had accepted a paper currency based on the government's pledge to redeem the currency in gold at $20 per ounce; then, when Roosevelt decided to betray that pledge, he also felt obliged to turn all citizens holding gold into criminals. Roosevelt stated that the ban on private ownership "was the first step also to that complete control of all monetary gold in the United States, which was essential in order to give the Government that element of freedom of action which was necessary as the very basis of its monetary goal and objective."[10] But the primary "freedom" government acquired was the freedom to default on its promises and to manipulate the lives of everyone depending on U.S. dollars in their daily transactions.

Senator Carter Glass of Virginia, chairman of the Senate Finance Committee, denounced the gold seizure: "It's dishonor. This great government, strong in gold, is breaking its promises to pay gold to widows and orphans to whom it has sold government bonds with a pledge to pay gold coin of the present standard of value. It is breaking its promise to redeem its paper money in gold coin of the present standard of value."[11] Historian Benjamin Anderson later observed: "The President's course in connection with the gold standard . . . represented an act of absolute bad faith. He had not dared to make any suggestion of anything but adherence to the gold standard in the [1932] campaign . . . "[12]

Similar righteousness permeated the National Industrial Recovery Act, another hallmark of Roosevelt's first hundred days. In a May 17, 1933, message, Roosevelt called for Congress to "provide for the machinery necessary for a great co-operative movement throughout all industry in order to obtain wide re-employment, to shorten the working week, to pay a decent wage for the shorter week and to prevent unfair competition and disastrous overproduction." Roosevelt demanded new power for the government because "employers cannot do this singly or even in organized groups, because such action increases costs and thus permits cut-throat underselling by selfish competitors unwilling to join in such a public-spirited endeavor."[13] In Roosevelt's New Ethics, the evil businessman was the one who charged low prices and the "public-spirited" businessman was the one who colluded with other businessmen to gouge customers.

The National Recovery Administration (NRA), created by the act, personified New Deal fairness: vesting unlimited arbitrary power in one person's hands and presuming that whatever he decreed was fair. Section 3 of the act allowed the president to personally impose codes of conduct on any industry. As a 1934 Brookings Institution study of the NRA noted,

> A further expansion of the President's powers . . . authorizes him, whenever he shall find that activities which he believes are contrary to the purpose of the law are being practiced in any trade or industry, to license business enterprises if he shall deem it essential to make effective a code of fair competition or agreement. No person shall, after a date which shall have been fixed in an announcement that licensing is required in an industry, engage in any business specified in such announcement unless he shall first have obtained a license pursuant to the regulations prescribed. . . . [C]arrying on of business without a license where a license is required is made a criminal offense. The penalty is a fine of not to exceed $500 or imprisonment not to exceed six months or both.[14]

The study noted that "the licensing provision, giving the President the power of life or death over business enterprises, is the ultimate weapon of enforcement and the capstone of the powers granted to the President . . . the most extraordinary extension of Presidential power in American history." The final provision of the bill vested in the president the power "from time to time to cancel or modify any order, approval, license, rule, or regulation issued under this title."[15] Senator Glass denounced "the utterly dangerous effort of the federal government at Washington to transplant Hitlerism to every corner of this nation."[16]

Roosevelt declared in 1933, "We recognize the right of the individual to seek and to obtain his own fair wage, his own fair profit, in his own fair way—just so long as in the doing of it he does not push down or hold down his neighbor."[17] And to protect people, Roosevelt's policies gave government a right to "push down or hold down" whatever group or industry it chose. The NRA restricted working hours, inflated prices, and obliged businesses to form committees to severely restrict competition. Federal officials proceeded to sanction codes for hundreds of industries, from the dog food industry (Code 450) to the shoulder pad manufacturing industry (Code 262). Code 348, governing the burlesque theatrical industry, dictated that no production could contain more than four stripteases.[18] Any violation of a code was an "unfair method of competition," and subjected the violator to a fine of up $500 for each offense, with each day considered a separate offense.[19] New Jersey tailor Jack Magid was jailed for "charging thirty-five cents for pressing a suit," in violation of the NRA code that mandated a 40 cent charge.[20] The NRA assumed that prosperity could be secured by restricting production and boosting prices—prosperity through "universal monopoly and universal scarcity," as critics quipped.

The inevitable result of Roosevelt's policies was to subjugate consumers to producers, to minimize freedom of contract in the name of social justice. The codes included the power to dictate minimum wages on an industry-by-industry basis; one result, according to a 1937 study, was that half a million black workers were thrown onto the relief rolls.[21] (Black workers were often the first to be tossed out of work because of bias in the job market, among other factors.) Record-high unemployment was an agonizing problem at the time Roosevelt took office—but it is tricky to create more jobs by mandating higher wages. (Unemployment remained extremely high through 1939, declining only after the onset of the Second World War.)

With the arrival of the NRA, the time had come when the nation could no longer afford to allow chicken buyers to choose their chickens. In 1934, the Schechter brothers, who ran the largest poultry slaughterhouse in Brooklyn, were arrested for violating the federal code of fair competition for the Live Poultry Industry of the Greater New York Metropolitan Area. Their case arrived at the

Supreme Court in 1935. The heart of the case—10 of the alleged 18 infrac-tions—involved violating the "straight killing" mandate, which the NRA defined as "the practice of requiring persons purchasing poultry for resale to accept the run of any half coop, coop or coops, as purchased by slaughter house operators, except for culls.'"[22]

Now, more than 60 years later, it is amusing to read the brief that the Roosevelt administration submitted to the Supreme Court in this case. The Roosevelt administration brief fretted about "cut-throat competition" in the chicken slaughter business. The brief stressed that, under the 1934 fair-conduct rules, "purchasers . . . shall not have the right to make any selection of particular birds."[23] The brief noted, "The 'straight killing' requirement of the Code is really a requirement of straight selling."[24] Letting buyers pick their birds, according to the Roosevelt administration, generated many "evils"[25]—primarily that it made it more difficult for sellers to charge higher prices for all chickens. It is difficult to comprehend why the New Deal Brain Trust assumed that the fewer choices the buyer had, the more ethical trade became.[26]

The administration's brief to the Supreme Court justified pervasive federal restrictions on chicken sales by quoting trial testimony: "One of petitioner's witnesses testified that members of the industry 'are looked upon as the worst type of businessmen in the world.'"[27] Yet, 64 pages later in the same brief, the administration asserted: "The [NRA] codes will therefore consist of rules of competition deemed fair for each industry by representative members of that industry—by the persons most vitally concerned and most familiar with its problems."[28] Apparently all that was necessary to make an industry ethical was to give "the worst type of businessmen" power to dictate rules for their competitors and customers and then have federal agents enforce the rules on everyone. (Ironically, the same presumption prevails today: many people assume that politicians are the "worst type of men," but allow politicians to impose edicts on everyone else and expect justice to result.)

The Supreme Court unanimously struck down the National Industrial Recovery Act (NIRA). The court decision asked,

> What is meant by 'fair competition' as the term is used in the act? Does it refer to a category established in the law, and is the authority to make codes limited accordingly? Or is it used as a convenient designation for whatever set of laws the formulators of a code for a particular trade or industry may propose and the President may approve . . . as being wise and beneficent provisions. . . ?[29]

The justices were dismayed at the sweep of the power granted in the act: "the discretion of the President in approving or prescribing codes, and thus enacting laws for the government of trade and industry throughout the country, is virtually unfettered."[30] The Court ruled that the act was "an unconstitutional delegation of legislative power."

However, in the subsequent years, after Roosevelt's court-packing threat of 1937, the justices swallowed whatever creative definition of fairness that Congress or federal agencies chose to proclaim. For instance, in 1942, Congress passed the Emergency Price Control Act, which created an Office of Price Administration with sweeping power to set or strike down prices in any industry or activity that it considered to be "defense-related"—a vague term that could have encompassed practically the entire national economy. The act contained no substantive guidelines for the administrator's decisions but merely required prices that "in his judgment will be generally fair and equitable."[31] The Supreme Court upheld the law in 1944; Justice Owen Roberts bitterly dissented that "it is plain that this Act creates personal government by a petty tyrant instead of government by law." [32] He also denounced the administrative system created by the statute as a parody of due process: "the court review is a solemn farce in which [courts] must go through a series of motions which look like judicial review but in fact are nothing but a catalogue of reasons why, under the scheme of the Act, the courts are unable to say that the Administrator has exceeded the discretion vested in him."[33] This comment summarizes the "due process" offered by scores of other federal administrative regimes set up in that period and afterwards.[34]

We will now examine some modern administrative triumphs of fairness.

AFFIRMATIVE ACTION:
FAIRNESS BY THE NUMBERS

President Lyndon Johnson declared in 1964, upon signing the Civil Rights Act, that the purpose of the act was "to promote a more abiding commitment to freedom, a more constant pursuit of justice, and a deeper respect for human dignity."[35] In the subsequent decades, the Equal Employment Opportunity Commission (EEOC) created by the Civil Rights Act has promulgated regulation after regulation governing the "fair" distribution of opportunity. The EEOC vigorously prosecutes any company that EEOC officials claim has failed to give enough opportunity to "protected" groups (which make up over half the population). However, an examination of the agency's records indicates that, for all practical purposes, "fairness" is whatever EEOC officials choose to impose.

The most positive impact of the 1964 Civil Rights Act was that the federal government prohibited lower levels of government from continuing to abuse and discriminate against blacks. Many southern state and local governments explicitly treated blacks as second-class citizens. This provision of the act was not primarily a triumph of government over private evil; rather, it was merely one level of government commanding other levels of government to cease violating the Constitution. (Unfortunately, state and local governments have no effective means to force the federal government to cease constitutional violations.)

The 1964 Civil Rights Act explicitly banned racial quotas and specifically required that an employer have shown an intent to discriminate in order to be found guilty.[36] However, by the late 1960s, the EEOC had intentionally subverted the law by establishing a definition of discrimination that was the opposite of the one that Congress had specified. EEOC chairman Clifford Alexander announced in 1968: "We . . . here at EEOC believe in numbers . . . our most valid standard is in numbers. . . . The only accomplishment is when we look at all those numbers and see a vast improvement in the picture."[37]

EEOC officials have proclaimed private companies guilty of violating or impeding "equal opportunity" because of their failure to race-norm test scores (covertly increasing the scores of "protected groups" to make them appear more qualified than other test takers);[38] failure to disregard employee theft; failure to disregard an employee's assaults on co-workers; failure by an upscale women's clothing chain to hire men for sales jobs that "included helping women try on clothes";[39] failure by a women's-only health club to hire male attendants who would work in locker rooms and shower areas (10,000 members of the chain signed letters threatening to quit if males were hired);[40] and failure to hire, in higher percentages, members of favored groups that were not qualified at the time but were, in the EEOC's judgment, "trainable." The EEOC capitalizes on the vagueness of the concept of equal opportunity to maximize its power to manipulate findings of guilt or innocence.

One of the most prominent prosecutions in EEOC history was its case against Sears. The EEOC spent 15 years threatening and harassing Sears, and the company reportedly spent over $10 million defending itself against charges of sex discrimination. The EEOC never produced a single witness at trial who alleged that Sears had discriminated against her. Instead, EEOC experts simply waved one statistical analysis after another in the air. A federal appeals court ruled in 1988 that "the EEOC statistics were plagued by arbitrary and false assumptions" and found Sears innocent on all charges.[41]

EEOC's dictatorial powers over "fairness" are exemplified in the settlements that it imposes on corporations. The EEOC devastated O & G Spring and Wire Forms Specialty Co., a metal-forming shop started by Ted Gryezkiewicz, who had immigrated to the United States from communist Poland. O & G hired mostly Polish immigrants who spoke no English, as well as many Hispanics, and had roughly 50 workers. The EEOC investigated the company and found it guilty of discriminating against blacks between 1979 and 1985. The only evidence the EEOC offered was statistical: based on the EEOC's analysis of the Chicago labor market, 22 percent of O & G's labor force should have been black. At trial, the EEOC could not produce one black witness who had applied to fill a job vacancy at the company.[42]

Yet, federal judge Harry Leinenweber found the company guilty. Leinenweber ordered the company to pay $8,000 for EEOC newspaper ads inviting blacks to file a claim for benefits regardless of whether they had ever applied for a job at O & G. Four hundred and fifty people responded to the ad. The EEOC made no attempt to check any of the claims for fraud. Some of the people who claimed to have been victims of discrimination were apparently in prison at the time (and thus could not possibly have worked at the company), as federal appeals judge Daniel Manion noted in a dissent to an appeals court decision in October 1994.[43] Yet, as long as they were black, that was enough for the EEOC to certify them as deserving victims of discrimination. The EEOC's sanctioning of payoffs to lying ex-convicts epitomizes the agency's habit of using government compulsion to change the racial distribution of income by fair means or foul.

In 1997, Joe's Stone Crab, a famous Miami restaurant, was found guilty of "unintentional discrimination" because the number of female servers on its staff was lower than 31.9 percent, which federal judge Daniel Hurley decreed was the percentage of females employed in comparable jobs in the local labor force. The EEOC spent several years investigating and prosecuting the restaurant, even though it had not received any complaints of discrimination from frustrated job applicants. As the *Washington Post* noted, "In the wake of his ruling, the judge took control of the restaurant's annual hiring process before the restaurant opened for the current season last fall. . . . The court supervised the placement and even the wording of help-wanted ads. After all that, the number of female applicants to the restaurant declined."[44] Judge Hurley in August 1998 ordered the restaurant to pay $150,000 to four women who had not been hired by the restaurant—including the payment of "lost wages" for time before the women applied for a job. When waiters at the restaurant protested the government action by wearing buttons stating "government approved," the EEOC threatened them with a contempt citation.[45]

The EEOC continually stretches its concept of social justice to further restrict freedom of association. The EEOC spent five years investigating and threatening the Hooters restaurant chain. Hooters, which has been described as a "Playboy Club for rednecks," sells titillation and flirtation along with its greasy burgers and fries. The restaurants hire only females as bartenders and waitresses.

Eagle-eyed EEOC investigators visited eight Hooters restaurants and surveilled the interaction between the staff and the customers. The EEOC issued its preliminary ruling on September 16, 1994: "The Commission finds [Hooters] longstanding policy of excluding men from the server, bartender and host positions to be evidence of *reckless indifference to federally protected rights.*"[46] The EEOC decreed that the business of Hooters was food, not Hooters girls, and that "no physical trait unique to women is required to serve food and drink to customers in a restaurant."[47]

The EEOC informed Hooters that it owed at least $22 million in back pay to guys who had never even worked at its restaurants. The EEOC also demanded that the restaurant chain revise the concept of Hooters and make it gender neutral.[48] The agency eventually backed down after the restaurant chain's propaganda counter offensive proved too embarrassing. But the fact that the EEOC avidly pursued Hooters symbolizes how civil rights enforcement has moved from crusading to allow blacks to sit at lunch counters to crusading to allow government employees to dictate the cup size of the person who serves the lunch.

Federal judge Stanley Sporkin complained in a 1997 decision that, because of labor and civil rights laws, "We are becoming the personnel czars of virtually every one of this nation's public and private institutions."[49] Affirmative action has generated a canon of law based on blind trust in the goodness and wisdom of government employees. Yet, the government agents in charge of enforcing the law have a vested interest in scorning fairness and procedural justice. The EEOC measures its own productivity by the amount of money it squeezes out of private companies. Any large settlement from a corporation, regardless of how meritless the charges or how undeserving the beneficiaries, makes the agency appear more successful. The agency's September 1997 "Strategic Plan" bragged:

> Last year the agency resolved more charges than in any time in its thirty-two year history. The rate of finding reasonable cause [i.e., of finding the accused guilty] during Fiscal Year 1997 is well ahead of what it was in Fiscal Year 1996. We have also collected over 425 million dollars for victims of discrimination in the past two and one-half years. . . . In Fiscal Year 1996 we filed half the number of cases filed in Fiscal Year 1995, but collected twice the monetary benefits.[50]

Later in the same report, the agency stressed that one of the "useful measures . . . to determine the degree of success we have achieved in reaching our goal of promoting equal employment opportunity" is "the actual benefits we have obtained for individuals, in terms of dollar amounts and jobs, and other opportunities, such as education and training. Indeed, in the past ten years,

EEOC has obtained 1.6 billion dollars for victims of discrimination."[51] Thus, every additional dollar squeezed out of any private company is automatically a triumph for equal employment opportunity.

PARITY: FARMERS'
KEY TO THE U.S. TREASURY

Federal farm policy has been driven for most of the twentieth century by the notion of "parity."[52] Agricultural Adjustment Administration chief Chester Davis declared in 1934, "Parity is justice now."[53] Parity is a doctrine of "fair exchange value:" if farmers receive less than so-called parity values, society has somehow wronged them.

Parity measurements were concocted by government agricultural economists in the 1920s to provide credibility to farm groups' demands for federal aid. The official parity calculation is based on the current ratio of farm prices to nonfarm prices, compared to the ratio of farm and nonfarm prices between 1910 and 1914. USDA chose some of the most prosperous years for farmers in American history, and then proceeded to implicitly condemn the nation for most of the twentieth century because farm prices were supposedly not as high as they had been during farmers' "golden age."[54] No one would try to drive across the country with a 1912 road map, but that is how the government made agricultural policy for much of the twentieth century.

And, as if its economically inane premises were not enough, parity calculations were further slanted by the Agriculture Department. The parity formula was designed to significantly understate farmers' income, since it completely disregarded all off-farm income of farmers (many of whom were part-time farmers); exaggerated business costs by counting half the cost of passenger automobiles as a farm expense; completely ignored the revolution in farm production and the fall in crop production costs that resulted from the introduction of tractors; ignored the increase in the quality and durability of other equipment that farmers bought, compared to that bought in 1910; and ignored the fact that roughly half of all farmers lived in the South, where people had both significantly lower incomes and lower living expenses than the national average.[55]

The doctrine of parity illustrates how bogus moral doctrines can be used to restrict freedom. The failure of farm prices to supposedly achieve "parity" in the early 1930s helped justify the Roosevelt administration's proclamation of a "national emergency" in regard to agriculture. The *New York Times* reported on March 12, 1933, shortly after Roosevelt's inauguration, that Agriculture Secretary Henry Wallace and farm leaders were appealing to Roosevelt for the appointment of a "farm dictator" to solve the farm crisis.[56] After the enactment of the Agricultural Adjustment Act in 1933, bureaucrats used the doctrine of parity to dictate how many pounds of peanuts each farmer could sell, how many acres of tobacco he could plant, how many boxes of oranges he could ship, and where he could sell his milk. Parity provided a noble-sounding pretext to justify giving hundreds of billions of tax dollars to landowners and farmers, to justify the forced shutdown of scores of millions of acres of farmland to inflate farm prices (and the resulting destruction of hundreds of thousands of jobs and the death of many small towns across the Midwest),[57] and to justify the arrest of thousands of farmers for planting or selling more of their harvest than the government permitted.[58] Once politicians claimed a duty to drive up prices, any farmer who disobeyed government orders was presumedly acting unfairly. Rep. James Polk on March 22, 1933, praised the Agricultural Adjustment Act, saying that the secretary of agriculture "will have at his command a weapon to whip into line selfish interests who decline to cooperate in helping to bring up the price of these farm commodities."[59]

While parity advocates have long declaimed that crop prices are unfairly low, crop prices have fallen primarily because modern technology, better seeds, better fertilizers and better-educated farmers have produced far higher yields and lower costs of production. Since 1910, the start of the parity base period, corn yields per acre increased more than 450 percent, wheat yields increased over 400 percent, and milk per dairy cow more than tripled.[60] Yet, farm subsidy advocates choose to completely ignore the technological revolutions of modern agriculture.

While parity has generally lost respect among agricultural economists, the parity formula is still used by the Agriculture Department and in federal laws to justify restrictions on what farmers can sell or on how farm products can be marketed. A February 20, 1998, *Federal Register* notice justified prohibiting producers of spearmint oil from selling half of their 1998 crop in part because spearmint oil prices were below "parity" prices.[61] A February 24, 1998, *Federal Register* notice justified federal prohibitions on the sale of so-called undersized dried prunes because prune prices were not at "parity levels."[62] (The restrictions are intended not to protect consumers but to drive up prune prices.) Restrictions on milk sales are perennially justified by references to parity prices.[63] Current farm legislation expires in 2002; if a new law is not passed before then, farm programs will automatically revert to the so-called permanent farm legislation of 1949 and parity calculations will be used to set mandatory support levels for all major subsidized crops.[64]

Agriculture laws provide "fairness" pretexts to lock people up. During the 1980s, federal import quotas (put in place to give lavish "fair" prices to farmers) drove U.S. sugar prices to five times the world price level (costing consumers $3 billion a year in higher prices), caused severe shortages of certain food specialty items, and made sugar smuggling immensely profitable. The Justice Department responded with a major sting operation named Operation Bittersweet, which caught 30 companies. Federal prosecutors were proud that the crackdown netted $16 million in fines for the government[65]—less than one-tenth of 1 percent of the amount consumers were forced to pay in higher prices during the 1980s because of federal sugar policies. The Justice Department was far more worried about businessmen importing cheap sugar than about the sugar lobby—which donated over $3 million to congressmen between 1984 and 1989[66]—bribing congressmen to allow them to extort billions of dollars from consumers. But because Congress dictates the rules—both for sugar imports and for campaign financing—there was nothing unfair or unethical about that.

FAIR HOUSING:
BINGO AND SOCIAL JUSTICE

In 1968, Congress passed the Fair Housing Act to outlaw discriminatory real estate practices. The act had a salutary effect in striking down local- and state-government barriers against blacks buying or renting the homes of their choice. However, the continual expansion of the list of "unfair" practices has made a mockery of any coherent concept of fairness or justice.

In 1988, Congress amended the Fair Housing Act to prohibit "discrimination" against drug addicts, alcoholics, the mentally ill, and families with children. Congress effectively labeled landlords' decisions not to rent to families with children as a hostile act that must be exterminated by increased federal power. Yet, rental "discrimination" against children is, in most cases, simply a rational economic decision based on the preferences of existing and would-be tenants. This ban on "familial discrimination" has resulted in legal nightmares for senior citizen trailer parks and apartment complexes around the country that were designed specifically for the peace and quiet of older folks. One of the first suits the Justice Department filed under the new law was against an apartment owner guilty of restricting families with children to ground-floor apartments.[67] HUD claimed this was an illegal unfair housing practice, though other tenants were likely grateful not to have children stomping on the floor over their heads. Having a seniors-only part of a building, or reserving one building out of a ten-building complex for seniors, is now a federal crime.

Fair-housing regulations illustrate how contemporary fairness increasingly depends on byzantine quibblings by government bureaucrats. Housing communities can be exempted from the rent-to-children mandate if 80 percent of the housing units each contain at least one person 55 years or older and provide "significant facilities and services specifically designed to meet the physical or social needs of older persons," according to federal law. On July 7, 1994, HUD issued 59 pages of proposed rules defining the law's terms. Among the examples that HUD gave of "significant services and facilities" necessary to qualify as adults-only were providing congregate dining services and daily meal delivery to residents; having a staff member assigned to read to the elderly; providing daily aerobic courses and tennis courses with rest areas and shaded trees; providing cleaning services for residents' units; reproducing material in large print and on audio tape (and providing residents with tape recorders), and offering arts and crafts and dancing classes. But mandating such services could easily double, triple, or quadruple the rent that old folks pay in mobile home parks. HUD's "fairness" regulations would have effectively banned low- and moderate-income elderly from seniors-only housing.

Comments received by HUD ran approximately 100 to 1 against the proposed regulations.[68] At meetings around the country, thousands of elderly turned out to denounce HUD's proposal. Swamped by the furor, HUD backed off and in 1995 proposed new requirements. Rather than mandating specific services, HUD offered a Chinese-menu approach: as long as housing providers provided at least two facilities or services each from five of twelve categories, the housing could be presumed not to be unfairly discriminating. Among options for the senior housing exemption were bingo clubs, bowling trips, and tai chi classes. To meet seniors' "educational needs," the housing provider could offer seminars on government benefit programs. The provider could also partially satisfy the law's requirements by providing certain HUD-recognized "leisure needs," such as having a "lawyer's office" on-site. (HUD's power grab created so much hostility among senior citizens that Congress repealed part of the law applying to senior citizens in December 1995, though HUD continues vigorously prosecuting apartment companies and others for violations.)

HUD bankrolls local government code-enforcement crackdowns to detect and punish slumlords who are deemed to be renting overcrowded housing. At the same time, HUD prosecutes apartment owners who are guilty of renting insufficiently crowded housing. HUD has recently filed numerous fair-housing cases against apartments that sought to limit apartment occupancy. In California, HUD prosecuted an apartment owner for refusing to rent a two-bedroom apartment to a family of four. A federal court denounced HUD's action as "reprehensible" and "appalling," since HUD had made "inconsistent and misleading representations to those regulated by the [act] and, in so doing, ha[d] led them down the garden path" to violating HUD's revised interpretation of the law.[69]

At a September 30, 1997 press conference, HUD Secretary Andrew Cuomo announced, "We will double the number of enforcement actions against [fair housing violators] in the president's second term." [70] One wonders if HUD investigators had previously ignored half the violators they detected, or if the standard for criminal conduct was going to be lowered to fulfill the new prosecution quotas. A doubling of lawsuits was portrayed by Cuomo as the equivalent of a doubling of justice.

In the name of fair housing, HUD is also conducting a war against free speech. HUD launched an investigation in 1994 of the members of the Irving Place Community Coalition, a group of New York City citizens opposed to placing another home for the mentally ill in a neighborhood already saturated with such homes. HUD investigators decided that the residents' civic activism was a crime and demanded membership lists, written messages, and other documents from the members—and even demanded to see the personal diaries of people involved in the opposition. Arlene Harrison, a member of the Irving Place Coalition, observed, "It was like Big Brother coming to your door with a hammer."[71] HUD assistant secretary for fair housing Roberta Achtenberg justified the crackdown: "HUD walks a tightrope between free speech and fair housing. We are ever mindful of the need to maintain the proper balance between these rights."[72](The Founding Fathers forgot to include the word "balance" in the First Amendment.)

HUD finances scores of fair-housing advocacy organizations to investigate, entrap, and sue private companies for alleged fair-housing violations. As *National Review* editor Rich Lowry noted in early 1998, "Some housing groups have been known to place allegedly biased housing ads in newspapers, then turn around and sue the papers for running them."[73] HUD does little or no policing of how fair-housing advocacy groups use their federal grants, apparently considering them above reproach. One Michigan landlord believed he had been defamed by a federally funded fair-housing council and threatened to sue. The Civil Rights Division of the U.S. Department of Justice promptly threatened to sue the landlord, claiming that merely by filing suit against the fair housing council, the landlord would violate a federal law that makes it "unlawful to coerce, intimidate, or threaten any person" exercising fair housing rights—apparently including the right to libel landlords.[74]

FAIR TRADE:
POLITICIANS' LICENSE TO STEAL

American consumers and businesses are paying tens of billions of dollars in higher prices because of U.S. trade barriers. Many of these trade barriers are justified in the name of "fairness"—as an integral part of U.S. fair trade policy. However, a cursory examination of the details of trade policy make a mockery of its moral pretenses.[75]

When politicians call for "fair trade" with foreigners, they routinely use a concept of fairness that is diametrically opposed to the word's normal usage. In exchanges between individuals, the usual test of fairness is the voluntary consent of each party to the bargain: "the free will which constitutes fair exchanges," as Sen. John Taylor wrote in 1822.[76] When politicians speak of unfair trade, they do not mean that buyers and sellers did not voluntarily agree, but that U.S. government officials disapprove of the bargains American citizens chose to make. Fair trade, as the term is now used, usually means government intervention to direct, control, or restrict trade. Fair trade means government officials deciding what Americans should be allowed to buy, and what prices they should be forced to pay. Fair trade means subjugating the economic interests of private citizens to the political values of government policymakers.

Anti-dumping penalties, for example, purport to prevent foreign companies from selling goods in the United States at "less than fair value." "Fair value" is determined according to whether the foreign company can pass dozens of arbitrary tests imposed by the U.S. government. Dumping occurs when a company charges a lower price for a product in an export market than in its home market, or when a foreign company sells products for less than the cost of production plus an 8 percent profit (a larger profit than most American corporations earn). When the Commerce Department finds a foreign company guilty of dumping, and the U.S. International Trade Commission also concludes that the dumped products injured competing American companies, the U.S. government imposes penalty tariffs on the imports equal to the alleged dumping margin.

In dumping cases, the Commerce Department is judge, jury, prosecuting attorney, and executioner, according to David Palmeter, one of the nation's preeminent trade lawyers.[77] The U.S. government has imposed more dumping penalties against low-priced imports in recent years than has any other government in the world. Federal law currently assumes that foreign competition that prevents American companies from raising their prices can unfairly injure them.[78]

The U.S. Commerce Department is very arbitrary in how it convicts foreign companies for selling at unfairly low prices. The Commerce Department penalized a Japanese company for selling typewriters in the United States for a fraction of a penny less than in Japan.[79] A federal judge slammed American TV manufacturers for using American fair-trade law to conduct an "economic war" against their Japanese competitors.[80] In a 1992 minivan dumping case, Commerce compared the price of new Mazda minivans sold in Japan with the price of used Mazda minivans sold in the United States.[81] Naturally, the used minivans sold for less than the new ones, which allegedly proved dumping.

Commerce convicted New Zealand kiwi farmers of dumping after it compared the price of small kiwis sold in the United States with larger kiwis from New Zealand sold to Japan.[82] The U.S. government has penalized foreign farmers for not paying wages to their wives and children, and penalized foreign companies for relying on part-time labor, making charitable donations, not having computerized sales records, and failing to charge their American customers the highest prices in the world.[83]

The Commerce Department sometimes blatantly rigs its dumping investigations. A 1993 federal court case revealed that Commerce Department officials changed the dumping margins on iron manhole covers from China as a result of "political considerations," as a confidential Commerce memo noted.[84]

The more unfair foreign practices American politicians claim to discover, the more power they seize over what Americans are allowed to eat, drink, drive, and wear. Each new definition of unfair trade becomes a pretext to further restrict the freedom of American citizens. Fair trade means a moral canonization of pure political arbitrariness. The ultimate basis of fair trade is the notion that the State is the fount of justice—that justice is whatever politicians say it is. Fair trade in practice consists of politically anointing a particular number or price and then commandeering the machinery of the State to enforce that political dictate. The definition of fair trade in practice has become simply trade controlled by politicians and bureaucrats.

THE META-ETHICS
OF UNFAIR LABOR PRACTICE

The National Labor Relations Board (NLRB) was created in 1935 to prevent "unfair labor practices" in employee-employer relations. However, the NLRB has never issued a clear definition of "unfair labor practice"; instead, it has made one ad hoc, inconsistent ruling after another. As a result, "unfair labor practices" have become whatever displeases the political appointees running the agency. The agency presumes that collectively bargained contracts are morally superior to contracts bargained directly between individual workers and employers. The NLRB often intervenes to block individual workers from negotiating directly with employers—apparently assuming that to allow some workers to negotiate directly is somehow unjust to other workers. In practice, fairness means subjugating individual workers to union hierarchies, regardless of how often union bosses have defrauded workers in the past.

The NLRB supervises union-management relations in part to ensure that companies do not coerce unions. NLRB officials have an expansive concept of coercion when it comes to management behavior; companies have been found guilty of "unfair labor practices" for merely criticizing unions or for offering raises to their workers before the workers vote on whether to join a union. Caterpillar was cited in 1996 for unfair labor practices because it gave free lunches to replacement workers during a United Auto Workers strike.[85] Though one of the goals of the federal labor law is to achieve higher pay for laborers, the NLRB will punish corporations—and impose injunctions—if the NLRB suspects that a pay raise for workers is not in a union's best interest. The NLRB has issued cease and desist orders to nullify companies' premium pay plans, and investigated one company for giving Christmas bonuses to employees without the union's permission.[86] In 1994, the NLRB accused Pony Express Courier Co. of committing an unfair labor practice because it set up a national toll-free telephone question line for its employees, thereby allegedly violating its obligation to have its employees deal with the company only through the Teamsters Union.[87]

While the NLRB uses creative concepts of "coercion" by management, it is often most forgiving when considering violence by some workers against other workers. According to the NLRB, violence by strikers is not an unfair labor practice unless the violence becomes excessive. The NLRB announced in 1979 "Although an employee may have engaged in misconduct [during a strike], he or she may not be deprived of reinstatement rights absent a showing that the conduct was so violent . . . as to render an employee unfit for future service."[88] The NLRB sometimes punishes businesses more harshly for hiring replacements for strikers than it punishes unions when their striking members shoot at the replacement workers, as happened in the Greyhound strike in the early 1990s.[89]

Murder threats are irrelevant in the NLRB's definition of unfair labor practices. In a 1991 case involving Precision Window Manufacturing Inc. of St. Louis, the NLRB ordered the company to rehire and award back pay to an employee who was fired after he threatened to kill his supervisor. The fired employee promised to come back at quitting time and kill his boss; the worker actually returned at quitting time, and remained outside the plant until police arrived. NLRB chairman James Stephens and board member Dennis Devaney ruled that the employee's "rambling, semicoherent mix of insult and threat"[90] were not so flagrant as to forfeit his right to favored treatment under federal labor law. A federal appeals court, overturning the decision in 1992, criticized the NLRB for ruling in the discharged employee's favor, especially since the ex-employee admitted to lying at the NLRB hearing on the case.[91] In another case, the NLRB ordered the Chicago Tribune Co. to give the home addresses of its pressmen hired as replacements to the local union, even though a strike a few years earlier had included mob violence, a stabbing, and death threats. (A federal appeals court in 1996 blocked the NLRB's order.)[92]

SUPERFUND:
DUE PROCESS TO THE GARBAGE DUMP

As the federal government has become more powerful and more interventionist, fair treatment of individuals is a luxury that it can no longer afford. Few programs better illustrate the modern contempt for due process than Superfund.

Congress enacted Superfund in 1980 to deal with the problem of abandoned hazardous waste sites. Since 1980, the Environmental Protection Agency (EPA) has cast the Superfund net over far more types of sites than Congress originally intended. The federal government has spent almost $10 billion for Superfund and forced private parties to spend up to another $80 billion.[93] Yet the program has cleaned up barely a third of the most dangerous landfills and chemical dumps identified by the EPA. The Congressional Office of Technology Assessment estimated that the total cleanup costs for all Superfund-designated sites could exceed half a trillion dollars.[94]

Thanks to EPA's interpretation of the law, EPA claims it has a right to impose the entire cost of cleaning up a hazardous waste site on any company, individual, or organization that contributed a single box of garbage or trash to that site. EPA can accuse almost any company of sending waste to a Superfund site, and it is up to the accused to somehow prove that they never dealt with the site. Even when the EPA has no reliable evidence that a company actually sent waste products to a Superfund site, it does not hesitate to file multimillion-dollar lawsuits against the company to bankroll its inefficient cleanup efforts. A Justice Department report on Superfund observed, "Joint and several liability frequently operates in a highly inequitable manner—sometimes making defendants with only a small or even de minimis percentage of fault liable for 100% of plaintiff's damage."[95]

Federal judge Norma Shapiro slammed EPA's Superfund enforcement practices as "an arrogance of power that is bureaucracy at its worst."[96] In Denver, after a recycling company improperly disposed of car batteries collected at a department store, EPA sued the individuals who had conscientiously brought their batteries to the store for proper disposal for the cost of cleaning up the mess.[97] Barbara Williams, a Gettysburg, Pennsylvania, restaurant owner, found herself sued to help pay the costs of a local Superfund site because she had put table scraps in her garbage; campgrounds, antique shops, pizza and ice cream shops, and book stores were also dragged into the liability mire.[98] One study estimated that 3,000 small businesses were hit with Superfund liability merely for sending household trash to sites later declared to be Superfund sites.[99] Lawyer James DeLong noted, "The operator of a municipal sewer system was recently held responsible under Superfund for the escape of hazardous substances that had been flushed down the drain by a research laboratory."[100]

Superfund is a retroactive law par excellence. Even though a company or individual may have obeyed all the laws existing at the time it disposed of its waste products, the company can still be forced to pay whatever cleanup costs EPA demands. In June 1997, EPA demanded that 71 Idaho mining companies provide the agency with "every scrap of paper they ha[d] produced in the last 117 years, from recent faxes and phone messages to notes scribbled as far back as 1880";[101] the EPA was trying to determine which companies were responsible for lead deposits at a mining-related Superfund site. The EPA gave the companies 14 days to provide copies of all their records from the last hundred-odd years, and promised fines of $27,500 a day if they failed to meet the agency's demand.[102] An editorial in the *Spokane Spokesman-Review* noted that the "cost of the paperwork alone to meet EPA's ultimatum could bankrupt tiny mining owners."[103]

The government increasingly defines justice in its own interest, as if its own needs give it an absolute right to as much of a corporation's assets as government lawyers can snare. State and local government are using the joint-and-several liability doctrine to force private companies to pay for cleaning up government landfills. This happens even in cases in which city employees are blatantly responsible for problems at the landfills. New York City "brought a Superfund suit to clean up its landfill, even though the illicit disposal resulted from one of its own employees dealing with organized crime."[104] EPA sued Shell Oil Company for total cleanup costs at Rocky Mountain Arsenal in Colorado, even though the contaminated ground had been used for years by the U.S. Army for chemical warfare tests.[105] In August 1997, the EPA issued new rules that limit the amount that town and city governments can be required to pay for cleanup of their own dumps; by creating special rules for governments, the EPA basically conceded the injustice of the Superfund liability scheme, but gave relief only to politicians and bureaucrats.[106]

THE NEW FAIRNESS

In the novel *1984,* George Orwell described how a totalitarian regime could use emotional manipulation of its subjects to generate bitter animosities towards foreigners, regardless of the government's previous allegiance to that foreign nation. A similar "1984" mentality now applies to political definitions of fairness. No matter how many times politicians and bureaucrats revise and reverse the official definition of fairness, the latest definition of fairness is presumed correct, and all previous definitions are to be forgotten. This is clear from the evolution of affirmative action, which began as a federal command of nondiscrimination, then degenerated into pressure to hire by racial numbers, and then descended into federal prosecution of companies that refused to rig applicant test scores to produce the right racial mix of winners and losers.

Prior to the hyperinterventionist policies of this century, fairness was defined largely by the common law—legal standards that had developed over many centuries. The Supreme Court in 1925 recognized the binding nature of the precedents from English common law: "The language of the Constitution cannot be interpreted safely except by reference to the common law and to British institutions as they were when the instrument was framed and adopted."[107] The common law was built upon the moral values of the English and American publics; the new definitions of fairness are built upon the dictates of today's bureaucrats and politicians. The common law was built upon the accumulation of practical experience over hundreds of years; the new fairness is slapped together for the bureaucratic convenience of the moment. The common law developed acceptable rules of conduct from the experience of thousands of cases; the new fairness is based upon whichever specific case is high-profile or politically most profitable. The common law sanctioned government criminal penalties only for individuals who violated clear, widely promulgated legal standards; the new fairness maximizes government officials' power to retroactively punish whomever they please. The common law sought to make the rules of fair conduct as clear and stable ("from time immemorial") as possible; the new fairness is preeminently an ad hoc fairness, maximizing government officials' power to scorn their own precedents for any reason. As University of Chicago law professor Richard Epstein observed, "The common law achieved a very high level of coherence and universality with its very few generative principles of rights and duties."[108] The general principles of the common law have been replaced with one general rule: politicians and bureaucrats must be empowered to decree who benefits and who loses. The protection offered against government abuses by the common law was far from perfect, and too many groups and classes of citizens were long denied equal rights. But at least it provided relatively known, predictable legal standards by which people could avoid falling under the penalty of law.[109]

When politicians put the prefix "fair" before a certain policy—be it in housing, trade, or other areas—they seek to give themselves a moral blank check to increase coercion. Yet, to accept any government edict as the final word on right and wrong is to be one definition away from servitude. Lawyer Alan Zarky observed in a 1993 brief to the Supreme Court:

> In an era when all or most of the laws reflected society's norms . . . almost any person violating the law had made a conscious choice to engage in blameworthy conduct, and it was fair to put the risk upon him that he was wrong about the law's ambit. But today, the reach of the regulatory statutes touches every facet

of people's lives. Behavior that is legal one day suddenly becomes illegal, and punishable by years in prison, with no effective notice. It would be grossly unfair to say that people act at their peril regarding the legality of their activity, when their conduct is comparable to other, totally legal actions taken in the business world every day. The unfairness increases when a person contemplating such conduct makes a good faith inquiry into the law's provisions, but happens to receive mistaken advice.[110]

Giving government officials the power to define fairness gives them the power to decree the limits of their own power. To expect bureaucrats to adopt a narrow interpretation of a law is to expect them to unilaterally disarm. The more unfairness they claim to discover, the more power they garner to impose their own will upon other Americans. For many government agencies, "achieving justice" simply means maximizing the number of fines they impose, arrests they make, and convictions they secure. Government agencies have a built-in conflict of interest in administering fairness, since their survival and budget growth depends on penalizing as many violators as possible.[111] The more accusations they make, the more power they acquire. The more private citizens a government agency punishes, the better it appears to be protecting the public.

If politicians began work on a new law by proclaiming, "Since we are the fairest people in American society, we automatically know what rules must be imposed on all other Americans," the public ridicule would be overwhelming. Yet, "we are the fairest of them all" is the unspoken preface of every law dictating new standards of fairness that ignore or overturn traditional or accepted standards of private conduct.

THE CONTINUAL
TILTING OF THE PLAYING FIELD

At the same time that government agencies are suppressing more types of private behavior as unfair, the government is increasingly exempting itself from traditional standards of decency.

Perjury provides one of the clearest moral dividing lines between the rulers and ruled. The FBI academy in 1997 added a course on ethics to its training for new recruits. According to the course's official syllabus, subjects of FBI investigations "have forfeited their right to the truth."[112] In other words, the mere fact that the FBI suspects that a person may have violated the law effectively grants FBI officials an unlimited right to deceive that person. (The FBI's "ethics" course only put into writing what is standard procedure for police departments across the nation.)

However, any citizen who utters a single false word to a federal agent faces five years in prison and a $250,000 fine. The false statement could occur in a casual street conversation. The federal false statements law conveys so much power that, according to Clinton administration solicitor General Seth Waxman, it allows federal agents to "escalate completely innocent conduct into a felony."[113] One federal judge complained that the law encourages "inquisition as a method of criminal investigation."[114] The federal statute is so broad that a person could even be prosecuted for making a false statement to an undercover federal agent.[115] (Congress amended the perjury law in 1996 to ensure that people who made false statements in congressional testimony could be prosecuted; naturally, statements made by congressmen at hearings and other public forums were exempted.[116])

In January 1998, the Supreme Court reinforced this power of federal agents when it upheld the conviction of a New York union official, James Brogan.[117] Brogan was surprised at home one evening by two federal investigators who asked him if he had received any cash or gifts from a real estate company whose employees were represented by his union. He answered "no"—which, the investigators knew, was false—and received a prison sentence for his one-word answer. (The jury also convicted him of receiving $150 in gratuities from the company—a misdemeanor.) Justice Ruth Bader Ginsburg, in a concurring opinion upholding the conviction, called attention to "the extraordinary authority Congress, perhaps unwittingly, has conferred on prosecutors to manufacture crimes."[118] She warned that broad interpretation of the law will result in "Government generation of a crime when the underlying suspected wrongdoing is or has become nonpunishable."

The government possesses an almost unlimited license to deceive the citizen—and a right to ruin the citizen's life if the citizen tries to deceive the government. The federal government has done so many things to destroy its own credibility that it is not surprising that some people have let their imaginations run wild. It is regrettable that some Americans believe absurd theories of United Nations black helicopters waiting to take over the country, but it is also regrettable that, as the CIA admitted in 1997, the U.S. government perennially made "misleading and deceptive statements to the public" about alleged UFO sightings; the agency conceded that most of the UFOs sighted in the late 1950s and 1960s were actually U.S. spy planes.[119] It is regrettable that many Americans see any trade-liberalizing agreement as an insidious element of a New World Order,[120] but it is also regrettable that the U.S. Interior Department is actively working to designate both private and public property as UN World Heritage Sites—thereby creating new pretexts to restrict owners' rights.[121] It may be surprising that so many veterans have no faith in the government's claims (and repeated revisions of claims) denying the existence of "Gulf War Syndrome," but it is also regrettable that the federal government failed to reveal until 1997 that a quarter of a million Americans were exposed to dangerous levels of radioactive fallout from nuclear tests in the 1950s and 1960s—up to 75,000 people may be struck by thyroid cancer as a result of the tests.[122] (A 1997 *New York Times* article noted that "through most of the 1950's, while the Government reassured the public that there was no health threat from atmospheric nuclear tests, the Atomic Energy Commission regularly warned the Eastman Kodak Company and other film manufacturers about fallout that could damage their products."[123]) It may be surprising that many Americans believe that the government shot down TWA Flight 800 over Long Island in 1996 to gin up support for new antiterrorist measures, but it is also surprising that confidential documents released by the John F. Kennedy Assassination Records Review Board in November 1997 revealed that the Pentagon developed plans in 1962 to concoct a "Communist Cuban terror campaign in the Miami area, in other cities and even in Washington" (including bombings and the shooting down of a civilian airliner) to create a pretext for a U.S. invasion of Cuba.[124] Not surprisingly, a 1995 poll found that 76 percent of Americans say they "rarely or never trust government to do what is right," and a 1997 poll found that only 6 percent of Americans placed "significant trust in the federal government."[125]

Law enforcement operations have become even more mendacious in recent decades. Thousands of elaborate sting operations have been set up in recent years to entice citizens to break the law—and to destroy their lives once they are caught. Since the 1970s, federal judges have become far more tolerant of government agents manufacturing crimes. As a *Kentucky Law Journal* article noted, courts have upheld law enforcement tactics such as "using a relative, sexual partner, or close friend as a government agent to convince the target to commit an offense; promises of legitimate and profitable business deals; . . . facilitating or encouraging a conspiracy and actually committing the offense; giving contraband to a defendant so that it can be exchanged for other contraband; [and] threatening a defendant or his friends."[126]

In one egregious case, the FBI paid $34,000 to Michael Fitzpatrick, a government informant who had previously been convicted of carrying out a bombing for the Jewish Defense League, to contact Qubilah Shabazz to entice her into authorizing him to kill Louis Farrakhan, who has been accused of masterminding the assassination of her father, Malcolm X.[127] Fitzpatrick called Shabazz dozens of times, continually raising the issue of killing Farrakhan; Shabazz, a struggling single mother, had the impression that Fitzpatrick was interested in marrying her, and Fitzpatrick encouraged her son to call him "my dad." Even though Shabazz was clearly backing away from the murder plot, FBI agents entered her apartment without a warrant on December 20, 1994, lied to her about the reason for their visit (claiming to be investigating Fitzpatrick), and pressured her into signing a confession. A federal magistrate subsequently ruled that the FBI had violated Shabazz's constitutional rights and threw her confession out of court. The FBI was further embarrassed when its informant admitted that he expected to be paid another $11,000 for his trial testimony to convict Shabazz. On the evening before the trial was to begin, the federal government agreed to drop the murder-for-hire charges, which could have landed Shabazz in prison for 90 years, if she would agree to undergo three months of psychiatric counseling. The *New York Times* described the settlement of the case as a "near rout" of the government.

The same government officials who are supposed to protect private citizens are routinely paid as bounty hunters, rewarded according to how many scalps they bring back to headquarters. Vice President Gore declared in 1996 that, until recently, Occupational Safety and Health Administration (OSHA) inspectors "were being rewarded on the basis of how many fines they issued."[128] Sen. William Roth of Delaware complained in 1997 that his investigation of the IRS found that "some officers who are able to collect the full amount of taxes due are often rated lower than those who have seized property. Seizures may be done for status and promotion as much as for enforcement."[129] IRS employees are also rated on the number of cases they refer for criminal prosecution; as Roth noted, "while there may be no basis in fact for a criminal referral, a taxpayer's life may well be turned upside down simply to keep an employee's, or district's, performance statistics up." One IRS revenue officer testified to the Senate Finance Committee in April 1998: "It appears to many of us that aggression [against taxpayers], coupled with an accumulation of high, arbitrary tax adjustments is the gateway to promotion." [130] A July 1998 IRS report on the agency's passion for enforcement statistics featured quotes by managers bragging about achieving their goals for the "number of fraud referrals," bragging that total additional dollars demanded during tax audits was "123% of the annual goal," and urging managers to "think of programs to bring in dollars. . . . What can we do as a group to bring up productivity?" A memo to managers in one IRS region declared that the "goal this year is $632 per hour [spent by auditors on taxpayers' returns] and easily within reach."[131] IRS auditors are rewarded based on how much additional taxes they impose on people, not on whether they follow federal tax law.[132] (Taxpayers who have additional taxes assessed on them during audits, and who then challenge the charges, have almost 70 cents of every dollar of such taxes dismissed by the IRS Office of Appeals.[133]) The District of Columbia Police Department launched a program in 1997 that evaluated officers according to how many arrests they made; arrests skyrocketed for petty offenses such as changing lanes without signaling. Police officer Kip Tate told the *Washington Post* that, prior to the new evaluation system, "Most officers weren't getting tied up with those minor offenses, but now, [police officials] want to see numbers, so we're arresting people and locking them up for almost anything."[134] After the District government ceased mailing notices to drivers reminding them of the date their drivers' licenses would expire, District police were able to arrest, handcuff, and jail thousands of District residents for a violation (expired license) that would not have received such punishment anywhere else in the United States.[135] After the police department in Redwood City, California, instituted a point system in 1997 that required each police officer to make at least seven arrests per month and issue one ticket per shift, one policeman told the *San Jose Mercury News:* "We're now looking at everybody as a point. You're a point. We joke around about it on the street, you hear it on the radio."[136] The same abuse—government agencies rewarding employees for the number of penalties imposed—perennially crops up, and politicians perennially claim that they have just banned such anti-citizen scoring by agencies once and for all.

One acid test of the honor and integrity of government is the behavior of prosecutors. As Attorney General Robert Jackson (later Supreme Court justice) observed in 1940, "The prosecutor has more control over life, liberty, and reputation than any other person in America. . . . With the law books filled with a great assortment of crimes, a prosecutor stands a fair chance of finding at least a technical violation of some act on the part of almost anyone."[137] Laws enacted in recent decades have greatly increased the power of federal prosecutors over defendants. A 1994 decree by Attorney General Janet Reno officially exempted federal prosecutors from the ethics guidelines that state bar associations required of all lawyers regarding contacting defendants directly without their lawyers present.[138] Reno's power grab for federal prosecutors was unanimously condemned by the Conference of Chief Justices, representing all the state supreme courts. Frederick Krebs, of the American Corporate Counsel Association, observed, "There is no evidence of the government's need to ignore the ethical constraints imposed on all other practicing attorneys."[139] Law professor Bennett Gershman observed: "There are hundreds, probably thousands, of glaring examples of prosecutorial concealment of evidence favorable to the defense, solicitation of false testimony or knowingly failing to correct false testimony, and the actual fabrication of evidence."[140] The number of formal complaints charging federal attorneys with prosecutorial misconduct has skyrocketed since 1990.[141]

Government's commitment to fairness can also be judged by the administrative gauntlets that private citizens must run.[142] For instance, federal agencies routinely confiscate a person's property without even filing criminal charges, and even in cases in which there is not even sufficient evidence to secure a search or arrest warrant. If the citizen wants his property back, he must sue the government and prove in court that his property is "innocent"; the government has no burden of proof. The citizen also must post a bond equal to 10 percent of the property's value (to cover the government's costs in defending itself against his lawsuit) and file a notice within 20 days of the seizure.[143] (Law enforcement agencies sometimes fail to formally notify the citizen of the seizure until after the deadline for such filings.) Legal costs for suing the government to recover one's property can easily exceed $5,000. Thus, if the government seizes only a small wad of cash or an old car, the citizen cannot possibly break even by suing to recover his property. Even if he wins in court and recovers his property, there is no provision for reimbursement of his attorney costs. A federal appeals court complained in 1992, "We continue to be enormously troubled by the government's increasing and virtually unchecked use of the civil forfeiture statutes and the disregard for due process that is buried in those statutes."[144]

Even in the relatively few cases in which federal courts strike down forfeitures, federal agencies still try to shaft their victims. The federal government confiscated $277,000 in cash from Ramon Montes on October 13, 1987. After years of legal wranglings, a federal court in 1992 ordered the money returned to Montes. Even though a judge ruled shortly after the initial seizure that "any interest accrued" from the seized money be included as part of the disputed property holdings, the government fought for three more years to seek to avoid paying the owner the interest on his wrongfully seized money. A federal appeals court denounced the Justice Department in 1995 for behavior "little short of scandalous" in its machinations, declaring that "the government will not be allowed to retain the fruits, once the tree has been ordered returned to its owner."[145]

The asset forfeiture laws are important not because of the total amount of property that the government has confiscated; a few billion dollars is a small amount compared to the total private property in the United States. However, the laws symbolize the power of government agents to destroy people with little or no evidence.

Federal policymakers are blase about stark conflicts of interest that could corrupt law enforcement. In 1996, the Justice Department announced that local and state law enforcement agencies would be permitted to use money they received from forfeiture funds to pay police salaries. The decision was harshly criticized by some law enforcement officials who believed it would encourage policemen to devote their time to seizing private property rather than protecting private citizens.[146] A report by the Arizona auditor general in 1993 concluded that many state agencies could not account for the property that they had confiscated and noted that law enforcement might "target suspects based on the value of the suspects' assets . . . before an investigation is begun or charges are filed."[147] A 1997 official investigation of high-profile New Jersey prosecutor Nicholas Bissell concluded that he had "created a climate where law enforcement and prosecutorial decisions were driven by forfeiture considerations and not necessarily the prosecution of the State's criminal business."[148] A congressional investigation of the U.S. Customs Service found that "Customs management has encouraged Customs employees to seize commercial merchandise. Entire Customs offices have been rated by Customs Headquarters' offices based on their seizure statistics."[149] Criminal courts in Louisiana are allowed to retain for their own court fund 40 percent of all private assets that they authorize to be seized.[150]

Some government agencies carry out de facto confiscations by surrounding themselves with bureaucratic quicksand. Local zoning and planning boards are renown for intentionally dragging out property use cases. One government attorney was quoted in a 1981 Supreme Court decision as explicitly advocating devious responses to private challenges to land-use restrictions: "If all else fails, merely amend the regulation and start all over again."[151] The process can drag on for decades before a property owner receives permission to use his land (or a final denial).[152] The frequent result of such long delays is that government employees get their pensions and private citizens either die or go bankrupt. A 1998 *Santa Clara Law Review* article noted that "when it suits them, federal land acquisition officials have been known to delay acquisition for years in a sometimes openly brazen effort to wear the property owners down and to acquire their land for thirty cents on the dollar, as one Park Service functionary put it."[153] Property owners can also be stripped of the value of their life savings by bureaucratic redefinitions. Arbitrary regulations on wetlands issued since 1989 effectively stripped scores of thousands of Americans of the right to control their own (dry) land; federal judge Roger Vinson in 1993 denounced federal agencies' contorted interpretations of the Clean Water Act—the basis of the wetlands restrictions—as "regulatory hydra . . . worthy of Alice in Wonderland."[154]

Modern administrative regimes create elaborate facades of due process that merely camouflage the arbitrary power of political appointees.[155] Most federal agencies effectively prohibit a citizen from taking a dispute between himself and the agency to an independent federal judge until he has exhausted his "administrative remedies." This "exhaustion of administrative remedies" requirement allows a federal agency to hold citizens or companies hostage for years, causing them to incur hundreds of thousands of dollars in legal fees regardless of how dubious the government's position may be.

The Labor Department's Office of Federal Contract Compliance Programs (OFCCP) routinely demands that private companies pay millions of dollars of back wages to people never hired by the company, based on legal interpretations that agency officials know federal judges would likely reject. According to former OFCCP director Ellen Shong Bergman, OFCCP officers are sometimes guilty of "attempted extortion" in their threats against businesses that fail to hire and promote sufficient numbers of minorities and women.[156] Before a federal contractor can get access to a federal judge to rule on the legality of the OFCCP's demands, the company must spend three or more years in the tar pit of Labor Department appeals processes.

Lawyers estimate that legal fees in OFCCP cases can easily exceed half a million dollars before companies reach a federal court.[157] Because of the high costs of reaching a federal judge, there have been few court rulings limiting the agency's power. As a result, OFCCP officials have free rein to twist the law to suit their purposes. And even in those areas in which federal judges have issued decisions limiting OFCCP's power, the agency has often ignored the rulings in subsequent enforcement actions. Administrative "court" proceedings are a farce when a political appointee (often with no expertise in the subject area) who disapproves of the "judge's" decision can overturn it with the mere flip of a memo.

Similar charades occur at the National Labor Relations Board. The Labor Policy Association noted in 1996 congressional testimony: "It is only when NLRB decisions reach the federal appeals courts that any impartiality begins to emerge in the law's enforcement."[158] In 1996 alone, 50 NLRB rulings were overturned by federal appeals courts; federal judges denounced the agency for a "warped interpretation of the facts," for a "flagrant disregard of judicial precedent," and for "abusing its discretion."[159]

To understand the morass of administrative law, imagine a world in which that process also applied to private legal disputes. Assume that a person had a conflict with some corporation; assume, for example, that he bought a supposedly new car from Chrysler dealer, and it turned out that the car actually had been previously owned and had several major defects about which the seller knowingly deceived the customer. If civil law worked like federal administrative law, the customer instead of simply taking the car dealer to the nearest court, would first have to file a formal complaint with the car dealer himself. After the dealer ignored the complaint for a few months, the customer would then have to write up a new complaint, with copies of all relevant documents, and send it to the district manager for Chrysler dealers. Then, after getting no response there, the person would be obliged to send it to the regional manager, wait a few more months, and then take his complaint to Chrysler headquarters. Perhaps someone there would respond, or perhaps not. Then and only then would the person be allowed to file a claim in a court of law. If someone proposed that people be required to go through all of a corporation's internal complaint procedures before suing that corporation— even if the procedures intentionally delayed the resolution of complaints for years—the proposal would be mocked far and wide.

Justice has also become a mirage for today's citizens because courts are overwhelmed by the immensity and complexity of government regulations and rulings. University of Chicago law professor Paul Bator observed, "Every day, Congress, the courts and the agencies are manufacturing new law with an energy unparalleled either in our own history or that of any modern society. . . . The opportunity for error, injustice, contradiction, uncertainty, and disuniformity proliferates as we have more law, more cases, more judges. . . . "[160] Bator detailed how access to the Supreme Court for private litigants has been curtailed in recent decades, while the Justice Department has acquired more power over which cases the Court will hear. Bator concluded, "The inevitable effect of the Supreme Court's limited time is that the resources to attend to the private sector simply do not exist. . . . The Government is the one consumer of law which is well served by the federal appellate system."[161]

The rising cost of getting due process from the government means fewer and fewer people can afford to say "no" to the demands of government officials. The vast majority of defendants in federal criminal cases cannot afford to hire their own attorneys.[162] Former deputy attorney general Arnold Burns observed in 1998, "More than 90% of criminal cases are resolved by plea agreements, without trials. Most often, defendants, even those who are not indigent, simply can't afford the staggering fees of a trial."[163] Warner Gardner, a lawyer who practiced in Washington before federal agencies for over 40 years, wrote in 1974, "The private citizen who has less than $20,000 at stake ordinarily would not be well advised to seek judicial review of agency action."[164] With inflation, $20,000 in 1974 would now amount to more than $50,000, which nearly equals the entire net worth of almost half of all American families. Former Treasury Secretary William Simon observed in 1978, "Unless an American business is immensely rich and can afford to fight the long battle to take its case to a higher court, it has little or no protection from the arbitrary decisions of the regulatory bureaucracies."[165] One 25-year IRS collections veteran, testifying anonymously before Congress in 1997, when asked about the effect of congressional legislation to protect taxpayers, replied, "It's had very little effect on the conduct of the IRS. The Taxpayer Bill of Rights is very positive . . . but who is going to enforce this for the taxpayer? If you're going to sue the IRS, it'll take 30, 40, 50,000 dollars."[166] IRS chief counsel Stuart Brown asserted in late 1997 that "there is relatively little controversy between the IRS and taxpayers, and almost all of this controversy is resolved without litigation."[167] The fact that it is so expensive to fight a government agency in court is thus offered as proof that the government abuses few citizens.

Because there can be no level playing field between the citizen and the State, every expansion of the State means increased subjugation of the citizen. Every increase in the cost of achieving justice from the State is a de facto subsidy for government oppression. The higher the cost of legal self-defense, the more likely that government agencies will abuse their power. Government employees who carry out vendettas against citizens almost never have to pay either the government's or the citizen's legal bills; their incentive is to stretch their power as far as possible. Every increase in the cost of traversing government administrative processes increases the arbitrary power of government employees over every citizen who cannot afford hefty legal bills. A. V. Dicey observed, "A right which an individual cannot enforce is to him no right at all; the dilatoriness of legal proceedings, and their exorbitant cost, or the want of an easily accessible Court, work greater and far more frequent injustice than the formal denial of a man's due rights."[168] Sen. John Taylor wrote in 1822: "There are no rights where there are no remedies, or where the remedies depend upon the will of the aggressor."[169] And, with the constantly expanding power and prerogatives of federal agencies, those remedies depend more than ever before on the bureaucratic aggressors.

ARBITRARY POWER
& THE DARK SIDE OF THE STATE

Arbitrary power means power without bounds, power that can be used at the whim of the government employee, power with sweeping discretion. Arbitrary power means the power to selectively target, cripple or destroy private targets. Some discretion in law enforcement is unavoidable. However, in the last 70 years, laws have proliferated that vest vast power in government agencies' hands and simply urge them to "do what they think best."[170]

The more arbitrary power government employees possess, the more they are transformed into a master class. Administrative law expert Kenneth Davis wrote: "Enforcement officers make more than ten times as many decisions involving justice or injustice as judges do, but we do not carve on their buildings 'Equal Justice Under Law.'"[171]

Arbitrary power has become more fashionable as government itself has been exalted. It is symptomatic of the contemporary attitude towards government that the term "czar" now has a positive connotation. The authors of the *Federalist Papers* neglected to use the term to symbolize their hopes for the executive branch of the government. Americans of earlier generations would be as shocked by the current adulatory use of the term "czar" as contemporary Americans should be shocked of the use of "fuehrer" as a compliment for a political leader. In an 1866 Supreme Court case involving the power of military governors in the conquered Southern states, one attorney declaimed to the court about his suffering plaintiffs: "So far as constitutional liberty is concerned, they might as well be living under a Czar or a Sultan, upon the banks of the Bosphorus or the Neva, as in this free country."[172] In an 1895 case, an attorney denounced a newly enacted income tax as conferring powers on the federal government "worthy of a Czar of Russia proposing to reign with undisputed and absolute power; but it cannot be done under this Constitution."[173]

Political and popular demands for appointments of a czar routinely stem from fundamental defects or contradictions in underlying federal laws. The first modern-era American "czar" was Energy Czar John Love, appointed by President Nixon in 1973 during the gas crisis, followed by other energy czars appointed by presidents Ford and Carter. Yet, while the appointment of an energy czar consoled some people sitting in gas lines, the fundamental cause of the energy shortages—federal price controls and other restrictions—were kept in place until Ronald Reagan took office in 1981.

When Congress enacted a law in 1982 that created a drug czar, President Reagan scorned the provision, complaining that

> The creation of another layer of bureaucracy within the Executive Branch would produce friction, disrupt effective law enforcement, and could threaten the integrity of criminal investigations and prosecutions—the very opposite of what its proponents apparently intend. . . . The so-called 'drug Czar' provision was enacted hastily without thoughtful debate and without benefit of any hearings.[174]

The drug czar remained a largely ceremonial post until President Bush appointed William Bennett; however, the chain-smoking, tough-talking Bennett did not find the magic words to make all Americans virtuous. President Clinton appointed a former general, Barry McCaffrey, as his second drug czar to prove that he was finally getting "tough" on drugs; the czar-general's grandest moment was his threat to revoke the medical licenses of California and Arizona doctors who mentioned cannabis to patients after citizens of those states endorsed legalizing the medical use of marijuana. In recent years, Americans have also been blessed by a "health care czar" (Ira Magaziner in 1993), an "AIDS czar" (various political appointees since 1993), and endless local "zoning czars" and "land use czars." But no matter how many czars are appointed, it is never enough. In August 1998, a government advisory panel called for the appointment of a "food czar" to "oversee the patchwork of food safety regulations."[175]

Faith in appointing czars presumes that there is no public policy snafu that cannot be fixed by vesting more power in some government official—that more power is the panacea for all problems caused by previous uses of power.

Arbitrary power has gone from being an outrage to being a commonplace. Few Americans realize how much discretion is vested in the hands of low- and mid-level federal employees. The Food and Drug Administration (FDA) requires pharmaceutical and medical device manufacturers to prove that new drugs and devices are both safe and effective, but the agency has refused to give a clear definition of efficacy. Lawyer Peter Barton Hutt, former FDA chief counsel, declared that FDA employees "don't have to prove anything. . . . The people who do premarket approval at FDA are like little kings and queens in their kingdom. They can have more power over the economy and technological development than the chairman of the board of the largest pharmaceutical company."[176] One FDA enforcement staffer told the *Food and Drug Insider Report* newsletter: "We have depended on the ability to selectively target companies . . . and to issue findings without fear of being second-guessed by some tinhorn judge."[177] A survey by the newsletter found that 84 percent of drug and medical device companies reported "declining to file a complaint against the FDA for fear of retaliation."[178] Kenneth Feather, chief of the FDA's Drug Advertising Surveillance Branch, explained the agency's goal: "We want to say to these companies that you don't know when or how we'll strike. We want to eliminate predictability."[179] The FDA even dictates the gender of voices that can be used in drug advertisements and pressures drug companies to get prior government approval for any communication they make to potential customers.[180] Under a 1998 FDA proposed rule, as former FDA biotechnology director Henry Miller observed, "even the most basic and innocuous communications between people in the industry could be labeled 'promotional' and prohibited by FDA censors."[181]

When Congress enacted the Insider Trading Sanctions Act in 1984, the new law did not define insider trading, largely because the Securities and Exchange Commission (SEC) vehemently opposed defining the crime that it had received more power to punish.[182] Despite decades of demands by critics, stock traders, and lawyers, the federal government has refused to define a crime that many federal officials are most avid to punish.[183] A federal appeals court slammed the SEC in 1998 for "almost deliberately obscurantist" interpretations of its insider trading regulations.[184] A *Wall Street Journal* article noted that the SEC "has done well pursuing cases based on its own unwritten—and, at times, vague—construction of the federal laws, because courts have traditionally shown deference to the agency's views."[185] In practice, "insider trading" can be almost any type of transaction that offends the sensitivities of SEC officials.

The near-incomprehensibility of federal regulations allows federal prosecutors to destroy citizens who make inadvertent mistakes. In 1993 the federal government sued George Krizek, an elderly psychiatrist, for $81 million, charging that he had made false Medicare and Medicaid claims for his treatment of patients. Federal judge Stanley Sporkin estimated that Krizek had overcharged the government for $47,000 over a seven-year period.[186] Krizek's lawyers said that the psychiatrist's sometimes imprecise billing (submitted by his Czech immigrant wife) also resulted in extensive undercharges to the government.[187] Sporkin highlighted one example of how the Medicare rule book tripped up Krizek: "The system cannot be so arbitrary, so perverse, as to subject a doctor . . . to potential liability in excess of 80 million dollars because telephone calls [regarding a patient] were made in one room rather than another."[188] Sporkin ruled that Krizek is "at worst, a psychiatrist with a small practice who keeps poor records."[189] Judge Sporkin also noted that it was "undisputed that Dr. Krizek worked long hours on behalf of his patients, most of whom were elderly and poor. Many of Dr. Krizek's patients were afflicted with horribly severe psychiatric disorders . . . "[190] While the feds sought to impale Krizek because of alleged errors in a small percentage of his bills, Medicare routinely refuses to compensate doctors for many of the services that they provide to its recipients, because of its own "deceitful" and "unfair" rules, the court decision noted.[191] Congress ignored the abuses that have occurred in cases such as Krizek's and in 1997 added a pathologically complex set of new paperwork requirements that carry fines of $10,000 for each form that doctors fail to fill out to the satisfaction of federal bureaucrats. As Dr. Jody Robinson observed in 1998, "The real purpose of these regulations is to find ways to reduce the payment for services provided to patients by applying the rule: If it isn't documented, it didn't happen."[192]

The fact that arbitrary power is no longer a major issue illustrates most political thinkers' lack of concern about limiting government power. At some point, the sheer accumulation of penalties and threats in the statute book fundamentally changes the citizen's relation to the government. Rather than a government of laws, it becomes a government of threats, intimidation, browbeating. When the law books reach a certain length, there is little or no difference between laws and arbitrary commands, because few people know what the laws or regulations actually are. One former high-ranking IRS attorney declared in 1996, "There is the general view that the more mysterious tax enforcement is, the more likely taxpayers will voluntarily comply."[193] The government employee spends his life amidst the rules and regulations and can invoke some obscure provision in order to trump private citizens.

Some contemporary political commentators are enthusiastic about unleashing government. Historian Alan Brinkley, in a Twentieth Century Fund book entitled *The New Federalist Papers,* derided the "fear of discretionary power . . . [of] lower-level officials," which he claimed was the result of "the relentless popular attacks on government."[194] One of the few protests about the danger of arbitrary power by a Statist liberal came from Robert Goodin, author of *Reasons for Welfare*. Goodin, seeking to allay fears of social workers' power over welfare recipients, declared: "The solution is to establish firm rules so that administrators and caseworkers have no discretion and hence no coercive power to threaten to withhold benefits."[195] Apparently social workers are the only government employees who could possibly have too much power.

Arbitrary power is a moral issue that goes to the heart of the relation of the citizen to the State. Benjamin Constant beautifully expressed the danger of arbitrary power in his 1815 book, *Principles of Politics*:

> Arbitrary power destroys morality, for there can be no morality without security. . . . Arbitrariness is incompatible with the existence of any government considered as a set of institutions. For political institutions are simply contracts; and it is in the nature of contracts to establish fixed limits. Hence arbitrariness, being precisely opposed to what constitutes a contract, undermines the foundation of all political institutions.[196]

The more arbitrary power bureaucrats acquire, the less likely fairness will result. The essence of arbitrary power is government's refusal to issue clear rules limiting its prerogative to punish private citizens. Because the affirmative action police, the housing police, and the trade police seek maximum discretion, rules are left vague, if not hopelessly confusing or impossible to comply with.

Big Government almost automatically destroys the moral foundation necessary for its credibility. Every arbitrary government action sends out shock waves that undermine government legitimacy. People learn to despise the State at the same time that the State is most adamant about imposing its moral judgments on the citizenry. The more fair that politicians claim to forcibly make society, the more unfair the average citizen perceives everyday life. According to a 1996 *Washington Post* poll, "Today, nearly two in three Americans believe that most people can't be trusted; three decades ago a majority of Americans believed that most people could be trusted."[197] This collapse in faith is, in part, the result of the growing chasm between common, everyday conceptions of fairness and the bureaucratic-political conceptions of fairness increasingly imposed on people's lives.

NIGHTSTICK ETHICS, OR BETTER LIVING THROUGH COERCION

According to Lord Chancellor Francis Bacon, a law should be "certain in meaning, just in precept . . . and productive of virtue in those that live under it."[198] (Bacon was convicted a few years after writing this for taking bribes from people whose cases he judged.) According to Samuel Johnson, law "is the last result of human wisdom acting upon human experience for the benefit of the public."[199] (At the time he wrote this, Johnson was a paid pamphleteer in the service of the absolutists in King George III's regime.)

The more closely one examines political reality, the more difficult it becomes to detect the State's nobility. Most theories of the State and morality presume that government can achieve moral ends via political-bureaucratic means—that government intervention, when inspired by a moral ideal, automatically becomes moral—that there is some way to take a redeeming sentiment, issue 50,000 words of regulations, and produce virtue.

Political thinkers often pretend that the State has a transcendent moral value apart from the actual machinery of government. According to T. H. Green, "The reason why certain powers should be recognized as belonging to the State . . . lies in the fact that these powers are necessary to the fulfillment of man's vocation as a moral being, to an effectual self-devotion to the work of developing the perfect character in himself and others."[200] But expecting moral progress via increased government coercion is the equivalent of the "hellfire and damnation" school of theology. The moralization of the State means the moralization of coercion— consecrating the power some people use to subjugate and shackle others.

What exactly is it about government intervention that supposedly produces this moral windfall? When does the moral sanctification from actions of the State first occur? When the politician receives official notification of his victory on election night, thus making all of his subsequent actions sacrosanct? When the federal employee starts his first day on the job—from then until he retires with full pension at age 55? When a bureaucrat first proposes to his supervisor a plan for expanding the agency's power? When new federal power is announced in the *Federal Register?* Or is the moral value not hatched until the first citizen is handcuffed and photographed for the local newspaper for violating the new edict? The sanctification of government power presumes ethical benefits each time that a policeman uses his shoe to persuade a bum to move along—and each time a salivating deputy sheriff shines his flashlight into a car of cavorting teenagers on Lover's Lane.

What exactly is there about being forced to submit to a government edict or restriction that makes a person a better human being? Is obedience the highest calling of mankind, or at least that part of mankind not born to be part of the ruling elite?

Contemporary public policy presumes that government agencies are advanced laboratories for the concoction of new, improved concepts of fairness, as if working in a government agency automatically enables a person to perceive the frontiers of moral progress and thus justifies endowing him with a regulatory bayonet to drive everyone else over that frontier.

"The State has morally killed everything smaller than itself," wrote Simone Weil of France in the 1930s. Statist ethics drive out private ethics. For instance, federal and state drug agencies have long pressured doctors to undermedicate people with severe pain. The federal Agency for Health Care Policy and Research released a special report in 1994 recommending that doctors treat cancer pain early and aggressively. Assistant Secretary of Health and Human Services Dr. Philip Lee declared that the new guidelines "put to rest the idea that narcotics should be held back out of an unrealistic fear of addiction. In fact, addiction almost never occurs."[201] A 1994 *New England Journal of Medicine* study concluded that "42 percent of cancer outpatients do not receive adequate pain treatment."[202] A 1997 report by the National Academy of Sciences' Institute of Medicine study concluded that "drug-prescribing laws, regulations, and interpretations by state medical boards frustrate and intimidate physicians" seeking to treat patients' pain.[203] The tragedy of undermedication of severe pain symbolizes a moral inversion in modern America. It is easier for drug bureaucrats to ban almost everyone from having access to morphine than to recognize its medical benefits to hundreds of thousands of suffering Americans.

Trusting the government to imbue moral values in the citizenry is absurd because some of the highest moral values—such as self-reliance and courage—do not make for docile citizens, and there is no trait that makes government employees' jobs easier than docility. In today's hyperinterventionist State, the type of virtue produced is the virtue of a citizen who kowtows when government agents snap their fingers, the virtue of someone afraid to complain of bureaucratic mistreatment for fear of retaliation, the virtue of someone resigned to suffer abuse because "you can't fight city hall."

While political philosophers speak of government lifting the citizenry's characters, day-to-day government administration often depends on frightening people into submission. For instance, the American Planning Association, composed largely of government bureaucrats, urged government inspectors to "carry cameras at all times" because of cameras' "intimidation effect—some citizens are more impressed by the formality of having their violations photographed than by the initial warning letter."[204] The federal Fish and Wildlife Service relies heavily on threats of draconian penalties—$100,000 per alleged violation of the Endangered Species Act—to pressure people into submitting to sweeping restrictions on the use of their own land. Many federal agents know that few of the threatened penalties could stand up in court, according to Ike

Sugg of the Competitive Enterprise Institute,[205] but because most landowners cannot afford savvy legal advice or protracted court battles, they bow to agents' demands. One IRS employee who had worked for its collection division for 25 years, testifying confidentially before a congressional committee in 1997, declared: "Many [IRS] revenue officers capitalize on the taxpayer's inherent fear of the IRS and the intimidation that they can inflict on taxpayers without any consequence for their improper enforcement."[206] (The American Institute of Certified Public Accountants complained in 1996 of IRS training materials on the Taxpayer Bill of Rights: "Every ethical issue presented finds the ethical result to be pro-IRS and anti-taxpayer. There is not one scenario where an IRS agent might act unethically against a taxpayer's interest."[207])

Contemporary public policy is based on nightstick ethics—the notion that anyone who possesses a badge is automatically morally superior to anyone who does not. The first principle of nightstick ethics is that someone who got whacked automatically deserved to be whacked, and every nightstick whacking is a triumph of good over evil. Thus, all that is necessary to maximize the amount of goodness in a society is to maximize the number of government officials with nightsticks, and to maximize the incentives to swing those nightsticks as often as possible. Contemporary moral thinking assumes a seesaw theory of public virtue: the heavier the penalties government imposes, the higher the people's character will rise.

We now have a concept of civic virtue based on compelled obedience to any government rule. Nowadays, "do the right thing" simply means to obey any dictate of any government employee—a triumph of the Prussian model of virtue. Public policy implicitly presumes that the more that people's lives are permeated by fear of offending any government official, the more moral they will be. This is why little effort is made to explain citizens' precise legal obligations; instead, the government relies on intimidation. The Internal Revenue Service, for instance, short shrifts spending on training its employees and on answering phone calls from taxpayers, yet has ample resources for high-profile prosecutions of celebrities suspected of underpaying taxes.

When government force is equated with morality, then any citizen who resists bowing down to the government is automatically presumed to be evil. Resistance to the government becomes a worse sin than practically anything a government agent could do to a private citizen. Yet, far greater crimes have been committed in this century by those obeying the government than by those resisting its power. Bogus definitions of fairness, by making people more submissive to government power, lead directly to new injustices. Insofar as people have been schooled to believe that government power is inherently just, thus far will people be abused and exploited by the State.

To presume an automatic moral benefit from government coercion is to presume that individual liberty is an inherently immoral condition—that whatever reduces liberty increases goodness. To equate morality with government power is to lay the foundation for totalitarianism. To believe that government force is morally uplifting is to believe that citizens are morally inferior to the government. And since they are inferior, then the government merely has to notice their existence—and shove them around a bit—for them to become better people.

Considering the contempt that politicians show for their own ethical conduct, they cannot be expected to lift other people's characters. After a 1998 public uproar about blatant conflicts of interest among Maryland politicians, the Speaker of the state House of Delegates responded with a "reform" bill that would require citizens to reveal their names and home addresses before being permitted to view a legislator's conflict-of-interest disclosure form.[208] The Joint Ethics Committee of the General Assembly responded to a deluge of media revelations of conflicts of interest by announcing that it was too busy to consider any more cases.[209] The *New York Times* summarized a 1998 study of conflicts of interest in the Illinois legislature: "In the Illinois State Capitol, in Springfield, farmer-legislators write the agriculture laws. Doctor-legislators propose the laws on H.M.O.'s. The beer-distributor-legislator sponsors a law limiting beer sales over the Internet. The law does not require disclosure of many potential conflicts. Business interests of legislators' spouses and dependents are not disclosed and neither are the amounts of stock holdings. Lawyer-legislators are not required to disclose their clients. . . . The state ethics law is little enforced."[210]

The moral nature of the State is shown clearly in international relations: *Regna regnis lupi,* the State a wolf unto the State, as the ancient Romans warned.[211] International relations have a long history of deceit, betrayal, and atrocities. Yet, the same governments that perennially cheat each other are assumed by idealists to have edifying effects when they deal with their own subjects, even though the average citizen lacks a military arsenal to make the government honor its word.

The debate over the moral nature of the State turns on the question: Does power corrupt, or does power ennoble? Are people likely to become more generous, benevolent, and evenhanded when they have another person under their thumb? As Benedict de Spinoza wrote, "It is absurd to believe that the only man not to be led astray by his passions will be precisely the one whose situation is such that he is surrounded by the strongest temptations, and for whom it is

SIDEBAR: INFLATION AND POLITICAL DECENCY

The stability of the value of government-issued currency is one of the clearest measures of the trustworthiness of a government. Earlier in this century, Americans clearly recognized the moral implications of inflation. Vice President Calvin Coolidge bluntly declared in 1922: "Inflation is repudiation." The morality of debasing a currency has been clear for over 500 years: Nicholas Oresme in a 1331 essay, declared, "To take or augment profit by alternation of the coinage is fraudulent, tyrannical and unjust, and moreover it cannot be persisted in without the kingdom being, in many other respects also, changed to a tyranny."[212] Inflation is a tax whereby government prints extra money to finance its deficit spending. The value of money is largely determined by the ratio of money to goods; if the quantity of money increases faster than the increase in the amount of goods, the result is an increase in the ratio of money to goods, and an increase in prices. Thus, the government's printing presses devalue people's paychecks and effectively allow government to default on the value of its debt. The threat of inflation was invoked in the early 1940s to justify imposing payroll tax withholding[213] (protecting people from their own paychecks) and in the 1970s to impose price controls over the entire economy. Apparently, politicians who decide to flood the money supply automatically become entitled to increase their coercion of their victims who hold increasingly worthless currency.

Considering the post-1933 inflation in this country, the federal government today, in one sense, has about 7 percent as much moral credibility as it had in 1933.[214] If someone proposed a law to give government the right to explicitly default by 2 to 3 percent a year on all its debts, the proposal would be widely denounced. Yet, this is what the government has been doing for decades. Though inflation has slowed since 1980, the purchasing power of the dollar has fallen by over 50 percent in subsequent years according to the government's own numbers (which slightly exaggerate the damage to the dollar), making a mockery of people's attempts to calculate the future or save for their retirements. A 1997 study by Congress's Joint Committee on Taxation found that, because of how capital gains taxes are calculated, many citizens are forced to pay taxes on investment "gains" when, in reality, they have actually suffered a loss, due to the deterioration of purchasing power of their original investment.[215]

easier and less dangerous to succumb to them."[216] Benjamin Constant, writing in the wake of the French Revolution's atrocities, ridiculed the pretensions of the modern Salvation State: "It is no longer enough to attribute to one man superior faculties and an unswerving equity. It is necessary to suppose the existence of one or two hundred thousand angelic creatures, raised above all the weaknesses and vices of mankind."[217]

PRIVATE CRIME
VERSUS POLITICAL-BUREAUCRATIC ABUSES

President Andrew Johnson observed in an 1868 message to Congress, "It may be safely assumed as an axiom . . . that the greatest wrongs inflicted upon a people are caused by unjust and arbitrary legislation."[218] America has suffered a deluge of crime in recent decades; the rate of assaults, robberies, rapes, and murder is three times higher than it was a few decades ago. Many Americans look at the crime wave and conclude that the government needs more power to control the citizenry.

However, it is worthwhile to compare the cost of private crimes with the losses and costs of abusive government policies. While many people are terrified of private crime, they have neglected to notice how government actions cost them far more.

According to the Justice Department, roughly 27 million Americans suffered economic losses from crime in 1992, the most recent year for which data is available. (For the Justice Department's breakdown of the losses see Table 5.1.)

The IRS has frequently been criticized by the General Accounting Office (GAO) and others for sending unjustified penalty and tax deficiency notices to citizens and businesses. The GAO found that the IRS made over 20 million unjustified changes to taxpayer accounts in 1994, many of which resulted in unjustified overcharges to taxpayers. *Worth* magazine reported: "According to a confidential agency report, only IRS demands for $25,000 or more are checked by humans for mistakes. IRS computers spit out bills charging lesser amounts with reckless abandon."[219] *Money* magazine estimated that the IRS wrongfully collected up to $7 billion in penalties it assessed in 1989 but were not owed by taxpayers.[220] Thus, Americans probably lose more each year from unjustified IRS payment demands than is stolen by all the burglars and armed robbers combined.

According to the federal government, cases of apparent arson destroyed roughly $1.5 billion in property in 1994. (Cases of proven arson destroyed just under $1 billion worth of property.)[221] These losses pale beside estimates of losses by property owners from government regulatory changes. Former White House environmental analyst Jonathan Tolman estimated, based on one study of the effect of wetlands designations on property values, that federal wetlands regulations could result in a decline in land values of over $100 billion.[222]

The Justice Department estimated that total losses from the 7,885 bank robberies nationwide in 1994 was approximately $28 million.[223] That same year,

TABLE 1

TOTAL ECONOMIC LOSS
TO VICTIMS OF CRIME, 1992

PERSONAL CRIMES	
CRIMES OF VIOLENCE	
RAPE	33,000,000
ROBBERY	680,000,000
ASSAULT	649,000,000
TOTAL	1,362,000,000
CRIMES OF PERSONAL THEFT	
LARCENY WITH CONTACT	76,000,000
LARCENY WITHOUT CONTACT	2,672,000,000
TOTAL	2,748,000,000
HOUSEHOLD CRIMES	
BURGLARY	3,970,000,000
HOUSEHOLD LARCENY	1,750,000,000
MOTOR THEFT	7,816,000,000
TOTAL	13,536,000,000
TOTAL	**$17,646,000,000**

Source: "The Costs of Crime to Victims: Crime Data Brief," Bureau of Justice Statistics, U.S. Department of Justice, February 1994.

federal prosecutors confiscated $2.1 billion in property, cash, and other goods in asset forfeiture proceedings. Since the procedures in forfeitures are so biased against private citizens, and since most people whose property is seized are never convicted of a crime, that a significant percentage of property confiscated in forfeiture proceedings is taken from innocent Americans. In other words, the nation's 5,000 federal prosecutors likely stole more from innocent citizens than the thousands of robbers stole from all the nation's banks.

The total economic losses from private crime also pales beside the cost to American consumers and businesses of political payoffs to domestic industries in U.S. trade laws. Author Albert Jay Nock observed, "The primary reason for a tariff is that it enables the exploitation of the domestic consumer by a process indistinguishable from sheer robbery." The United States now has over 8,000 different tariffs, with levies on imports as high as 451 percent of their value.[224] According to the Institute for International Economics, U.S. trade barriers cost Americans $70 billion.[225] For every dollar that robbers steal in broad daylight or in dark allies, the U.S. Congress mugs consumers and businesses for $80.

JUSTICE AND THE STATE

Many evaluations of the justice of government action begin with a presumption that, as Thomas Hobbes wrote, "no Law can be Unjust. The Law is made by the Sovereign Power, and all that is done by such Power, is warranted. . . ."[226] Or, as Hitler declared, "The total State must not know any difference between law and ethics."[227]

Such Statist presumptions permeated much of twentieth century political thought. Sidney and Beatrice Webb, in their 1936 paean to the U.S.S.R., discussed Soviet ethical doctrines: "Paramount is the injunction to abstain from and to resist 'exploitation,' meaning any employment of others at wages for the purpose of making a profit out of their labor." The Webbs observed that "abstention from exploitation is the ethical duty that is . . . most forcibly and frequently impressed on the youthful mind."[228] The Webbs' comment exemplifies the tendency to presume that all private contracts are exploitative and all political commands just. Making money off of someone else's labor is the worst sin—regardless of the wages that a person might receive—and regardless that the job may be the best option available to the worker. The Webbs wrote in the aftermath of a five-year plan during which Stalin intentionally slashed the living standard of his subjects to finance state investment. The Webbs had no problem with the minuscule wages paid by the Soviet state because those wages were dictated by an institution that supposedly incarnated justice—and thus was incapable of exploiting people. And the proliferation of vast slave labor systems and the Gulags was not a moral issue because the internees were merely being forced to labor for the good of society. (Leon Trotsky captured the meaning of Soviet employment ethics: "In a country where the sole employer is the State, opposition means death by slow starvation. . . . who does not obey shall not eat."[229])

American political thinkers have often routinely viewed government as the fount of justice. American Civil Liberties Union national director Burt Neuborne observed, "From Marxist ideas of control of production and distribution, to the reforms of the New Deal, to the mildly redistributionist policies of the Kennedys, left-leaning reformers had placed their faith in government as the principal engine for achieving real justice."[230] Coercion—at least by government officials—has become almost completely irrelevant to contemporary considerations of fairness. The fact that a proposed government intervention will increase the compulsion of private citizens by government employees is rarely raised as an issue in itself. Ignoring the coercive nature of government allows Statists to change radically the moral calculus of government intervention, since government coercion is thereby made the moral equivalent of voluntary agreement. And since government is inherently superior to private citizens, why not maximize fairness by maximizing government intervention?

Virtue is now something to be mass produced by government compulsion. President Clinton is crusading for a national Kiddie Draft—urging all government schools to require high schools students to perform a certain number of hours of "community service" before being allowed to receive a high school diploma. After Chicago adopted "mandatory volunteer" requirements for its high school students, Chicago schools spokesman Bruce Marchiafava declared that students "need to know that community is about giving, not just getting."[231] Unfortunately, Chicago school employees are often too busy getting for themselves, thus accounting for the appalling quality of education in parts of the city. At the 1997 Philadelphia Summit on Volunteering, Clinton announced that America needs "citizen servants" and asserted that "the era of big government may be over, but the era of big challenges for our country is not, and so we need an era of big citizenship."[232] Apparently, the fact that the average citizen is forced to work more than four months a year just to pay taxes does not count: politicians also want to seize control of people's free time. "Mandatory volunteerism" presumes that submitting to political commands is more virtuous than free citizens voluntarily helping others. Over 90 million Americans already spend time each year volunteering. But Clinton is not nearly satisfied and insists that goals and timetables be established to pressure and compel more Americans to give up their free time for politically approved causes.

The more injustices the government commits against the citizenry—the more bogus accusations, the more unjustified confiscations, the more devious entrapments—the more iniquity appears to exist in the private sector. And, since iniquity is pervasive, the obvious solution is to vest more power in the hands of government agents. Thus, the more crimes the government commits against the people, the more power the government appears to need over the people.

To see the scams that government uses in dealing with citizens—to see the contempt for any reasonable concept of fairness in common government administrative practices—should extinguish any residual notions of government's moral superiority. There is no inherent virtue to bowing to government threats. Coercion might occasionally be necessary to preserve social peace, but it will not edify its victims. True moral progress consists of something other than the slaughter of private interests on the altar of political self-interest. Moral value can be produced only by the free action of individuals, not by the commands of rulers. The only "virtue" that modern governments can produce is the virtue of obedience gained by threats—the same virtue a dog shows when he abstains from soiling the kitchen floor because he knows he will otherwise be beaten.

Voluntary agreements are generally fairer than official edicts because the necessity for agreement curbs the power of all parties to the agreement. In the political sphere, the harshness or inequity of the terms of an agreement are limited solely by the amount of coercive power officialdom possesses.

Freedom maximizes fairness because allowing each person to control his own life minimizes the injustices that a person suffers from others. The justice of liberty is based on each man's ownership of himself and his life. No man has a right to dispose of what he does not own. Unnecessary coercion is inherently unjust. The wrongful use of force is the key concept for understanding the justice of the free society.

The expansion of the realm of compulsion means the triumph of political machinations over private responsibility. The more power politicians and bureaucrats acquire, the more blurred their moral vision becomes. As Professor Bruce Benson observed, "Because increasing criminalization leads to greater potential payoffs to corruption, the incentives to be corrupt become stronger as the government grows."[233]

Insofar as government is the institution of coercion, and insofar as coercion is morally inferior to voluntary agreement, thus far is the government sphere morally inferior to the voluntary sphere of life. Moral goodness cannot be created by coercive action and pervasive subjugation. At best, by curtailing aggression between private citizens, government can safeguard room for private virtue to develop and flourish. There are no moral benefits from the expansion of government power beyond a minimum necessary to protect individual rights.

CONCLUSION

Government cannot make people's lives more fair by making them less free. Government coercion is not an exercise in moral fine-tuning. To recognize the moral void at the center of government power and to cease presuming that fairness lurks in the bowels of regulatory and legislative proceedings are the prerequisites for honest thinking about justice and fairness.

We must not define or measure the Good Society by the number of people that the government has the option to imprison. Politicians are not priests and are unfit to judge the goodness or evil of fellow citizen's behavior. Especially in a representative government, politicians should be chosen and elected to serve narrowly proscribed functions, not to promenade as moral saviors.

Government cannot morally rise above its coercive origins and its day-to-day subjugation and exploitation. To politicize moral issues is almost certainly to drag them down. Government is a tool to enforce restraints, not an all-wise machine to promulgate values. Those who seek to take their moral values from the government will lower society to the level of the conniving political class, rather than raising it to the ideals of philosophers.

As morality and goodness are increasingly presumed to rest in the State, the contradiction grows between what it means to be a good man and a good subject. The good man tells the truth; the good subject repeats the lies that his rulers tell him. The good man cherishes his word and honors his contract; the good subject accepts that government officials and politicians renounce their promises at their convenience. The good man seeks to stand on his own two feet; the good subject relishes his dependence on his political overlords and cherishes each new promise his rulers make. The good man takes responsibility for his own actions and minds his own business; the good subject is the informant, ready to call the recycling police about any neighbor who fails to separate his tin cans from his plastic bottles.

SIX

SOVEREIGNTY
& POLITICAL SLAVERY

Prerogative is the sovereign's right to do wrong.
—Ambrose Bierce[1]

Were not the King a God to man, one man would be a wolf to another.
—English pamphleteer, 1660[2]

THE CONCEPT OF SOVEREIGNTY may be the most dangerous Pandora's box in the history of political thought. Sovereignty seems to be something that the government soaks up like a sponge, getting fuller and fuller year by year—until at last all the rights of the people have been drained away. Nowadays, governments act as if they possess "natural rights" to demand the obedience of their victims.

The Founding Fathers had a vivid concept of governmental authorities "going too far." The early state constitutions and the U.S. Constitution and Bill of Rights sought to craft institutions to keep government forever humbled to the citizenry. When governments were less powerful in the United States, most controversies regarding sovereignty occurred over whether state or federal governments had supreme jurisdiction within their domains. But, as government power multiplied, sovereignty became far more important. In the same way that every military invasion raises questions of national sovereignty, regulatory incursions by politicians and bureaucrats must raise questions about the sovereignty of individuals over their own lives. What pretexts justify government massively transgressing the borders of the individual's own life?

We have seen that the consent of the governed is, in most cases, a mirage. The fact that people live in a certain place indicates that they consent to the weather as much as that they consent to the government. The mere invocation of the people's name cannot automatically legitimate an unlimited amount of coercion of the people. In order to live in a society and under a government, is it necessary that people be "ridden like horses, fleeced like sheep, worked like cattle, and fed and clothed like swine and hounds," as John Adams wrote?[3] Does the fact that one person has a badge and a uniform give him an unlimited right to forcibly intrude into other people's lives—to kick down their front doors, to strip search their children,[4] to tap their phones, and to manipulate them into breaking laws and destroying their futures?

We must now consider whether government inherently possesses some higher sanction that legitimizes its coercion of the citizenry. What is a State entitled to, by mere fact of its existence—by the mere fact that it has managed to suppress armed resistance against itself?

SOVEREIGN IMMUNITY

To better understand the concept of sovereignty, we will examine some of the injuries that government permits itself to inflict. Justice Oliver Wendell Holmes declared in 1907: "A sovereign is exempt from suit . . . [because] there can be no legal right as against the authority that makes the law on which the right depends."[5] Federal court decisions on lawsuits against federal agencies routinely include the following boilerplate: "Where a suit has not been consented to by the United States, dismissal of the action is required."[6] As a result of such immunity, "The Secretary of the Interior has an absolute privilege to include malicious defamation in a press release concerning official business, and the Secretary of the Treasury is not liable for 'arbitrary, wanton, capricious, illegal, malicious, oppressive, and contemptuous' action," as University of Chicago law professor Kenneth Davis observed.[7]

Such judicial genuflection to government was not always the case. In 1793, in the first case involving a lawsuit against a state government, four of five Supreme Court justices ruled that governments could be sued regardless of whether they deigned to permit such suits.[8] But, in 1821, Chief Justice John Marshall, offering no evidence, rewrote the rule book: "The universally received opinion is, that no suit can be commenced or prosecuted against the United States; that the judiciary act does not authorize such suits."[9] A 1945 Supreme

Court opinion declared that sovereign immunity is "embodied in the Constitution."[10] However, neither law professors nor private citizens victimized by the government have ever been able to find precisely where in the Constitution this doctrine is "embodied."[11] As Professor Jeremy Travis noted, "It is a magnificent historical irony that America, a republic whose independence was declared in a document indicting the sovereign for treasonous acts, should adopt without serious examination the doctrine of sovereign immunity."[12]

There are scores of thousands of government agencies and government-sponsored entities in the United States that enjoy some degree of legal immunity. The largest government-sponsored enterprise is the U.S. Postal Service, which has claimed immunity from lawsuits charging it with false advertising (regarding its deceptive claims for Priority Mail), trademark infringements of its competitors, or other unfair trade practices.[13] Yet, when the Postal Service sues its competitors, it claims that it is a private entity.[14] A federal appeals court in 1998 thumped the agency's efforts to evade legal responsibility: "The Postal Service has hastily elevated the shield of governmental privilege when accused of competitive wrongdoing."[15]

Thanks to a 1991 Supreme Court decision, state and local government officials are exempt from federal antitrust laws even when they conspire with private companies and engage in illegal anticompetitive activities.[16] When the Tennessee Valley Authority (TVA), a federally owned, federally subsidized electric utility, began selling power in competition with nearby utility companies (in violation of federal law), several companies lobbied Congress to reform the law governing the TVA's actions. The TVA responded in 1997 by formally requesting that the Justice Department investigate its competitors for violating an obscure law that carries heavy fines and five year prison sentences for entering into any "conspiracy, collusion or agreement, express or implied with intent . . . wrongfully and unlawfully, to defeat the [TVA's] purposes."[17] Though the TVA is exempt from antitrust laws, it sought to invoke the same laws to thwart its competition.[18]

With sovereign immunity, the devil is often in the details of seemingly innocuous laws. In 1985, the Ohio legislature enacted a law exempting local governments from liability for traffic accidents caused by police responding to emergencies. The law set off a scramble by local governments to chisel their victims. The *Columbus Dispatch* editorialized in 1997 that "the Columbus Division of Police has a record of twisting the law, sometimes deceitfully, to deny accountability for crashes."[19] In dozens of cases, the *Dispatch* found that "victims had been told that officers were responding to emergencies when they were not." The city even charged impoundment fees when seizing the vehicles of victims crashed into by wayward cops. The 1985 law specified that cities would be liable only for damage not covered by victims' insurance policies—usually only a few hundred dollars' deductible. There was no scintilla of justice in this edict, but state politicians felt entitled to help themselves to the assets of insurance companies.

Police were at fault in most crashes, as an expose by *Columbus Dispatch* reporter Michael Berens showed. Yet, police denied any compensation to victims in over 75 percent of crashes in which the police were at fault. The police department offered some novel exculpations; for instance, "When an officer drove the wrong way on a one-way street [the police department found that] the victim had enough time to get out of the way." Almost all the accidents were investigated solely by the police department itself, with no oversight from any outsiders. When the city council wavered and considered compensating one victim in 1992, it was dissuaded by an assistant city attorney, who warned that though the "claim may seem fair, by paying the $1400 that the city can certainly afford, the city runs the risk that the next emergency run immunity claim is $1.4 million."[20] Obviously, the city was obliged to provide equal injustice to all its victims. And, thanks to a 1993 ruling by an assistant city attorney, the city became absolutely immune from any injury done to citizens by cops riding horses or bicycles.[21] Why? Because horses and bikes are not motor vehicles, so no one injured by a cop on a horse or bike has any legal rights.

Sovereign immunity can provide a license to kill with impunity. The *Atlanta Journal* reported in 1996:

> Barbara Starr and her husband, John, were helping volunteers plant trees in Atlanta's Adams Park in October 1993 when a runaway dump truck rolled down a hill and crushed them. Barbara Starr, 46, of Norcross, died instantly. John Starr spent 2 ½ months in the hospital and had to learn how to walk again. If the truck had belonged to a private company the Starr family might already have collected a huge personal injury settlement. But the dump truck belonged to the city of Atlanta, and under city policy the family was eligible for no more than $2,000—$1,000 per person—for the accident. . . . Many of Georgia's larger local governments, including most in metro Atlanta, declare themselves immune from big monetary damages in auto accidents—even when they are at fault.[22]

Everyone is equal, except when government employees kill private citizens. For instance, in 1994, D.C. police officer Roosevelt Askew shot car thief Sutoria Moore. Askew and other police on the scene wrote up an official report claiming that Moore was killed as he was on the verge of running over another policeman. However, after subsequent investigation by others, Askew admitted the report was a complete fraud. Askew told prosecutors that his gun had gone off accidentally as he approached Moore, who had stopped his car and was waiting for the policeman to approach. Prosecutors allowed Askew to plead guilty to filing a false police report and promised not to file manslaughter or murder charges. No such light penalty would ever be contemplated for someone who pointed a gun at a policeman and "accidentally" pulled the trigger.[23] New York police officers who are accused of wrongdoing—such as killing innocent civilians—are entitled to delay answering any questions about their conduct for 48 hours after the incident. The *New York Times* editorialized, "The rule gives officers who are involved in crimes two days to coordinate their stories—or try to influence witnesses."[24]

On July 12, 1998, a squad of six Houston police smashed into the apartment of Pedro Oregon in the middle of the night. The 23-year old Hispanic fled into his bedroom; police smashed down the door and, when they saw that Oregon had a handgun, unleashed a volley of 30 shots. Oregon died, shot 9 times in the back. The police had no warrant for the search but claimed that a confidential informant said that he witnessed a drug deal occur at the address. (No drugs were found.) Harris County (Houston) District Attorney John Holmes observed that the police who killed Oregon might not be indicted: "I don't know of any authority at this point that gave [the police] the right to be in that residence. But that doesn't make the shooting a crime." Holmes explained that the police "do not have to sit still for a citizen pointing a firearm at them, even if they entered unlawfully."[25] Thus, the mere possession of a weapon of self-defense in a person's own bedroom is sufficient to justify death by police firing squad.

The Justice Department's view of the untouchability of federal lawmen is clear from its action in the Idaho trial of FBI sniper Lon Horiuchi. Horiuchi gained renown in 1992 after he shot and killed 42-year-old Vicki Weaver as she stood in the door of her cabin holding her ten-month-old baby.[26] (Moments earlier, Horiuchi had shot her husband, Randy Weaver, in the back without warning or provocation; Ms. Weaver posed no threat to anyone at the time Horiuchi killed her.) The FBI initially labeled its Ruby Ridge operation a big success and indicated Ms. Weaver was a fair target; later, the agency claimed that her killing was accidental.[27] Boundary County, Idaho prosecutor Denise Woodbury filed manslaughter charges against Horiuchi in 1997, just before the statute of limitations expired. (Many Idaho residents believed Horiuchi should have been charged with first-degree murder.) FBI Director Louis Freeh was outraged that a local court would attempt to hold an FBI agent legally responsible for the killing. He declared that Horiuchi had an "exemplary record" and is "an outstanding agent and continues to have my total support and confidence."[28]

This raises the question: How many mothers holding babies does an FBI agent have to gun down before an FBI director loses faith in him? Freeh declared: "The FBI is doing everything within its power to ensure [Horiuchi] is defended to the full extent and that his rights as a federal law enforcement officer are fully protected."[29] Justice Department lawyers persuaded a judge to move Horiuchi's case from a state court to a federal court, where federal agencies have far more procedural advantages. Although a confidential Justice Department report concluded that Horiuchi acted unconstitutionally,[30] Justice Department lawyers argued vigorously that Horiuchi was exempt from any state or local prosecution because he was carrying out federal orders at the time he gunned Ms. Weaver down. The Justice Department and the FBI warned in March 1998 that permitting Horiuchi to be prosecuted would have "an enormously chilling effect on federal operations, especially law enforcement."[31]

On May 14, 1998, federal judge Edward Lodge decreed that the state of Idaho could not prosecute Horiuchi for killing Vicki Weaver, that what the agent had done was "necessary and proper." Lodge focused on Horiuchi's "subjective beliefs": as long as Horiuchi supposedly did not believe he was violating anyone's rights or acting wrongfully, then he could not be tried. The judge blamed Vicki Weaver for her own death. Lodge decreed that "it would be objectively reasonable for Mr. Horiuchi to believe that one would not expect a mother to place herself and her baby behind an open door outside the cabin after a shot had been fired and her husband had called out that he had been hit."[32] Thus, if an FBI agent wrongfully shoots one family member—the government receives a presumptive right to slay the rest of the family unless they run and hide. A citizen's duty to bow before law enforcement, in Judge Lodge's view, trumps a spouse's duty to a mate in mortal danger.

On the morning of April 2, 1994, 20 IRS agents and state alcoholic beverage control agents stormed into one of the best known restaurants on the Virginia Beach, Virginia, waterfront—the Jewish Mother. Federal agents in flak jackets, duly accompanied by police dogs, waved automatic weapons in the air and yanked utensils out of the hands of patrons who did not move fast enough for their pleasure. The agents then proceeded to ransack the restaurant; a truck pulled up a few hours later and all the restaurant's business records were hauled away. Federal agents also raided and ransacked the homes of restaurant manager Scotty Miller and owner John Colaprete. [33] The raid was the result of unsubstantiated allegations by a former restaurant employee and convicted felon, Deborah Shofner, who later pled guilty to embezzling $30,000 from the restaurant. (She had been convicted of grand larceny two years before being hired by the restaurant.) After the restaurant fired her, Shofner went to the IRS and state beverage control and claimed that the restaurant was dealing with "Jamaican hit squads," had bags of cocaine stacked five feet high on premises, and was laundering large amounts of money. The IRS knew of the woman's criminal record but her uncorroborated allegations were sufficient to launch the raid. Five months after the raid, the government returned most of the seized contraband (a valuable watch given to Colaprete by his father "vanished") and dropped all charges. The restaurant owners and Miller are suing the IRS agents and state agents for $10 million in compensatory damages and $10 million in punitive damages. The IRS cannot be sued in this case because the federal government has not waived its immunity; the Justice Department hired expensive legal representation for the IRS agents, and lawyers on both sides conceded there is little chance the government agents will be found liable.[34]

Sovereign immunity is also a bulwark of public education. The government routinely effectively confiscates parents' money to pay for schools and then fails to educate their kids, yet faces no liability for their de facto breach of implied contract. A 1995 investigation by the New Jersey State Department of Education concluded: "The Newark School District has been at best flagrantly delinquent and at worst deceptive in discharging its obligations to the children enrolled in public schools."[35] Public high schools graduate an estimated 700,000 functionally illiterate teenagers each year.[36] Regardless of how badly school officials fail to serve students, parents are left no recourse but to file complaints with the same unresponsive bureaucracy. Parents are compelled to pay for public schools, but the public schools have no liability to the parents. As law professor Judith Berliner Cohen observed, "No plaintiff to date has been able to convince a court that a school owes him or her any more than 'a chair in a classroom.' . . . Insofar as they have been 'deluded' into believing that it is not necessary to find alternate means of education, the students are arguably worse off than they otherwise would have been."[37]

Government officials sometimes bluntly claim a prerogative to damage or destroy the property of private citizens. Customs Service agents are renowned for destructive "searches" of import shipments. In one case, agents used a chain saw to "inspect" a cigar-store wooden Indian for drugs (no drugs were found).[38] The Customs Service never compensates property owners for the damage its agents do, regardless of how irresponsibly or maliciously its agents have acted. Deputy Assistant Attorney General Stephen Bransdorfer, testifying before the House Judiciary Committee on October 23, 1991, opposed holding the Customs Service liable for "negligent destruction" of commercial cargo because "standard marine cargo insurance . . . is available at readily affordable rates."[39] The same rationale would justify torpedoing ships with suspected contraband as soon as they enter U.S. territorial waters.

Congress sometimes invokes sovereign immunity to default on federal contracts. Instead of closing failing thrifts (whose accounts were covered by federal deposit insurance) in the 1980s, the government preferred to arrange to have them taken over by credit-worthy, solvent thrifts, thereby minimizing the cost to the government. Federal banking agencies signed written agreements promising specific benefits to institutions in return for their assistance in taking over failing thrifts. But in 1989 Congress, as a cost-saving measure, nullified many of these contracts, forcing many otherwise solvent savings and loans into liquidation. Several savings and loans sued the government for breach of contract, but lawyers for the U.S. government denied that previous agreements were still binding after Congress specifically declared that the agreements were not in the public interest. U.S. Claims Court Chief Judge Loren Smith ruled against the government, declaring, "On the government's reasoning, any statute breaching a contract would be immune . . . merely because its purpose was to breach the contract."[40]

The Clinton administration appealed Smith's decision (and other court defeats) to the Supreme Court. Since the vast majority of potential defendants cannot afford to battle "the world's largest law firm," the Justice Department's interpretation of the Constitution is often more important than the Supreme Court's interpretation. The government's brief declared: "Even if respondents had unmistakably obtained the promises they allege, those promises would be invalid and unenforceable because the thrift regulators who would have made them would not have had the authority to bind future Congresses."[41] According to the Justice Department, Congress has an unlimited right to revoke any commitment a federal agency makes. The Justice Department warned: "A governmental obligation to pay substantial damages as the price for exercising regulatory authority unquestionably carries the danger that needed future regulatory action will be deterred."[42] The Supreme Court sided with Judge Smith and rebuked the federal government in 1996 in *U.S. v. Winstar*.[43] Despite this decision, the Justice Department continued fighting tooth and nail to avoid paying compensation to most of the injured savings and loans. In December 1997, Judge Smith again lambasted the government for its shady legal tactics: "Because the dollars at stake appear to be so large, the government has raised legal and factual arguments that have little or no basis in law, fact or logic."[44]

Congress has at various times enacted legislation purportedly to curb the injustices of sovereign immunity. Congress enacted the Federal Tort Claims Act (FTCA) in 1946 to permit lawsuits against the federal government. However, Congress specifically exempted 13 different classes of tort claims from government liability.[45] Citizens are not permitted to sue the federal government for "any claim arising out of assault, battery, false imprisonment, false arrest, malicious prosecution, abuse of process, libel, slander, misrepresentation, deceit, or interference with contract rights."[46] In effect, the FTCA covered only "accidental" wrongs or abuses or injuries that were inflicted by government agencies or agents on citizens. If some government agent actually intended to shaft or oppress a private citizen, then the citizen is almost certainly out of luck.

The futility of this "remedy" was made stark in the 1987 Supreme Court decision in the case of James Stanley, an army sergeant who volunteered in the late 1950s for a program supposedly testing protective clothing. The Army covertly drugged Stanley and many other soldiers with LSD to study the drug's effects. As Martin Schwartz noted in the *New York Law Journal*, "As a result of his exposure to LSD Stanley suffered from hallucinations, periods of incoherence and memory loss and, on occasion, engaged in violence against his wife and children. He was not informed of the administration of LSD until 1975."[47] The Supreme Court, by a five-to-four margin, rejected Stanley's claims against the government. Solicitor General Charles Fried hailed the Court's ruling as a triumph of "justice according to law."[48] Justice O'Connor dissented: "In my view, conduct of the type alleged in this case is so far beyond the bounds of human decency that as a matter of law it simply cannot be considered a part of the military mission."[49] Justice Brennan also dissented: "The Government of the United States treated thousands of its citizens as though they were laboratory animals, dosing them with this dangerous drug without their consent."[50] (This Supreme Court decision came at a time when the federal government was leading a crusade to make America "drug free"—except for drugs government covertly administered to people.)

In 1971, in *Bivens v. Six Unknown Agents of the Federal Bureau of Narcotics,* the Supreme Court ruled for the first time that individual federal employees could be sued for civil damages for violating citizens' rights.[51] Webster Bivens was an innocent Cleveland man who was roughed up, handcuffed, and dragged out of his house in front of his wife and children after an illegal search. In *Bivens,* the Court declared that the "very essence of civil liberty certainly consists in the right of every individual to claim the protection of the laws, whenever he receives an injury."[52] However, subsequent court decisions made it practically impossible for any citizen to gain a *Bivens*-type victory in court. In the first 17 years after the Supreme Court decision, 12,000 Americans filed *Bivens* suits against federal employees; only 30 of the "cases resulted in judgments on behalf of plaintiffs . . . and only four judgments have actually been paid by the individual federal defendants."[53] And in recent years, it is even more difficult to win in court on a *Bivens* action. As law professor Sandra Bandes noted in 1995, "Less than twenty-five years later, in the wake of [subsequent Supreme Court decisions], there is little left of the *Bivens* principle."[54] The fact that the Supreme Court has effectively gutted the *Bivens* remedy indicates either that the justices had a completely wrongheaded notion of civil liberty in 1971—or perhaps that federal agents no longer violate citizens' rights.

The essence of sovereign immunity is that "the king can do no wrong." But as Professor Jeremy Travis noted, "The oldest purported rationale for the immunity of the sovereign . . . is a perversion of its historical intendment, which was that the king was privileged to do no wrong."[55] As one English lawyer explained in the wake of James II's fall, "When a king . . . does wrong, he thereby ceases to be king. . . . God and the law are above the king."[56] But, in the contemporary Statist interpretation, a phrase intended to prevent kings from injuring subjects becomes a license for government abuses of the citizenry.

Sovereign immunity creates a two-tier society: those above the law and those below it; those whom the law fails to bind and those whom the law fails to protect. Sovereign immunity presumes that the more evils government officials are permitted to commit, the more good they will achieve. Sovereign immunity presumes that in order to protect people, government must be permitted to destroy them: to crash into their cars, to break into their homes and businesses, and to drug them at its convenience. Although doctrines of immunity might be carved out by legislators and judges when considering cases involving accidental injuries, such exemptions soon metastasize into a license to intentionally inflict harm. The fact that government can recklessly endanger people's lives with little or no financial responsibility for the resulting deaths means that the further government control extends, the more citizens will be killed or injured.

The doctrine of "sovereign immunity" illustrates how power corrupts. Unless government officials already felt far superior to private citizens, they would not have the audacity to claim a right to injure them without compensation. That some government agents are punished on rare occasion merely shows that the power of contemporary governments is not absolute. Even tyrants occasionally find it in their interest to sacrifice one of their underlings to placate public wrath.

MODERN POLITICAL SLAVERY

In 1977, East Germany ransomed hundreds of its leading intellectuals and artists to West Germany, partly because it did not wish to endure public criticism by its own citizens during an International Rights Conference.[57] In spite of the human sale, there was no general revulsion against the East German government in the international community. The East German regime was considered by many social scientists to have more legitimacy than the West German government, because of its more expansive social welfare system and its grandiose paternalist pretensions. (Romania engaged in similar sales during the 1980s with its Jewish and ethnic-German subjects.) How many of its citizens does a government have to sell before it loses legitimacy? How many of its subjects does a government have to sell "on the world market" before all subjects of that government are recognized as essentially slaves?

During the 1980-88 Iraq-Iran war, the Iranian government used thousands of children to clear minefields for its precious tanks. Children were rounded up, given small silver keys to assure them that they would quickly enter Paradise, chained together, and sent to clear minefields in front of Iranian tanks.[58] Older draftees were used in human wave attacks explicitly designed to exhaust the ammunition of Iraqi defenders.[59] If the government possesses the right to throw children into a minefield for the convenience of its military operations, then are not all children slaves of the political rulers?

Consider the experience of the U.S. citizens during the Vietnam War. Some American politicians had laudable intentions at the start of the U.S. involvement in Vietnam, seeking to prevent the people of South Vietnam from falling under communist tyranny. But conscription effectively gave politicians unlimited power over the lives of millions of young American males. Had it not been for the military draft—and perennial government lies—presidents Johnson and Nixon and the U.S. Congress could not have squandered the lives of tens of thousands of Americans in the jungles and rice paddies of Vietnam. Defense Secretary Robert McNamara described Vietnam as a "social scientists' war"[60]—and apparently, the professors had a right to deceive the students and send them to their deaths. In his 1995 book, which largely exculpated himself for responsibility for the disaster in Vietnam, McNamara announced: "Underlying many of these errors [in how the U.S. conducted the war] lay our failure to organize the top echelons of the executive branch to deal effectively with the extraordinarily complex range of political and military issues . . . associated with the application of military force under substantial constraints over a long period of time."[61] But, as army major and Gulf War veteran H. R. McMaster, author of the 1997 book *Dereliction of Duty,* argued, "This [failed war strategy] was not due just to overconfidence, not due just to arrogance, this was due to deliberate deception of the American public and Congress based on the president's short-term political goals."[62] McMaster also observed, "The Great Society, the dominant political determinant of Johnson's military strategy, had nothing to do with the war itself."[63] McNamara, in a 1995 interview, justified not being honest with both Congress and the American people regarding the winnability of the war: "I was a servant of our president. He appointed me; he was elected by the people. My obligation to our people was to do what their elected representative wanted."[64] McNamara also insisted that citizens must obey:

"Where you're asked to follow instructions by an elected representative of your government, follow them . . . I believe that we all have an obligation to serve our government or take the penalty, take a jail sentence, if we violate the law."[65] Apparently, no amount of government lies can reduce the citizens' obligation to follow government orders.

It was politically cheaper to send tens of thousands of young people to die in vain than to risk being called soft on communism. According to a December 21, 1970, entry in the diary of Nixon White House chief of staff H. R. Haldeman,

> K [Henry Kissinger, Nixon's national security adviser] came in and the discussion covered some of the general thinking about Vietnam and the [president's] big peace plan for next year, which K later told me he does not favor. He thinks that any pullout next year would be a serious mistake because the adverse reaction to it could set in well before the '72 elections. He favors instead a continued winding down and then a pullout right at the fall of '72 so that if any bad results follow they will be too late to affect the election."[66]

When Haldeman's diary was published posthumously in 1996, Kissinger hotly denied making such comments. The peace treaty was signed in early 1973; South Vietnam was conquered two years later when the North Vietnamese government ignored the treaty and sent its army directly into Saigon.

Politicians frittered away the lives of American pilots in order to make political statements to the North Vietnamese government and the American people. As retired air force colonel and Vietnam veteran Samuel Dickens bitterly complained:

> [McNamara] would not let our forces bomb North Vietnamese airfields for fear we would kill Soviet or Chinese advisers. Enemy aircraft could only be attacked once airborne. We were prohibited from bombing fuel storage tanks at Haiphong for fear of damaging Soviet ships in the harbor. . . . Surface-to-air-missiles (SAMs) could not be destroyed in transit . . . and were not targeted for destruction until they were mounted on their launching rails, this for fear we would kill Soviet or Chinese advisers accompanying the shipments.[67]

This illustrates how political slavery differs from economic slavery: few private slaveowners would have cast off their prized possessions in the same cavalier way that some politicians disposed of the lives of citizens.

In some jurisdictions, politicians appear to have granted police de facto unlimited power over citizens. Despite the scandal of the Mollen Commission report, the New York Police Department dismissed only 8 officers for brutality in the following three years—including two who were dismissed after they were convicted for unjustifiably killing private citizens. A 1997 *New York Times* editorial noted that "wrongful arrests, strip-searches and even beatings can be triggered by talking back to an officer, asking for a badge number or merely inquiring why."[68] After NYPD detectives savagely beat Manuel Villa (who was innocent of any crime) during an interrogation, handcuffing him, pinning him to the floor, and punching him more than 50 times—resulting in hemorrhaging in both of his eyes, seizures, severe bruises, and permanent injuries—the police department concluded the detectives used excessive force, and docked them 20 vacation days as the penalty.[69] Police who decide to bludgeon someone who does not kowtow to them routinely charge them with either resisting arrest, disorderly contempt, or obstruction of government administration—charges which, as the *Times* noted, are later dropped—after the person has spent the night in jail or in a holding pen.[70] Only one officer out of 38,000 New York City cops has been dismissed as the result of complaints to the Civilian Complaint Review Board.[71] A 1998 Human Rights Watch report observed, "Police officers engage in unjustified shootings, severe beatings, fatal chokings, and unnecessarily rough physical treatment in cities throughout the United States, while their police superiors, city officials, and even the Justice Department fail to act decisively to restrain or penalize such acts or even to record the full magnitude of the problem."[72]

Taxation is another area in which politicians' power is often boundless. John Locke based his political philosophy on each person's ownership of himself and right to the fruits of his labor. Currently, the fact that someone is born or works in America provides politicians with a right to confiscate the lion's share of that person's income. The Sixteenth Amendment to the Constitution effectively gave Congress unlimited power to tax, since it authorized taxes on income without limit. In 1943 the Supreme Court declared that "an income tax deduction is a matter of legislative grace."[73] This statement, quoted hundreds of times in subsequent federal court decisions, confirms that Congress can seize any citizen's income simply by legislative decree. Nor does due process provide effective limits on politicians' power to commandeer property. In 1994, the Supreme Court upheld retroactive taxation, ruling that "tax legislation is not a promise, and a taxpayer has no vested right in the Internal Revenue Code."[74] Tax law implicitly presumes that the taxpayer is always wrong in any dispute with the government. Tax courts and federal courts bend over backwards to give the IRS the benefit of the doubt; the IRS often introduces no evidence whatsoever but merely asserts that a taxpayer had XXX dollars of unreported income and therefore owes XXX dollars in taxes, penalties, and interest.

Trade policy also illustrates how politicians perceive no limits to their legitimate power. Congresswoman Helen Bentley, who displayed her subtle trade philosophy in 1987 by sledgehammering a Japanese TV on the steps of the Capitol, bewailed in 1994: "Under the new GATT [General Agreement on Tariffs and Trade], Congress will have [only] limited power over trade. . . . We cannot allow this to happen."[75] Rep. Joseph Gaydos of Pennsylvania, chairman of the House steel caucus, declared in 1988, "We're not going to allow domestic companies, if we can help it, to buy [steel] overseas."[76] Politicians talk as if they have the right to dispose of the dollars of any American company or citizen that needs to buy an imported product. Rep. Charlie Rose of North Carolina demanded to know in 1985: "Who has the right to send shirts into my district in my stores that sell for $18, $20, that cost $4 to make in Hong Kong when it costs over twice as much to make that shirt in American textiles?"[77] Rep. Rose apparently believed that he should have direct power over what items are sold at what price in North Carolina stores. For politicians to allocate market share is to treat consumers like serfs who can be freely traded by their lords.

Most proposed restrictive trade legislation is based on the idea that because someone is a congressman, he should have a right to impose punitive taxes or prohibitions on what 270 million American citizens are allowed to buy and own. Because 90,000 people in eastern Ohio voted for some individual as the lesser of two evils on a rainy November day, that individual somehow automatically acquires the right to try to impose a 40 percent oil import fee, embargo all imports from some disfavored nation, or ban all peanut butter imports. Currently, congressmen have arbitrary power to restrict Americans' freedom to buy from and sell to 96 percent of the world's population. What gives one person a right to arbitrarily and forcibly reduce another person's standard of living? Should election into office automatically give a person the right to dictate the food other people eat, the clothes they wear, and the cars they drive?

Firearms prohibitions also illustrate politicians' pursuit of absolute power. New York City, Washington, Chicago, and other large cities effectively ban any citizen from owning a pistol, even in their own homes for their own protection. Sen. John Chafee of Rhode Island proposed a bill to require government confiscation of almost all of the 60-plus million privately owned handguns in the nation.[78] Rep. Major Owens of New York proposed the "Public Health and Safety Act of 1997" to ban all private citizens from owning handguns or ammunition.[79] Supreme Court justice John Paul Stevens, in a 1995 dissent, declared, "In my judgment, Congress' power to regulate commerce in firearms includes the power to prohibit possession of guns at any location because of their potentially harmful use."[80]

Government officials have invoked federal firearms laws to justify attacking any group that might resist federal power. After the 1993 Waco debacle, the

Treasury Department issued a report on its actions against the Branch Davidians; an appendix to that report laid out the rationale for the ATF assault:

> In a larger sense, the raid fit within an historic, well-established and well-defended government interest in prohibiting and breaking up all organized groups that sought to arm or fortify themselves. . . . From its earliest formation, the federal government has actively suppressed any effort by disgruntled or rebellious citizens to coalesce into an armed group, however small the group, petty its complaint, or grandiose its ambition.[81]

The mere possibility of resistance from any group, however "petty its complaint," is sufficient to justify government crushing them.

Robert Cottrol, a professor who has done pathbreaking work on the racist origins of gun control statutes, observed in 1997, "For most of human history . . . the individual has all too often been a helpless dependent of the State, dependent on the State's benevolence and indeed competence for his physical survival. The notion of a right to arms . . . takes the individual from servile dependency on the State for survival to the status of participating citizen capable of making intelligent choices in defense of one's life and ultimately one's freedom."[82] Jews for the Preservation of Firearms Ownership, a U.S. advocacy organization, warns that widespread private gun ownership is necessary to deter government tyranny or genocide.[83] The only way that firearms could be less vital to defending freedom now than in the past is if politicians were no longer dangerous. But there is no trigger guard on political ambition.

Some defenders of government authority do intellectual somersaults to dismiss the traditional right to self-defense. Professor Stephen Holmes wrote in 1995: "The social contract, according to Locke, *required* individuals to surrender the right of violent self-defense to the State."[84] Actually, Locke explicitly endorsed violent self-defense: "It is the brutal force the aggressor has used, that gives his adversary a right to take away his life, and destroy him if he pleases. . . . I may kill a thief that sets on me in the highway. . . . "[85] According to the FBI, 5 million Americans were the victims of violent attacks—assaults, rapes and attempted rapes, and murders—in 1995. To assume that none of those 5 million had the right of "violent self-defense" is to entitle every predator to successfully carry out his crime. John Lott, a fellow at the University of Chicago Law School, concluded in his 1998 book, *More Guns, Less Crime: Understanding Crime and Gun Control Laws,* that the rising numbers of Americans authorized to carry concealed weapons is reducing crime; Lott observed that if all states "had adopted right-to-carry concealed-handgun provisions in 1992, about 1,500 murders and 4,000 rapes would have been avoided."[86]

Political writers of the seventeenth and eighteenth centuries clearly recognized that unlimited government power meant slavery. Locke wrote, "Nobody can desire to have me in his Absolute Power, unless it be to compel me by force to that which is against the Right of my Freedom, i.e., make me a slave."[87] John Trenchard and Thomas Gordon, writing in 1721, declared, "Liberty is, to live upon one's own terms; slavery is, to live at the mere mercy of another."[88] William Pitt declared that if Americans bowed to the Stamp Act, they would "voluntarily . . . submit to be slaves."[89] The second Continental Congress, when it issued the "Declaration of the Causes and Necessity of Taking Up Arms" in 1775, declared, "We have counted the cost of this contest, and find nothing so dreadful as voluntary slavery."[90] James Madison described "people who submit to . . . laws made neither by themselves nor by authority derived from them" as slaves.[91] Historian John Phillip Reid wrote, "The word 'slavery' did outstanding service during the revolutionary controversy, not only because it summarized so many political, legal and constitutional ideas and was charged with such content. It was also of value because it permitted a writer to say so much about liberty."[92]

Slavery is not a question of political intent. Consider the cases in the previous discussion of sovereign immunity. If politicians and government employees were explicitly allowed by legislators to maliciously commit the same acts that they now commit "accidentally," government employees would clearly be a master class. But in court, the intent to maliciously injure or damage is extremely difficult to prove, especially since government officials and government agencies routinely receive so many procedural advantages over private citizens.

The greater the State's legal superiority over the citizen, the closer the citizen is to a slave. Modern political slavery means politicians having absolute power over citizens—power to transform individual citizens into fodder for their rulers' social, economic, and military schemes, into disposable building blocks for their rulers' fame and glory. The question of whether people are essentially political slaves does not turn on how often government agents beat them, but on whether government agents possess the prerogatives and immunities to inflict such harm. The measure of slavery is the extent of the slaveowner's power, not the number of lash marks on the slave's back. Slavery is not an all-or-nothing condition. There are different gradations of slavery, as there are different gradations of freedom. The fact that Americans do not wear shackles 24 hours a day does not prove that they are free citizens with inviolable rights. Political slavery is revealed at those moments when the paths of the citizen and the State cross, and the citizen suddenly becomes aware of his complete legal insignificance.

Given the vast power that politicians exercise and claim over private citizens, how could subjects not be considered in some sense slaves? Philosophers have sought to reason out this quandary for centuries. Benedict de Spinoza, writing in 1670, after declaring that citizens must waive all their rights to the government, asked, "Will it perhaps seem to someone that by this principle we are making men slaves?" Spinoza observed,

> Action in obedience to orders does take away freedom in a certain sense, but it does not, therefore, make a man a slave, all depends on the object of the action. If the object of the action be the good of the State, and not the good of the agent, the latter is a slave and does himself no good: but in a State or kingdom where the weal of the whole people, and not that of the ruler, is the supreme law, obedience to sovereign power does not make a man a slave, of no use to himself, but a subject. . . . A slave is one who is bound to obey his masters' orders, though they are given solely in the master's interest . . . a subject obeys the orders of the sovereign power, given for the common interest, wherein he is included.[93]

In essence, the only thing that prevents the citizen with no inviolable rights from being a slave to his government is wishful thinking—the delusion that the government is repressing, plundering, and punishing the citizen for the citizen's own good, not for the good of the government. The only thing necessary to convert slaves to freemen is to fine-tune political rhetoric.

ORDER BY
AGREEMENTS OR BY IRON FISTS

"To obey the King who is God's lieutenant, is the same as to obey God . . . we shall have no peace till we have absolute obedience," warned Hobbes.[94] Many contemporary Statists share Hobbes's assumption that near-total control is the only way to avoid near-certain destruction—that without a policeman, a bureaucrat, and a politician watching over their every move, citizens would beat their wives, starve their children, poison their customers, and blow up city hall. Supposedly, it is only the restraining hand of government that prevents the total dissolution of civilization, and the more power the restraining hand possesses, the safer civilization becomes.

Before addressing the question of sovereignty, we must ask: How much power does government actually need to maintain order? And can politicians be trusted to rightly and intelligently impose order on other citizens?

How much subjugation is necessary to preserve civil peace? At what point does force and threat of force subvert order? French philosopher Pierre Bayle wrote, "It is not tolerance, it is intolerance that causes disorder."[95] Bayle wrote at a time when many monarchs felt obliged to violently suppress religious nonconformity, a practice that drenched Europe in blood during the seventeenth century. Bayle's epigram is as true for social and economic behavior as it is for religious beliefs. Government-imposed social and economic edicts and orthodoxies are, in many cases, as disruptive today as government-imposed religious orthodoxies were several centuries ago. Many laws and government programs stem from politicians' intolerance of people living as they choose.

Most government interventions are not a question of achieving or safeguarding order, but of forcibly changing people's behavior for political profit. Before assessing government's role in preserving order, we must first recognize the extent of government-caused chaos.

Rent control, which currently exists in New York City and over a hundred other American cities, epitomizes how political solutions incite private conflicts. The rental market in New York City is marked by much lower vacancy rates, far more animosity and legal battles, and far more fraud (both by tenants and landlords) than exists in most other American cities.[96] A 1997 study by a pro-subsidy group, the National Low Income Housing Coalition, claimed that more people in New York were unable to afford their apartments than in any other state in the country.[97] Because politicians forcibly imposed a system designed to sacrifice owners to renters, the entire housing market has gone to hell, with the lowest rate of construction of new apartment housing of any American city. As professor and Manhattan Institute fellow Peter Salins observed, "The city has strangled its housing market in a web of regulation unmatched in any other large municipality."[98] New York currently has a two-tier market: a favored minority with rents below the market price, and a majority with rents significantly higher than they otherwise would have been, thanks to the politically created shortage. Rent control provides the largest benefits to those who need aid least: middle- and upper-class long-term renters.

When it comes to economic policy, the phrase "mindless intervention" is often redundant. "Political order" sows chaos in American agriculture. G. Edward Schuh, the chairman of the agricultural economics department at the University of Minnesota, observed, "Ultimately it is the instability of government policy and government intervention that cause the instability in commodity markets."[99] Private citizens, dealing with each other, reach agreements that balance crop supply and demand for most crops at market-clearing prices. Politicians, on the other hand, perennially disrupt the markets of a handful of subsidized products to give windfalls to their favorites. Federal dairy policy was notorious for decades for producing inflated prices and mountains of rotting surpluses. In 1997, secret tapes were made public in which President Nixon explained in 1971 how his administration made policy: "We've given them [the dairy industry] the 85 percent of parity thing. . . . We're going all out, all out. . . . [Treasury Secretary John Connally] knows them well, and he's used to shaking them down, and maybe he can shake them for a little more [illegal campaign contributions]."[100] Federal controls are profoundly disruptive for crops like peanuts; every few years, a drought hits the peanut-growing areas, and the supply restrictions, combined with draconian import quotas, guarantee that domestic peanut prices skyrocket far higher than they otherwise would have.[101]

Government sometimes sacrifices order to maximize revenue. Federal Highway Administration traffic-safety engineers Samuel Tignor and Davey Warren concluded in a 1990 study that most speed zones were "posted 15 m.p.h. below the maximum safe speed; that, on average, speed limits are set too low to be accepted as reasonable by most drivers, and that the posted speeds make violators out of motorists who drive reasonably and safely."[102] Politicians profit from unnecessarily low speed limits because of the increase in the number of drivers eligible for speeding tickets. Accidents and traffic jams result from police's fixation on ticketing drivers who pose no threat to public safety.[103]

In 1974, Congress imposed a 55 mile per hour speed limit on all interstate highways. In 1987, Congress permitted states to raise speed limits to 65 miles per hour on rural portions of interstates. Economists Charles Lave and Patrick Elias examined the consequence and concluded that allowing people "to drive faster reallocates traffic from side roads to the safer interstate highways, and a higher speed limit permits highway patrols to shift manpower from speed enforcement to other safety activities." Lave and Elias concluded that "the fatality rate dropped by 3.4%-5.1% following the speed limit increase" in states with higher speed limits.[104] Higher speed limits are safer in part because they decrease the speed variance among drivers. In late 1995, Congress gave states full authority to set interstate speed limits, and, according to Lave, total fatalities further declined as a result.[105]

Government power does not guarantee order because political pressure often subverts efforts to protect the rights of innocent citizens. Public school systems are notorious for refusing to expel violent students, regardless of how many other students they injure. All 23 high school principals in Montgomery County, Maryland, signed a petition complaining that the school system refused to eject violent students who had assaulted teachers, committed arson, or thrown other students through plate glass windows; the system even refused to eject a group of students who assaulted one passive victim so badly that he suffered permanent brain damage, as the *Washington Post* reported. Principals recommended over a thousand students for expulsion in 1996, but the school system authorized expelling only 3 students.[106] Private schools are almost universally recognized for providing far better order—as well as safety for both students and teachers—than do public schools. Students who severely or perennially misbehave in private schools are expelled, even though most private schools depend heavily on tuition payments from students' parents, and thus lack an incentive to be overly punitive. This illustrates how voluntary association can produce order more reliably than the police power of the State.

Politically imposed "order" is also often far more expensive than most Americans realize. Gary Bauer, chief of the Family Research Council (labeled "Washington's most formidable conservative" by the *Weekly Standard*)[107] denounced in 1997 a proposal to legalize marijuana as "anarchy."[108] Law enforcement agents prevented "anarchy" by arresting 624,000 people for marijuana violations in the United States in 1996, according to the FBI.[109] However, there is far more violence involving marijuana in the United States than there is in Holland, where marijuana is legal. Almost 19,000 state and local law enforcement officials are assigned to the drug war on a full-time basis[110]— at a time when most big cities have record numbers of unsolved murders on the books. Florida State University economists Bruce Benson and David Rasmussen concluded that one consequence of shifting resources to the drug war is that "violent and property criminals are not caught until they have committed a relatively large number of crimes, if they are caught at all."[111]

Politicians appear far more anxious to control citizens than to protect them. The number of people sentenced to prison for drug offenses in 1996 significantly exceeded the number of people sentenced for violent crimes.[112] Three-quarters of people sentenced to state prisons on drug charges have no history of criminal violence.[113] Under federal sentencing guidelines, a person is entitled to the same five-year prison ticket for possession of five grams of crack that he would receive for embezzling between $10 million and $20 million from a bank, or for using a threat of violence to extort between $2.5 million and $5 million from someone, or for kidnapping someone and seriously injuring the victim.[114] The disparity between mandatory sentences for drug possession and the lenient sentences for assorted heinous acts vivifies how breaking the commandments of the Paternalist State is a worse crime than terrorizing, maiming, and robbing private citizens.[115]

The more laws, the more uncertainty that permeates private lives, and the more difficult it becomes for citizens to order their own affairs. Between 1981 and 1993, over 9,000 subsections of the federal tax code were amended.[116] In June 1997, the congressionally appointed National Commission on Reform of the IRS reported that the tax code's complexity placed a severe burden on citizens who sought to honestly fulfill their legal obligations. Congress responded a few weeks later with the Taxpayer Relief Act of 1997, which contained 36 retroactive changes, 114 changes effective August 5, 1997, 69 changes effective January 1, 1998, 5 changes effective thereafter, and 285 new sections and 824 Internal Revenue Code amendments.[117] IRS officials can take five, seven, or more years to write the regulations to implement a new tax law—and Congress routinely changes the law before new regulations are promulgated. Much of current tax law is provisional, either waiting to be revised according to the last tax bill passed, or already targeted for change in the next tax bill. The changes to the tax code illustrate politicians' tendency to manipulate private lives for their own political advantage—to secure the latest campaign contributions. By continually yanking back and forth the demarcation between legal and illegal behavior, Congress assures that many citizens will be left in tax purgatory. (Humorist Dave Barry wrote that tax laws "are constantly changing as our elected representatives seek new ways to ensure that whatever tax advice we receive is incorrect.")[118]

Governments can safeguard order by maintaining a legal system that allows citizens a forum to peacefully resolve the inevitable disputes that arise in any society. But, the more criminal penalties politicians create, the more government neglects its traditional role as umpire and referee for private disputes. Thanks to the explosion in drug prosecutions, it is far more difficult and expensive for average citizens or businessmen to get their civil cases heard in courts. As Yale professor Steven Duke and Albert Gross noted in *America's Longest War,* "In many court systems, the right to trial by jury has all but disappeared, especially in civil cases. Indeed, since criminal cases have priority, many courts are unable to reach their civil dockets at all."[119]

Politicians have also sacrificed order to laws that subvert individual and corporate responsibility. The tort system in the United States has become the laughingstock of the world. The proliferation of nonsense tort suits— everyone seems to have a right to dump hot coffee on their lap and then sue the coffee shop—epitomizes the collapse of rationality in injury suits. By promulgating the notion that no one can be held responsible for their own behavior, the legal system multiplies the number of irresponsible individuals. By subverting tort law, government makes it far more difficult and expensive for people to gain speedy recompense for injuries imposed by other citizens or businesses.

For politicians, a "good order" maximizes government's opportunities to penalize and mulct the citizenry. For citizens, a "good order" minimizes conflict between citizens and coercion by government. A good order is any system of sustaining human interaction that satisfies participants without violating other people's rights. The danger of disorder lies in the violation of rights of citizens, not in the diminishing of the prestige of government officials. "Government order" is sometimes little more than politicians rampaging through other people's lives, searching for photo opportunities and votes. It is a choice between an order that allows each person to, as far as possible, go his own way and make his own decisions and contracts, and an order designed to keep people in their place—to hold some people down for other people's benefit.

The greater the unnecessary submission, the greater the deadweight loss of any system of order—the loss of new discoveries, personal satisfaction, and other benefits. The more that a system of order is based on political commands, the more people's lives are forcibly limited by the wisdom or judgment of the people at the top. History is replete with civilizations that sank into the mire because of excessive obedience.

Disobedience to foolish laws is not "disorder" in a negative sense. For example, many sub-Saharan African governments until recently imposed grain monopolies and paid ruinous low prices to farmers, leading to catastrophic food shortages; the more people evaded such government controls, the fewer people starved.

The further politicians extend their attempts to control personal behavior, the more likely that government will subvert true order; the proliferation of penalties creates its own chaos. People have been schooled to vastly exaggerate government's role in generating order. Bertrand de Jouvenel observed:

> Men have found it hard to believe that the immense benefits conferred by the exercise of authority derived from small modifications introduced under its aegis into their own behaviors; they have not viewed the social benefits conferred as the fruit of their own adjustments, but supposed that these benefits rained down from on high thanks to the mediation of the rulers.[120]

Most of the ordering that occurs in everyday life is not the result of political edicts; instead, it is the result of traditional, evolved compromises between people. The vast majority of benefits of contemporary economic and social order are the result of the habits, consideration, courtesy and responsibility of individuals treating each other with respect and fair play. Left to their own devices, most people will usually find ways to reach mutually beneficial agreements or accommodations with others. It is not a question of natural harmony, but of people recognizing their own self-interest in following general rules of conduct and respecting other people's rights.

There is no known social or political system in which conflict disappears. In a good system, people will be aware of the general rules that will decide any conflict, thereby minimizing the number of conflicts. The more that an "order" is the result of voluntary agreements among citizens, the stronger the self-interest of all parties involved to perpetuate that order. And the fact that the order results from voluntarily agreements gives it a stamp of legitimacy that no number of official edicts can provide. If the rules upon which order derives are considered fair and are generally accepted, the government will need minimal power to help enforce those rules, since there will be few violators. It is only when government seeks to enforce rules that are not generally accepted by the populace that it will need vast power to impose its dictates.

WHAT DO CITIZENS OWE THE STATE?

Before considering the issue of sovereignty itself, we will briefly examine what citizens owe the State. Every extension of the Welfare State results, directly or indirectly, in politicians and bureaucrats feeling entitled to demand more obedience from people. What does the government do for citizens that citizens could not do as well or better for themselves? This is the first question that must be answered before gauging how much obedience people might owe a government. Insofar as government busies itself doing things worse for the citizen than he could have done himself, the citizen is justified in viewing government as a nuisance, a predator, and a poacher.

In the vast majority of cases, governments possess only what they seize from private citizens. How can citizens owe government when practically everything the government has it first took from them? The fact that people are forced to pay for certain goods and services indirectly, via taxation, cannot create an ineradicable debt to the people who seized their paychecks. People who are government dependents have a debt not so much to the government itself, but to their fellow citizens who earn the money the government seizes and then renders to them.

Some Statists insist that the citizen should be grateful for such government services as mail delivery. Yet, the government is more vigilant in attacking private threats to its monopoly over first-class mail than in expediting the mail. First-class mail service is significantly slower than it was 30 years ago, in part because of an intentional policy of reducing next-day mail deliveries adopted in the early 1990s.[121] In areas in which the Postal Service competes directly with private companies, such as overnight express mail and parcel post, the government has been shamed. Citizens cannot be indebted to the government for mail service when it is federal restrictions that prohibit a far wider array of private services.[122]

Others will insist that people are indebted to government for public schools. But the parents of most children pay more in taxes than government spends educating their kids. Besides, since schools have lately shown more talent for brain numbing than for education, how can that create a debt? (A February 1998 international comparison revealed that, despite sharp increases in government spending for education in the last 15 years, American high school students scored at the rock bottom in math and science compared to students in other countries.[123]) Without quasi-monopoly public schools, a far more extensive network of private schools would be available—schools that would be responsive to parents' desire for their children to learn. The rapid spread of the home-schooling movement (whose students consistently outscore public school students on standardized tests) vivifies how parents can do better on their own.[124]

Nor are citizens indebted to government for providing goods such as roads. Despite heavy federal taxes levied on gas buyers, politicians are allowing more and more of the interstate highway system to deteriorate to Third World road conditions. Roughly three-fifths of all interstate highways are in poor or mediocre condition, according to the Federal Highway Administration.[125] Drivers pay over $140 billion in gas taxes each year, but only about half of that money is actually spent on maintaining and building roads; the rest is spent on other political wish lists.[126] Roads are a good example of the contempt that government shows for citizens in the services it forces them to finance. As road expert and author Gabriel Roth observed, "U.S. roads suffer from the typical command economy characteristics: poor maintenance, congestion, and insensitivity to consumer needs."[127] Because traffic jams cost government employees nothing, government agencies scorn sound traffic control measures. A 1997 federally funded study found that traffic congestion in the Washington, D.C., area imposes the equivalent of an $860 annual tax for each person living in the region.[128] (Will Rogers suggested long ago: "The way to deal with traffic congestion is to have business provide the roads and government the cars."[129])

Do citizens owe a vast debt to the State for keeping the peace? Many big city police departments have effectively abandoned serious efforts to solve robberies and other cases of nonlethal violence; the District of Columbia police, for instance, make arrests in less than 10 percent of burglaries and robberies.[130] (But the D.C. police did set a record in 1997 for arrests of citizens detected drinking alcohol on their front porches.[131]) Insofar as government prohibits people from owning or carrying weapons for self-defense—it is scant consolation that a policeman arrives after the crime to chalk off the body. There are more than twice as many private security guards as uniformed policemen in the United States. More citizens than ever before are living in gated communities or relying on home alarm systems. Private citizens use guns to defend themselves over 2 million times a year, according to Florida State University criminologist Gary Kleck.[132]

Citizens are indebted to the government for national defense. The defense against, and resistance to, the Soviet Union during the Cold War was one of the stellar achievements of the U.S. government in this century. And, considering the number of rogue governments currently around the world, citizens will continue to need protection from foreign enemies for the foreseeable future. However, if a government busies itself making enemies, and then praises itself for pledging to protect citizens from the enemies it made, there is less than a transcendent benefit. The United States currently has troops stationed in a hundred different nations.[133]

Yet, while the U.S. government rarely misses a chance to intrude into foreign disputes, the Clinton administration refuses to erect any type of defense against incoming missiles—even though 25 nations, some of them intensely hostile to the United States, now possess ballistic missiles.[134]

What have politicians given to the citizenry that they did not originally take from them? This is the bottom line that must permeate all thinking about the "goods" that government "provides" to the citizenry. In reality, in the vast majority of cases, politicians give back far less in value than they took. The more the government takes, the less the citizen owes to the government.

THE LIMITS OF LEGITIMACY

Many politicians apparently believe there is no limit to their right to control and punish other people's behavior. Consider recent legislation on youth smoking. In North Carolina, youths under the age of 18 who try to buy cigarettes now face a $1000 fine and 30 days of community service. In 1997, Idaho enacted a law sentencing young people caught smoking to up to six months in a juvenile detention center.[135] (Six months is a longer sentence than first-time juvenile robbers or muggers would get in many places in the United States.) Other politicians, such as the mayor of Friendship Heights, Maryland, have proposed bans on outdoor smoking within city limits, fearing that permitting outdoor smoking could set a bad example for young children.[136]

Government control means political control, which means politically mandated punishments. What gives some people the right to punish other people? The question of sovereignty is the question of the rightful limits of government power. Every intervention is premised on the State's right to punish those who do not obey. No self-respecting nation would sign a treaty with another nation that gave the latter carte blanche to invade its borders, seize its assets, and humiliate its citizens. Yet some political thinkers imply that there is such a "treaty" between the citizen and the State—a "social contract" in which both the rights of the State and the duties of the citizen are unlimited. Governments now possess far more power over people than could be justified by any social contract—unless people are presumed to have implicitly contracted for their own destruction.

Bureacratic aggression is necessary to compel citizens to submit to political dictates. What legitimizes this aggression? How do some people acquire the right to dictate how others must live?

The current extent of government power is partly the result of doctrines of sovereignty developed before the birth of the United States. French thinker Jean Bodin defined sovereignty in 1576 as "supreme power over citizens and subjects, unrestrained by law"[137]—sovereignty was "the most high, absolute, and perpetual power over the citizens and subjects of a commonweal."[138] Sir Robert Filmer, in his 1648 essay "The Power of Kings," declared, "We see the principal point of sovereign majesty and absolute power to consist principally in giving laws unto the subjects without their consent."[139] Hobbes declared that "there can happen no breach of Covenant on the part of the Sovereign; and consequently none of his subjects, by any pretence of forfeiture, can be freed from his subjection."[140] Hobbes offered "Suicide Pact Sovereignty": to recognize a government's existence is to automatically concede the government's right to destroy everything in its domain.

Sovereignty is a word practically devised to induce delusions of grandeur and nullify political common sense. As historian William Dunning observed, "The definition and development of sovereignty, as a concept of political science, had been almost entirely the work of those who, like Bodin and Hobbes, were defending absolute monarchy. By the liberalizing school of Locke and Montesquieu the idea of sovereignty was evaded as unnecessary in theory and dangerous in practice—a mortal foe to liberty."[141] Bertrand de Jouvenel wrote, "The theory of popular sovereignty, as Rousseau left it, offers rather striking parallels to the medieval theory of divine sovereignty."[142]

In contrast, American colonists focused on the limits to rightful government power. As a 1768 Massachusetts Circular letter declared, "In all free states the Constitution is fixed, and as the supreme legislative derives its power and authority from the Constitution, it cannot overleap the bound of it, without destroying the foundation; that the Constitution ascertains and limits both sovereignty and allegiance."[143] Supreme Court justice James Wilson commented in 1793 that "to the Constitution of the United States the term sovereignty is totally unknown."[144] Chief Justice John Jay declared in the same case that "at the Revolution, the sovereignty devolved on the people; and they are truly the sovereigns of the country, but they are sovereigns without subjects . . . and have none to govern but themselves; the citizens of America are equal as fellow citizens, and as joint tenants in the sovereignty."[145] Unfortunately, sometime between 1793 and Chief Justice Marshall's proclamation of government immunity in 1821, sovereignty was conveyed from the people at large to a lockbox in some federal office. The more time that has passed since the ratification of the Constitution, the more rights people are presumed to have surrendered, and the fewer binding obligations government appears to have.

Archaic notions of sovereignty occasionally pop up in court decisions, such as the 1973 federal appeals court ruling on the Nixon White House tapes: "Sovereignty remains at all times with the people and they do not forfeit through elections the right to have the law construed against and applied to every citizen."[146] But this notion of sovereignty has little or no influence on the vast majority of judges or government agencies. As the sovereign immunity cases show, sovereignty is now routinely invoked to justify violating people's rights, rather than to curb government power. Insofar as sovereignty is something separate from and above the people, the greater the sovereignty, the greater the oppression.

James Wilson, writing in 1774, declared that citizens' "obedience is founded on the protection derived from government: for protection and allegiance are the reciprocal bonds, which connect the prince and his subjects."[147] And conversely, the less protection a person needs, the less obedience he owes. Once it is recognized that the life of the average citizen is not simply one long episode of the "perils of Pauline," then the government's right to take over his life vanishes.

The fact that a government unjustly and unnecessarily decreases people's freedom cannot miraculously increase the people's obligation to their rulers— any more than slaves would owe more obedience after their master built a higher fence around their quarters. Government never deserves the benefit of the doubt when it is using force against the citizenry—any more than one gives the benefit of the doubt to someone who pushes another person in front of an oncoming subway train.

The rightful extent of sovereignty cannot extend beyond the necessary extent of the government. Unnecessary compulsion means wrongful control. There can be no just exercise of sovereign power beyond defending the rights of citizens. If there are no injuries, there can be no justified punishments. Nor is government justified in punishing someone for, in the government's opinion, not acting properly in its own self-interest, since politicians do not own citizens.

The duty to respect the rights of other citizens and to honor one's promises is above and separate from the duty to obey the government. Regardless of whether any government has earned a citizen's obedience, no citizen has a right to steal his neighbor's cow. Civil society depends not on people obeying government but on how people treat each other on a day-to-day basis.

THE RIGHT OF RESISTANCE

Throughout history, governments have occasionally overstepped the bounds of their legitimate power. What should be done when government betrays its promises?

John Locke's *Two Treatises of Government* was written in the 1680s, when Englishmen were chafing under the growing tyranny of the Stuart kings. Locke wrote, "That *subjects,* or *foreigners* attempting by force on the properties of any people, may be *resisted* with force, is agreed on all hands. But that *magistrates* doing the same thing, may be *resisted*, hath of late been denied: as if those who had the greatest privileges and advantages by the law, had thereby a power to break those laws, by which alone they were set in a better place than their brethren. . . . "[148] Locke showed how the power of a ruler must not be placed on a higher moral plateau than that of any other potential criminal:

> Should a Robber break into my House, and with a Dagger at my Throat, make me seal Deeds to convey my Estate to him, would this give him any title? Just such a title by his Sword, has an unjust Conqueror, who force some into Submission. The injury and the Crime is equal, whether committed by the wearer of a Crown, or some petty villain. The title of the offender, and the number of his Followers make no difference in the Offence, unless it be to aggravate it.[149]

No concept of sovereignty can justify extending government power beyond the bounds of political right.

It is absurd to expect governments to descend gradually, step-by-step into barbarism—as if there was a train schedule to political hell and people could get off at any stop along the way. People forget how quickly the forms of political power can turn civilized behavior into unrestrained pillage and mass violence. Most people strolling the streets of German towns in the late 1920s would never have suspected that, within a few years, the government would launch a policy of genocide. Similarly, someone visiting Moscow in 1913 or Pnomh Penh in 1969 would likely not have seen the barbarity just around the bend. Politicians rarely give formal warnings of how they intend to abuse the power they acquire.

Once ideas and principles consecrating unlimited power are accepted, it is only a matter of time until that power is used in ways that shock those who acquiesced to its expansion. As Sen. John Taylor observed, "Tyranny in form is the first step towards tyranny in substance."[150]

Discussions of political right are mere parlor talk unless citizens have a right to resist tyranny. The New Hampshire Bill of Rights, written in 1784, declared: "The doctrine of nonresistance against arbitrary power, and oppression, is absurd, slavish, and destructive of the good and happiness of mankind."[151] Yet much of the political and academic establishment shudders at even considering the right to resist. Some friends of government have the same horrified reaction today against mentions of such resistance that some Christians had against heresy in the sixteenth century. At a 1997 American Society of Criminology conference, one professor argued that among signs of "hate group ideology" were "discussion of the Bill of Rights, especially the Second Amendment or the Federalist Papers," "discussion of military oppression, in the U.S. or elsewhere," and "discussion of the Framers of our Government."[152] Professor Joyce Lee Malcolm, who attended the conference session, observed that the professor "was anxious to have militia classified as hate groups because then federal legislation on hate groups would apply to them."[153] Malcolm was surprised that the proposed expansive definition of hate groups elicited no objections from the scholarly audience.

Any discussion about the right of resistance must begin by recognizing the extent to which government is already the aggressor. As Locke wrote, "There is only one thing which gathers people for sedition, and that is oppression."[154]

History is replete with tyrannical governments that deserved to be destroyed by their victims. At what point can we say that a government has placed itself in a state of war with the citizenry? By what standard or measure can people know when they have a right to forcibly resist illegitimate power? In Bosnia, in Rwanda, or in other areas where mass murders have recently occurred, the citizen obviously may use as much deadly force as necessary to prevent himself and his family from being slaughtered by rampaging government forces or by murderous private mobs acting with government sanction. And in the United States, blacks clearly had a right to peacefully resist segregationist restrictions in the 1950s and 1960s and had a right to violently resist attacks on them by sheriffs and private citizens.[155] Unfortunately, there is no lucid standard for a citizen to use to know precisely when he must cease obeying. And, regrettably, much of the political establishment, like the Anglican Church in the 1680s, will preach the duty of passive resistance all the way to the entrance of the political slaughterhouse.

Nonviolent action is, in most cases, a far more effective means to curb power than is violent resistance.[156] Killing an oppressive politician usually only generates more sympathy and sanctity for the engine of coercion that he commanded. Many attempted or successful assassinations became pretexts to redouble oppression. The first necessity for peaceful reform is for people to realize how much power they have to bring government to its knees. At the height of the Vietnam War protests, fewer than 5 percent of the American public were actively protesting the war, yet those protests psychologically paralyzed the Johnson administration and played a role in the Nixon administration's paranoia of dissent that led to Watergate.

Intelligent, targeted, decisive protests can puncture the sense of legitimacy that cossets both Leviathan's commanders and employees. And once the government's aura of legitimacy is shattered, the "transaction costs" of tyranny skyrocket. Each person who understands his rights and liberties is another barrier against the wrongful expansion of government power. As de la Boetie observed, "It is the inhabitants themselves who permit, or, rather, bring about their own subjection, since by ceasing to submit they would put an end to their servitude."[157]

In the final analysis, the government's sovereignty is limited by the character strength of its subjects. If the citizens have self-respect and courage—and the means to defend their rights—government abuses will be curbed. Historian Thomas Babington Macaulay, writing in 1832, asserted that the English in the 1500s were "beyond all doubt, a free people. They had not, indeed, the outward show of freedom; but they had the reality. They had not a good constitution . . . but they had that . . . which, without any constitution, keeps rulers in awe— force, and the spirit to use it."[158]

There may come a time when peaceful resistance becomes futile. As Locke wrote, "Men can never be secure from tyranny, if there be no means to escape it, till they are perfectly under it."[159] In the same way that any citizen has a right to defend himself against a mugger or a murderer, so citizens in general have a right to defend themselves against violent political predators.

As Joyce Lee Malcolm showed in her 1994 book, *To Keep and Bear Arms: The Origins of an Anglo-American Right,* the Second Amendment was based on recognition that people had the right to possess the means to resist government tyranny.[160] Discussions on federal gun control measures often focus on whether specific guns serve "sporting purposes." However, if the Founding Fathers had added a clause to the Second Amendment specifying that people will be "permitted to own guns for hunting rabbits"—the Constitution would have been overwhelmingly rejected as Americans would have been alerted to how far politicians intended to stretch their power.

The citizen's right to resist government is directly proportionate to the amount of force government uses against the citizen. If the government generally respects the rights of the citizen, then the citizen should give the government the benefit of the doubt when it occasionally errs or exceeds its legitimate power. When abuses do occur, citizens are obliged to seek every peaceful remedy before forcibly resisting. Regardless of whether Americans consider the federal government illegitimate, attacks that kill innocent people are never justified. The 1995 bombing of the Oklahoma City federal building was inexcusable and the people who carried out the bombing deserve death sentences. Citizens have as little right to kill innocent government agents as government agents have to kill peaceful private citizens.

If resistance becomes necessary, citizens must not seek merely to anoint a new oppressor. The goal of resistance should not be a nominal change in rulers, but a fundamental rollback of coercive power—a defanging of the State.

If Statists fear popular resistance to government, then perhaps government should violate fewer rights. The militia movement in this country became highly active only after the federal killings at Ruby Ridge, Idaho and Waco, Texas. The fact that no federal officials have been held legally responsible for the deaths at Ruby Ridge and Waco made many people presume, not surprisingly, that the government was out of control and a dire threat to their rights and safety.

CONCLUSION

The more commands government issues, the less presumption of obedience it deserves. "Sovereignty" is little more than some people's prerogative to exploit and coerce other people with power consecrated by political hocus-pocus. The doctrine of "sovereignty" often does nothing more than provide a respectable gloss for some people's lust to control other people's behaviors, or to seize the fruits of other people's labor. When politicians or bureaucrats invoke sovereignty, they are almost always trying to seize more power than they deserve. By invoking a "right" of the State, they disparage the rights of the citizens.

The State does not have rights in itself, but only possesses such powers as are necessary to safeguard and uphold the rights of the citizens. The more power that sovereignty supposedly confers upon government, the more the doctrine of sovereignty defeats the entire purpose for which government was created. Sovereignty must be limited by the superior rights of real individuals over abstract political entities.

The more often a government invokes sovereign immunity, the less fit it is to hold power over citizens. By stretching their power beyond reasonable bounds, politicians destroy the legitimacy of the State. It is the power-hungry politicians who subvert the State, not the citizens who rise up against political oppression.

If one opposes slavery, then one must oppose any concept of sovereignty that is unlimited. As Hannah Arendt observed, "If men wish to be free, it is precisely sovereignty they must renounce."[161] The challenge of our times is to limit the power of government so that citizens can reclaim sovereignty over their own lives.

SEVEN

PATERNALISM VERSUS THE BLESSINGS OF LIBERTY

Now the country suffered from its laws, as it had hitherto suffered from its vices.

—Tacitus[1]

LIBERTY WILL BE VIGOROUSLY DEFENDED only where its value is clearly understood. Freedom must be judged by what it prevents as well as by what it produces. We will examine the claims of contemporary paternalism and conclude with a few observations on the benefits of liberty.

DOMESTIC TRANQUILITY VIA RECIPROCAL PLUNDER

Throughout the twentieth century, politicians have shrugged off the danger of concentrated power by asserting that it is inconceivable that government would abuse the citizenry. In 1928, Stalin, justifying new grain requisitions that would eventually depopulate the Ukraine, declared: "Are the peasants capable of bearing this burden? They undoubtedly are . . . because this additional tax is being levied . . . under Soviet conditions, when exploitation of the peasants by the Socialist State is out of the question."[2] Sympathy for the high ideals proclaimed by the Soviet government muffled Western criticisms of Stalin's terror-famine.

Modern political thought often presumes that politicians are virtuous and then asks what form of government best permits citizens to benefit from the goodness of their rulers. Since government is the supreme protector, the idea of protection from the protector is a logical absurdity, like the notion that a Christian would need protection from God.

Paternalism "deals people a better hand" by taking away more of their cards every year. The word "paternalism" originally referred to a father's power over his children; contemporary paternalism means government treating citizens like children. The more paternalist policies are adopted, the further the citizenry is infantilized. As children grow older, they acquire more autonomy and are less restricted by their parents' rules and values. In contrast, the Welfare State piles rule upon rule, edict upon edict—and the only certainty is that citizens will be presumed less competent next year than they were last year.

But to label most contemporary interventionist policies "paternalist" is dubious at best. Law professor H. L. A. Hart defined paternalism as "the protection of people against themselves."[3] According to Donald VanDeVeer, author of *Paternalistic Intervention,* "A paternalistic act is one in which one party *interferes* with another for the sake of the other's own good."[4] Few government laws and regulations are intended to protect a person from himself; instead, most mulct some people's freedom or rights for other people's benefit.

The essence of the Welfare State is to control some people for other people's benefits, and to allow politicians to decree who wins and loses. Contemporary Statists measure progress by the rising number of bodies that other people are forced to carry through life. The Welfare State inevitably becomes the Political Warfare State. Economist Aaron Director formulated a law of public income redistribution: "Any government will redistribute resources to benefit whatever group can take command of its machinery."[5] Each group of citizens must devote more time and effort to protect the tattered remnants of their paychecks, or to sink their teeth into other people's paychecks. "Reciprocal plunder," in Bastiat's phrase, becomes the soul of political life.[6]

"To enjoy a good reputation, give publicly and steal privately," advised nineteenth-century humorist Josh Billings.[7] The credibility of modern paternalism rests on the immaculate handout—on pretending that the coercion necessary to finance the handouts has no adverse effect on anyone. And since the misery engendered by seizing of the paychecks doesn't count, any happiness of the handout recipient vindicates the entire system. The scant attention paid to tax burdens and the enormous attention paid to government handouts accounts for much of the good reputation of government.

Politicians deserve no credit for seizing and bestowing what they did not produce. Modern governments have mastered the pretensions of benevolence. Politicians rarely explicitly ask for more power. Instead, they talk of all the good deeds they could do if only this or that law was enacted. President Franklin

Roosevelt declared in 1936, "Better the occasional faults of a government that lives in a spirit of charity than the consistent omissions of a government frozen in the ice of its own indifference."[8] Government generosity is the great fiction of contemporary moral thinking. The only way government can "live in a spirit of charity" is by presuming that taxes are mere conveyances or accounting adjustments between two ledgers on the same page. Governments cannot be generous because governments have no right to dispose of the goods private citizens produce, any more than one person can be generous by giving a homeless person a bogus title to his neighbor's house.[9]

The Paternalist State advances by multiplying its levers over private behavior. These levers are enforced by government penalties: the more the government claims to protect citizens, the more it must punish them. Yet, at some point, the sheer number of threats government makes purportedly to protect the citizen destroys the citizen's "domestic tranquility." This is the vicious cycle of paternalism: the more power the government acquires to control people, the more the citizen naturally fears the government.

A 1996 Gallup Poll revealed that 50 percent of Americans believe that "the federal government has become so large and powerful that it poses an immediate threat to the rights and freedoms of ordinary citizens."[10] The poll found that roughly equal percentages of liberals, conservatives, and centrists perceive government as a dire threat. The citizen's fear of the Paternalist State is understandable, since bureaucracies in action are often not calibrated to notice nuances such as guilt or innocence. The more the government tries to take care of every aspect of the citizens' lives, the more hours citizens spend fearing that they will be pounced on by some bureaucrat needing to fill his quota of violators.

According to Montesquieu: "As virtue is necessary in a republic . . . so fear is necessary in a despotic government."[11] Montesquieu identified fear as "the spring" of despotism—the principle upon which it was based and the key to its survival. The fact that scores of millions of Americans now fear government does not by itself prove that the government is despotic. Yet, some government agencies openly strive to intimidate citizens. Sen. William Roth of Delaware, chairman of the Senate Finance Committee, denounced the IRS in 1997 as "an agency in which a subculture of fear and intimidation has been allowed to flourish."[12] At a minimum, that contemporary benevolence increasingly mocks its victims.

GOVERNMENT-ISSUE HAPPINESS

Paternalism delivers happiness via an iron fist. Individuals *pursue* happiness, governments *impose* happiness. Paternalism presumes that people will be happier doing what they are told than what they choose. Kant declared, "Nobody may compel me to be happy in his own way. Paternalism is the greatest despotism imaginable."[13] Kant based his ethics on the moral value of each person as an end in himself; paternalism necessarily sees people as plug-ins to fulfill political visions and bureaucratic timetables. Once paternalism gets rolling, individual preferences cannot be allowed to delay the official advance of progress. Whole-wheat bread is more nutritious than white bread, but would that justify government food police going into each recalcitrant's home, seizing his white bread, and jamming wheat bread down his throat? The damage done by forcing even healthy morsels down someone's throat—in all but extreme cases, in which the beneficiary is on the verge of death—will almost certainly exceed the nutritional benefits of the food itself.

There is more to life than the avoidance of toe stubs, more to life than not paying the bill for your own doctors' visit, more to life than being certified as handout-worthy by the nearest social worker. The Welfare State concept of happiness is based on forced flight from the realities of everyday life— happiness via minimal expectations, submission, and gratitude for whatever benefits one's master deigns to provide—a happiness that is practically the mirror image of human dignity.

Paternalists perceive happiness as deriving solely from a final result—higher average intake of broccoli, more motorcyclists wearing helmets, etc. The happiness of the Welfare State is necessarily based on passivity—on people queuing up to accept their officially allocated fair share of government benefits or opportunities or parking spaces. But happiness is also the result of an active pursuit of one's own values. Often the difference in results between what a person achieves or produces and what the paternalist believes the person should have achieved is simply a result of a difference in values between that person and the paternalist.

The people must be subdued before they can be saved. The prerequisite of paternalism is breaking resistance to the government's good deeds. The Welfare State offers the social-economic equivalent of happiness through political conquest and obedience—happiness via surrendering the keys to one's own life to one's political overlords.

Paternalists often denigrate the people government must save. The hatred of the Soviet elite for the peasantry begot the savagery of forced collectivization.[14] The disdain that many congressmen and local politicians felt towards blacks and Puerto Ricans in the 1950s and 1960s permeated urban renewal programs that bulldozed thousands of neighborhoods and displaced over a million Americans (most of whom received little or no compensation for their losses).[15] The wider the difference between the government planner's and the private citizen's concept of happiness, the greater the contempt of the planner for the private citizen, and the more easily the planner justifies brutality.

The Welfare State seeks to permit citizens to have as much happiness as their rulers think they deserve. British socialist Harold Laski declared, "The real meaning of democratic government is the equal weighing of individual claims to happiness by social institutions [i.e., government]."[16] Some paternalists, rather than seeking to increase the sum total of happiness, aim instead to change control over its distribution. But, in the same way that socialists err by conceiving of the distribution of goods as a process completely divorced from their production,[17] so paternalist thinking on the distribution of happiness is hopelessly flawed. Socialist economic thinking routinely ignores economic incentives; similarly, paternalist thinking scorns the importance of not stifling each person's peaceful efforts to achieve happiness in their own lives.

Contemporary Welfare States are based on the nationalization of the pursuit of happiness. This nationalization presumes that everyone will have more happiness if they surrender their own goals and efforts to those of political masterminds—that a person's happiness will rise in proportion as he loses control over his own life.

Faith in the Welfare State depends on faith in the pursuit of happiness through political action. What are the precise mechanisms by which government is to deliver happiness to the citizenry? At what precise moment does government action produce happiness in citizens? When an edict is promulgated, when the enforcement agents arrive, or perhaps when a violator is handcuffed? How does putting more people in jail make people happier, since most popular songs (except for Elvis Presley's *Jail House Rock*) do not portray incarceration as a joyful condition? Should we presume that people are made happy by being punished, or that they become happy by watching government punish other people? Are people supposed to be gratified by the sight of government agents swarming all over the land—by the rising number of government agents carrying weapons, by the rising number of government lawsuits against citizens on the slightest pretext? By the rising number of confiscations of the property of innocent owners? By the fact that EPA agents who find a wet spot on a parcel of land can try to ruin the landowner's life?[18]

The Welfare State seeks to maximize happiness by maximizing submission, as if confinement were the key to contentment. Are modern citizens supposed to be made happy *because* government coerces and restricts them in so many ways—or *despite* that? Is the subordination of the individual to the State supposed to make the individual happy, or supposed to make the State happy?

How can we distinguish between coercion to punish and subjugate people and coercion to make them happy? Is the difference due to the preambles of statutes that impose new penalties, or to the organization charts among the enforcing agencies? The sanction of coercion matters less to most citizens than how often and harshly they are coerced.

Welfare State happiness must be a type of happiness that can be mass-produced by inefficient government bureaucracies—a "close enough for government work" happiness, a happiness that exists because government agency annual reports claim to have fulfilled their goals. Paternalists envision a happiness that can be weighed, spliced, and distributed in little packages. Paternalism presumes that individuals are "welfare receptacles" waiting to be filled to the correct level by their superiors.[19]

The goal of the welfare State is not to make people happy, as people themselves understand their own happiness; instead, it is to make them "happy" in ways their superiors think they should be happy. According to philosopher Hans Kelsen, "happiness in an objective-collective sense" means "the satisfaction of certain needs, recognized by the social authority, as needs worthy of being satisfied, such as the need to be fed, clothed, housed, and the like."[20] Thus, the "social authorities" (i.e., government employees) are granted sweeping discretion to decree which desires or aspirations of private citizens are "worthy of being satisfied." (Chinese communist leaders defended their regime during the Cultural Revolution with the slogan: "A bowl of rice is all the people need.")[21]

How do citizens benefit from Big Government? It does not make citizens better off when politicians confiscate more of their paychecks to provide lavish early retirement benefits to government workers. It does not make citizens better off when politicians confiscate their paychecks so that two policemen can ride in each patrol car (to placate police unions and reduce on-the-beat loneliness). It does not make citizens better off when Customs Service inspectors are paid "night-pay" bonuses for the time they spend on vacation.[22] It does not make citizens better off when generous welfare payments dissuade recipients from getting a job. So many of the uses that government makes of tax revenues are either completely unrelated or directly contrary to citizens' well being.

The more often government acts, the further it intrudes. The more expansive the government, the more the values of government employees will preempt the values of private citizens in daily life. The spontaniety of private life is increasingly squeezed out by the structures of the civil service.

The more power government acquires over people, the more that the system of governance rests upon a blind faith in the rulers' benevolence. Paternalism presumes that government will serve the people even better than the people could have served themselves. And why? Because government knows best. But, this old saw means nothing more than "government employees know best." And why do they know best? Because they work for the government.

A 1995 national survey conducted for the federally funded Council for Excellence in Government found that 72 percent of respondents agreed that "the federal government creates more problems than it solves," while only 21 percent believed that it solves more problems than it creates.[23] The poll asked over a thousand Americans: "Do government programs and policies do more to help or more to hinder your family in trying to achieve the American dream?" Fifty-six percent of the respondents said "hinder" and only 31 percent said "help."[24] The same poll surveyed people receiving government handouts; as *New Democrat* magazine summarized the results, "47 percent of those whose everyday existence relies to some extent on government aid replied that this same government was a hindrance to their achieving the American dream."[25] (Perhaps paternalists would invoke the poll as proof of the unfitness of average citizens to judge their own happiness.)

THE MISSING FULCRUM

The limits of coercion are the limits of paternalism. How much good can one person forcibly impose on another person? Faith in the benevolence of Big Government presumes that there is some political genius who can turn coercion from a scourge into a blessing.

President Clinton, in a 1997 San Francisco political fund raising speech, declared that Americans must decide whether they are "for the people who try to drive you down or the people who try to lift you up. . . . [W]hether you believe the purpose of politics is to elevate the human spirit . . . or whether you believe the purpose of it is to carve out power."[26] How exactly is government supposed to lift people up? Before the government can coddle the citizenry, it must first financially plunder them. Government action always starts by restraining citizens, punishing them, or seizing their earnings—and after that, government can get around to lifting people up.

The more coercion government uses in the name of progress, the more oppressed people will feel. Government is often like a lifeguard who begins a rescue by standing on the shoulders of an allegedly drowning person. The bigger the government, the heavier the political dead weight on the average citizen. In order to lift himself, the citizen must also lift "his fair share" of the entire government. The heavier the weight of government, the greater the odds against self-help. The more power government acquires to rescue people, the more people will sink under the weight of supporting government itself. The expansion of government by itself, of itself, becomes an increasingly negative factor in the life of the individual. Citizens are left to glean the remnants of their own lives from what the politicians have not already seized.

Some philosophers, such as Harvard's Michael Sandel, advocate that government pursue a policy of "soulcraft" to lift the people's values. This is a theological view of the role of government—as if politicians were demigods, if not full-feathered gods. Sandel favors American character renewal by means such as citizen-activist "sprawlbuster" campaigns banning new Wal-Mart stores and local lobbying campaigns by low-income people to get more government spending in their neighborhoods.[27] Sandel praised as "cultivating virtue" a 1940 Supreme Court ruling that upheld compelling all government school children to stand and repeat the Pledge of Allegiance each morning; Sandel regretted the Court's reversal on that issue in 1943.[28] But this is, at best, "virtue" based on uniformity, blind obedience, and suspension of one's critical faculties. Virtue depends on more than maximizing the number of times subjects salute their rulers.

Why presume that politicians and bureaucrats would give the average citizen higher values than he would find on the street? Politicians typically begin seeking to raise people's souls by emptying their wallets. What sort of soulcraft can we expect from politicians who cannot even be honest about the budgets they draft, the taxes they impose, or the wars they send citizens to fight? Without a prying, preening government, the average citizen will not be as honest as Lyndon Johnson, as trusting as Richard Nixon, as chaste as Bill Clinton, and as conscientious as congressmen who vote for bills they have not read.

Boosting government power is often portrayed as the key to progress. President Johnson's chief economic adviser, Walter Heller, declared: "The Less Developed Countries are caught in a vicious circle of poverty. To break out of this circle, apart from foreign aid, calls for vigorous taxation and government development programs; on this point expert opinion is nearing a consensus."[29] However, the confiscatory taxation subsequently adopted throughout Africa and many parts of Asia and Latin America, as well as the deluge of foreign aid, allowed kleptocracies to wreck the lives and living standards of their victims.[30] The Congressional Budget Office concluded in 1997: "In many cases, foreign aid has sustained governments in their pursuit of economically counterproductive political and economic policies."[31] Former deputy assistant Treasury secretary Bruce Bartlett observed, "Insofar as foreign aid is linked to poverty, the adoption of bad economic policies may even encourage additional flows of aid."[32] Professor George Ayittey, a native of Ghana, wrote in 1998 that "in many African countries, 'government' as Westerners understand it simply does not exist. These nations are ruled by gangsters, crooks and scoundrels who use the instruments of state to enrich themselves, their cronies and their tribesmen. The dispensation of patronage to buy political support has resulted in soaring government expenditures and bloated bureaucracies."[33] Sidya Toure, the prime minister of Guinea, complained that, when he took office in 1996, "This country had 50,000 civil servants who were consuming 51% of the nation's wealth."[34]

Coercion is a far better tool for repressing people than for raising them. Political force will always be administered by people in authority—from above. There is no fulcrum by which government coercion can be transformed into an uplifting force on the people coerced.

How much wiser or smarter must one person be to justify vesting in him coercive power over others? At what point do differentials in intelligence outweigh the advantages of letting people live their own lives, follow their own values, and make their own choices? With children and people who indisputably are mentally incompetent, parents and guardians can be justified in exercising jurisdiction over their actions and decisions. But the difference between government employees and private citizens cannot be equated to the difference between adults and seven-year-olds, or between the sane and the psychotic. Any purported difference in intelligence between government employees and private citizens is likely less than the perennial inefficiency of government.[35] ("The king's cheese goes half away in pairings" was an English proverb 300 years.)

Some paternalists stress the benevolent characters of government policymakers. But the effect of most politicians' good intentions ceases when a law is signed and the television cameras are turned off. The speeches that a politician makes on the floor of the House of Representatives do not hover like an angel over all subsequent enforcement of the law. The good intentions are transient, while the rise in coercion is permanent. Most congressmen's apathy about performing oversight belies their "good intentions"; they are far more interested in being credited with doing good than with actually doing it.

The Welfare State makes government employees the czars of the risks in everyone else's life. The Consumer Product Safety Commission (CPSC), for example, is currently examining standards for bicycle reflectors that aid drivers in noticing bicyclists at night. But bicycle reflectors are only a second-best solution. CPSC official Ron Medford told the *Washington Post*, "We don't think people should ride at night, though we realize people do."[36] "Fear of the dark" thus appears to be the epitome of bureaucratic wisdom: risk avoidance is the supreme good, even if it means no one riding their bike at night. According to CPSC chairman Ann Brown, "There can be stupid consumers and they deserve to be protected as well as smart consumers."[37] (Ms. Brown made this comment during an interview in which she called for a federal mandate for "fire-safe cigarettes" because some people fall asleep while smoking in bed.) Unfortunately, the federal government seeks to impose village-idiot standards on products that any American can buy. Brown even takes her job to include the role of movie censor, publicly complaining in 1994 about the movies *Lassie* and *Richie Rich* because they featured scenes showing children in all-terrain vehicles in chase scenes. The CPSC general counsel announced that the agency may seek jurisdiction over movies as "consumer products," which would give the agency a legal club to prohibit portrayals of any unsafe behavior.[38] Yet, despite the CPSC's benevolent image with the mainstream media, it has done far less to improve product safety than have the hundreds of private standards-setting organizations and the incentives in the legal code for companies not to kill customers. The United States benefits from hundreds of private organizations that set standards for consumer products. As former CPSC commissioner Carol Dawson observed, "All available evidence, including injury data and marketplace monitoring, indicate that non-government standards have an excellent record. They are often more stringent than federal regulations. . . . Compliance with non-government standards is usually very high—a feat achieved not through coercion but by the twin market forces of competitiveness and the threat of liability suits."[39] Paul Rubin, the agency's former chief economist, wrote in 1996 that "There is no reliable public evidence that any of the CPSC's policies has saved any lives."[40]

The more helpless citizens are presumed to be, the more sanctified government power becomes. Government agencies seek to persuade people to think of themselves as mental invalids. In 1993, the Federal Trade Commission ruled that the logos for smokeless tobacco painted on racing cars were illegal because the cars did not also have warning labels painted on them.[41] The FTC feared that people who relished watching races might get ideas about unsafe lifestyles from seeing snuff advertisements on the cars before and after the crashes. The FTC cracked down on Beck's Beer in 1998 for a television commercial that showed people on a boat holding beer bottles and "engaging in acts that pose a substantial risk of falling overboard and drowning;" commissioner Mozelle Thompson declared, "In my view, a reasonable young consumer could be deceived by not appreciating the danger involved in imitating such behavior."[42] Government agencies increase their power by persuading people that they cannot hope to resist sinister forces such as the Joe Camel cartoon advertisements.[43]

The arrogance bred by government power can be fatal. FDA Commissioner David Kessler declared in 1992, "If members of our society were empowered to make their own decisions . . . then the whole rationale for the agency (FDA) would cease to exist. . . . To argue that people ought to be able to choose their own risks, that government should not intervene . . . is to impose an unrealistic burden on people."[44] While some banned drugs do pose deadly risks, the FDA has likely done more harm than good. Stanford University professor Dale

Geringer observed, "In terms of lives, it's quite possible that the FDA bureau-cracy could be killing on the order of three to four times as many people as it saves."[45] According to Robert Goldberg of George Washington University, "By a conservative estimate, FDA delays in allowing U.S. marketing of drugs used safely and effectively elsewhere around the world have cost the lives of at least 200,000 Americans over the past 30 years."[46]

"The benevolent have a tendency to colonize, whether geographically or legally," observed law professor Arthur Allen Neff.[47] A. V. Dicey observed, "'Protection' . . . is tacitly transformed into guidance."[48] The Welfare State, in its daily operation, appears more devoted to controlling people than to benefiting them. Every extension of benefits is premised on an increase of controls—sometimes on the person to be benefited, sometimes on other people (taxpayers, businesses). In 1982, the federal government imposed price controls on hospitals and doctors treating Medicare patients; the result was an explosion in paperwork and a decrease in health care quality. In 1997, Congress decreed that no doctor could accept direct payments from any elderly patient without permission from the federal government. Robert Moffit, a former deputy assistant secretary at the Department of Health and Human Services, observed, "This assault on the doctor-patient relationship is deliberately designed to make private contracts with Medicare patients all but impossible."[49] The *Wall Street Journal* editorial-ized that the new provision "makes clear that seniors are being locked into a government-run system of one price and one choice for anything Medicare covers, even if they want to use their own money to buy privacy, convenience or more expert care."[50] Once politicians start giving a benefit, they entitle themselves to do anything they choose to "hold down the cost" of that benefit. The federal government in 1997 began paying hundreds of millions of dollars to the nation's teaching hospitals to curtail training programs—seeking to reduce future Medicare outlays by slashing the supply of doctors.[51]

The character traits necessary to capture political power are unrelated to those portending the benevolent use of that power, once acquired. This is a contradiction upon which all schemes to boost happiness via increased coercion run aground. The people in command of government policies will likely enjoy power as much as, if not more than, they enjoy benevolence. To presume that government is inherently benevolent is like presuming that anyone who wants power over you is automatically your friend. Thus, whichever politician demands the most power is the most kind hearted. And the more power the government acquires, the more benevolent government employees will become . . . which is why prison guards are renowned as the highest specimens of humanity.

There is no virtue in forcibly taking care of people who otherwise would have taken care of themselves. Many paternalist policies are the equivalent of

Boy Scouts kidnapping little old ladies and forcing them to cross streets so that the Scouts can fill their quota of good deeds. Some governments seem driven to the brink of insanity by the desire to run up statistics proving their benevolence. Montgomery County, Maryland, offers "grief counseling" to all victims of crime, including 11-year-old boys whose bicycles are stolen.[52] Federal subsidies for local adult midnight basketball programs became a progressive rallying cry in 1994, regardless that late-night hoop shooting skews the odds against arising the next morning to go to work. After the California Northridge earthquake in 1994, the Federal Emergency Management Agency blanketed thousands of residents with unsolicited checks of up to $3,450, simply because they lived in zip codes that reportedly had been hard hit. (Many of the lucky recipients had suffered little or no damage to their homes.)[53]

Government is far more effective at reducing incentives for people to help themselves than it is at actually helping them. The gap between the politicians' promises and the performance of the State is the maw into which the lives of more and more citizens are falling. The Comprehensive Employment and Training Act (CETA), which consumed over $40 billion between 1974 and 1983, produced "significant earnings losses for young men of all races and no significant effects for young women," according to the Urban Institute.[54] A Labor Department-financed study concluded in 1992 that the Job Training Partnership Act, CETA's successor, "actually reduced the earnings of male out-of-school youths."[55] Insofar as people are taught to expect government to provide them with opportunity, or with education, or with job skills, or with practically anything else, they will correspondingly decrease their own efforts to acquire such opportunities or skills, and the people who relied on political promises are left with no skills, shameful housing, and blighted lives.

POLITICAL ACCOUNTING
VERSUS GOOD GOVERNMENT

"Political language . . . is designed to make lies sound truthful and murder respectable, and to give an appearance of solidity to pure wind," observed George Orwell.[56] Professor Ruth Grant wrote that "hypocrisy and politics are inextricably connected on account of the peculiar character of political relationships."[57] Since government is coercion, then politics is largely the exercise of deception regarding the intended use of coercion.

The benevolence of government rarely transcends the venality of politics. Paternalism seeks to generate mass happiness by forcibly sacrificing as many people and groups as necessary to the Greater Good. And who defines the Greater Good? The same people who benefit from maximizing the sacrifices.

SIDEBAR: PROTECTIONISM AS PARADIGM OF PATERNALISM

Protectionism has long dominated the trade policy of most of the nations of the world. Trade paternalist policies helped divide the nation and cause the Civil War, were a primary cause of the Great Depression, and created a byzantine system of unearned privileges that last to our times. While "protection" was often endowed with transcendent virtues, in reality it consists of nothing more than political aggression against consumers for the benefit of favored industries. William Graham Sumner declared in 1884, "Congress passes taxes [on imports], as big as the conflicting interests will allow, and goes home, satisfied that it has saved the country. Taxes can do it all."[58] But, as Henry George quipped, "A discriminating pirate, who would confine his seizures to goods which might be produced in the country to which they were being carried, would be as beneficial to that country as a tariff."[59] Joseph Jones, in his 1934 book, *Tariff Retaliation*, noted, "Makers of American tariffs have legislated consistently without regard for our foreign trade, taking foreign markets for granted. . . . In 1930 the United States was clearly vulnerable and Congress did not recognize the fact."[60]

Trade barriers debilitate beneficiaries: those American industries that have been most protected have had among the slowest increases in productivity.[61] Every trade barrier undermines the productivity of capital and labor throughout the economy. A 1979 Treasury Department study estimated that trade barriers routinely cost American consumers eight to ten times as much as they benefit American producers.[62] A 1984 Federal Trade Commission study estimated that tariffs cost the American economy $81 for every $1 of adjustment costs saved.[63] Restrictions on clothing and textile imports cost consumers $1 for each 1 cent of increased earnings of American textile and clothing workers.[64] A U.S. International Trade Commission study concluded that abolishing restrictions on domestic shipping would save consumers $17 for each $1 of foregone profits of domestic shippers benefiting from the restrictions.[65]

Protectionism is a consummate example of paternalism because it unites know-nothing politicians, profoundly deceptive rhetoric, and a blind faith in coercive restrictions. Protectionist politicians throughout history have been seemingly incapable of seeing or reasoning past the immediate, direct effect of imposing a restriction; similarly, today's paternalist politicians seemingly refuse to consider anything other than the promised benefits of new restrictions.

The amount of power a politician can seize is often inversely related to the politician's honesty. If the politician openly tells people how much more coercive power he seeks and how he intends to use it, there will likely be strong opposition to the expansion of government. Politicians rarely wish to admit that they are pursuing a larger "market share" in the life of the average citizen. Because politicians and government officials often seek more power than they publicly admit, many, if not most, of their analyses of government policies are skewed. Politicians will always have an incentive to understate the cost of increasing their own power.

But if a politician camouflages his plans, then people may fail to resist the increased power until it is too late. This is the thumbnail history of Social Security, a program that illustrates the natural combination of paternalism with political fraud.[66] As the Brooking Institution's Martha Derthick observed, "In the mythic construction began in 1935 and elaborated thereafter on the basis of the payroll tax, Social Security was a vast enterprise of self-help in which government participation was almost incidental."[67] The Social Security Administration for decades told people that their Social Security taxes were being held for each citizen in individual accounts; in reality, as soon as the money came in, politicians found ways to spend it.[68] Social Security Commissioner Stanford Ross, after he announced his resignation, conceded in 1979 that "the mythology of Social Security contributed greatly to its success. . . . Strictly speaking, the system was never intended to return to individuals what they paid."[69] Ross said that Americans should forget the "myth" that Social Security is a pension plan and accept it as a tax on workers to provide for the "vulnerable of our society." But Sen. Patrick Moynihan of New York accurately characterized Social Security taxes as "outright thievery" from young working people.[70] American citizens now shoulder over $12 trillion in unfunded Social Security liabilities.[71] If the defenders of Social Security insist that the fraud was justified, the question arises: What future limits should exist on government's prerogative to deceive the people? If Social Security is an acceptable fraud, what would government have to do before it was considered to have gone too far? Social Security is a perfect symbol of political generosity: it robs scores of millions of young people, it halves the national savings rate and thereby sabotages investment and productivity increases,[72] and it maximizes bureaucratic and political control over people's fortunes. If the average worker had a dollar for every time a congressman lied about Social Security, his retirement would be safe. There is no "Honesty in Intervention Act" governing new laws or political action. Current taxpayers are still paying for the lies that politicians told to get reelected in 1936, 1938, 1940, *ad nauseam*. The fact that politicians replace old lies with new lies does not reduce the burden on citizens of laws that were enacted on false pretenses generations ago.

Paternalism will always be based on political accounting, which is practically the opposite of private accounting. Businesses prosper by reducing costs; politicians prosper by denying that costs exist. For politicians, it is more important that spending forecasts be popular than accurate. The more that politicians and bureaucrats underestimate the cost of their favored policies, the easier it becomes to hustle those policies to voters and other legislators. (Medicare—one of the largest expansions of government power since the New Deal—steamrolled through Congress in 1965 in part because of a spending forecast that made the expansion of handouts seem easily affordable; by 1990, however, Medicare was costing almost ten times more per year than the 1965 forecast had predicted it would cost).[73]

The political concept of waste is almost diametrically opposed to the economic concept of waste. In economics, if an activity produces something that other people value, it can be successful. In politics, if a program garners votes, campaign contributions, or power, it is successful. This is the black hole into which the benevolence of many government programs vanishes. Government programs are often effectively designed to waste money because politicians benefit from an inefficient, spendthrift program as much or more than they would benefit from an efficient, well-targeted program. Congressmen brag about the amount of federal money spent in their district, not about the lack of fraud in programs they champion.

Political accounting means that government leaders will be ignorant or misled or dishonest about the true cost of policies they impose. The General Accounting Office (GAO) released the first consolidated financial report on the federal government as a whole in early 1998. GAO found that "significant financial systems weaknesses, problems with fundamental record keeping, incomplete documentation, and weak internal controls . . . prevent the government from accurately reporting a large portion of its assets, liabilities, and costs."[74] GAO concluded that "amounts reported in the consolidated financial statements and related notes do not provide a reliable source of information for decision-making by the government or the public."[75] Sen. Fred Thompson of Tennessee declared, "We are spending almost $2 trillion a year and managing a $850 billion loan portfolio based on erroneous or non-existent information. It means basically that we don't know what the government's assets are, we don't know what the government's liabilities are, we don't know what it costs to run government."[76] After the audit was released, a senior Clinton administration official told the Associated Press, "This is an old closet that we haven't cleaned out in 200 years."[77] If politicians are going to have the closet cleaned out only once every couple centuries, maybe they have no right to control the house. A report that should have been proof of the political class's incompetence instead merely evokes another round of promises to "try harder next time."

Paternalism presumes that government agencies judiciously weigh costs and benefits before extending their power. However, many bureaucracies have little or no curiosity about the impact of agency actions on private citizens. The House Commerce Committee surveyed federal agencies and concluded in a 1997 report, "Where costs [of regulation to private companies] are addressed, they represent only the smallest and most insignificant portion of total costs . . . With little or no documentation on the costs of regulation, agencies have no basis to judge whether any possible benefits from a new regulation would outweigh the possible costs of the regulation."[78] Because government agencies do not have to pay for the costs they impose, they have no incentive to track the burdens. The Committee warned that "federal agencies may inadvertently be exposing our Nation to incalculable economic harms."[79] The only way such government ignorance could not be harmful is by presuming that government dictates are always superior to private decisions.

The value of liberty and personal independence is almost never factored into the calculus of paternalism. Social scientists, politicians, and bureaucrats consider the expected benefits of any proposed new rule and ignore the effect of its forcible imposition. Every government program, every intervention, every penalty carries a hidden cost of preemption. If the costs do not show up on the official government budget outlays, the costs do not officially exist.

Whatever increases political power will be considered a success by many politicians. If a policy increases the number of people beholden to their favor, then it is good as an end in itself. The ultimate conflict of interest that subverts paternalism is that government officials want power and citizens want freedom.

How much brighter would life be if politicians had not intruded into so many places on so many false pretexts? No one can precisely calculate the costs of paternalism and political control. No one can know the old-age provisions and annuities that were never created because of Social Security, the new types of health insurance and payment systems that never came into being because of federal tax and Medicare and Medicaid polices, the new systems of job training that did not arise because of scores of federal training programs, the types of communication systems that have been squelched or long delayed or crippled by the Federal Communications Commission, the revolutions in education that were thwarted or stillborn because of the quasi monopolies of the government schools, the types of innovative, peaceful methods of allocating land uses that would have developed without pervasive political zoning strangleholds. Trying to know what the social and economic landscape would have been like without pervasive government power is like trying to figure out what would have happened to a nation if it had not been invaded and ravaged by a foreign military power. No one can know precisely what could have developed if the government had not politically conquered area after area of private life. The only certainty is that the actual costs are far greater than the apparent costs, and far greater than what government admits.

THE VALUE OF LIBERTY

To better understand the value of liberty, we will consider the views of some contemporary skeptics of the value of individual freedom.

The remnants of contemporary freedom are often derided. A 1996 review in the *Nation* commented, "Today, 'freedom' is invoked mainly by proponents of lower taxes, the right to bear arms and a 'free market' offering the choice between Burger King and McDonald's."[80] Michael Lerner, the editor of *Tikkun,* asserted, "The freedom obtained through [market economies] increasingly feels empty, and people in fact are trapped and dominated by a subtler but equally coercive power, now operating by shaping their consent rather than by opposing it."[81] Some communitarians simply dismiss the value of contemporary freedom. According to Professor Amitai Etzioni, the 1995 president of the American Sociological Association, "Today, everybody's free to do anything, but it's not what they want. It's not liberating. It's not freedom."[82] (It would surprise many readers of the *Federal Register* to learn that they are "free to do anything.") Apparently, the question of whether a person is free turns on whether a college professor with a political agenda believes that existing choices convey a personal sense of "liberation." Because the professor scorns the lifestyle choices of the unwashed masses, he proclaims that the people are not "liberated" by their freedom, and thus lose nothing when government further subjugates them. (Etzioni favors government making freedom more meaningful by prohibiting private citizens from possessing firearms, requiring them to submit to urine tests, and letting government automatically seize and use their bodies after they die by allowing "organ harvesting" from any dead citizen who had not specifically prohibited such 'harvest.'")[83] For Etzioni, freedom means being part of a herd, free to do only those activities that have been precertified as virtuous or meaningful by the herd administrators. Etzioni believes that there is danger even in proclaiming the value of liberty in contemporary America: "To promote liberty in a society teetering on the edge of anarchy is like removing the police when rioting, arson and looting erupt."[84] Implying that Americans have too much freedom today makes as much sense as asserting that East Germans had too much freedom in the 1980s because every now and then someone managed to escape over the

Berlin Wall. Etzioni and other contemporary Statists appear obsessed with the areas of conduct that government does not currently control and oblivious to all the restrictions government already imposes. They are far more anxious about the potential abuses of liberty than about the actual abuses of government.

Similarly, Harvard's Michael Sandel laments, "The triumph of the voluntarist conception of freedom has coincided with a growing sense of disempowerment."[85] But is a "sense of disempowerment" a result of the meaninglessness of freedom, or is it a result of the loss of freedom in many areas of people's lives? The "voluntarist conception of freedom" has not triumphed in the lives of average Americans who find themselves more regulated, taxed, and punished than ever before. Some Statists sound as if all the power government possesses somehow does not exist or is irrelevant, as long as the government does not possess the power to advance their own pet project.

Practically the only "ideal" that Lerner and other Statists offer citizens is, "trust your rulers to impose more meaning into your life." Presumably, the more intolerant government becomes, the more meaningful life will be. But people do not need to be on their knees for their lives to have meaning. It may gratify the rulers when other people are compelled to follow their values, but their gratification is not synonymous with the quality of life for the common man.

Liberty is sometimes denounced for its role in fomenting inequality. According to Ronald Dworkin, a prominent legal philosopher, "A more equal society is a better society even if the citizens prefer more inequality."[86] Cornell political scientist Andrew Hacker declared, "Citizens should be given the blessings of equality whether they want them or not."[87]

Compulsory equalization policies are in effect a declaration of war against anyone who aspires to achieve above the average, as if personal excellence were an act of aggression against all the underachievers in a society. How many hostages should politicians be allowed to take in the name of equality?

Whenever individuals are allowed to choose, they will choose differently and inequality will result. As long as people are allowed to choose their occupation, spouses, living arrangements, and personal goals, individual incomes and happiness will vary. The only alternative to free choice in such matters is for government to impose uniform misery on everyone.

Inequality is no betrayal of liberty because people have no right to do as well as their neighbors. All people should have equal freedom to speak as they please, but listeners have no duty to equally appreciate their thoughts. All people have equal freedom to worship as they please, but are not entitled to equal solace from their deity; or equal chances of admission to heaven, regardless of their personal conduct. All people should be equally free to accept the work or contracts they choose, but their employers or contractors are not bound to equally value and reward their efforts.

Equalization is a punitive policy: the more equality government purports to impose, the more the entire political order is poisoned by the resulting arbitrary power. A 1998 *New York Times* survey of political and court battles over the equity of school financing within states observed that "there is no consistency in the decisions, no single standard has emerged by which to gauge how much equity is required, and how much has been achieved."[88] In Vermont, the court ruling that gave the state government control over local education spending and policies in the name of equality has deeply embittered much of the citizenry.[89]

It is fashionable to fret that stressing the value of liberty and individual rights somehow subverts community. Al Gore, writing in 1992 (shortly before he became vice president), declared, "The emphasis on the rights of the individual must be accompanied by a deeper understanding of the responsibilities to the community that every individual must accept if the community is to have an organizing principle at all."[90] But the same people who anoint themselves to assess responsibility are often the ones who benefit most from destroying freedom. The political class can continually proclaim new "responsibilities," and, regardless of whether government is respecting people's rights, can load onerous new duties on citizens. Citizens must act responsibly to deserve freedom: but this responsibility consists largely of not injuring other citizens, not in fulfilling politicians' ever-growing wish lists. The alternative is to make people's liberties rest on something so insecure as politician's shifting opinions about whether each person or group of persons "did their duty."[91]

In a similar vein, British prime minister Tony Blair declared in 1997, "I tell you, a decent society is not based on rights, it is based on duty—our duty to one another. To all should be given opportunity, from all responsibility demanded."[92] Blair presumes that politicians should have unlimited control over the distribution of opportunity. Politicians do not give people "opportunity": in reality, politicians are primarily giving some people the tattered remnants of other people's paychecks. And even though politicians are distributing other people's property, they still have the right to burden recipients. Politicians win on both sides of the bargain: they have two blank checks—one on how much they take, the other on how much they give.

The opportunities created by free citizens are worth far more than the favors doled out by paternalist regimes. The opportunities are limited only by the creativity, resolution, courage, and hard work of free citizens; the privileges of paternalist regimes are limited by the narrowness of bureaucrats' minds and politicians' self-interest, the amount of resources they confiscate to bankroll the privileges, and the dead loss resulting from funneling goods through government coffers.

Freedom is far more bountiful than political commands. Much of the debate over the value of liberty comes down to a dispute between the value of government action versus private initiative. Governments are far less productive than many people have been taught. Herbert Spencer wrote in 1884:

> It is not to the State that we owe the multitudinous useful inventions from the spade to the telephone; it is not the State which made possible extended navigation by a developed astronomy; it was not the State which made the discoveries in physics, chemistry, and the rest, which guide modern manufacturers; it was not the State which devised the machinery for producing fabrics of every kind, for transferring men and things from place to place, and for ministering in a thousand ways to our comforts. The world-wide transactions conducted in merchants' offices, the rush of traffic filling our streets, the retail distributing system which brings everything within easy reach and delivers the necessaries of life daily at our doors, are not of governmental origin. All these are the results of the spontaneous activities of citizens, separate or grouped.[93]

In the time since Spencer wrote, private ingenuity has produced automobiles, microwave ovens, televisions, refrigerators, indoor plumbing, well-insulated homes, low-priced clothing, affordable food,[94] stunning breakthroughs in health care technology and pharmacology, telecommunications, computers, ad infinitum. The vast majority of achievements that have made modern life far more comfortable, safe, and long lasting are due to the hard work, sagacity, and creativity of private citizens.

By contrast, mass murder is the most memorable achievement of governments in the twentieth century. The *Black Book of Communism*, a 1997 French scholarly compendium, detailed how between 85 million and 100 million people came to die at the hands of communist regimes in the Soviet Union, China, Cambodia, and elsewhere.[95] Professor R. J. Rummel, in his book *Death by Government*, declared: "Almost 170 million men, women, and children have been shot, beaten, tortured, knifed, burned, starved, frozen, crushed, or worked to death; buried alive, drowned, hung, bombed, or killed in any other of the myriad ways governments have inflicted death on unarmed, helpless citizens and foreigners."[96] Gerald Scully, writing for the National Center for Policy Analysis, concluded that "perhaps as many as 360 million have been murdered by their own governments in this century."[97] Of course, every such slaughter is the "exception that proves the rule" of government benevolence.

Government can claim more technological successes in recent decades than in earlier centuries. Yet, considering how many private resources the government is confiscating and consuming, the government's productivity looks as feeble as it did in earlier centuries. From 1981 to 1990, according to a Tufts University study, private industry was the first to synthesize 92 percent of all new drug products; government, a mere 1 percent. According to the Pharmaceutical Research and Manufacturers of America, 99 of the 100 most prescribed drugs in 1995 were patented by private industry; only 1 was patented by a public university.[98] Contemporary Statist conventional wisdom presumes that any benefit from government-funded research is a bargain, regardless of the cost. Presumably, if politicians had not confiscated the money from the people who earned it, citizens would have buried it in their backyard or squandered it all on hot dogs and Diet Pepsi. Taxation to finance government research preempts private research. How many private inventions have been foregone because of federal tax and regulatory burdens?

Government-financed research has hit a few home runs. U.S. government military research laid the foundations for what later became the Internet. But a worldwide mass communications system was the last thing the Pentagon intended to create when it began work in the 1960s on a communications system that could survive a nuclear holocaust. The federal government has probably spent less than $2 billion on the Internet's development, according to National Science Foundation spokesman Lee Herring.[99] What has made the Internet a vehicle for mass communication is not the Pentagon's original master system, but the invention of the personal computer and powerful new software, both of which were private sector triumphs.

Government agencies measure their achievements by how much they prohibit; private companies gauge their accomplishments by how much they produce. Government bureaucracies brag about the number of fines they have imposed, while private companies brag about the number of inventions they have created. Government bureaucrats pride themselves on forcing private citizens to obey orders, while private companies pride themselves on discovering ways that help each person find his own path.

At this point in modern history, there should be little debate that economic freedom is far more bountiful than the commands of dictators or bureaucrats. As economist Gottfried Haberler declared in 1981:

> The striking difference in the economic performance as measured by the standard of living or output per capita of such pairs of countries as West and East Germany,

Austria and Czechoslovakia, Greece and Yugoslavia, Thailand and Burma, and China and Taiwan, can be explained only in terms of their different economic regimes: for the paired countries are similar in state of development, climate and resource endowment (both human and material), and they had enjoyed roughly the same standard of living in the pre-communist period.[100]

Since Haberler wrote, most of the communist regimes in the world have collapsed, largely thanks to their own gross economic incompetence and daily oppression of citizens.

After the fall of the East Bloc, the failure of political control of economies should be as indisputable as futility of censorship has been for decades. But what have many of today's thinkers deduced from that fall? Mainly that government needs to try different methods of economic coercion, or that the coercive programs need to have more uplifting names, or that another reorganization or reinvention of government agencies will square the economic circle, or that more senior bureaucrats should have a master's degree in public administration, or that the other political party deserves a chance to test its preferred scheme of expropriation.

Governments do not fizzle away money in a vacuum. The more of an economy that is subject to political command and control, the greater the foregone opportunities and the less the private prosperity. Wasteful government spending crowds out productive private investment; as a result, the entire society becomes increasingly impoverished, compared to what people could have achieved.

The supposed tradeoff between freedom and welfare is based almost entirely on the bogus premise that politicians will provide more welfare (after seizing increased power over everyone else) than private citizens can generate through their voluntary agreements and hard work. A 1998 report by economist James Gwartney and colleagues for the congressional Joint Economic Committee found that since 1960, average government expenditures for the 23 major industrial countries had risen from 27 percent of GDP to 48 percent of GDP in 1996—while the average economic growth rate "fell from 5.5% in the 1960s to 1.9% in the 1990s." Gwartney observed: "While growth has declined in all [23] countries, those countries with the least growth of government have suffered the least."[101] Gwartney concluded, "If government expenditures as a share of GDP in the United States had remained at their 1960 level, real GDP in 1996 would have been $9.16 trillion instead of $7.64 trillion, and the average income for a family of four would have been $23,440 higher." Gwartney notes that the share of GDP consumed by governments in the United States rose by more than 6 percent since 1960—and that increased "transfers and subsidies by themselves fully account for the growth of government as a share of GDP in the United States." [102] The rise in living standards has also been thwarted by government regulations. A 1995 study by the Employment Policy Foundation found that half of the long-term American productivity slowdown since the early 1970s can be tied to government regulations.[103]

Freedom provides vast benefits even to those who are afraid to take risks. As Ludwig von Mises wrote, "The virtue of the profit system is that it puts on improvements a premium high enough to act as an incentive to take high risks."[104] While few Americans use their garages to build new inventions, the fact that Steven Jobs and Stephen Wozniak did so—and pioneered the personal computer—sparked a revolution that helped make life more productive and entertaining for scores of millions of Americans. Regardless of whether someone has the skill to develop new computer software, he can benefit because many other people have the courage to gamble on their own talent. While much attention is paid to the external harms resulting from certain types of economic activity, many people neglect the vast external benefits from peaceful economic interactions.

Market economies, backed by a sound liability system, make each person responsible for his own failures but allow others to share in his successes. It is easier for a successful private innovation to spread than for a failed political intervention to stop. Liberty limits the collateral damage from mistaken judgments and bad ideas. Government agencies, unlike private individuals, rarely pay the price for their own mistakes. What was the last federal agency abolished as the result of its perennial gross incompetence? One of the bright sides of the market economy is that stupid or inept businessmen go bankrupt. Foolish businessmen sink their own ships, while foolish bureaucrats sink everyone else's ships.

Freedom of contract is the great escape mechanism for social problems and economic stagnation. Freedom of contract allows each person to seek out the other party who would most value what they have to offer. Freedom of contract allows people with stifling jobs to try their luck with their own company. Since 1980, tens of millions of Americans have started their own businesses or have become independent contractors, a triumph of courage that means a vast quality-of-life difference to people who prefer to make a living contracting with customers rather than taking orders from superiors ("boss diversification," in the words of Dilbert cartoonist Scott Adams).[105]

Individual freedom is not merely a question of maximizing wealth. Freedom means not needing a permit to find and roam the open spaces within one's own life. Freedom means not having a person's life plan dictated by some superior who doesn't like the length of his hair or the glint in his eye. Freedom means each person having a chance to live for what he considers to be his highest value. Freedom means being able to invest in the tools of one's trade without permission from some government planning agency or telecommunications or computer monopoly. Freedom means having the option to buy an old Volkswagen bus and go roam the country for months on end, working odd jobs to make ends meet. Freedom means not being fated to be an economic or social underling because of the petulant judgment of some government official. Freedom means not being confined to the rut of what other people think best. Freedom means the chance to upgrade one's life above the standards that satisfy bureaucrats aging at their desks. Freedom means being able to gamble on one's own talents, character, and luck—to "set one's life upon a cast and stand the hazard of the die."

A person's sense of freedom is more dependent on how he lives and what he values than on his income. Henry Thoreau wrote, "I am convinced, both by faith and experience, that to maintain one's self on this earth is not a hardship but a pastime, if we will live simply and wisely. . . . There is no more fatal blunderer than he who consumes the greater part of his life getting a living."[106] Thoreau felt freer than most of his affluent Concord townsmen, even though he was chronically and proudly "dirt poor." One of his acquaintances told him that "he should live as I did, if he had the means"[107]—but Thoreau's primary means were a will to make the maximum opportunity out of his surroundings and not to squander his time acquiring luxuries and fulfilling pointless social obligations.

A free society minimizes the number of bows and curtsies that a person must perform in daily life. Liberty is vital to individual dignity, to self-respect, to individual pride in "being one's own man." A free society has no legal caste system—no officialdom with its pretexts to bring everyone else to their knees. Liberty means a social system in which people live as they please, restrained only by their duty to respect the equal freedom of others.

Freedom encourages the maximum number of people to attempt to find a better way to do something, a better way to live, a better way to produce, a better way to build, a better way to thrive. Freedom is supremely valuable because, in most areas for most people, government does not know best. Each person must find out what is best for themselves drawing on custom, the experience of others and his own trials and errors. The value of liberty lies in the value of not shackling people who could otherwise raise themselves, of not locking people in a box. To vest vast power in the hands of one class necessarily severely limits everyone else's horizons in life.

Liberty breeds strong wills. The American character in the early days of the Republic—when the burden of government was far lighter—was renowned for courage and resilience. Emerson wrote in his essay "Self-Reliance" of the "sturdy lad from New Hampshire or Vermont, who in turn tries all the professions, who teams it, farms it, peddles, keeps a school, preaches, edits a newspaper, goes to Congress, buys a township, and so forth, in successive years, and always like a cat lands on his feet. . . . He has not one chance but a hundred chances."[108] But the further government power extends, the more futile individual effort becomes. The higher government raises the barriers, the fewer people will even try to make something of themselves. Every new unnecessary regulatory or licensing barrier effectively closes the door on some people's dreams.

Liberty spurs mental growth. In a free country, every man can profit from his own intelligence to master the challenges he faces. As economist Julian Simon showed in his book *The Ultimate Resource,* people have repeatedly overcome crippling shortages by finding new technologies, new materials, and new applications.[109] The creativity of the human mind can overcome the vast majority of obstacles that it comes across, as long as it is not fettered. On the other hand, if government officials have unlimited sway, then society will be victimized by whatever harebrained enthusiasm sweeps the political ruling class. (In 1930, Soviet engineers were convicted of being "wreckers" because of their devotion to quality at a time when Stalin was obsessed with maximizing output in statistical terms.)[110]

Freedom must be defended as the highest political value because otherwise it will be nickel-and-dimed to death by every political and bureaucratic ploy in the book. As Hayek wrote:

> Since the value of freedom rests on the opportunities it provides for unforeseen and unpredictable actions, we will rarely know what we lose through a particular restriction of freedom. Any such restriction, any coercion other than the enforcement of general rules, will aim at the achievement of some foreseeable particular result, but what is prevented by it will usually not be known. . . . We shall never be aware of all the costs of achieving particular results by such interference. And so, when we decide each issue solely on what appear to be its individual merits, we always over-estimate the advantages of central direction. Our choice will regularly appear to be one between a certain known and tangible gain and the mere probability of the prevention of some unknown beneficial action by unknown persons. If the choice between freedom and coercion is thus treated as a matter of expediency, freedom is bound to be sacrificed in almost every instance.[111]

Rather than stand on principles, many contemporary politicians prefer to proclaim themselves "pragmatists." Charles Pierce, the father of American pragmatism, defined pragmatism as "merely a method of ascertaining the meanings of hard words and of abstract concepts."[112] William James, the most prominent exponent of pragmatism, wrote in an essay "What Pragmatism Means" that "ideas become true just in so far as they help us to get into satisfactory relation with other parts of our experience."[113] This may work as a method for washing one's hands of pointless metaphysical disputes—but it is unfit for resolving political disputes. Historian Henry Adams astutely noted: "Practical politics consists of ignoring the facts." Combining a denial of facts with pragmatism does not produce practical results; instead, it merely generates more plausible lies.

Pragmatists create an atmosphere in which the most unprincipled politicians win. Pragmatism subverts honesty since policymakers recognize that it would be impolitic to publicly admit how much of people's rights and freedoms they have destroyed. The ultimate expressions of contemporary pragmatism are pretending that government is not coercive, pretending that people pay taxes voluntarily, pretending that politicians are honest, and pretending that most government employees are hard-working public servants. Pragmatism might make sense if the apex of good government was nothing more than the consecration of deals to split the booty among competing bands of brigands.

The fact that "pragmatic" is usually a term of praise shows the implicit Statism of contemporary political thinking. Contemporary pragmatists ignore the batting average of the State. Pragmatists usually begin by working from accepted Statist premises and degenerate into tinkering within the narrow boundaries of politically correct alternatives. Pragmatists devote themselves to debating over whether to marginally extend political control or make minor adjustments to existing interventions—not on the question of whether the current extent of control makes any sense. In the same way that pragmatic communist reformers in Hungary and elsewhere in the 1980s perpetuated the misery of communism with half-hearted attempts to fix its incurable defects, contemporary pragmatists seek ways to ameliorate or hide the worst failings of western Leviathans. Pragmatists seek to fine-tune agencies and laws which can only be corrected by being abolished or repealed. Many pragmatists seem desperate to be accepted and empowered by the existing political establishment, further suppressing whatever curiosity they might have about the legitimacy of contemporary governments.

The glory of freedom is the opportunity for people to make the best of themselves. The terror of freedom is that it leaves people with few excuses for their failure to make something of their own lives. The choice between freedom and government control is a choice of a social system based on human courage or on human fear.

Liberty is a political fire wall that limits the damage government can do to the individual. Freedom limits some people's power to ruin other people's lives.

The curtailment of freedom of speech makes it more difficult to inform people of government abuses, and thus rally public resistance. The curtailment of trial by jury makes it easier to railroad people on trumped-up charges, and thus makes it more risky to oppose the government. The decimation of property rights makes it more difficult for a person to find a place of his own to stand against government onslaughts. To reduce people's freedom is essentially to place government on an honor system—as if the less chance people have to escape or resist government power, the more benevolent government will become. Statists presume that regardless of how many freedoms government destroys, it will still respect people's rights—except for their right to freedom.

Liberty provides the strongest incentives for the person most likely to solve a problem to actually solve it. The value of liberty is limited only by each person's ability to help himself. Liberty will not somehow spontaneously generate the strength of character in every citizen to take full advantage of all his opportunities in life. The fact that some people become drug addicts or alcoholics, or beat their spouses, or neglect their children is no proof of the failure of liberty. The fact that some people crash and burn is no reason to give bureaucrats power to prohibit anyone from soaring beyond mediocrity. No amount of private errors can create a presumption of government omniscience.

A free society gives people the chance to be their own disciplinarians. Rather than being molded by their masters, people can impose their own strictures on themselves in pursuit of their chosen goals. As Nietzsche wrote, "He who cannot obey himself will be commanded."[114] To understand the spur of freedom, contrast the work habits and hours of the average self-employed entrepreneur with those of the average tenured government clerk. There will always be some people who need or desire to work within an organization with strict discipline, and in a free society, such people can find their niche.

Real moral values and real moral progress will not arise from further subordinating private citizens to the political class. The preservation of freedom is a moral starting place—it allows each person to create his own goodness, and to create goodness in association with others. Liberty permits each person to build his own moral utopia or to wallow in his own moral squalor, to live according to his own moral values or lack thereof. Liberty allows each person to be as good as he chooses to be. Liberty also maximizes opportunities to encourage other citizens to get out of the gutter. But as long as people indulge themselves with their own property and without injuring others, that is their business.

A free society is based on the idea that it is more important to be able to do as you like than to force your neighbor to do as you approve. Yet freedom is compatible with harsh moral judgments on the private behavior of others. A citizen in a free society has no obligation to approve or sanction other people's behavior that he finds offensive or destructive or wrong. The question of whether someone is free is not a question of whether he is criticized by his fellow citizens. John Stuart Mill, in his classic *On Liberty,* portrayed conformist social pressure as the greatest threat to individual freedom. Mill stated that individual liberty in England suffered more at that time from "invasion" from "public opinion" than it did from "invasion from the government." [115] Mill also wrote that "the interference of government is, with about equal frequency, improperly invoked and improperly condemned."[116] Mill's work beautifully captured how individuals are the source of creativity, innovation, and progress. Unfortunately, by focusing excessively on the threat of hostile opinion, Mill encouraged many people to neglect the danger of political power. Liberty requires stoutness; if one assumes that people dissolve like a sugar cube in the rain each time they hear a harsh word, then a free society is impossible.

The alternative to freedom is not some warm, fuzzy, social-economic womb, provided by benevolent politicians, where people can avoid the sometimes painful choices of daily life—a place where people will be completely safe because their rulers continually remind them that they are being well-cared for. People do not have a choice between being free and being cosseted. It is much easier to find "enlightened despotism" in college textbooks than in government agencies. The alternative to freedom is government control, which means manipulation and exploitation by liars and hypocrites. The loss of freedom does not occur in a vacuum; instead, it sets off a chain reaction that is sure to drag people lower than they expect. The opening of the borders of private lives to government intrusion is not the final act of some grandiose political drama, but merely the beginning of a sordid, predictable farce. The loss of freedom does not simply mean that people will have fewer choices in how they live; instead, it means that other people will have new prerogatives to command how they live and to punish them for disobeying. And the greater the power at stake, the more noxious the people who are likely to eventually get the grip on the reins.

CONCLUSION

Contemporary paternalism presumes that no citizen has a legitimate claim to the fruits of his own labor or control of his own life. Almost everyone recognizes the injustice when an innocent person is falsely convicted because of government foul play and sent to prison. Why do people not also recognize the gross injustice of politicians' lying and seizing power to destroy freedom in area after area? New government laws and edicts are often the equivalent of confining another part of people's lives to a political prison, of consigning another part of a person's life to political control and bureaucratic manipulation. If it is clearly an outrage to imprison an innocent man, why is it not also an outrage to unnecessarily subject another portion of a person's life to political control? If it is an outrage to lock up an innocent man for a year in jail, why is it not also an outrage to compel people to surrender four months of their yearly earnings to the government?

Paternalism presumes that political power is more reliable than self-help. Paternalism is a desperate gamble that lying politicians will honestly care for those who fall under their power. Paternalism collapses on at least three counts: first, the presumption of the superior wisdom of government employees and politicians; second, the notion that government employees and politicians have a burning desire to benefit others; and third, the assumption that there is a mechanism by which good intentions could combine with coercion to automatically improve the lives of the intended beneficiaries. The fact that political programs must be carried into practice via coercion, punishment, and penalties nullifies much of their supposed good.

To presume that the Paternalist State will increase citizens' happiness is to presume that it will use its accumulated force only to make people happy, not for its own ends. Yet, there is practically no State that has followed this standard. History offers catalog after catalog of crimes committed by governments against their subjects, or against the subjects of other governments.

If progress is measured by the greater contentment and satisfaction of people with their own lives, then coercion is almost certain to be retrogressive. The amount of coercion necessary to impose a government policy is often a shorthand measure of how much that policy's victims believe government is sacrificing their own happiness.

Where is the political value-added? This is the question that proponents of the Welfare State can rarely answer, at least for the majority of citizens and the vast majority of interventions. Instead, as William Graham Sumner wrote, "The prosperity which we enjoy is the prosperity which God and nature have given us minus what the legislator has taken from it."[117]

EIGHT

A Few Thoughts on
an Ideal Political Order

THERE IS NO WAY TO CRIMINALIZE OUR WAY TO UTOPIA. To speculate about an ideal form of government is almost inherently a self-delusion—like speculating on the ideal form of canine abuse. What is needed is not a political philosophy that promises the moon but merely one that limits havoc on Earth. Politicians will always be with us. The goal must be to minimize the coercive power that some people hold over other people.

No amount of fine-tuning can turn Leviathans into servants of those whom they control. As Professor Ruth Grant observed in her masterful study of John Locke, "Locke keeps the reader constantly aware of the gravity of the political problem and of the fragility of human solutions to it. The political problem arises because there is no natural political order. . . . There is no natural common authority to ensure that force is always coupled with right."[1] The "political problem" is essentially how to limit coercion so that it does not destroy those who it is sanctioned to protect. Though this problem is unsolved, politicians continue expanding government power as if the dilemma was a relic of the barbaric past.

This is not the place for a detailed road map on how to move from contemporary Leviathans to higher ground. However, there are a few general principles and guides that should be considered.

BILL OF RIGHTS: What is necessary to make a government legitimate? At a minimum, government must honor the pledges that it has made to the citizenry. This is why Americans need a far better understanding of the Bill of Rights. As Thomas Jefferson wrote in 1787, "A bill of rights is what the people are entitled to against every government on earth . . . and what no just government should refuse, or rest on inference."[2] Insofar as government officials violate the rights recognized by the Founding Fathers and codified in the Constitution, then the government is illegitimate. Congressmen and the president take an oath of office to uphold the Constitution. When as they scorn that oath, they transform themselves into a predator class, and politics becomes little more than promising and pilfering.

RULE OF LAW: As A.V. Dicey wrote in 1885, the Rule of Law means that "no man is punishable or can be lawfully made to suffer in body or goods except for a distinct breach of law established in the ordinary legal manner before the ordinary Courts of the land . . . the absolute supremacy or predominance of regular law as opposed to the influence of arbitrary power . . . equality before the law, or the equal subjection of all classes to the ordinary law of the land administered by the ordinary Law Courts."[3] The Rule of Law provides an invaluable standard to recognize abuses at all levels of government. Most of the administrative law regimes that have spread like crabgrass since the 1930s violate the Rule of Law. The Rule of Law is no guarantee that government will not suppress freedom. A theocratic government can impose the same religious commandments on all citizens—but equal oppression will not make everyone free.[4] Minimizing arbitrariness and preventing government from setting up phony bureaucratic courts can do much to curb government abuses.

There must be no classes of legal superiors or legal inferiors. Sovereign immunity is one of the gravest threats to a free society. Law professor Rodolphe J. A. de Seife observed in 1996 that "anywhere between six to eight million people in this country enjoy some sort of immunity, including the absolute immunity granted to prosecutors . . . some five percent of the American population end up being above the law in one way or another."[5] In some parts of this nation, laws against abusing pets are probably better enforced than are laws against government employees abusing citizens. The more public officials who are effectively above the law, the more citizens should fear the government. To require government to compensate its victims will, almost overnight, sharply reduce the number of people government injures.

TAXATION: "Unnecessary taxation is unjust taxation,"[6] declared the 1884 Democratic Party National Platform. This is a principle of justice that has long since vanished from American understanding. Supreme Court justice Oliver Wendell Holmes expressed the modern enlightened attitude in 1927: "Taxes are what we pay for civilized society. . . ."[7] But insofar as civilization means people living and dealing with each other peacefully, insofar as taxes epitomize coercion and enable government agencies to hire agents and build prisons and shackle citizens—thus far are taxes the bane of civilization. Tax levels measure the deficit of voluntary cooperation within a society.

Edmund Burke declared in 1775 that "the great contests for freedom in this country were from the earliest times chiefly upon the question of taxing."[8] What is needed is not just tax cuts—but a radical rethinking about taxation in general, about the right of politicians to take other people's income. Politicians will always find ways to spend as much as they seize. Mandatory payroll tax withholding must be abolished. Payroll-withholding delivers windfall profits to politicians every time someone works harder or longer and increases their own income. The State cannot have any presumptive claim to the citizen's income— any more than a servant can lay claim to a large chunk of a mansion owner's capital gains. Federal tax collections rose from $1.09 trillion to $1.72 trillion between 1992 and 1998—a 58 percent increase, more than three times greater than inflation.[9] Did members of Congress and President Clinton deserve this raise? How many Americans would have voluntarily delivered so much more of their own money to Washington?

Every tax rise provides new sinews to subjugate citizens. Citizens who wish to be free must pay strict attention to all exactions politicians impose. Ending politicians' unlimited taxing power is the first step towards liberating the citizenry. The current tax code is a monument to the bad faith presidents and congresses have long shown towards the American people. A good tax system will provide sufficient revenue and nothing else—no inside lane on everyone's personal lives, no pretext to penalize scores of millions of people for inadvertent errors, and no hash of regulations to empower every would-be bureaucratic tyrant. There is no way for any tax system that raises as much revenue as does that of the federal government to be "fair," because government can in no way render equivalent benefits to the average taxpayer.

Taxation is unjust if politicians spend tax revenues on actions for which government possesses no visible competence. Congressmen are personally liable for every dollar which they authorize the IRS to seize. Programs such as public housing fail year after year; even Vice President Gore proclaimed that "these crime-infested monuments to a failed policy are killing the neighborhoods around them."[10] And after each new failure, politicians and experts commiserate over how they almost got it right that time. If politicians have a right to seize and squander other people's money, how can citizens be anything more than beasts of burden for political ambition? The failure of a government policy does not merely reduce the number of bureaucrats who receive "outstanding achievement" job evaluations. Every waste of tax dollars undermines the legitimacy of the entire political system. Governments cannot waste tax dollars without squandering part of the lives of the people who earned those dollars. There are human costs to every government snafu. A billion tax dollars wasted preempts 10,000 families from buying starter homes, or preempts 100,000 people from buying bottom-of-the-line new cars, or preempts a million people from taking a summer vacation, or preempts citizens from buying 40 million new books or 80 million cases of beer.

FEDERALISM: A federalist structure of government allows the benefits of common defense and a large free-trade area without subjection to the same laws or political infestations. Local provision of necessary government services minimizes the distance that citizens must throw their lassos to rein in politicians and bureaucrats. Though a federal system is far superior to a centralized monolith, by itself it provides little assurance that politicians' power will not become excessive. The issue of how much power government possesses is far more important than how that power is divided. A federalist division of government powers must be back-stopped by judges with the power to nullify unconstitutional laws. Unfortunately, many of the disputes regarding federalism in the United States from the 1850s onward focused on which level of government had the supreme right to abuse citizens, not on whether any level of government possessed such right.

FOREIGN POLICY: It is difficult to craft an ideal foreign policy, since foreign policy consists largely of dealing with other predator entities/governments. However, a recognition of the legitimate role of government should minimize disputes. If people did not believe that a government had a right to confiscate the property and regiment the lives of its subjects, they would be less prone to kill over imaginary lines. Regardless of where national boundaries are drawn, people should be able to speak the language they please, use the currency they choose,[11] send their children to schools they approve, and practice any religion or peaceful lifestyle. A sound foreign policy must respect other nations' rights to mangle their own destinies. President John Quincy Adams declared that America should be the "well-wisher to the freedom and independence of all, but the champion and vindicator only of her own."[12] No single nation in the world has all the answers, and thus no nation has the right to forcibly impose its values on other nations. America has a great opportunity to influence the rest of humanity by becoming a shining example of tolerance and liberty. But insofar as the United States wantonly intrudes in foreign nations—such as bankrolling candidates in foreign elections, as the National Endowment for Democracy has done[13]—this nation deserves the hostility it harvests.

However, in the meantime, before political enlightenment triumphs around the globe, national defense is the preeminent task of national government. A good defense policy must reduce the number of foreign enemies by minimizing the provocations of and injuries to foreign citizens. National defense must be subordinated, as far as possible, to individual liberty: people should ever be on guard both against foreign predators and against domestic politicians seeking to frighten people out of their freedom. Military conscription is simply a means to allow politicians to confiscate the value of part of young people's lives: a nation that claims to value freedom cannot honorably defend itself with slave labor.

AID TO HELPLESS CITIZENS: In a hypothetical ideal society, government would have no role in aiding those who cannot help themselves. Private assistance efforts are far more cost-effective and far less likely to create golden handcuffs than are government welfare agencies.[14] Private relief can achieve far more than governments choose to currently recognize. And the vast reduction in tax levels that would occur after the cessation of inept and illegitimate government programs would leave people with far more resources with which to aid the truly needy. As private aid rises, government aid can be sharply phased down. However, government can prevent people from perishing from destitution without dragging an entire society into the mire of political control. For centuries, governments provided some aid to the helpless without becoming massive spigots of redistribution. The current vast number of government dependents should be recognized, as Professor Richard Epstein wrote, as "evidence of the [welfare] system's manifest failure to constrain the demands for its services. . . . [I]f the state had never undertaken welfare programs, the demand for them would be a tiny fraction of what it is today."[15] Unfortunately, politicians lack an incentive to honestly define neediness. Instead, they exaggerate people's hardships to maximize their own power to buy votes. As de Jouvenel observed, "Redistribution is in effect far less a redistribution of free income from the richer to the poorer, than a redistribution of power form the individual to the State."[16] As long as government aids only those who truly cannot help themselves, and as long as the level of aid is lower than entry-level wages, and as long as aid is not delivered in ways that destroy freedom of contract (such as minimum wage laws), then the relief system should have little negative impact on the economy or society. Fewer people will need help once government ceases lavishly rewarding irresponsibility.

AID TO BUSINESSES: Government cannot rightfully seize some people's wages to boost other people's profits. Business welfare bleeds taxpayers for more than the combined cost of food stamps. No government should give a dime in aid to any business. Government must end all bankrolling of stadiums for professional sports teams, end all loan programs to favored groups, end all attempts to manipulate crop prices or prop up farm income, and end attempts to rig markets. Every intervention is more disruptive than it first appears. While government may have a role in preventing starvation, it must have no role in encouraging people to launch business ventures for which they have little or no competence. Government paperwork burdens likely drown far more businesses than are aided by government handouts. Government cannot help one industry or business without indirectly disadvantaging all others. Banning all aid to business would do more to reduce corruption than all the ethics laws that politicians have enacted to govern their conduct since the Progressive era. The surest way to clean up government is to get politicians out of people's pockets—either taking or "giving."

VICES/CRIMES: Far more coercion is necessary to purportedly protect people from themselves than to protect them against other people. An ideal political order must distinguish between vices and crimes. As Lysander Spooner wrote in 1875, "Vices are those acts by which a man harms himself or his property. Crimes are those acts by which one man harms the person or property of another. Vices are simply the errors which a man makes in his search after his own happiness."[17] Someone or some group is not a public enemy simply because politicians can win votes by tarring them. Many of the worst law enforcement abuses stem from politicians' wars on people's vices—from drug or alcohol use, to gambling, obscenity, and prostitution. The more consensual the crime, the more intrusive law enforcement efforts to suppress it must become. For instance, in July 1998, the District of Columbia city council, seeking to suppress prostitution, decreed that anyone on D.C. streets who repeatedly attempts to engage passersby in conversation can be arrested.[18] This ban, if strictly enforced, could result in the jailing of many befuddled foreign tourists seeking directions. Politicians' efforts to suppress private vices routinely harm far more innocent bystanders than the vices themselves. The government is already promising to protect everyone against practically everything and many people are busy destroying their lives anyway.

Decriminalizing narcotics, for instance, would sharply reduce the violent crime rate in American cities. The easier access to decriminalized drugs would be countervailed, at least in part, by the vast decrease in the profits from dealing drugs. Some drug laws, such as stiffer penalties on crack than cocaine possession, affect far more blacks than whites; blacks and Hispanics are also far more likely to be the targets of no-knock raids, arbitrary searches, and other abusive practices. Ending the war on drugs will reduce tension between law enforcement and minority groups and lower the fatality rate among law enforcement (many police die each year in vain efforts to suppress drugs). Repealing the national minimum drinking age of 21 will end such charades as squadrons of police attacking groups of college students who are simply drinking a few beers. When cops are concerned primarily with protecting people against murderers, rapists, and robbers, they will not need the armored vehicles and mechanized battering rams that are the prides of some big city police departments. It will require far fewer government agents to protect people than to control them. As government policies become less intrusive, police will become more respected.

While adults are entitled to choose their own vices, children are not similarly capable of exercising individual responsibility. Prohibitions against selling alcohol or narcotics to young children and against adults from becoming sexually involved with young children are justified. Government can rightfully intervene to stop parents from brutalizing their children—though laws passed since 1974 have given social workers sweeping prerogatives that have been greatly abused.[19] An understanding of the damage done by government's bogus rescues and by terrible conditions in foster homes and government child-care facilities should permeate government policies regarding children. And politicians must not be allowed to invoke "the children" as cover for schemes to stretch their power over people of all age groups.

PUBLIC HEALTH, PUBLIC SAFETY: From controls on harmful bacteria in the water supply to efforts to detect and curb outbreaks of serious illnesses, government can safeguard public health with scant impact on the paychecks or liberties of private citizens. The government could continue to fund some medical research; the federal Centers for Disease Control have done some excellent work. However, federally funded medical research will suffer from the usual defects of government work; the National Institutes of Health, for example, was harshly criticized for politicizing its research agenda in a July 1998 report by the National Academy of Sciences.[20]

The type of activities for which government may actually have a comparative advantage in efficiency or reliability are, in general, those which have very little cost. Any government intervention or program must be structured to minimize impact on the possibilities for voluntary agreement and for the development of better solutions than any bureaucrat can imagine.

Some type of organization or entity or system is necessary to referee private disputes and to punish private violence. But, simply because such an organization appears necessary does not prove that it must be vested with "sovereignty," or that accolades and power must be heaped upon it. Most of the tasks government now performs could be handled by private companies. Private arbitration services, for instance, are providing faster and more reliable civil dispute resolution than government courts provide. Citizens in various parts of the nation already benefit from the superior services and reduced costs of private mass transit, trash pickup, road maintenance, and fire departments.

There is no reason for government to provide any service that can be reliably provided by a private business. Privatizing government services will mean that more activities can be determined by private agreements instead of political finagling.

IMPROVING DEMOCRACY: Voting in a democracy nowadays often means trusting one's life, liberty, and property to one of two candidates, neither of whom seems trustworthy. Politicians and majorities must recognize that they have no right to control what they do not own. Any proposal for the reform of democracy must also recognize the limits of both voters and legislators. Neither will be significantly more attentive in the future than in the past. A momentary lapse of public attention routinely results in a permanent expansion of government power. This is part of the reason why many of the worst laws are enacted in the end-of-legislative-session stampedes, both in Washington and in state capitols. We must choose between continued inept, oppressive government and a much smaller government.

People must change their attitude towards the nation's highest elected officials. People who expect their leaders to save them on a daily basis are already unfit for self-government. The longing for a wiser, more honest leader presumes that most of the problems in people's lives can be solved by vesting the right person with power, as if the foremost challenge in life is to find a good master. Finding one good politician—or even a few hundred good politicians—cannot redeem the character of a government with millions of employees and scores of thousands of enforcement agents. The more fixated people become on the supreme leader, the less attention is devoted to all other government officials, and the easier it becomes for them to engage in petty oppression.

At elections, each voter, each citizen must ask: "Does any candidate deserve broad coercive power over me? Is there any candidate sufficiently superior to me, both morally and intellectually, that he should receive a right to shackle me or seize the bulk of my paycheck?" Each politician must be judged by how much power he believes government deserves over private citizens. Each politician championing an intrusive new law must be asked: "What gives you the right to coerce, compel, or restrain other people according to your own whim?" Citizens must ask of any proposed law or economic/political system: How much competence, wisdom, and virtue does it presume of the people who will command its levers? As Benjamin Constant wrote in 1815, "It is the degree of force, not its holders, which must be denounced. It is against the weapon, not against the arm holding it, that it is necessary to strike ruthlessly. There are weights too heavy for the hand of man."[21] The extent of government power should be the preeminent issue for people fighting to regain their liberties. The issue is not which party holds office, but how much power any officeholder has to punish and shackle other Americans.

Political action will always be a feeble, delusory substitute for self-help. The opportunity to engage in political finagling is no substitute for direct control over one's own life. Pursuing one's goals through one's own efforts, versus relying on representatives, is a choice of seeking to directly improve one's life, or of acting through a dozen intermediaries, any one of which might betray, deceive, or ignore one's concerns. Contrast how individuals try to influence and manipulate the political process, with all its uncertainty and dishonesty, with the direct efforts a person makes to achieve a goal in his own life. People can send $100 in campaign contributions to a congressman and hope that their letter with a grievance towards the government makes it past the newest intern, and hope that the congressman's staffer's contacts at a federal agency will pay attention, and, if they do pay attention, hope that word will pass from the agency headquarters to the regional office and then down to the local office, the source of the grievance. Or, at a higher level, someone can pay $50,000 and have coffee at the White House, and hope that the president or one of his minions pays attention and will express appropriate gratitude. It is a choice of exerting themselves to pull political strings that might or might not be connected to something real and of putting one's shoulder behind improving one's own life.

It is naive to expect politicians as a class to suddenly develop an allergy to political power. The bulk of the current crop of politicians will not voluntarily deactivate the legal minefields they and their predecessors have strewn in all directions around people's lives. Voters must purge those who shackled them. Limitations on how many terms a politician can hold an office can deter the buildup of a permanent governing class with interests distinct from the citizenry. But term limits, without a profound change in attitude, will amount to only a scoundrel-rotation-in-office policy.

NECESSARY NOT TO COERCE: Coercion is an evil. If coercion is not absolutely necessary, then it is necessary not to coerce. To say "there ought to be a law" is to say "there ought to be a penalty" and that some people must have more power to punish other people. Any unjustified law amounts to wrongful aggression against the citizenry. Judges do not give the benefit of the doubt to private citizens who shoot into a crowd in hopes of hitting a criminal, and nor should politicians receive the benefit of the doubt when they use compulsion for their shot-in-the-dark economic or social schemes. When government power extends beyond keeping the peace, the government ends up making war on the citizenry that it was created to protect. The more power government acquires, the more that it subverts the purpose of its existence.

But how can we know whether it is necessary to coerce? Coercion is justified only to prevent greater coercion. Government power must be limited to protecting citizens from others' aggression, not from their own stupidity or weakness. Coercion is a blunt instrument that produces many ill effects aside from the purported government goal. To rely on coercion to achieve progress is like relying on bulldozers and steamrollers for routine transit. The question is not whether a person can eventually reach a goal driving a steamroller, but how much damage is left in his wake, and how much faster the destination could be reached without crushing everything along the way.

REPEAL, REPEAL, REPEAL: To restore government to its proper place requires repealing most current statutes and regulations. If laws are not repealed and programs not abolished, the danger remains that new abuses will follow the betrayal of old promises. A new political order should seek to build upon the principles and insights of common law, to turn back the clock to a time when laws respected contracts and the individual's right to autonomy and control of his own destiny, and sought to maximize each person's responsibility for his own actions. Unfortunately, such principles were largely abandoned earlier in this century. Cleaning up the legal code by repealing unneeded laws and reforming court procedures will also reduce the advantage accruing to businesses or citizens who can afford the most expensive lawyers. The statute books should be as lean as people's lives are bountiful. Where there is peace and respect for individual rights, the positive side of human nature will naturally flourish.

If the power of government is not radically decreased, then no administrative, electoral, or other reform will safeguard the citizenry. As long as government power is nearly boundless, the defense of the individual against the State will be nearly hopeless. Politicians as a class should have as little power as possible over the rest of humanity. From airwaves, to land, to children's minds, politicians must be compelled to relinquish their grip on other people's lives.

A minimal government is the only just government. Government is the most powerful and dangerous special interest in society—it controls the courts and authorizes itself to use coercion against any private party. There is no system in which government can supervise and investigate itself the same way that private citizens are investigated. Thus, the bigger the government, the greater the injustices that will likely go unpunished.

"Peace in our time" must be the goal: not only peace between nations, but peace between people within a nation. A nonaggression pact between politicians and citizens is needed to minimize some people's pretexts to interfere in other people's lives. People should respect politicians only insofar as politicians respect their right to live their own lives. The further politicians' power extends, the more contemptible they become.

Political progress depends on distrust of politicians. The more credulous people are, the more attractive political life becomes to charlatans and demagogues. People must recognize the inevitable tendency of coercive power to corrupt human nature. People cannot sit idly by waiting for politicians to enact laws to end political abuses. Governments should have sufficient power to protect people against force and fraud, and people should have sufficient gumption to keep government in its place. Good laws are no substitute for vigilant citizens.

Government coercion is not the only evil that people face in their lives. Even if governments adopt ideal policies, there will still be human beings who try to cheat, rob, and assault other human beings. And, far more frequently, there will still be people who fail in their fundamental duties to themselves and their families. But government and political action are by far the clearest source of evil that can be decisively reduced.

The better that government respects citizens' right to peacefully live their own lives, the less glory there will be for politicians. When government does only what it can competently and rightfully do, then its achievements are mundane—low crime rates, no foreign invasions, and safe water. These are all vital goods and the government that secures them to a citizenry—with minimum coercion and scant taxation—is a true benefactor. Government only becomes "glorious" when it attempts tasks far beyond its competence. This is why the fevered pursuit of national greatness by the political class is ever a reliable shortcut to national ruin.

NINE

TAKING COERCION SERIOUSLY

When men build on false grounds, the more they build, the greater is the ruin.

— Thomas Hobbes[1]

GOVERNMENT IS OURSELVES—ARMED WITH CLUBS. Therefore, the achievements of government will forever be limited by the primary tool of government—coercion.

Conventional political wisdom is based on a series of farces. First, we pretend that citizens control the government. Next, we pretend the citizen is indirectly controlling himself when the government controls him. Then we pretend that any control imposed must be in the public interest, or else it would not have been imposed. Finally, the people are irrevocably labeled as "free" until the government completely wrecks the economy or slaughters a statistically significant percentage of the population.

People have worshipped government too long. The halo that hovers over the State must be banished. It is time to demystify and desanctify the State—to see it as merely another human institution that relies on force and fear mongering. It is time to take the State off its pedestal, especially in the minds of those people who do not recognize that they have placed it on a pedestal. It is time to stop confusing what the State is with what its champions claim it can be.

The average citizen should cancel any debt of gratitude to his political captors. Abstract intellectual errors produce real chains and fetters. A political philosophy that is not grounded in reality is like an electric power wire dangling from a telephone pole. Unfortunately, modern political philosophy has resulted in the electrocution of one hapless populace after another. People must cease wiping the slate clean after each new atrocity. Citizens must cease presuming that people who are seeking more power over them are acting in good faith. Government must be judged in light of all the lies politicians have told, all the rights government agents have violated, and all the wealth bureaucracies have squandered.

Citizens must choose between "government-issue liberty" and "self-reliant liberty." The choice is between a concept of freedom based on government handouts and a concept of freedom based on restraint of government—between a liberty in which people are perpetually treated as children needing to be restrained and a liberty in which they are allowed to experiment, adventure, and pay for their own bloody noses. It is a choice between a freedom in which each person can make his own mistakes and a freedom in which each person becomes another statistic in the government's mistakes. Americans need a concept of freedom that does not intellectually disarm the citizen in the face of the State. A good definition of liberty draws a line in the sand that even 10,000 enforcement agents are not allowed to cross.

The burden of proof must be upon those who promise great things from vesting vast power in some people to punish and subjugate other people. In the preface of any new political philosophy, the writer should specify his conception of government; if he intends to discuss government as an ideal, he should make his intentions clear and explain why the ideal will become the real under his system. Philosophers who choose to ignore the coercive nature of the State must show why coercion is irrelevant—or why their ideals are more important than the coercion. The fancies of philosophers are not more sacrosanct than the hides of citizens.

At this point, marginal reforms should suffice only for those who believe citizens deserve marginal lives—lives consisting of what politicians choose not to confiscate and bureaucrats deign not to prohibit. To be overgoverned means lives thwarted, hopes dashed, creativity suppressed, potential squandered, character subverted, and dignity destroyed.

There can be no final victory in the fight for freedom. Faith in the State will continue reviving as long as some people feel entitled to run other people's lives. Whenever old truths are forgotten, old follies will rise again from the intellectual graveyard. Regardless of reforms, government will still be an evil to be controlled, rather than a blessing to be multiplied. As soon as people drop the reins on government, government will leash the people.

The capture of political power confers as much legitimacy to run other people's lives as the purchase of a Good Humor ice cream truck gives to dictate the diets of all the children in a town. Most current governments receive the same sanction that most governments have received throughout history—the mere fact that they have not been violently overthrown by the people. The State has no right to impose thousands of restrictions on individuals for the benefit of politically favored groups, and no right to turn average citizens into sacrificial animals for political ambition.

Politicians do not have the power to save men's souls: political apparatuses cannot redeem otherwise banal and purposeless lives. We should expect as little from political action as we do from any other form of mendacious behavior. People should expect as little from the government as they would from brute force—or, more accurately, brute force accompanied by sonorous phrases. And once people expect far less from government, they will recognize that government has no right to most of the power it has seized. Paternalism is impossible without either a deluded conception of the State or a degraded conception of the people. Since government cannot produce happiness, the most helpful thing it can do is get out of the way.

People should not take their values from their political masters. Politicians' moral claims can have no more credibility than their campaign promises. Individuals must rise above the corrupt morality offered by the State—rise up to self-respect, self-reliance, and honor. People can have fulfilling lives without the intervention of politicians and bureaucrats. Citizens can do good deeds as individuals without being cogs in great masses orchestrated by political overlords. People can help their fellow man without government agents intervening as bagmen for every good deed. The focus of moral effort must shift from political action and mass movements to the actions of individuals resolved to becoming better human beings.

H. L. Mencken concluded his 1934 *Treatise on Right and Wrong:* "The great failure of civilized man is his failure to fashion a competent and tolerable form of government. Most of our worst vexations are not in the field of morals, properly so called, but in that of law."[2] From a different perspective, the continual failure of government is a tribute to the richness of the human character—to people unwilling to spend their lives as pawns on planners' playboards. The vibrancy and resilience of human nature has continually confounded the schemes of political saviors. Human beings have overcome a staggering amount of misgovernment to reach new heights on their own.

We need to expect less from government and more from humanity. It is not cynical to have more faith in freedom than in subjugation. It is not cynical to have more faith in individuals vested with rights than in bureaucrats armed with power. It is not cynical to suspect that governments that have cheated so often in the past may not be dealing straight today. We do not say that an animal that escapes from a zoo is depraved, and nor should we so characterize human beings who refuse to bow to their self-appointed overlords.

To blindly trust government is to automatically vest it with excessive power. To distrust government is simply to trust humanity—to trust in the ability of average people to peacefully, productively coexist without some official policing their every move. The State is merely another human institution—less creative than Microsoft, less reliable than Federal Express, less responsible than the average farmer husbanding his land, and less prudent than the average citizen spending his own paycheck.

Politicians and bureaucrats have perennially devoted vast amounts of tax dollars to deceive taxpayers. But, ultimately, much of the responsibility for the expansion of coercive government power rests on average Americans—who failed in their duty of oversight of the government and whose greed for unearned benefits blinded them to unforeseen costs.

There is no safe political refuge for those afraid to take responsibility for their own lives. No amount of character defects in the political class can absolve citizens of their duty to keep an eye on politicians. In the early 1930s, many Germans became so disgusted with politics that they embraced Hitler, in part because he promised to suppress politics once and for all.[3] Germans swallowed the antipolitician rhetoric and acquiesced to the vast increase in government power. The question is not whether a candidate swears to despise other politicians but whether he seeks more power over voters.

Yet, to recognize this is emphatically not to say that "we" are all responsible for whatever coercive or criminal action any government employee commits. Simply because many people lack the wisdom or foresight to recognize the machinations of their rulers does not convert them into willing co-conspirators. Simply because a person does not throw himself in the path of a juggernaut does not make him responsible for all the damage it does.

Government will take aggressive action against citizens, regardless of whether citizens are politically aware or active.[4] Politicians and bureaucrats understand how to advance their own power better than citizens understand how to defend their rights and liberties. Since good government is ever the exception in human history, the good citizen must intellectually arm himself against the likely depredations of the political class.

The surest effect of exalting government is to make it easier for some people to drag other people down. Government is worth far less than people are being compelled to pay for it. We have the choice between the minimal State and the parasitical State.

Government's grasp on power—in the minds of tens of millions of Americans—may be far more precarious than politicians realize. Once people begin asking the right questions about government, the intellectual and moral foundations of today's Leviathans will dissolve.

People must summon the will and resolution to drive politicians out of their own lives. What is needed now is the same passion and outrage over political and bureaucratic aggrandizement that existed towards chattel slavery 140 years ago. We must recognize that possession of government office does not confer ownership rights over human beings. If that can be done, then the stage will be set for a vast rollback in political power over private citizens. John Adams, writing in the summer in which the Declaration of Independence was issued, declared of his fellow Americans: "Idolatry to Monarchs, and servility to Aristocratical Pride was never so totally eradicated from so many Minds in so short a Time."[5] If contemporary Americans can cease idolizing the State, a rebirth of the spirit of freedom will begin.

ACKNOWLEDGMENTS

I began work on this book about 20 years ago, but its completion was slightly delayed by other tasks.

I am indebted to many people who helped me better understand the issues with which I wrestled in this book. I would like to thank Jim Moody, the late Julian Simon, Gideon Kanner, Tom Miller, Sam Kazman, Jacob Hornberger, Doug Bandow, Jeff Tucker, Barbara Phillips, Jim Powell, Jim Petersen, Andrea Millen Rich, Robert Cihak, Tom Palmer, Joyce Lee Malcolm, Karlyn Keene Bowman, Wladyslaw Pleszczynski, and Robert Meier.

I would also like to thank Matt Gaylor, Mark White, John McPherson, and Greg Ransom for allowing me to post requests for research assistance on their excellent email lists, and thank everyone who sent me their suggestions and ideas. I want to especially thank Daniel Russell, Goncala Fonseca, and Mark Brandly for their key suggestions. I want to thank John M. Jaworsky for suggesting the book title and thank everyone else who took the time to send along their ideas for a title. I wish also to express my gratitude to Gordon Woods for allowing me to reprint a long section from a brilliant 1996 speech he gave.

During the time I was working on this book, I benefitted from a 10-month fellowship with the Competitive Enterprise Institute in 1996-97 that allowed me the chance to concentrate on property rights and environmental policy; I also benefitted from a brief stint at the Hoover Institution at Stanford University in the summer of 1996.

This is the third book I have published with St. Martin's Press and I am continually impressed by that publisher's competence and high standards. I am indebted to senior editor Michael Flamini for his hard work, enthusiasm, insightful suggestions, and willingness to go against the conventional wisdom; to Bill Berry and Christopher Cecot for their excellent copy-editing; and to production editor Alan Bradshaw for his good-natured patience and judicious conversion of the manuscript into final book form.

NOTES

CHAPTER 1

1. Hans Morgenthau, "The Evil of Politics and the Ethics of Evil," *Ethics*, vol. 56, October 1945, p. 1.
2. "Remarks by President Bill Clinton at Democratic National Committee Meeting," Federal News Service, January 21, 1997.
3. Speech by Attorney General Janet Reno, Newark, New Jersey, May 5, 1995. Quoted in James Bovard, "Waco Must Get a Hearing," *Wall Street Journal*, May 15, 1995.
4. *U.S. v. Kozminski*, 487 U.S. 931, 972 (1988).
5. Food and Drug Administration Commissioner David Kessler, commencement speech, College of William and Mary, Williamsburg, Virginia, May 16, 1993.
6. One medical publication noted, "Newspaper reports have also speculated that his resignation has to do with a congressional investigation of his allegedly padded expense accounts." David Woods, "The Scourge of the Tobacco Industry Steps Down," *British Medical Journal*, January 4, 1997, p. 11. Kessler denied that he resigned as a result of the controversy over his expense account.
7. James F. Byrnes, "Great Decisions Must be Made," *Vital Speeches of the Day*, July 15, 1949, p. 580.
8. "Tax Burden on American Families Rises Again," Special Report No. 74, Tax Foundation, Washington, 1998.
9. John Locke, *Two Treatises of Government* (1690; reprint, Cambridge: Cambridge University Press, 1960), p. 446.
10. Etienne de la Boetie, *The Discourse of Voluntary Servitude*, ed. Murray Rothbard (1575; reprint, New York: Free Life Editions, 1975), p. 56.

CHAPTER 2

1. Bertrand de Jouvenel, *On Power: The Natural History of Its Growth* (1948; reprint, Indianapolis: Liberty Fund Press, 1993, p. 19. Jouvenel used the term "power" to denote "the totalitarity of the components of government."
2. Quoted in H. L. Mencken, *A New Dictionary of Quotations* (1942; reprint, New York: Alfred Knopf, 1984), p. 1145.
3. Quoted in H. L. Mencken, *Prejudices,* 2nd ser. (New York: Knopf, 1924), p. 221.
4. Quoted in Friedrich Hayek, *Constitution of Liberty* (1960; reprint, Chicago: Henry Regnery, 1972), p. 246.
5. *The Complete Madison: His Basic Writings,* Saul Padover, ed., (New York: Harper & Brothers, 1953), p. 340.
6. Christopher Daly, "Rhode Island's Image: Down in the Dumps," *Washington Post,* December 24, 1995. See also David Segal, "Rogues Island," *New Republic,* November 25, 1991.
7. Quoted in Dennis Coyle, *Property Rights and the Constitution* (Albany: State University of New York, 1993), p. 240.

8. Carl J. Friedrich, "Modern Man's Golden Calf," in Waldo Browne, ed., *Leviathan in Crisis* (New York: Viking, 1946), p. 84.

9. Arthur Lionel Smith, "English Political Philosophy in the Seventeenth and Eighteenth Centuries," in *Cambridge Modern History,* vol. 6 (Cambridge: Cambridge University, 1909), p. 802.

10. Harold Laski, *The State in Theory and Practice* (London: George Allen & Unwin, 1935), p. 61-62.

11. Jean-Jacques Rousseau, *The Social Contract and Discourses* (New York: Dutton, 1950), p. 198.

12. Ibid., p. 17.

13. Ibid., p. 38.

14. Quoted in Robert Wokler, "Rousseau and His Critics on the Fanciful Liberties We Have Lost," in Robert Wokler, ed., *Rousseau and Liberty* (Manchester: Manchester University Press, 1995), p. 208.

15. Maurice Cranston, "Rousseau's Theory of Liberty" in Robert Wokler, ed., *Rousseau and Liberty* (Manchester: Manchester University Press, 1995), p. 241.

16. Rousseau, *The Social Contract and Discourses,* p. 32.

17. Rousseau, *The Social Contract and Discourses,* p. 19-20.

18. Quoted in William Ralph Inge, "The God-State" (1922) in Browne, ed., *Leviathan in Crisis,* p. 150.

19. G. W. F. Hegel, *Philosophy of History* (New York: P. F. Collier & Son, 1902), p. 87.

20. Ibid.

21. Ibid., p. 61.

22. Quoted in Laski, *The State in Theory and Practice,* p. 64.

23. Quoted in L. T. Hobhouse, *The Metaphysical Theory of the State* (London: George Unwin, 1918), p. 24.

24. G. W. F. Hegel, *The Philosophy of Hegel,* Carl Friedrich, ed. (New York: Modern Library, 19540, p. 323.

25. Ibid., p. 283. Historian William Dunning noted in 1920: "The ineffable majesty predicted by [Hegel] of the State as idea, was inevitably transferred by the followers to the State as a concrete fact. In the heyday of Hegel's popularity at Berlin (1818-1831) there was no lack of philophasters to whom the Prussian monarchy was 'perfected rationality,' or who saw the 'eternal and necessary essence of spirit' in the stodgy Hohenzollern then on the throne." William Archibald Dunning, *A History of Political Theories from Rousseau to Spencer* (1920; reprint, New York: Macmillan, 1936), p. 159.

26. Quoted in J. K. Bluntschli, *The Theory of the State* (Oxford: Clarendon Press, 1895), p. 74.

27. Quoted in J. Salwyn Schapiro, *Liberalism: Its Meaning and History* (Princeton: Van Nostrand, 1958), p. 173.

28. F.S.C. Northrup, *The Meeting of East and West,* (New York: MacMillan, 1946), p. 199.

29. Ernst Cassirer, *The Myth of the State* (New Haven: Yale University Press, 1946), p. 248.

30. Ibid., p. 263.

31. Thomas Hill Green, *Lectures on the Principles of Political Obligation* (London: Longmans, 1895), p. 136.

32. David Ritchie, *The Principles of State Interference* (1891; reprint, Freeport, NY: Books for Libraries Press, 1969), p. 102.

33. Bernard Bosanquet, *The Principle of Individuality and Value* (London: Macmillan, 1912), p. 316.

34. Bernard Bosanquet, *The Philosophical Theory of the State* (1899; reprint, New York: St. Martin's Press, 1965), p. 139.

35. Adam Ulam, *Philosophical Foundations of English Socialism* (1951; reprint, New York: Octagon Books, 1964) p. 59.

36. Quoted in Schapiro, *Liberalism: Its Meaning and History,* p. 172.

37. Hobhouse, *The Metaphysical Theory of the State,* p. 24.

38. Wadia wrote, "When a political philosopher talks of the State, he cannot possibly be expected to mean by it all the varying and mutually conflicting types of it. Hence he uses it only in its ideal sense, as the perfected State wherein all the associations have a harmonious life and all the individuals find the most perfect means for their moral development. Such a State has not so far existed, but the conception of it serves as the standard, whereby to test the relative worth of historic and existing states. . . ." A. R. Wadia, "The State Under a Shadow," *International Journal of Ethics,* vol. 31, 1921, pp. 325 and 327.

39. Laski, *The State in Theory and Practice,* p. 45.

40. Guido de Ruggiero, *The History of European Liberalism* (1927; reprint, Boston: Beacon, 1959), p. 342.

41. Benito Mussolini, "The Political and Social Doctrine of Fascism," *Political Quarterly,* vol. 4, July-September 1933, p. 352. This article is a translation of a 1932 *Encyclopedia Italiana* article written by Mussolini.

42. Carmen Haider, "The Meaning and Significance of Fascism," *Political Science Quarterly,* vol. 48, December 1933, p. 562.

43. Friedrich Nietzsche, *Thus Spoke Zarathustra* (New York: Penguin, 1969), p. 76.

44. Ralph Raico, "Keynes and the Reds," *The Free Market,* April 1997.

45. Quoted in Paul Craig Roberts and Karen LaFollette, *Meltdown: Inside the Soviet Economy* (Washington: Cato Institute, 1990), p. 129.

46. Quoted in Paul Hollander, *Political Pilgrims* (Lanham, MD: University Press of America, 1990), p. 128.

47. Quoted in Robert Conquest, *The Great Terror* (London: Macmillan, 1968), p. 183.

48. Ibid., p. 230.

49. Virgil Michel, "Liberalism Yesterday and Tomorrow," *Ethics,* vol. 49, 1939, p. 419.

50. Adam Ulam, *Stalin: The Man and His Era* (New York: Viking, 1973), p. 688.

51. Jo Durden-Smith, "Rose-Colored Soviet Russia," *Moscow Times,* October 1, 1996.

52. "When Political Scientists Gather," *National Journal,* September 16, 1978, p. 1465.

53. Paul Johnson, "Terror Unlimited," *Daily Mail* (London), November 29, 1997.

54. Quoted in James Bovard, "Trim the Civil-Service Pension Bonanza," *Wall Street Journal,* February 14, 1985.

55. James M. Beck, *Our Wonderland of Bureaucracy* (New York: Macmillan, 1933), p. 118.

56. Motto from a St. Gaudens presentation metal, 1905-06, on display at the Cornell University Art Museum, 1997.

57. William James, "The Moral Equalivalent of War," in *Essays on Faith and Morals* (Cleveland: World Publishing, 1962), p. 322. (emphasis added)

58. Herbert Croly, *The Promise of American Life* (1909; reprint, Cambridge: Harvard University Press, 1965), p. 267.

59. Larry Arnn, "No Right to Do Wrong," *Policy Review,* fall 1995, p. 54.

60. Quoted in Hayek, *The Constitution of Liberty,* p. 246.

61. John Dewey, "Force and Coercion," *International Journal of Ethics,* vol. 26, April 1916, p. 364.

62. Ibid.

63. Ibid.

64. Quoted in Alan Brinkley, "The New Deal and the Idea of the State," in Steve Fraser and Gary Gerstle, eds., *The Rise and Fall of the New Deal Order, 1930-1980* (Princeton: Princeton University Press, 1989), p. 92.

65. Benjamin Anderson, *Economics and the Public Welfare* (1949; reprint, Indianapolis: Liberty Press, 1979), pp. 100-291.

66. Robert Skidelsky, *The Road from Serfdom* (New York: Penguin, 1997), p. 53.

67. James Bovard, *The Farm Fiasco* (San Francisco: ICS Press, 1989), pp. 12-24.

68. Milton Friedman and Anna Schwartz, *A Monetary History of the United States, 1867-1960* (Princeton: Princeton University Press, 1963).

69. *The Public Papers and Addresses of Franklin D. Roosevelt, 1936* (New York: Random House, 1938), p. 233.

70. *The Public Papers and Address of Franklin D. Roosevelt, 1933* (New York: Random House, 1938), p. 47.

71. Quoted in Robert Reich, Review of *Liberal: Adolf A. Berle and the Vision of an American Era,* by Jordon Schwartz, *New Republic,* March 7, 1988.

72. *The Public Papers and Addresses of Franklin D. Roosevelt, 1936* (New York: Random House, 1938), p. 16.

73. *The Public Papers and Addresses of Franklin D. Roosevelt, 1936* (New York: Random House, 1938), p. 235.

74. *Nothing to Fear: The Selected Addresses of Franklin Delano Roosevelt 1932-1945,* ed. B. D. Zevin (Boston: Houghton Mifflin, 1946), p. 365.

75. Ibid.

76. Rexford Tugwell, *Our Economic System and Its Problems* (New York: Harcourt Brace, 1934), p. 541.

77. Rexford Tugwell, "Design for Government, " *Political Science Quarterly,* Vol. 68, September 1933, p. 330.

78. William E. Leuchtenberg, *Franklin D. Roosevelt and the New Deal* (New York: Harper & Row, 1963), p. 77.

79. Rexford Tugwell, *Our Economic System and Its Problems,* pp. 541-42.

80. *Political Quotations,* ed. Daniel Banker (Detroit: Gale Research, 1990), p. 118.

81. Quoted in Ludwig von Mises, *Liberalism in the Classical Tradition* (Irvington-on-Hudson, New York: Foundation for Economic Education, 1985), p. v. Clark also declared: "A liberal believes government is a proper tool to use in the development of a society which attempts to carry Christian principles of conduct into practical effect."

82. *Public Papers of the Presidents of the United States—John F. Kennedy, 1963* (Washington: Government Printing Office, 1964), p. 326.

83. Frank S. Meyer, *In Defense of Freedom: A Conservative Credo* (Chicago: Regnery, 1962), p. 134.

84. *The World Almanac of Presidential Quotations: Quotations from America's Presidents,* ed. Elizabeth Frost-Knappman (New York: Pharos Books, 1993), p. 166.

85. Edward J. Erler, "Public Policy and the 'New Equality,'" *Political Science Reviewer,* vol. 8, fall 1978, p. 258.

86. "Remarks to a Democratic National Committee Meeting," *Public Papers of the Presidents,* January 21, 1997, p. 66.

87. Myrna Blyth and Becky Cain, "In the White House; President and Mrs. Bill Clinton; The Clintons and the Doles. Exclusive LHJ Interviews," *Ladies Home Journal,* November 1996.

88. Anna Quindlen, "America's Sleeping Sickness," *New York Times,* October 17, 1993.

89. Editorial, "White House Dishonesty," *Arizona Republic,* January 3, 1998.

90. Harold Laski, *The State in Theory and Practice,* pp. 26-27.

91. George Gilder, *Wealth and Poverty* (New York: Bantam, 1981), p. 106.

92. George Stigler, *The Economist as Preacher and Other Essays* (Chicago: University of Chicago Press, 1982), p. 126.

93. George Stigler, *The Citizen and the State* (Chicago: University of Chicago Press, 1975), p. 53.

94. Frank Chodorov, *Fugitive Essays* (Indianapolis: Liberty Fund Press, 1980), p. 42-43.

95. James Gwartney, Robert Lawson, and Randall Holcombe, "The Size and Functions of Goverment and Economic Growth," report prepared for the Joint Economic Committee, April 1998.

96. Quote is from copy of 1936 introduction provided by Ball State University economics professor Mark Brandly.

97. Eli Heckscher, *Mercantilism* (London: George Allen & Unwin, 1937), p. 353. Heckscher, a Swedish economist, observed that it was "symptomatic of present-day tendencies that

Keynes does not mention anywhere the real reason for the excess of currency which has been characteristic of such a large part of the history of western civilization. This was of course quite simply that governments needed money to finance wars and other sate expenditures. Nine times out of ten this was the reason both for the debasement of coinage and for the over-issue of paper. . . ."

98. Theodore J. Lowi, *The End of Liberalism* (New York: Norton, 1969), p. 85.
99. *Political Quotations,* ed. Banker, p. 94.
100. *Redlands Foothill Groves v. Jacobs,* 30 F. Supp 995, 998 (1940).
101. *American Banana Company v. United Fruit Co.,* 213 U.S. 347, 356 (1909).
102. *National Data Collection on Police Use of Force,* published jointly by the National Institute of Justice (Washington) and the Institute for Law and Justice (Alexandria, VA), April 1996.
103. Carmen Haider, "The Meaning and Significance of Fascism," *Political Science Quarterly,* vol. 48, December 1933, p. 559.
104. "Tax Foundation Announces May 10 as Tax Freedom Day," *Tax Notes Today,* April 16, 1998.
105. For the 1980 earnings figure, see Patrick Fleener, ed., *Facts & Figures on Government Finance* (Washington: Tax Foundation, 1995), p. 17. For the 1998 tax figure, see "Total Tax Collections to Reach $2.667 Trillion in 1998, Tax Foundation Says," *Tax Notes Today,* June 11, 1998.
106. "The Hidden Tax Bite in Everything You Buy," Americans for Tax Reform, Washington, 1998.
107. Internal Revenue Service, *1992 Annual Report* (Washington: Government Printing Office, 1993), p. 7.
108. For instance, Treasury Secretary Robert Rubin, in a September 22, 1997 letter, asserted: "Although the great preponderance of taxes owed are paid voluntarily, enforcement is a critical part of the job of the IRS. First, additional moneys owed but not voluntarily paid are collected through enforcement." "Rubin Asks Roth to Watch Rhetoric on Eve of IRS Abuse Hearings," *Tax Notes Today,* September 23, 1997.
109. General Accounting Office, "Financial Audit—Examination of IRS's Fiscal Year 1994 Financial Statements," August 1995, p. 52.
110. "Prepared Statement of Charles Rossotti, Commissioner of Internal Revenue Service before the Senate Finance Committee," Federal News Service, May 1, 1998.
111. Daniel Pilla, "Why You Can't Trust the IRS," Cato Institute Policy Analysis no. 222, April 15, 1995.
112. Quoted in "Tax Notes," *Wall Street Journal,* September 14, 1979.
113. "Public Debt Reduction Fund Has Drawn in $38.6 Million, Congressional Research Service Report Says," *Tax Notes Today,* June 13, 1994.
114. Interview with IRS information officer Don Roberts, January 13, 1998.
115. General Accounting Office, "Tax Administration: Extent and Causes of Erroneous Levies," December 21, 1993.
116. "Bank Statements Provided Notice of IRS's Seizure," *Tax Notes Today,* December 6, 1995.
117. Nancy Roman, "Gephardt Rolls Out Tax Cut," *Washington Times,* December 14, 1994.
118. Another example of this thinking comes from a commentary by Los Angeles Times contributing editor Robert Scheer: "The mood of the Republican congressional leadership is so ideologically obtuse as to doom even this modest first step down the path of responsibility. They would rather kill people than raise taxes." Robert Scheer, "Why Fight a Sin Tax to Aid Child Health?" *Los Angeles Times,* April 22, 1997. I first became aware of this quotation through "The Best Notable Quotables of 1997," Media Research Center, December 15, 1997.
119. Senate Minority Leader Daschle whined: "We're sending the wrong message [about the IRS] by this incessant concentration on the abuse and not the enforcement." "White House, Dems Confer, Preparing for IRS Hearings," *Tax Notes Today,* April 23, 1998.
120. Paul Bedard, "Clinton Labels Tax Cut 'Selfish,'" *Washington Times,* November 4, 1997.

121. Interview with Sam Kazman, March 14, 1995.

122. Daniel Levine, "This Law Might Kill You," *Reader's Digest,* March 1993.

123. Editorial, "The Perils of CAFE," *New York Times,* August 4, 1991.

124. *Competitive Enterprise Institute and Consumer Alert v. National Highway Traffic Safety Administration,* 956 F.2d 321, (1992).

125. Jim Powell, "Why Housing Investors are Brave—or Foolish," *Wall Street Journal,* August 18, 1994.

126. Hamil Harris, "D.C. Is Raking In the Fines; New Ticket Effort Targets Leaf-Law Violators," *Washington Post,* April 13, 1996.

127. Ibid.

128. Ibid.

129. Editorial, "Getting Away with Murder in D.C.," *Washington Post,* September 14, 1997.

130. Dennis O'Brien, "Some Firms Charge City Used Iron Fist on Fences," *Chicago Tribune,* August 23, 1996.

131. Gideon Kanner, "Clear Views—and a Total Lack of Insight," *Los Angeles Times,* February 1, 1998.

132. Karl Vick, "A Cutback, Literally; Stop Using 'G' Word, Duncan Tells County," *Washington Post,* October 20, 1995.

133. Memo from Bruce Romer to all department heads, Montgomery County, Maryland, government, September 29, 1995.

134. "Maryland School Enforces Quota System," CBS Evening News, September 12, 1995.

135. Manuel Perez-Rivas, "Is Rockville Pike at Its Peak?" *Washington Post,* December 26, 1997.

136. Lara Jakes, "Duncan's Pro-Business Pledge Wows," *Washington Times,* January 16, 1995.

137. Cass Sunstein, *After the Rights Revolution: Reconceiving the Regulatory State* (Cambridge: Harvard University Press, 1990), p. 40.

138. Interview with Gerald Arenberg, September 10, 1996.

139. A so-called drunk driving checkpoint erected by Florida police near Orlando in 1994 resulted in 65 drivers receiving fines for crimes such as not carrying proof of insurance, not wearing seat belts, having non-functioning horns or loud mufflers, and failure to have the correct residential address on drivers license—almost ten times as many drivers were fined for such violations as were fined for drunk driving. "Seven People Arrested for DUI at a Volusia Checkpoint," *Orlando Sentinel,* December 31, 1994.

140. Phillip J. O'Connor, "Too Loud, Too Late, You Lose Your Car; More Suburbs Seize Cars in Crackdowns on Minor Lawbreakers," *Chicago Sun-Times,* March 31, 1996.

141. James Bovard, "Blown Away," *Playboy,* August 1996.

142. Kristan Trugman, "Police put Brakes on Car Seizures," *Washington Times,* October 23, 1997.

143. For an overview of forfeiture abuses, see E. E. Edwards, "Governmental Abuse of Forfeiture Powers: Three Cases," *Journal of Legislation,* vol. 21, 1995, p. 229.

144. State and local governments have also jumped on the bandwagon, increasing their confiscations of private property by a hundredfold since the 1970s. Interview with Steven Kessler, September 21, 1993. Kessler's study on forfeiture is *Civil and Criminal Forfeiture: Federal and State Practice* (New York: Clark, Boardman, and Callaghan, 1993).

145. Shannon Noya, "Hoisted by Their Own Petard: Adverse Inferences in Civil Forfeiture," *Northwestern School of Law Journal of Criminal Law & Criminology,* vol. 86, winter, 1996, p. 493.

146. Oral hearings before the Supreme Court, *U.S. v. Bajakajian,* no. 96-1487, November 4, 1997.

147. Press Release, FBI, October 4, 1997.

148. The number of prisoners increased from 196,000 in 1972 to 1,244,000 in 1997. Interview with Felicia Hobbs, National Criminal Justice Reference Service, Justice Department, August 10, 1998.

149. "Lifetime Likelihood of Going to State or Federal Prison," Bureau of Justice Statistics, NCJ-160092, March 1997.

150. Interview with IRS press spokesman Larry Blevins, January 12, 1998. Also, various IRS annual reports and GAO reports.

151. Letter from Jim Baxter of the National Motorist Association to author, May 7, 1998. Baxter noted: "There is no centralized source of ticket data. Much of the numerical data is deliberately hidden or destroyed, mostly by local units of government that don't want to share the revenue with state government."

152. Gordon Wood, *The Creation of the American Republic, 1776-1787* (Chapel Hill: University of North Carolina Press, 1969), p. 283.

153. U.S. Congress, Senate Judiciary Committee, *Reorganization of the Federal Judiciary: Adverse Report from the Senate Committee on the Judiciary Submitted to Accompany S. 1392,* June 7, 1937 (Washington: Government Printing Office, 1937), p. 8.

154. *Breithaupt v. Abram,* 352 U.S. 432, 442 (1957).

155. *Arizona v. Fulminante,* 111 S. Ct. 1246, March 26, 1991.

156. *U.S. v. Carolene Products Co.,* 304 U.S. 144 (1938).

157. Geoffrey P. Miller, "The True Story of Carolene Products," in Philip Kurland, Gerhard Casper and Dennis Hutchinson, eds., *Supreme Court Law Review,*(Chicago: University of Chicago, 1987), p. 399.

158. Ibid., p. 422.

159. *U.S. v. Carolene Products Co.,* 304 U.S. 144, 152 (1938).

160. James DeLong, *Property Matters* (New York: Free Press, 1997), p. 87.

161. "Brief for Appellants on Reargument, *Wickard v. Filburn, Charles Fahy, Solicitor General,* September 1942," reprinted in Philip Kurland, ed., *Landmark Briefs and Arguments of the Supreme Court of the United States: Constitutional Law,* vol. 39, (Washington: University Publications of America, 1975), p. 111.

162. Wickard v. Filburn, 317 U.S. 111, 125 (1942).

163. "Brief for Appellants on Reargument, *Wickard v. Filburn,*" *Landmark Briefs and Arguments,* p. 771.

164. *Wickard v. Filburn,* 317 U.S. 111, 118, 131 (1942).

165. *Wickard v. Filburn,* 317 U.S. 111, 127 (1942).

166. Martin Anderson, *The Federal Bulldozer* (Cambridge: MIT Press, 1964), pp. 189-90.

167. Berman v. Parker, 348 U.S. 26, 33 (1954).

168. Coyle, *Property Rights and the Constitution,* p. 44.

169. Michael Powell, "Showing Dubious Progress in a Deadly District," *Washington Post,* April 19, 1998.

170. John Nivala, "Constitutional Architecture: The First Amendment and the Single Family House," *San Diego Law Review,* vol. 33, winter 1996, p. 291.

171. *Chevron v. Natural Resources Defense Council,* 461 U.S. 956, (1983).

172. Michael Greve, Speech at American Enterprise Institute, November 7, 1996, on occasion of the publication of his book, *The Demise of Environmentalism in American Law* (Washington: American Enterprise Institute, 1996).

173. E. P. Krauss, "Unchecked Powers: The Supreme Court and Administrative Law," *Marquette Law Review,* vol. 75, summer 1992, p. 837.

174. James W. Ely, Jr., *The Guardian of Every Other Right* (New York: Oxford University Press, 1992), p. 127.

175. Ibid., p. 140.

176. *United Steelworkers of America v. Weber,* 443 U.S. 193 (1979).

177. Deborah Billings and Pamela Prah, "Labor Department Expects Data to Show Major Difference from Affirmative Action," *Daily Labor Report,* March 20, 1995.

178. Herman Belz, *Equality Transformed* (New Brunswick, NJ: Transaction, 1991), p. 163.

179. *United Steelworkers of America v. Weber,* 443 U.S. 193, 224, 226 (1979).

180. Belz, *Equality Transformed,* p. 168.

181. *Congressional Record,* March 13, 1996, p.H2129.

182. *Congressional Record,* July 28, 1995, p. S10902.

183. *Congressional Record,* November 13, 1995, p. S 17000.

184. *Congressional Record,* January 3, 1996, p. S 14.

185. Quoted in John Phillip Reid, *The Concept of Representation in the Age of the American Revolution* (Chicago: University of Chicago Press, 1989), p. 30.

186. *D.A.R.E. Officer's Guide, Grades K-4; Lesson 3 (DARE K-1-2),* p. 25.

187. Bureau of Justice Assistance, "An Invitation to Project DARE: Drug Abuse Resistance Education," Program Brief, U.S. Department of Justice, June 1988, p. 4.

188. James Bovard, "DARE Scare: Turning Children into Informants?" *Washington Post,* January 30, 1994.

189. Renee Ordway, "Police Chief Must Face Lawsuit, *Bangor Daily News,* July 15, 1997. The judge was not ruling on the facts in the case but on whether the student's allegations were sufficient to go to trial; the Searsport Police Department claimed that the officer should be legally immune even if all the allegations were truthful. The Searsport Police Department settled the case with a cash payment to the student's family a week before jury selection was scheduled to begin in October 1997. Walter Griffin, "Searsport Settles Informant's Suit," *Bangor Daily News,* October 4, 1997.

190. Dennis Cauchon, "Study Critical of D.A.R.E. Rejected," *USA Today,* October 4, 1994.

191. Denise Hamilton, "The Truth About D.A.R.E.," *New Times Los Angeles,* March 20, 1997.

192. William Booth, "Exploding Number of SWAT Teams Sets Off Alarms," *Washington Post,* June 17, 1997.

193. Peter Cassidy, "Police Take a Military Turn," *Boston Globe,* January 11, 1998.

194. William Booth, "Exploding Number of SWAT Teams Sets Off Alarms," *Washington Post,* June 17, 1997.

195. Ibid.

196. House of Representatives, *Investigation into the Activities of Federal Law Enforcement Agencies Toward the Branch Davidians,* Report 104-749, August 2, 1996 (Washington: Government Printing Office, 1996), p. 94.

197. Transcript, "Joint Hearing of the Crime Subcommittee of the House Judiciary Committee and the National Security International Affairs and Criminal Justice Subcommittee of the House Government Reform and Oversight Committee, Subject: Review of Siege of Branch Davidians' Compound in Waco, Texas," Federal News Service, July 24, 1995.

198. Lee Hancock, "Agent Acknowledges Changing Story on Raid," *Dallas Morning News,* January 19, 1994.

199. Ellen Cantarow, "Not Tears Alone; Toxic Effects of CS, or o-chlorobenzylidene malonitrile, a Tear Gas," *Technology Review,* October 1988, p. 16.

200. House of Representatives Report, *Investigation into the Activities of Federal Law Enforcement Agencies Toward the Branch Davidians,* p. 96.

201. Interview with John Mica, July 26, 1995.

202. Interview with Carol Moore, August 5, 1998. Moore is the author of a book on the confrontation between the Davidians and the federal government. Brooks made this comment during a recess of a congressional hearing; Brooks was not aware the C-SPAN microphones were on at that time. Brooks' statement was used against him in the 1994 congressional race.

203. "Day Ten of Oversight Hearings into Actions of Federal Agents at Waco, Texas," House Judiciary Subcommittee on Crime, August 1, 1995.

204. Mark Smith, "5 Davidians Get Maximum Prison Terms," *Houston Chronicle,* June 18, 1994.

205. Sam Howe Verhovek, "11 in Texas Sect are Acquitted of Key Charges," *New York Times,* February 27, 1994.

206. The jury apparently mistakenly convicted the defendants on a firearms charge tied to a conspiracy charge that the defendants were found innocent on. The *New York Times*

reported on March 1, 1994: "Judge Smith set aside convictions on one count for seven defendants, including one woman who was acquitted on all other charges, saying the jury had misunderstood his instructions. He said it should not have found the defendants guilty of using a firearm in furtherance of a conspiracy when it had effectively decided that there was no conspiracy." Sam Howe Verhovek, "Juror Says Doubts Determined Verdict in Sect Trial," *New York Times,* March 1, 1994.

207. Steve McGonigle, "FBI Chief Praises Agents' Work in Branch Davidian Crisis," *Dallas Morning News,* October 14, 1993.

208. CNN, "Capital Gang," transcript no. 176, April 22, 1995.

209. James Bovard, "Waco Must Get a Hearing," *Wall Street Journal,* May 15, 1995.

210. "Statement of Larry A. Potts, Assistant Director of the Criminal Division, FBI, House Judiciary Hearing, Federal Actions at Waco, Texas," Federal Document Clearing House, July 27, 1995.

211. James Bovard, "Hearings Show Waco Defense is Wacky," *Wall Street Journal,* August 2, 1995. Most of the media coverage hailed Reno as a heroine for refusing to budge from her official line in the face of questioning from Republicans.

212. Editorial, "Janet Reno, Torchbearer," *Washington Times,* May 1, 1997.

213. Transcript, "Hearing of the Senate Judiciary Committee, Subject: Federal Raid at Ruby Ridge, Idaho," Federal Documents Clearing House, September 19, 1995.

214. Clyde Wayne Crews, "Ten Thousand Commandments: A Policymaker's Snapshot of the Federal Regulatory State," Competitive Enterprise Institute, Washington, January 1998, p. 13.

215. Robert Rogowsky, "Sub Rosa Regulation: The Iceberg Beneath the Surface," in Roger E. Meiners and Bruce Yandle, eds., *Regulation and the Reagan Era* (New York: Holmes and Meier, 1989), p. 210.

216. Anthony Faiola, "Liquor Ads on TV," *Washington Post,* November 9, 1996.

217. A. V. Dicey, *Lectures on the Relation Between Law and Public Opinion in England During the Nineteenth Century* (1905; reprint, London: Macmillan, 1952), p. 42.

218. Wood, *The Creation of the American Republic,* p. 5.

219. Wood, *The Creation of the American Republic,* p. 4.

220. James Castello, "The Limits of Popular Sovereignty: Using the Initiative Power to Control Legislative Procedure," *California Law Review,* March 1986, vol. 74, p. 548.

221. Stephen Holmes, *Passions and Constraints: On the Theory of Liberal Democracy* (Chicago: University of Chicago Press, 1995), p. xi.

222. Sunstein, *After the Rights Revolution,* pp. 230 and 233.

223. "Prepared Statement of Susan Berresford, President, Ford Foundation, Before the House Committee on Government Reform and Oversight," Federal News Service, October 31, 1997.

224. David Kopel and Christopher Little, "Communitarians, Neorepublicans, and Guns: Assessing the Case for Firearms Prohibition," *Maryland Law Review,* vol. 56, March 1997, p. 438.

225. PBS, "Supreme Court Watch," *The NewsHour with Jim Lehrer* (Public Broadcasting Service), transcript no. 5837, May 27, 1997.

226. Robert Kuttner, "A Government to Be Trusted," *Sacramento Bee,* April 15, 1996 (distributed by the Washington Post Writers Group).

227. Aleksandr Solzhenitsyn, "What Kind of 'Democracy' Is This?" *New York Times,* January 4, 1997.

228. Matthew Brzezinski and Scott Kilman, "The Red Earth," *Wall Street Journal,* January 12, 1998.

229. Bob Herbert, "War Games," *New York Times,* February 22, 1998.

230. Ibid.

231. Alexander Hamilton, James Madison, and John Jay, *The Federalist Papers* (New York: New American Library, 1961) pp. 282-83.

232. See, for instance, Steven Duke and Albert Gross, *America's Longest War* (New York: Putnam, 1993), and James Bovard, *Lost Rights: The Destruction of American Liberty* (New York: St. Martin's, 1994), pp. 227-248.

233. James Bovard, "Don't Touch That Style!" *American Spectator,* April 1997.

234. Julie Chao, "Seattle's Landmarks Aren't All That Old, but City Isn't Either," *Wall Street Journal,* September 19, 1995.

235. Sara Rimer, "Vermont Debates Value of Saving a Rural Image," *New York Times,* July 4, 1993.

236. Beck, *Our Wonderland of Bureaucracy,* p. 223.

237. Senate Committee on Environment and Public Works, *Federal Highway Beautification Assistance Act of 1979,* July 17, 1979 (Washington, D.C.: Government Printing Office, 1979), p. 353.

238. "Current Penalties—Federal-Aid Highway Program," American Highway Users Alliance, 1997.

239. Robert Pear, "Vast Worker Database to Track Deadbeat Parents," *New York Times,* September 22, 1997.

240. General Accounting Office, "Health Insurance Standards—New Federal Law Creates Challenges for Consumers, Insurers, Regulators," March 10, 1998.

241. Sheryl Gay Stolberg, "Health Identifier For All Americans Runs Into Hurdles," *New York Times,* July 20, 1998.

242. Anthony DePalma, "New Rules at U.S. Borders Provoke Criticism," *New York Times,* November 14, 1997. Anna Marie Gallagher, a lawyer with the American Immigration Law Foundation, observed: "The most frightening aspect of it is the power it gives to low-level Government officials. They are judge, jury and executioner."

243. Rep. Ron Paul and Rep. Bob Barr, along with the Free Congress Federation, took the lead in challenging these regulations in 1998.

244. Editorial, "Fix Communications Law," *New York Times,* February 9, 1996.

245. "FCC Adopts 'V-Chip' Standards," Associated Press, March 12, 1998.

246. James Bovard, "Disarming Those who Need Guns Most," *Wall Street Journal,* December 23, 1996.

247. Tim Weiner, "CIA Taught, Then Dropped, Mental Torture in Latin America," *New York Times,* January 29, 1997.

248. John Diamond, "Revised CIA Manual Discourages Use of Torture by Interrogators," Associated Press, January 29, 1997.

249. Tom Herman, "Tax Report," *Wall Street Journal,* June 17, 1998.

250. Philosopher Bertrand Russell wrote in 1916: "The extent of the tyranny thus exercised is concealed by its very success: few men consider it worth while to incur a persecution which is almost certain to be thorough and effective." Bertrand Russell, "The State as Organized Power," in Browne, ed., *Leviathan in Crisis,* p. 45.

251. See, for instance, "Address Before a Joint Session of the Congress on the State of the Union," *Public Papers of the Presidents,* February 4, 1997, p. 136.

CHAPTER 3

1. Quoted in Jacques Ellul, "Politicalization and Political Solutions," in Kenneth S. Templeton, Jr., ed., *The Politicalization of Society* (Indianapolis: Liberty Press, 1979), p. 232.

2. Gurney Benham, *Benham's Book of Quotations* (New York: G. P. Putnam's, 1946), p. 542b. The Latin version is: Beneficium accipere libertatem est vendere.

3. Bloch further noted, "In the formation of the network of personal subjections so characteristic of the age, the houses of prayer were among the most powerful centers of

attraction." Marc Bloch, *Feudal Society*, vol. 2 (Chicago: University of Chicago Press, 1961), p. 347.

4. John Phillip Reid, *The Concept of Liberty in the Age of the American Revolution* (Chicago: University of Chicago Press, 1988), p. 65.

5. Forrest McDonald, *Novus Ordo Seclorum: The Intellectual Origins of the Constitution* (Lawrence, KS: University Press of Kansas, 1985), p. 10.

6. Reid, *The Concept of Liberty*, pp. 56, 65, and 114.

7. John Trenchard and Thomas Gordon, in David Jacobson, ed., *The English Libertarian Heritage*, (San Francisco: Fox & Wilkes, 1994), p. 127-8.

8. Adam Smith, *The Wealth of Nations* (New York: Modern Library, 1937), p. 651.

9. Jean-Jacques Rousseau, *The Social Contract and Discourses* (New York: Dutton, 1950), p. 37.

10. Ibid., p. 18. (emphasis added)

11. Quoted in Ernst Cassirer, *The Question of Jean-Jacques Rousseau*, ed. Peter Gay (New Haven: Yale University Press, 1989), p. 10.

12. Maurice Cranston, *The Mask of Politics and Other Essays* (London: Allen Lane/Penguin, 1973), p. 74.

13. Quoted in Robert Hausheer, "Fichte," in *Conceptions of Liberty in Political Philosophy*, edited by Zbigniew Pelcynski and John Gray (New York: St. Martin's, 1984), p. 138.

14. Ibid., p. 139.

15. As professor Andrzej Walicki noted, "In Fichte's Utopia (considered to be a socialist Utopia by the Marxists of the Second International) the rational, totalitarian state was treated as an instrument of freedom-an instrument of collective ego, which controls and determines itself, subjects itself to laws, and in this way liberates itself from the humiliating power of blind necessity governing the world of things." Andrzej Walicki, "The Marxian Conception of Freedom," in Pelcynski and Gray, eds. *Conceptions of Liberty in Political Philosophy*, p. 227.

16. G. W. F. Hegel, *Hegel's Philosophy of Right* (New York: Oxford University Press, 1967), pp. 107 and 259-60.

17. Ibid., p. 144.

18. G. W. F. Hegel, *Philosophy of History* (New York: P. F. Collier & Son, 1902), p. 87.

19. G. W. F. Hegel, *Hegel's Philosophy of Right*, p. 280.

20. Professor Avital Simhony noted that "Green's advocacy of a positive conception of freedom is the watershed in the evolution of liberal theory, dividing the classical and the modern versions." Avital Simhony, "Beyond Negative and Positive Freedom: T. H. Green's View of Freedom," *Political Theory*, vol. 21, February 1993, p. 29.

21. Quoted in Ibid., p. 37.

22. Quoted in Ibid., p. 37.

23. Quoted in Adam Ulam, *Philosophical Foundations of English Socialism* (1951; reprint, New York: Octagon Books, 1964) p. 28.

24. David Nicholls, "Positive Liberty, 1880-1914," *American Political Science Review*, March 1962, vol. 56, p. 127.

25. Ibid., p. 114.

26. David Ritchie, *The Principles of State Interference* (1891; reprint, Freeport, NY: Books for Libraries Press, 1969), p. 85.

27. Ibid., p. 116.

28. Ibid., p. 85.

29. Quoted in Gertrude Carman Bussey, "Dr. Bosanquet's Doctrine of Freedom," *Philosophical Review*, vol. 25, September 1916, p. 712.

30. Bernard Bosanquet, *The Philosophical Theory of the State* (1899; reprinted, New York: St. Martin's Press, 1965), p. 132.

31. Quoted in George Crowder, "Negative and Positive Liberty," *Political Science*, vol, 40, December 1988, p. 64 (emphasis added).

32. John Dewey, *Liberalism and Social Action* (New York: G. P. Putnam's, 1935), p. 27.

33. Ibid., pp. 30-31.

34. Ibid., p. 54. (Emphasis in original.)

35. John Dewey, "Force and Coercion," *International Journal of Ethics*, vol. 26, April 1916, p. 366.

36. Dewey, *Liberalism and Social Action*, p. 48.

37. Quoted in James Stever, "Technology , Organization, Freedom," *Administration and Society*, vol. 24, February 1993, p. 434.

38. Quoted in Stephen Holmes, "Practically Wisdom," *New Republic*, March 11, 1996.

39. Alexander Meiklejohn, *What Does America Mean?* (New York: Norton, 1935), p. 208.

40. Ibid., p. 106.

41. Ibid., p. 111.

42. Ibid., p. 131.

43. Ibid., p. 221.

44. *The Public Papers and Addresses of Franklin D. Roosevelt, 1934* (New York: Random House, 1938), p. 422.

45. *The Public Papers and Addresses of Franklin D. Roosevelt, 1936* (New York: Random House, 1938), p. 232-233.

46. *Nothing to Fear: The Selected Addresses of Franklin Delano Roosevelt 1932-1945*, ed. by B. D. Zevin (Boston: Houghton Mifflin, 1946), p. 266.

47. See, for instance, Donald B. Kates, Jr., "Handgun Prohibition and the Original Meaning of the Second Amendment," *Michigan Law Review*, vol. 82, November 1983, p. 204, and Sanford Levinson, "The Embarrassing Second Amendment," *Yale Law Journal*, vol. 99, December 1989, p. 637. The vast majority of law journal articles that have examined the meaning of the Second Amendment in the past fifteen years have concluded that the Founding Fathers intended the amendment to protect the right of citizens to possess firearms.

48. For an excellent primer on the contemporary importance of the Ninth Amendment, see Randy Barnett, ed., *The Rights Retained by the People: The History and Meaning of the Ninth Amendment* (Fairfax, VA: George Mason University Press, 1989).

49. *Nothing to Fear: The Selected Addresses*, p. 265.

50. "Remarks at the 50th Anniversary Observance of Franklin D. Roosevelt's Four Freedoms Speech," *Public Papers of the Presidents*, January 30, 1991, p. 96.

51. "Text of Presidential Proclamation of Roosevelt History Month," U.S. Newswire, October 7, 1996.

52. *The Public Papers and Addresses of Franklin D. Roosevelt, 1944-45* (New York: Russell and Russell, 1950), p. 41.

53. Ibid.

54. Author Ralph Robey, writing in 1934, observed, "The New Deal [farm] program has frozen in the inefficient producer. . . All possibility of the public getting the benefits of continued improvements in agricultural technique has been stalemated." Ralph Robey, *Roosevelt vs. Recovery* (New York: Harper & Brothers, 1934), pp. 117-18.

55. *The Public Papers and Addresses of Franklin D. Roosevelt, 1944-45*, p. 37.

56. Ibid., p. 43.

57. Ibid., pp. 38-39.

58. Ibid., p. 32.

59. Norman Davies, *Heart of Europe: A Short History of Poland* (New York: Oxford University Press, 1984), p. 75.

60. "Remarks by the President in MTV's 'Enough is Enough' Forum on Crime," Office of the Press Secretary, White House, April 19, 1994.

61. Alexander Hamilton, James Madison, and John Jay, *The Federalist Papers* (New York: New American Library, 1961) p. 322. (Federalist no. 51)

62. "Research by CBO Director Dr. June O'Neill shows that an increase in monthly AFDC and Food Stamp benefit levels of 50 percent will cause an increase of 43 percent in the number of illegitimate births within a state." "Prepared Testimony of Robert Rector, Heritage Foundation, Before the House Ways and Means Committee, Hearing on Welfare Dependency and Illegitimacy," Federal News Service, May 23, 1996.

63. George Crowder, "Negative and Positive Liberty," *Political Science*, vol. 40, December 1988, p. 70.

64. Charles Taylor, "What's Wrong with Negative Liberty," in Alan Ryan, ed., *The Idea of Freedom*, (Oxford: Oxford University Press, 1979), pp. 177 and 180. (emphasis added)

65. Ibid., p. 185.

66. Ibid., p. 186.

67. *Public Papers of the Presidents, Lyndon B Johnson, 1963-64* (Washington: Government Printing Office, 1965), p. 820.

68. *Public Papers of the Presidents—Lyndon B. Johnson, 1965* (Washington: Government Printing Office, 1966), p. 57.

69. General Accounting Office, Review of Economic Opportunity Programs, March 18, 1969.

70. *Congressional Record*, October 11, 1966, p. A 5230. A September 17, 1996, article in the *Chicago Tribune* reported: "Police and municipal officers have complained in city after city that poverty war money and personnel have been used to produce a climate of hatred leading to race warfare."

71. Alexis de Tocqueville, *Democracy in America*, vol. 2 (Garden City, NY: Doubleday, 1969), p. 673.

72. Cass Sunstein, *After the Rights Revolution: Reconceiving the Regulatory State* (Cambridge: Harvard University Press, 1990), p. 40.

73. "Remarks by the President," Office of the Press Secretary, White House, November 5, 1996.

74. Sunstein, *After the Rights Revolution*, p. 40. (Emphasis added.)

75. Ibid., p. 41.

76. This was the name of a PBS special aired during a fund-raising marathon in 1996.

77. Robert Goodin, *Reasons for Welfare* (Princeton: Princeton University Press, 1988), p. 319.

78. "Prepared Testimony of Sam Kazman, Competitive Enterprise Institute, Before the House Committee on Commerce-Subject: Reauthorization of the National Highway Traffic Safety Administration," Federal News Service, May 22, 1997. Claybrook made the quoted comment on a CNN television program on November 21, 1983.

79. David Ottaway and Warren Brown, "From Life Saver To Fatal Threat; How the U.S., Automakers And a Safety Device Failed," *Washington Post*, June 1, 1997.

80. Joan Beck, "Switching Gears," *Chicago Tribune*, June 15, 1997.

81. "Prepared Testimony of Sam Kazman," May 22, 1997.

82. Editorial, "Mandate Mania," *Orange County Register*, June 20, 1997.

83. "House Leaders Not Buying Hatch/Richardson Supplement Bills," *Food Labeling News*, August 5, 1993.

84. For examples of FDA abuses, see the 1993 staff report by the office of Sen. Orrin Hatch: "False and Misleading: FDA's Report, 'Unsubstantiated Claims and Documented Health Hazards in the Dietary Marketplace.'"

85. See, for instance, Jane Brody, "High Intake of 2 Vitamins May Lower Coronary Risk," *New York Times*, February 4, 1998, and Jane Brody, "Vitamin E May Enhance Immunity, Study Finds," *New York Times*, May 7, 1997.

86. *The Speeches of Adolph Hitler, April 1922-August 1939*, vol. 1 (Oxford: Oxford University Press, 1942), p. 244.

87. Quoted in Fritz Machlup, "Liberalism and the Choice of Freedoms," in *Roads to Freedom: Essays in Honour of Friedrich A. von Hayek*, in Erich Streissler, ed. (London: Routledge & K. Paul, 1969), p. 126.

88. Sidney and Beatrice Webb, *Soviet Communism: A New Civilization?*, vol. 2 (New York: Charles Scribner's Sons, 1936), pp. 1038.

89. Ibid., vol. 2., p. 563.

90. Quoted in Dorothy Fosdick, *What is Liberty? A Study in Political Theory* (New York: Harper and Brothers, 1939), p. 28.

91. James Gregor, *The Ideology of Fascism* (New York: Free Press, 1969), p. 212.

92. *The Public Papers and Addresses of Franklin D. Roosevelt, 1937* (New York: Macmillan, 1941), p. 361.

93. Leslie M. Pape, "Some Notes on Democratic Freedom," *Ethics,* vol. 51, April 1941, p. 26.

94. Edward Hallett Carr, *The New Society* (London: Macmillan, 1951), p. 107.

95. Ibid., p. 108.

96. John Jewkes, *The New Ordeal by Planning* (New York: St. Martin's, 1968; book included verbatim reprints of several chapters from the 1948 edition, along with introductory chapters that helped readers understand historical developments), p. 213.

97. Ibid., p. 213.

98. Gideon Kanner, "Tennis Anyone?" *California Political Review,* March-April 1998, p. 17.

99. William Grimes, "History Explains Disparity Between English and French Cuisine," *New York Times,* May 9, 1998.

100. Quoted in Friedrich Hayek, *Law Legislation, and Liberty, vol. 2, The Mirage of Social Justice* (Chicago: University of Chicago Press, 1976), p. 184.

101. Quoted in Marvin Gettleman and David Mermelstein, eds., *The Great Society Reader* (New York: Random House, 1967), p. 256.

102. Henry Hazlitt, *The Conquest of Poverty* (New Rochelle, NY: Arlington House, 1973), p. 99.

103. U.S. Department of Agriculture, *Food and Nutrition,* February 1972.

104. James Bovard, "Feeding Everybody," *Policy Review,* Fall 1983.

105. "The Welfare Bill: Excerpts from Debate in the Senate on the Welfare Measure," *New York Times,* August 2, 1996.

106. "Radio Address of the President," Office of the Press Secretary, White House, December 7, 1996.

107. Robert Rector and William Labuer, *America's Failed $5.4 Trillion War on Poverty* (Washington: Heritage Foundation, 1995), p. 5.

108. Ibid, p. 26.

109. Blaine Harden, "Rejuvenation of Cities: Was It Just Cosmetics?" *Washington Post,* March 15, 1998.

110. Michael Tanner, Stephen Moore and David Hartman, "The Work versus Welfare Trade-Off," Cato Institute, September 19, 1995.

111. Rector and Lauber, *America's Failed $5.4 Trillion War on Poverty,* p. 26.

112. Robert Rector, "Welfare Reform Deception," Washington Times, August 17, 1997.

113. "Total Tax Collections to Reach $2.667 Trillion in 1998, Tax Foundation Says," *Tax Notes Today,* June 11, 1998.

114. "Prepared Statement of Lawrence Lilly Before the Senate Finance Committee-Subject: Oversight Hearing on the Internal Revenue Service," Federal News Service, September 24, 1997.

115. Goodin, *Reasons for Welfare,* p. 313.

116. Edgar Browning, "The Marginal Cost of Redistribution," *Public Finance Quarterly,* vol. 21, January 1993, p. 3.

117. Ibid., p. 3.

118. Amy Gutmann, *Liberal Equality* (Cambridge: Cambridge University Press, 1980), p. 8.

119. Ibid., p. 123.

120. Alan Wolfe, Review of *Passions and Constraint: On the Theory of Liberal Democracy,* by Stephen Holmes, *New Republic,* May 1, 1995.

121. "Special Supplement: The Full Text of Clinton's FY 1995 Budget Submitted to Congress Feb. 7, 1994. Analytical Perspectives: Generational Accounting," *Daily Report for Executives*, February 10, 1994, p. d90.

122. *See* briefs for U.S. Government in the case of *Nestor v. Fleming,* 363 U.S. 603 (1960).

123. The first quote is from Cass Sunstein, "Speech in the Welfare State: Free Speech Now," *University of Chicago Law Review*, vol. 59, winter 1992, p. 265, and the second is from Sunstein, *After the Rights Revolution*, p. 39.

124. Friedrich Hayek, *Law Legislation and Liberty*, vol. 1, *Rules and Order* (Chicago: University of Chicago Press, 1973), p. 123.

125. Julian Simon, "What the Starvation Lobby Eschews," *Wall Street Journal*, November 18, 1996.

126. Doug Bandow, "Foreign Aid: Repeating History," Copley News Service, June 17, 1997.

127. Kim Holmes, Bryan Johnson, and Melanie Kirkpatrick, *1997 Index of Economic Freedom* (Washington: Heritage Foundation and Dow Jones, 1997) p. 18.

128. Etienne de la Boetie, *The Discourse of Voluntary Servitude,* edited by Murray Rothbard (New York: Free Life Editions, 1975), p. 70.

129. "Excerpts from President Clinton's FY 1996 Budget Submitted to Congress Feb. 6, 1995; Part 1 of 2," *Daily Report for Executives*, February 7, 1995, p. d139. Emphasis added.

130. William P. Shaw, "Rebuilding the Nation's Public Housing," *Indianapolis Star*, November 12, 1995.

131. U.S. Department of Housing and Urban Development, Office of Policy Development and Research, *Fiscal Year 1998 Income Limits and Section 8 Fair Market Rents*, October 1997.

132. HUD Secretary Henry Cisneros had heatedly denied such rental excesses in a response to a 1994 Wall Street Journal article. See James Bovard, "Clinton's Wrecking Ball for the Suburbs," *Wall Street Journal*, August 4, 1994.

133. Judith Havemann, "Rescue for Low-Income Housing Approved," *Washington Post*, October 9, 1997.

134. William Goldschlag, "Rent Program a Real HUD Dud," *New York Daily News*, April 29, 1997.

135. Letter to Docket Clerk, Department of Housing and Urban Development, Washington, from Bertha M. Conger, Davenport, Iowa, May 28, 1993.

136. Quoted in Lars-Erik Nelson, "Housing Vouchers a Noble Idea that Hits Working Poor," *New York Daily News*, May 1, 1996.

137. Kirstin Downey, "HUD Report Renews Debate on Rent Rates," *Washington Post*, June 1, 1991.

138. U.S. Department of Housing and Urban Development, Office of Policy Development and Research, *Fiscal Year 1998 Income Limits and Section 8 Fair Market Rents*, October 1997.

139. Terry Pristin, "Battery Park City to Give Middle-Income Renters a Break," *New York Times*, March 24, 1998.

140. James Brooke, "Subsidies for High-Income Families," *New York Times*, May 17, 1998.

141. Manuel Perez-Rivas, "Montgomery Housing Agency Fights Back," *Washington Post*, February 15, 1998.

142. Alice Thomas, "Audit of Section 8 Finds Problems," *Columbus Dispatch*, December 22, 1997. See also the report of Abt Associates Inc., "Recommendations on Ways to Make the Section 8 Program More Acceptable in the Private Rental Market," January 31, 1994.

143. Howard Husock, "The Inherent Flaws of HUD," Cato Institute, December 22, 1997.

144. E. Thomas McClanahan, "The Housing Fiasco," *Kansas City Star*, June 1, 1997.

145. Serge Kovaleski, "Illegal Rent Subsidy Vouchers Were Easy to Obtain," *Washington Post*, May 2, 1994.

146. David Josar, "Ex-Housing Official, 2 Associates Found Guilty in Bribery Scheme," *Detroit News*, October 4, 1996.

147. "Former U.S. Housing Agency Worker Indicted," *Los Angeles Times*, September 27, 1996.

148. "Proclamation 6708: Anniversary of the Americans with Disabilities Act, 1994," *Public Papers of the President*, July 26, 1994, p. 1559. President George Bush used similar rhetoric when he signed the original bill in 1990: "With today's signing of the landmark Americans for Disabilities Act, every man, woman, and child with a disability can now pass through once-closed doors into a bright new era of equality, independence and freedom." "Signing of the American with Disabilities Act by President George Bush," Federal News Service, July 26, 1990.

149. *Code of Federal Regulations*, title 29, subtitle B, chapter 14, appendix to part 1630.

150. Michael Slackman, "New Shapes for Cop Candidates," *Newsday*, March 6, 1996.

151. *Federal Register*, July 26, 1991, p. 35726.

152. Equal Employment Opportunity Commission, "New EEOC Policy Guidance Explains that Applications for Disability Benefits do not Bar Claims under the ADA," press release, February 12, 1997.

153. Mental Health Association of Southeastern Pennsylvania, "Training Offered for Employers of Mentally Ill at Work," PR Newswire, November 5, 1991.

154. Equal Employment Opportunity Commission, "Enforcement Guidance on Pre-Employment Disability-Related Inquiries," May 1994.

155. Equal Employment Opportunity Commission, "EEOC Enforcement Guidance on the Americans with Disabilities Act and Psychiatric Disabilities," no. 915.002, March 25, 1997.

156. Michael Reznicek, "A Recipe for Creating Disabilities," *Weekly Standard*, December 29, 1997, p. 27.

157. Ann Saccomano, "Bias Charges Hit UPS," *Traffic World*, March 31, 1997.

158. Kathi Wolfe, "Handicapped by a Law that Helps," *Washington Post*, July 26, 1998.

159. Paul Fahri, "Battle Looms Over What Cable Will Carry," *Washington Post*, June 17, 1993.

160. Thomas Hazlett, "Making Room for Reruns," *Journal of Commerce*, April 16, 1997.

161. Turner Broadcasting System v. Federal Communications Commission, 512 U.S. 622 (1994). Emphasis added.

162. Matthew D. Bunker and Charles N. Davis, "The First Amendment as a Sword: The Positive Liberty Doctrine and Cable Must-Carry Provisions," *Journal of Broadcasting and Electronic Media*, vol. 40, 1996, p. 87.

163. "Remarks to Members of the National Baptist Convention in New Orleans, Louisiana," *Public Papers of the Presidents*, September 8, 1989, p. 1341.

164. "Remarks by President Bush to the American Legion Convention, Baltimore Maryland," Federal News Service, September 7, 1989.

165. Norm Brewer, "Liberals have Misgivings About Tough Crime Bill," Gannett News Service, November 6, 1991.

166. Jim McGee, "Military Seeks Balance in Delicate Mission: The Drug War; As Involvement Expands, Law and History Are Basic Guides," *Washington Post*, November 29, 1996.

167. "Remarks by President Bush at the Dedication of the DEA New York Headquarters," Federal News Service, June 29, 1992.

168. Milton Friedman, "A War We're Losing," *Wall Street Journal*, March 7, 1991.

169. Michael Isikoff, "Bennett Exits Drug War With Potshots; Rep. Rangel a 'Gasbag,' City of Washington a 'Basket Case'," *Washington Post*, November 9, 1990.

170. Guy Gugliotta, "Clinton Lets Police Raid Projects," *Washington Post*, April 17, 1994.

171. Tracey Maclin, "Warrantless Sweeps are an Erosion of Freedom," *Houston Chronicle*, April 22, 1994.

172. Stephen Braun, "Chicago Police Seek Warrantless Sweeps to Seize Guns," *Los Angeles Times*, April 7, 1994.

173. Herbert McCann, "Federal Judge Nixes Warrantless Gun Sweeps," Associated Press, April 8, 1994.

174. Tom Raum, "Clinton Says Court Decision May Undermine Anti-Crime Efforts," Associated Press, April 11, 1994.

175. "Remarks to the Community at Robert Taylor Homes in Chicago," *Public Papers of the President*, June 17, 1994, p. 1296.

176. David Kopel, letter to the editor, *Policy Review*, fall 1994, p. 93.

177. Ira Glasser, "Why Unwarranted Searches are Wrong," *Cleveland Plain Dealer*, May 11, 1994.

178. Tom Raum, "Clinton Tours High-Crime Housing Project to Promote Gun Ban," Associated Press, June 17, 1994.

179. "Teleconference on Community Policing Grants and an Exchange with Reporters," *Public Papers of the Presidents*, May 13, 1994, p. 1058.

180. *Budget of the United States Government, Fiscal Year 1995*; section: "The Agenda Remaining; Personal Security: Crime, Illegal Immigration, and Drug Control," unpaged Lexis-Nexis version of budget. The document stated that "the administration also supports a ban on semi-automatic firearms."

181. A survey of public housing complexes in Boston found that 40 percent of the residents considered it "very dangerous" to be alone in their apartments at night. U.S. Department of Housing and Urban Development, *Crime in Public Housing: A Review of Major Issues and Selected Crime Reduction Strategies*, vol. 1, (Washington: Government Printing Office, 1979), p. 3.

182. "Remarks to the American Society of Association Executives," *Public Papers of the Presidents*, March 8, 1994, p. 454.

183. Grace-Marie Arnett, "Cops and Doctors," *Washington Post*, December 19, 1993.

184. "Testimony of Kenneth McLennan, President, Manufacturers' Alliance for Productivity and Innovation, House Ways and Means/Health Care Reform," Federal Document Clearing House, February 4, 1994.

185. Merrill Matthews and Molly Hering, "The Clinton Plan; Health Care Reform," *National Review*, December 13, 1993.

186. "Clinton Radio Text," Associated Press, February 24, 1996.

187. The line in the text is a variation from a quip reported in the "Laugh Lines" column in the *Los Angeles Times*, February 5, 1996.

188. Randal Archibold, "School Uniform Plan Approved in NYC," *New York Times*, March 19, 1998.

189. Katharine Seelye, "Dole Says President Defends Old Elites Seeking Largesse," *New York Times*, January 24, 1996.

190. Bertrand de Jouvenel, *On Power: The Natural History of its Growth* (1948; reprinted, Indianapolis: Liberty Fund Press, 1993), p. 381.

191. Ronald Bailey, ed., *The True State of the Planet* (New York: Free Press, 1995).

192. James Bovard, "The EPA's Latest Power Grab," *Wall Street Journal*, October 17, 1996.

193. John Locke, *Two Treatises of Government* (New York: New American Library, 1965), p. 320.

194. Baron de Montesquieu, *The Spirit of the Laws* (New York: Hafner, 1949), p. 150.

195. Economist J. M. Robertson observed in 1928, "All France lay under a stupid fiscal system which was always impoverishing and starving the people in some province; and where the harvest was good the farmers were hindered from selling to the provinces where it was bad, wherefore they would sow less the next year." J. M. Robertson, *The Political Economy of Free Trade* (London: P. S. King & Son, 1928), p. 31.

196. Franklin Pierce, *The Tariff and the Trusts* (New York: Macmillan, 1909), p. 20.

197. *Public Papers of the Presidents of the United States-John F. Kennedy, 1962* (Washington: Government Printing Office, 1963), pp. 727-728.

198. David Adams, "Secondhand Cuban Smokes Find Market," *Dallas Morning News*, July 19, 1997.

199. John Phillip Reid, *Constitutional History of the American Revolution* (Madison, WI: University of Wisconsin Press, 1986), p. 31.

200. Quoted in Richard Epstein, "History Lean: The Reconciliation of Private Property and Representative Government," *Columbia Law Review*, vol. 95, April 1995, p. 595.

201. Locke, *Two Treatises of Government*, p. 460.

202. John Taylor, *Tyranny Unmasked* (1822; reprinted, Liberty Fund Press, 1992), p. 233.

203. Quoted in James W. Ely, Jr., *The Guardian of Every Other Right* (New York: Oxford University, 1992), p. 26.

204. *Chicago, Burlington & Quincy R.R. v. Chicago*, 166 U.S. 226, 236 (1897).

205. Dewey, *Liberalism and Social Action*, p. 34.

206. Jerome Gilison, *The Soviet Image of Utopia* (Baltimore: Johns Hopkins University Press, 1975), p. 149.

207. Quoted in Robert Skidelsky, *The Road from Serfdom* (New York: Penguin, 1997), p. 99.

208. Ibid., p. 119.

209. James Bovard, "Eastern Europe, The New Third World," *New York Times*, December 20, 1987, and James Bovard, "The Hungarian Illusion," *Journal of Economic Growth*, January 1987.

210. *The Writings of James Madison*, vol. 6, ed. Gaillard Hunt (New York: G. P. Putnam's Sons, 1906), p. 103. The quote is from an article Madison wrote for the *National Gazette*, March 29, 1792.

211. Alan Wolfe, "Review of Stephen Holmes' *Passions & Constraint: On the Theory of Liberal Democracy*," *New Republic*, May 1, 1995.

212. Tom Bethell, *The Noblest Triumph: Property and Prosperity Through the Ages* (New York: St. Martin's Press, 1998), pp. 272-289.

213. James Bovard, "Assistance to Flood Victims Invites Further Disaster," *Los Angeles Times*, June 18, 1997.

214. Richard Epstein, *Takings* (Cambridge: Harvard University Press, 1985), p. 66.

215. *Oliver v. United States*, 466 U.S. 170, 179 (1984).

216. Ibid., p. 180, fn. 11.

217. Ibid., p. 192.

218. *The National Law Journal* reported in 1995 that between 1980 and 1993, the number of federal search warrants relying exclusively on an confidential informants nearly tripled, from 24 percent to 71 percent and that "from Atlanta to Boston, from Houston to Miami to Los Angeles, dozens of criminal cases have been dismissed after judges determined that the informants cited in affidavits were fictional." Mark Curriden, "Secret Threat to Justice," *National Law Journal*, February 20, 1995.

219. *Florida v. Riley*, 488 U.S. 445 (1989).

220. Evelyn Nieves, "I.N.S. Raid Reaps Many, But Sows Pain," *New York Times*, November 20, 1997.

221. Associated Press, "Agent Fired During Raid on Migrants, Report Finds," *New York Times*, December 12, 1997.

222. Craig Hemmens, "I Hear You Knocking: The Supreme Court Revisits the Knock and Announce Rule," *University of Missouri at Kansas City Law Review*, vol. 66, Spring 1998, p. 562.

223. Michael Cooper, "As Number of Police Raids Increase, So Do Questions," *New York Times*, May 26, 1998.

224. Ibid.

225. Barney Rock, "Kicking in Doors New Trend among Thieves," *Arkansas Democratic Gazette*, Jan. 21, 1995,

226. Craig Hemmens, "I Hear You Knocking: The Supreme Court Revisits the Knock and Announce Rule," *University of Missouri at Kansas City Law Review*, vol. 66, Spring 1998, p. 584.

227. Brief for the United States as Amicus Curiae Supporting Respondent, *Wilson v. Arkansas*, no. 94-5707, February 23, 1995, p. 26.

228. Ibid., p. 28.

229. Craig Hemmens, "I Hear You Knocking: The Supreme Court Revisits the Knock and Announce Rule," p. 601.

230. Litigation Backgrounder, "Searching without Consent: Government's Assault on the Sanctity of the Home," Institute for Justice, Washington, D.C. , 1997.

231. *Kenneth Black et. al v. Village of Park Forest,* 1998 U.S. Dist. LEXIS 2427, February 23, 1998.

232. Goodin, *Reasons for Welfare,* p. 307.

233. James Buchanan, "Book review of *Democracy's Discontent: American in Search of a Public Philosophy,*" *Reason,* February 1997, p. 59.

234. Arthur Fredheim, "IRS Audits Digging Deeper Beneath the Surface," *Practical Accountant,* March 1996, p. 20.

235. See, for instance, Tracey Maclin, "The Decline of the Right of Locomotion: The Fourth Amendment on the Streets," *Cornell Law Review,* vol. 75, September 1990, p. 1258, and Mark Kadish, "The Drug Courier Profile: In Planes, Trains, and Automobiles; and now in the Jury Box," *American University Law Review,* vol. 46, February 1997, p. 747.

236. See, Sue Blevins, "Medical Monopoly: Protecting Consumers or Limiting Competition?", *USA Today* (magazine), January 1998, p. 58.

237. Interview with Federal Trade Commission spokesman Howard Shapiro, July 28, 1998.

238. Quoted in Richard Epstein, *Forbidden Grounds* (Cambridge: Harvard University, 1992), p. 134.

239. *Yick Wo v. Hopkins,* 118 U.S. 356, 369 (1886).

240. *Budd v. New York,* 143 U.S. 517, 551 (1892).

241. *Meyer v. Nebraska,* 262 U.S. 390 (1923).

242. Goodin, *Reasons for Welfare,* p. 309.

243. Francis Bacon, *The Complete Essays of Francis Bacon* (1625; reprinted, New York: Washington Square Press, 1963), p. 134.

244. See, for instance, Hannah Arendt, *Between Past and Future* (New York: Penguin, 1968), pp. 143-69.

245. Immanuel Kant, *The Science of Right* (1790) (translated by W. Hastie) internet edition.

CHAPTER 4

1. "Quote of the Day," *The Hotline* (American Political Network), November 3, 1994. Clinton made this statement during an interview on Black Entertainment Television, November 2, 1994.

2. Lysander Spooner, *The Lysander Spooner Reader* (San Francisco: Fox & Wilkes, 1992), p. 85.

3. Friedrich Hayek, *The Essence of Hayek* (Palo Alto, CA: Hoover Institution, 1984), p. 352.

4. Clarence Carson, *The Rebirth of Liberty* (New Rochelle, NY: Arlington House, 1973), pp. 82-3.

5. Quoted in Gordon Wood, *The Creation of the American Republic, 1776-1787* (Chapel Hill: University of North Carolina Press, 1969), p. 348.

6. Nicholas Kittrie and Eldon Wedlock, eds., *The Tree of Liberty: A Documentary History of Rebellion and Political Crime in America,* vol. 1, (Baltimore: Johns Hopkins University Press, 1998), p. 50.

7. Ibid.

8. Quoted in John Phillip Reid, *The Concept of Representation in the Age of the American Revolution* (Chicago: University of Chicago Press, 1989), p. 224.

9. Quoted in Ibid., p. 73.

10. John Phillip Reid, *The Concept of Liberty in the Age of the American Revolution* (Chicago: University of Chicago Press, 1988), p. 111.

11. Reid, *The Concept of Representation,* p. 135.

12. Wood, *The Creation of the American Republic*, p. 348.

13. Quoted in Reid, *The Concept of Representation*, p. 11.

14. Quoted in Ibid., p. 81.

15. Quoted in Wood, *The Creation of the American Republic*, p. 266.

16. Irving Babbitt, *Democracy and Leadership* (1924; reprint, Indianapolis: Liberty Fund Press, 1978), p. 141.

17. Jean-Jacques Rousseau, *The Social Contract and the Discourses* (New York: Dutton, 1950), p. 32.

18. William Archibald Dunning, *A History of Political Theories from Rousseau to Spencer* (1920; reprint, New York: Macmillan, 1936), p. 39.

19. Quoted in Iain Hampsher-Monk, "Rousseau and Totalitarianism—With Hindsight?" in Robert Wokler, ed., *Rousseau and Liberty* (Manchester: Manchester University Press, 1995), p. 272.

20. Quoted in Wood, *The Creation of the American Republic*, p. 63.

21. Quoted in Ibid., p. 406.

22. Quoted in Ibid., p. 367.

23. Ibid., p. 195.

24. Alexander Hamilton, James Madison, and John Jay, *The Federalist Papers* (New York: New American Library, 1961,) p. 77. (Federalist no. 10)

25. Spooner, *The Lysander Spooner Reader*, p. 109.

26. This quote is from a source which I read many years ago and, regrettably, have not been able to track down. Historian Brad Thompson of Ashland University, author of a book on Adams's political thought, stated that the published collections of Adams's 1790s writings were "woefully inadequate." Interview with Brad Thompson, August 21, 1998.

27. Kittrie and Wedlock, *The Tree of Liberty: A Documentary History*, p. 89.

28. Wilson made this comment while he was arguing that the German people must be held responsible for actions such as Kaiser Wilhelm's 1914 decision to invade Belgium. *The Papers of Woodrow Wilson*, ed. Arthur S. Link, vol. 63 (Princeton: Princeton University Press, 1990), p. 8.

29. Arthur Link, *Woodrow Wilson and the Progressive Era* (New York: Harper & Row, 1954), p. 65. Further information on Wilson's racist policies can be found in David Bernstein, "The Law and Economics of Post-Civil War Restrictions on Interstate Migration of African-Americans," George Mason University, Law and Economics Workings Paper no. 96-03, 1995.

30. *The Public Papers and Addresses of Franklin D. Roosevelt, 1938* (New York: MacMillan, 1942), p. 489. (emphasis added)

31. "Remarks to Business Leaders in Stamford, Connecticut," *Public Papers of the Presidents*, October 7, 1996, p. 1999.

32. "Farewell Address to the Nation," *Public Papers of the Presidents*, January 11, 1989, p. 53.

33. Clyde Wayne Crews, "Ten Thousand Commandments," Competitive Enterprise Institute, Washington, January 1998, p. 6.

34. Alice McGillivary and Richard Scammon, *America at the Polls 1960-1992* (Washington: Congressional Quarterly, 1994), p. 1.

35. Quoted in Jennifer Bensch, "Government in the Sunshine Act: Seventeen Years Later: Has Government Let the Sun Shine In?" *George Washington Law Review*, June 1993, vol. 61, p. 1477.

36. *Public Papers of the Presidents of the United States: John F. Kennedy, 1963* (Washington: Government Printing Office, 1964), p. 408.

37. Quoted in Michael Delli Carpini and Scott Keeter, *What Americans Know About Politics and Why It Matters* (New Haven: Yale University Press, 1996), p. 43.

38. Ibid., p. 189.

39. Pew Research Center Survey, May 15, 1997, Public Opinion Online, Accession no. 0279499. While few Americans recognize the name of the FBI director, many have been

imbued with FBI-certified propaganda. For instance, tens of millions of people regularly watched the ABC television series *The FBI*, but few of them realized that the FBI had absolute control over the program's content. Ron Kessler, *The FBI* (New York: Pocket Books/Simon & Schuster, 1994), p. 434.

40.   George Will, "Flippant Foreign Policy," *Washington Post,* March 12, 1998.

41.   Linda L. M. Bennett and Stephen Earl Bennett, "Looking at Leviathan: Dimensions of Opinion About Big Government," in Stephen Craig, ed., *Broken Contract?* (Boulder, CO: Westview Press, 1996), p. 42.

42.   Richard Morin and Dan Balz, "Americans Losing Trust in Each Other and Institutions," *Washington Post,* January 28, 1996.

43.   Ibid.

44.   Stephen Earl Bennett, "'Know-Nothings' Revisited: The Meaning of Political Ignorance Today," *Social Science Quarterly,* June 1988, p. 480.

45.   Richard Morin, "Who's In Control? Many Don't Know or Care," *Washington Post,* January 29, 1996.

46.   Ibid.

47.   William Safire, "Broadcast Lobby Triumphs," *New York Times,* July 23, 1997.

48.   Clyde Wayne Crews, "Ten Thousand Commandments: A Policymaker's Snapshot of the Federal Regulatory State," Competitive Enterprise Institute, January 1998. The $668 billion figure is from a Small Business Administration study.

49.   James Bovard, "Plowing Deeper," *Barron's,* April 12, 1996. See also James Bovard, *The Farm Fiasco* (San Francisco: ICS Press, 1989).

50.   Richard Morin, "Who's In Control? Many Don't Know or Care," *Washington Post,* January 29, 1996.

51.   Roper Center at University of Connecticut, December 7, 1979 poll, Public Opinion Online, accession no. 0028805.

52.   "Survey Reveals Americans Unfamiliar with Bill of Rights," *St. Petersburg Times,* December 15, 1991.

53.   Delli Carpini and Keeter, *What Americans Know About Politics and Why It Matters,* p. 98. Also, Stanley Twardy, "Connecticut Opinion: Learning and Living the Constitution," *New York Times,* June 7, 1987.

54.   Delli Carpini and Keeter, *What Americans Know About Politics and Why It Matters,* p. 43.

55.   Press Release, "Voters Underestimate Tax Burden," Grassroots Research, November 28, 1995.

56.   Tom Herman, "Tax Report," *Wall Street Journal,* February 4, 1998.

57.   Richard Morin, "Who's In Control? May Don't Know or Care," *Washington Post,* January 29, 1996. The *Post* noted: "Overall, surveys indicate that Americans know about as much about politics and government today as they did during the 1940s. But these results hide a more distressing trend: in the past 50 years, the average number of years an American spends in school has increased from less than nine to more than 12, yet political knowledge has not grown."

58.   Richard Morin, "Dumbing Down Democracy," *Washington Post,* February 11, 1996.

59.   Tax Foundation, *Facts and Figures on Government Finance,* 30th ed. (Washington: Tax Foundation, 1997).

60.   Robert Samuelson, "The Regulatory Juggernaut," *Newsweek,* November 7, 1994, p. 43.

61.   For the 1948 number, see Lee Sigelman and Marcia Lynn Whicker, "The Growth of Government, the Ineffectiveness of Voting, and the Pervasive Political Malaise," *Social Science Quarterly,* vol. 69, June 1988, p. 304.

62.   *Congressional Record,* March 29, 1995, p. H 3944.

63.   *Bates v. Jones,* U.S. App., Lexis 36791, December 19, 1997.

64.   Joseph A. Schumpeter, *Capitalism, Socialism and Democracy* (New York: Harper, 1950), p. 262.

65. See James Buchanan and Gordon Tullock, *The Calculus of Consent* (Ann Arbor, MI: University of Michigan Press, 1962), and James Buchanan, *Democracy in Deficit* (New York: Academic Press, 1977).

66. Quoted in Fritz Morstein Marx, "State Propaganda in Germany," in Harwood Childs, ed., *Propaganda and Dictatorship* (Princeton: Princeton University Press, 1936), p. 30. The Goebbels quote was from an article in the *Hamburger Fremdenblatt,* March 20, 1934.

67. John Rawls, *A Theory of Justice* (Cambridge: Harvard University Press, 1971), p. 136.

68. Mark Green and Andrew Feinstein, "The Trouble with Sunset Laws," *Washington Post,* October 23, 1977.

69. "To an Enduring Wit, Election Day Was More Fun Than Halloween," *New York Times,* November 3, 1996.

70. Guy Gugliotta, "Reporting on a Practice That's Ripe for Reform," *Washington Post,* February 11, 1997.

71. Eric Felten, "Feeding Frenzy at the Public Trough," *Washington Times,* November 18, 1994.

72. Susan Cornwell, "Clinton asks for Prayers for Crime Bill," Reuters, August 14, 1994.

73. Weston Kosova, "Where's the Pork?" *New Republic,* September 5, 1994.

74. *Congressional Record,* September 30, 1996, p. S11818.

75. *Congressional Record,* September 30, 1996, p. S 11835.

76. Quoted in David Mason, "Reforming the Imperial Congress," Heritage Foundation, October 27, 1992.

77. Editorial, "Stuffing a Turkey," *Washington Post,* October 15, 1998.

78. Raymond Hernandez, "Frustrated N.Y. Legislators Know When to Vote, Not for What," *New York Times,* July 2, 1996.

79. Raymond Hernandez, "Cry for Help: 'Paul, How do I vote?" *New York Times,* July 13, 1996.

80. Editorial, "Do Less in Albany," *New York Times,* June 4, 1996.

81. Ibid.

82. The *Times* noted of the last day of the 1996 summer session: "Some newly printed bills were rushed to the floors of the Senate and Assembly so quickly that lobbyists and even some lawmakers had trouble getting copies before voting began." James Dao, "Legislature Finally Ends Its Long Session and Passes Budget," *New York Times,* July 14, 1996.

83. Editorial, "An Appalling Finale," *New York Times,* August 7, 1997. The editorial observed, "Symbolically, most of the Assembly bills were approved by computerized votes in which absent lawmakers were automatically recorded as yes votes. In the Senate, the computer was still voting while most of the senators left to play golf at a $1,000 a person Republican campaign fundraiser."

84. Dana Milbank, "Part-Time Legislators Ask: Should We Make Laws or Make a Living?" *Wall Street Journal,* January 8, 1997.

85. Ibid.

86. Ibid.

87. H. L. Richardson, *What Makes You Think We Read the Bills?* (Ottawa, IL: Caroline House, 1978), pp. 38-39.

88. Linda Wheeler, "Mutts Ado About Nothing," *Washington Post,* January 30, 1997.

89. Amy Gutmann and Dennis Thompson, *Democracy and Disagreement: Why Moral Conflict Cannot Be Avoided in Politics, and What Should Be Done About It* (Cambridge: Harvard University Press, 1996), p. 1.

90. Ibid., p. 4.

91. Quoted in James A. Gardner, "Shut up and Vote: A Critique of Deliberative Democracy and the Life of Talk," *Tennessee Law Review,* vol. 63, Winter 1996, p. 421.

92. *Federal Register,* March 10, 1998, p. 11585.

93. *Federal Register,* March 18, 1998, p. 13036.

94. *Federal Register,* February 19, 1997, p. 7602.

95. Sam Howe Verhovek, "In Small-Town Texas, the Sewing Stops," *New York Times,* January 15, 1996.

96. *Federal Register,* January 30, 1998, p. 4802.

97. *Federal Register,* March 7, 1997, p. 10527.

98. *Federal Register,* March 3, 1997, p. 9351.

99. *Federal Register,* March 5, 1997, p. 9959.

100. *Federal Register,* March 7, 1997, p. 10545.

101. *Federal Register,* March 7, 1997, p. 10481.

102. *Federal Register,* March 4, 1997, p. 9685.

103. *Federal Register,* March 7, 1997, p. 10473.

104. *Federal Register,* March 6, 1997, p. 10247.

105. *Federal Register,* March 7, 1997, p. 10420.

106. *Federal Register,* March 6, 1997, p. 10308.

107. *Federal Register,* March 6, 1997, p. 10312.

108. *Federal Register,* March 3, 1997, p. 9374.

109. Wilson added, "I have never, in my own mind, admitted the distinction between the other departments of life and politics." *The Papers of Woodrow Wilson,* ed. Arthur S. Link, vol. 35 (Princeton: Princeton University Press, 1990), p. 443.

110. Quoted on the *Economist* Screen Saver, http://www.economist.com

111. *Letters and Other Writings of James Madison,* vol. I, 1769-1793, (New York: Worthington, 1884), p. 325.

112. Editorial, "Congress Holes Out," *Wall Street Journal,* October 7, 1991.

113. "Reachback Tax Hits Scores of Virginia Companies," PR Newswire, November 11, 1993.

114. Jack Deutsch, "Miners' Health Law Debated," *Charleston Daily Mail,* June 22, 1995.

115. Robert Pear "Small Items in Budget Bills Yield Big Benefits for Special Interests," *New York Times,* November 6, 1995.

116. "Dear Colleague Support for HR 878," Sen. Thad Cochran, Congressional Press Releases, July 19, 1995.

117. *Eastern Enterprises v. Kenneth S. Apfel, Commissioner of Social Security, et. al.,* no. 97-42, June 25, 1998.

118. Bertrand Russell, "The State as Organized Power," in Waldo Browne, ed., *Leviathan in Crisis* (New York: Viking, 1946), p. 51.

119. Alan Ehrenhalt, *The United States of Ambition* (New York: Times Books, 1991), pp. 272-3. Ehrenhalt further noted: "By and large, faith in the possibilities of government to do good has been one of the underlying values of the professionals [political candidates] who have come to dominate that system in the last two decades."

120. Adam Clymer, "G.O.P. Rebellion Scuttles Accord on Budget Talks," *New York Times,* December 21, 1995.

121. Mark Liedl, "Congress' Busywork: Constituent Service has Replaced Governing," *Washington Post,* January 28, 1990.

122. John Burnheim, *Is Democracy Possible?* (Berkeley: University of California Press, 1985), p. 97.

123. *Scoundrels All,* ed. Ferdinand Lundberg (New York: Lyle Stuart, 1968), p. 53.

124. Quoted in Jeffrey Rogers Hummel, *Emancipating Slaves, Enslaving Free Men* (La Salle, IL: Open Court, 1996), p. 314.

125. Howard Kurtz, "Quotable," *Washington Post,* February 18, 1996.

126. Tom Sherwood, "Barry Disavows '78 Remark," *Washington Post,* October 30, 1986.

127. Ibid.

128. Linda DiVall, "Women of the Year," *New York Times,* May 14, 1992.

129. Survey sponsored by Henry J. Kaiser Family Foundation, Harvard University, and The *Washington Post,* "Question No. 81," December 1995, Public Opinion Online, Accession no. 0272485.

130. Karlyn Keene Bowman, "Widespread Dissatisfaction," *American Enterprise*, November-December 1994, p. 86. Survey by ABC News-*Washington Post*, March 1994.

131. Donald Kaul, "Public Trusts Lying TV Geeks More than It Does the Press?" *Houston Chronicle*, March 4, 1994.

132. Burns W. Roper, "Democracy in America: How Are We Doing?" *The Public Perspective*, March 1994.

133. Ibid.

134. Alexis Simendinger, "Of the People, for the People," *National Journal*, April 18, 1998, p. 850.

135. "Transcript of Clinton Remarks at Luncheon for Sen. Boxer," U.S. Newswire, June 23, 1997.

136. Council for Citizens Against Government Waste, "National Taxpayer Watchdog Group Condemns Congressional Pay Increase," PR Newswire, September 23, 1997. The press release cited as survey by *Roll Call* that showed that 67 of 73 newly elected members of Congress in 1994 received a pay increase.

137. "Transcript of Clinton Remarks at Luncheon for Sen. Boxer," U.S. Newswire, June 23, 1997.

138. Public Opinion Online, June 20, 1997, Accession no. 0280594, (data from a poll taken on November 5, 1996). Only 43% of the voters replied "yes" when asked "do you think Bill Clinton is honest and trustworthy." Since almost 50% of the roughly 95 million voters voted for Clinton, at least five million of his votes came from people who believed he was untrustworthy.

139. Roper Center at University of Connecticut, Public Opinion Online, accession no. 0266715. (poll taken October 1996).

140. Roper Center at University of Connecticut, Public Opinion Online, accession no. 0266716. (poll taken October 1996).

141. Roper Center at University of Connecticut, Public Opinion Online, accession no. 0271322. (Poll taken from October 19 to October 22, 1996.)

142. Richard Stengel and Eric Pooley, "Masters of the Message," *Time*, November 18, 1996.

143. Paradoxically, exit polls showed that 25 percent of voters who believed "government should do less" also voted for Clinton-even though the president campaigned on a laundry list of new federal programs, including new job training vouchers, more college aid handouts, a new college scholarship program to any student maintaining a B average, new federal scholarships for anyone graduating in the top 5 percent of their high school class, a multibillion-dollar literacy program for younger school children, massive increases in drug testing, massive increases in government subsidies for health care, and a federal mandate for public school uniforms. Editorial, "The Promising Game," *Investor's Business Daily*, October 14, 1996.

144. "CNN/USA Today/Gallup: Approval Remains High for Clinton," The Hotline, March 28, 1997.

145. Malcolm E. Jewell and David Breaux, "The Effect of Incumbency on State Legislative Elections," *Legislative Studies Quarterly*, vol. 13, November 1988, p. 495.

146. Ibid., p. 507.

147. Donn Esmonde, "State Government Works for Insiders, but How About Us?" *Buffalo News*, May 1, 1997.

148. Garry Wills, "The Clinton Principle," *New York Times Magazine*, January 19, 1997, p. 28. An October 1996 *Wall Street Journal*/NBC News poll found similar results; When asked why they are "voting for Bill Clinton and not Bob Dole," and given the opportunity to list multiple reasons, only 16% said they "Agree with Clinton's stands on issues." Question No. 009, Public Opinion Online, accession no. 0268969.

149. A more accurate result would have been garnered if voters had been asked their views on five of Clinton's key positions, which could then have been compared to the last positions Clinton took immediately prior to the election. (Or, to get a precise measurement, the

question could have been: How many voters flip-flopped on the major campaign issues simultaneously with Clinton?)

150. James Bennet, "Campaigns Fail to Stir Passions Among Voters," *New York Times*, November 4, 1996.

151. Daniel LeDuc, "A Blurred Line on Ethics; Md. Law Open to Wide Interpretation," *Washington Post*, April 6, 1998.

152. Interview with Gideon Kanner, August 24, 1998.

153. Bennett and Bennett, "Looking at Leviathan," p. 32. "On the eve of Reagan's election in 1980, approximately half the public believed that the federal government was too powerful for the good of the nation and the individual person. . . . Only a small percentage of the public (7 percent) felt that Washington should become more powerful, and about one-tenth was satisfied with the status quo."

154. Ibid., p. 33.

155. Richard Morin and Dan Balz, "Americans Losing Trust in Each Other and Institutions," *Washington Post*, January 28, 1996.

156. "Poll Update," The Hotline, November 11, 1996. This 49 cents consensus is a nip higher than polls quoted in Vice President Gore's 1993 report on "reinventing government," which stated: "The average American believes we waste 48 cents of every tax dollar." *Report of the National Performance Review and Vice President Al Gore, Creating a Government That Works Better And Costs Less* (Washington: Government Printing Office, 1993), p. 1.

157. "Remarks on Signing the National Voter Registration Act of 1993," *Public Papers of the Presidents*, May 20, 1993, p. 914.

158. Editorial, "Mentally Incompetent Should Not Be Voting," *Chicago Sun-Times*, February 18, 1997.

159. Ruth Larson, "INS Workers Forced to Halt Check of Voters," *Washington Times*, June 4, 1997.

160. Paul Craig Roberts, "Building a Class Warfare Army," *Washington Times*, March 18, 1993.

161. Editorial, "Electoral Fraud," *Dallas Morning News*, July 22, 1997.

162. Most information in this paragraph is from the Social Security Administration Internet site, August 1998.

163. Matthew Miller, "In Welfare Fuss, Real Cheats Run for Office," Austin American-Stateman, May 31, 1996.

164. Robert Rector and William Lauber, *America's Failed $5.4 Trillion War on Poverty* (Washington: Heritage Foundation, 1995), p. 1.

165. James Bryce, in his classic *Modern Democracies*, warned in 1921: "The larger the number of State undertakings and State employees, the larger is the influence which the latter can exert through their votes. They become a powerful class, with personal pecuniary interests opposed to those of the community as a whole, and Ministers have in many countries found it hard to resist their demands." James Bryce, *Modern Democracies*, vol. 2 (New York: MacMillan Co, 1921), p. 576. For an analysis of the power of government unions in the U.S., see Leo Troy, *The New Unionism in the New Society* (Fairfax, VA: George Mason University, 1994).

166. Peter Brimelow and Leslie Spencer, "The National Extortion Association," *Forbes*, June 7, 1993, p. 72.

167. Robert J. Barro, "Can Public Schools Take Competition?" *Wall Street Journal*, March 10, 1997. See also, "Prepared Testimony of Caroline M. Hoxby, Assistant Professor of Economics, Harvard University, before the Senate Budget Committee, Subject: What is Now Needed in Education Reform," Federal News Service, February 5, 1997.

168. Katherine Boo, "Reform School Confidential," *Washington Monthly*, October 1992, p. 17.

169. *Business Mailers Review*, September 17, 1990.

170. Clifford Krauss, "Police Contend PBA Leaders Hindered Stings," *New York Times*, February 3, 1995.

171. Editorial, "A Bad Bill on Police," *New York Times*, July 2, 1997.

172. Peter Davis, "Rodney King and the Decriminalization of Police Brutality in America," *Maryland Law Review,* vol. 53, Winter 1994, p. 271.

173. Interview with Joe McNamara, July 3, 1997.

174. Kenneth Weinstein, "Official Time: How Taxpayers Are Forced to Pay for Union Activities," Heritage Foundation, April 7, 1997.

175. Dan Miller, letter to editor, *Washington Times,* June 3, 1997.

176. Press Release, "Personal Income and Outlays," Bureau of Economic Analysis, U.S. Department of Commerce, September 25, 1998.

177. H. Erich Heinemann, "The Dog that Didn't Bark," *Journal of Commerce,* October 9, 1996. Both figures are in "constant" dollars.

178. Barbara Vobejda, "Elderly Lead All in Financial Improvement," *Washington Post,* September 1, 1998.

179. Interview with Wendell Cox, April 24, 1998.

180. "Corporate and State Taxes Show Biggest Gains in Decade," *Tax Notes Today,* August 28, 1992.

181. Joel Popkin, "Improving the CPI," *Business Economics,* July 1997, p., 42.

182. John Stuart Mill wrote in 1861: "Representative institutions are of little value, and may be a mere instrument of tyranny or intrigue, when the generality of electors are not sufficiently interested in their own government to give their vote, or, if they vote at all, do not bestow their suffrages on public grounds, but sell them for money. . . . " John Stuart Mill, *Utilitarianism, Liberty, and Representative Government* (New York: Dutton, 1951), p. 241.

183. Bruce R. Dold, "GOP Foolishness Overshadows Clinton's Errors," *Chicago Tribune,* July 25, 1997.

184. Plutarch, *The Lives of the Noble Grecians and Romans* (New York: Modern Library, 1935), p. 943.

185. Montesquieu, *The Spirit of the Laws,* p. 110.

186. Wood, *The Creation of the American Republic,* p. 24.

187. Herbert Croly, *The Promise of American Life* (1909; reprint, Cambridge: Harvard University Press, 1965) p. 178.

188. J. Allen Smith, *The Spirit of American Government* (1907; reprint, Cambridge: Harvard University, 1965), p. 306-7.

189. Quoted in Paul Johnson, *The Recovery of Freedom* (Oxford: Basil Blackwell, 1980), p. 70.

190. Quoted in Friedrich Hayek, *Law Legislation & Liberty,* vol. 2, *The Mirage of Social Justice* (Chicago: University of Chicago Press, 1976), p. 176.

191. Hans Kelsen, *General Theory of Law and State* (Cambridge: Harvard University Press, 1945), p. 285.

192. Robert Bork, *Slouching Toward Gomorrah* (New York: HarperCollins, 1997), p. 115.

193. Ibid., p. 117.

194. Ibid.

195. Quoted in Sheldon Richman, *Separating School and State* (Fairfax, Virginia: Future of Freedom Foundation, 1994).

196. John J. Goldman, "Parents Kept from Paying N.Y. Schoolteachers' Salary," *Los Angeles Times,* September 24, 1997.

197. Mary Beth Lane, "Texans Wrangle Over School Funds," *Cleveland Plain Dealer,* February 2, 1997.

198. Edward B. Fiske, "Commission on Education Warns 'Tide of Mediocrity' Imperils U.S.," *New York Times,* April 27, 1983.

199. See Myron Lieberman, *The Teacher Unions: How the NEA and the AFT Sabotage Reform and Hold Parents, Students, Teachers and Taxpayers Hostage to Bureaucracy* (New York: Free Press, 1997).

200. "Clinton, Dole in Their First Face-to-Face Showdown," *USA Today,* October 7, 1996. Dole was referring to inflation-adjusted spending.

201. Gordon Wood, "The Success of the American Revolution," paper presented at "The Meaning of Modern Revolutions" conference, University of Chicago, May 17, 1996, pp. 26-27 and 47-48.

202. Arthur Ekirch, *The Decline of American Liberalism* (New York: Longmans, Green & Co., 1955), p. 143.

203. Ibid., p. 144. Ekirch noted: "Discrimination was more a demand of the poorer white elements of the population, which felt keenly the threat of Negro competition. The reactionary regimes of the Redeemers, on the other hand, had even allowed Negroes the suffrage when their votes could be controlled, and for 20 years after 1865 no southern state had segregation laws in respect to railroad travel. But beginning in 1887, such laws multiplied as the anti-Negro populists gained influence in the South."

204. Fareed Zakaria, "The Rise of Illiberal Democracy," *Foreign Affairs*, November-December 1997.

205. Karen Lange, "In Liberia, the People Choose an Awful Hope for Peace," *Washington Post*, August 10, 1997.

206. *The State of the Union Messages of the Presidents, 1790-1966*, Vol. I (New York: Chelsea House, 1966), p. 916.

207. Alexander Meiklejohn, *What Does America Mean?* (New York: Norton, 1935), p. 98.

208. Bruno Leoni, *Freedom and the Law* (1961; reprint, Indianapolis, IN: Liberty Fund Press, 1991), p. 131.

209. John Locke, *Two Treatises of Government* (Cambridge: Cambridge University Press, 1963), p. 170-303.

210. Frank Chodorov, *Fugitive Essays* (Indianapolis: Liberty Fund Press, 1980), p. 49.

211. Quoted in Hannah Arendt, *Between Past and Future* (New York: Penguin, 1968), p. 150.

212. Thomas Babington Macaulay, *The History of England*, vol. 1 (Philadelphia: Porter & Coates, 1860), p. 90.

213. Economist G. Warren Nutter has made a similar observation: "The more that government takes, the less likely that democracy will survive." G. Warren Nutter, *Political Economy and Freedom* (Indianapolis: Liberty Fund Press, 1983), p. 52.

CHAPTER 5

1. Thomas Szasz, *The Untamed Tongue* (La Salle, IL: Open Court, 1990), p. 155.

2. A. R. Wadia, "The State Under a Shadow," *International Journal of Ethics*, vol. 31, no. 3, 1921, vol. 31, p. 327.

3. *The Public Papers and Addresses of Franklin Roosevelt, 1936* (New York: Random House, 1938), p. 232-233.

4. Gustav Cassell, *The Downfall of the Gold Standard* (1936; reprinted, New York: Augustus Kelley, 1966), p. 118-19.

5. Barry Eichengreen, *Golden Fetters: The Gold Standard and the Great Depression, 1919-39* (New York: Oxford University Press, 1992), p. 321.

6. Cassell, *The Downfall of the Gold Standard*, p. 124.

7. *The Public Papers and Addresses of Franklin D. Roosevelt, The Year of Crisis, 1933* (New York: Random House, 1938), pp. 110-11.

8. *The Public Papers and Addresses of Franklin D. Roosevelt, 1933*, p. 112.

9. *The Public Papers and Addresses of Franklin D. Roosevelt, 1933*, p. 114.

10. *The Public Papers and Addresses of Franklin D. Roosevelt, 1933*, p. 115.

11. Benjamin Anderson, *Economics and the Public Welfare* (1949; reprint, Indianapolis: Liberty Fund Press, 1979), p. 314.

12. Ibid., p. 316.

13. Charles Dearing, Paul Homan, Lewis Lorwin, and Leverett Lyon, *The ABCs of the NRA* (Washington: Brookings Institution, 1934), p. 113.

14. Ibid., p. 19.
15. Ibid., p. 23. The Brookings study noted, "The President, it appears, is thus authorized to remake in any way any code at any time during the life of the law."
16. William Leuchtenburg, *Franklin Roosevelt and the New Deal* (New York: Harper & Row, 1963), p. 67.
17. *Public Papers and Addresses of Franklin D. Roosevelt, 1933,* p. 518.
18. Leuchtenberg, *Franklin Roosevelt and the New Deal,* p. 68.
19. Dearing et al., *The ABCs of the NRA,* p. 17.
20. Susan Love Brown et al., *The Incredible Bread Machine* (San Diego: World Research, 1974), pp. 49-50.
21. Anderson, *Economics and the Public Welfare,* p. 337.
22. *U.S. v. Schechter Poultry,* 295 U.S. 495, 527 (1935).
23. "Brief of the United States, A.L.A. Schechter Poultry Corp. v. U.S., Stanley Reed, Solicitor General, 1935," in Philip Kurland, ed., *Landmark Briefs and Arguments of the Supreme Court of the United States: Constitutional Law,* vol. 28, (Washington: University Publications of America, 1975), p. 620.
24. Ibid., p. 625.
25. Ibid., p. 639.
26. The Roosevelt Administration appeared traumatized by the fall in the price of freshly slaughtered poultry—but, as its own brief noted, "In the past for or five years there has been a decline of about 25,000,000 pounds in the amount of live poultry sold in New York, and a corresponding increase in the amount of dressed poultry sold there. . . . Kosher killed poultry is sold with the feathers on and it is very hard for a person who does not know poultry to distinguish an ordinary bird from a poor one after it has been killed." Ibid., p. 648. It should not have been a mystery that, as orthodox Jewish immigrants in New York City became more prosperous, they preferred to buy prepared poultry instead of dead birds covered with feathers.
27. Ibid., p. 648.
28. Ibid., p. 732.
29. *U.S. v. Schechter Poultry,* 295 U.S. 495, 531 (1935).
30. *U.S. v. Schechter Poultry,* 295 U.S. 495, 542 (1935).
31. Quoted in Eric Felten, *The Ruling Class* (Washington: Heritage Foundation, 1993), p. 72.
32. *Bowles v. Willingham,* 321 U.S. 503, 537 (1944).
33. Ibid.
34. Interview with lawyer James Moody, April 18, 1997.
35. *Public Papers of the Presidents of the United States—Lyndon B. Johnson, 1963-64* (Washington: Government Printing Office, 1965), p. 446.
36. Hugh Davis Graham, *The Civil Rights Era* (New York: Oxford University Press, 1990), p. 191. Senator Hubert Humphrey declared, "The express requirement of intent is designed to make it wholly clear that inadvertent or accidental discriminations will not violate the title or result in entry or court orders. It means simply that the respondent must have intended to discriminate."
37. Herman Belz, *Equality Transformed* (New Brunswick, NJ: Transaction, 1991), p. 28.
38. EEOC v. Atlas Paper Box Company, 680 F. Supp. 1184 (1987).
39. Michael Fletcher, "Men Waited Tables, and Women Waited," *Washington Post,* February 24, 1998.
40. "Court Clears Way for Trial in EEOC Suit Challenging Hiring in All-Female Health Clubs," *Daily Labor Report,* April 23, 1993, p. d7.
41. *EEOC v. Sears,* 839 F. 2d 302 (1988).
42. *EEOC v. O & G Spring and Wire Forms Specialty Company,* 38 F.3d 872, 885 (1994). (Dissent by Judge Daniel Manion.)
43. Ibid.

44. Michael Fletcher, "Men Waited Tables, and Women Waited," *Washington Post,* February 24, 1998.

45. Vin Suprynowicz, "What's In a Name?" *Las Vegas Review Journal,* August 14, 1998.

46. Equal Employment Opportunity Commission, "Ruling in Re: Commissioner R. Gaull Silberman v. Hooters," September 16, 1994, p. 12. (Emphasis added).

47. Ibid.

48. Letter from Hooters counsel Pat Casey, Akin Gump, to EEOC's Carol Pullum-Crews, September 26, 1995. For further discussion of this case, see James Bovard, "The EEOC's War on Hooters," *Wall Street Journal,* November 17, 1995.

49. Kirstin Downey Grimsley, "Job Discrimination Lawsuits on Upswing," *Los Angeles Times,* May 12, 1997.

50. Equal Employment Opportunity Commission, *Strategic Plan 1997–2002,* September 1997.

51. Ibid.

52. Lowi noted in 1969: "High price supports with crop controls, the center of farm policy for a generation, are supported by 'liberals'; but these policies are 'liberal' because and only because they are governmental." Theodore J. Lowi, *The End of Liberalism* (New York: Norton, 1969), p. 65.

53. Chester Davis, "The Problem of Agricultural Adjustment," *Farm Economics,* February 1934, p. 88.

54. Parity presumed that there was no significant change in the value of items that farmers purchased. But in the *Index Numbers of Prices Paid by Farmers for Commodities Bought,* published in 1935, the USDA admitted that "the quality and utility of many of the farm machinery items, as well as other items the farmers buy, change over a period of years. Engineers have estimated that the wearing quality and capacity of 25 items of farm machinery in 1932 averaged about 170 percent of prewar machinery. This means that the prices in recent years represent machines of greater producing capacity than in the prewar years." Cited in Robert F. Martin, *Income in Agriculture, 1929-35* (New York: National Industrial Conference Board, 1936), p. 123.

55. Ibid. For further discussion of the origin and evolution of parity, see James Bovard, *The Farm Fiasco* (San Francisco: ICS Press, 1989), chapters 2 and 3.

56. "Roosevelt is Urged to Ask Wide Power as 'Farm Dictator,'" *New York Times,* March 12, 1933, p. 1.

57. Isabel Wilkerson, "With Rural Towns Vanishing, States Choose Which to Save," *New York Times,* January 3, 1990. Sen. Kent Conrad of North Dakota complained that the Conservation Reserve Program, one of the largest acreage-idling programs, has "absolutely wiped out small town after small town as we took land out of production." "The Conservation Reserve," *The Cargill Bulletin,* January 1993.

58. In 1954, Congress set the U.S. price support for wheat at roughly double the world price and imposed new mandatory production controls on wheat and corn farmers. In 1955-56, the USDA arrested or sued more than 1,500 farmers for growing more wheat than was permitted. Stanley Yankus, a Michigan farmer arrested for illegally growing wheat illegally to feed his chickens, told the House Agriculture Committee in 1959, "I am not fighting for the right to grow wheat. I am fighting for the right to own property. If I am forbidden the use of my land, then I do not own it. How can you congressmen justify the laws which have destroyed my means of making a living?" Cited in Paul Findley, *Federal Farm Fable* (New Rochelle, NY: Arlington House, 1968), p. 106.

59. Quoted in Carl Pescosolido, *An Analysis of the Legislative History of the Agriculture Adjustment Act* (Exeter, CA: privately published, 1984), p. 87.

60. Lloyd D. Teigen, "Agricultural Parity: Historical Review and Alternative Calculations," report prepared for the U.S. Department of Agriculture (Washington, D.C.: Government Printing Office, 1987), p. 59. Productivity has increased significantly since the publication of Teigen's report.

61. *Federal Register,* February 20, 1998, p. 8559.

62. *Federal Register,* February 24, 1998, p. 9160.

63. See, for instance, *Federal Register,* January 30, 1998, p. 4802.

64. James Bovard, "Plowing Deeper," *Barron's,* April 12, 1996.

65. Kevin McGill, "23 Plead Guilty in Sugar Scam," Associated Press, July 11, 1985.

66. Public Voice for Food and Health Policy, "Too Sweet to Resist: The Congressional Appetite for Sugar PACs," 1990.

67. Joseph D. Rich, "Enforcement of the Fair Housing Act," *Business Lawyer,* May 1991, p. 1335.

68. This estimate is based on the author's perusal of the comment file at the general counsel's office, Housing and Urban Development headquarters, 1994 and 1995.

69. *Pfaff v. U.S. Department of Housing and Urban Development,* 88 F. 3d 739 (1996).

70. "Clinton Administration Cracks Down on Housing Discrimination with New Charges, $15 Million in Grants," U.S. Newswire, September 30, 1997.

71. Andrea Hamilton, "Residents Protest HUD Moves," Associated Press, February 12, 1995.

72. Roberta Achtenberg, "Sometimes on a Tightrope at HUD," *Washington Post,* August 22, 1994.

73. Richard Lowry, "Testing Bias," *National Review,* February 9, 1998, p. 4.

74. Letter to Joseph Vogan, Varnum, Riddering, Schmidt & Howlett, Grand Rapids, Michigan, from Paul Hancock, U.S. Department of Justice, May 23, 1996. This letter was provided to the author by George Leef and Sheldon Rose of Michigan.

75. For further details, see James Bovard, *The Fair Trade Fraud* (New York: St. Martin's Press, 1991).

76. John Taylor, *Tyranny Unmasked* (Washington: Davis and Force, 1822), p. 38.

77. Interview with David Palmeter, January 7, 1990.

78. See, for instance, the rulings in the following two trade cases: U.S. International Trade Commission, "Certain Fresh Atlantic Groundfish from Canada," ITC publication no. 1844, May 1986, p. 16; and U.S. International Trade Commission, "Certain Light-walled Rectangular Pipes and Tubes from Taiwan," ITC publication no. 2169, March 1989, p. A-33.

79. *Federal Register,* November 13, 1989, p. 47249.

80. *Zenith Radio Corp. v. Matsushita Elec. Indus. Co.,* 513 F. Supp. 1100, 1333 (1981).

81. James Bovard, "Miniban: Detroit's victory over Mazda," *New Republic,* June 22, 1992.

82. James Bovard, "Let's Have Fair Play for Foreign Kiwis," *New York Times,* February 9, 1992.

83. Bovard, *The Fair Trade Fraud,* pp. 107-168.

84. James Bovard, "Clinton's Dumping Could Sink GATT," *Wall Street Journal,* December 9, 1993.

85. Peter Kilborn, "Company Told to Pay Strikers for Perks it Gave to Workers," *New York Times,* December 27, 1996.

86. *NLRB v. John Zink Co.,* 551 F. 2d 799 (1979).

87. "Pony Express Calls NLRB complaint 'Baffling,'" *Daily Labor Report,* March 24, 1994, p. d18.

88. Armand J. Thieblot, Jr. and Thomas R. Haggard, *Union Violence: The Record and the Response by Courts, Legislatures, and the NLRB* (Philadelphia: University of Pennsylvania, 1983), p. 334.

89. James Bovard, "Union Goons' Best Friend," *Wall Street Journal,* June 2, 1994.

90. "Divided NLRB Orders Reinstatement of Worker Who Threatened to Kill Boss," *Daily Labor Report,* August 16, 1991, p. A-14.

91. "Threat to Kill Supervisor Forfeits Labor Law Protections, Court Holds," *Daily Labor Report,* May 14, 1992, p. A-10.

92. *Chicago Tribune Company v. National Labor Relations Board,* 79 F. 3d 604 (1996).

93. Tom Diemer, "Superfund has Little to Show for 13 Years," *Cleveland Plain Dealer,* May 9, 1993.

94.   Maria Berthoud, "Protecting agents' stake in the Superfund debate," *Best's Review: Property-Casualty Insurance*, April, 1995, p. 54.

95.   U.S. Department of Justice, *Causes and Policy Implications of the Current Crisis in Insurance Availability and Affordability*, 1986, pp. 64-65.

96.   *Industrial Park Dev. Co. v. EPA*, 604 F. Supp. 1136 (1985).

97.   Warren L. Dean, "Just Follow the Law," *Journal of Commerce*, October 14, 1997.

98.   "Prepared Statement of Barbara Williams, Owner, Sunnyray Restaurant on behalf of the National Federation of Independent Business before the House Commerce Committee Finance and Hazardous Materials Subcommittee," Federal News Service, March 5, 1998.

99.   Ibid.

100.   James DeLong, "Privatizing Superfund," Cato Institute Policy Analysis no. 247, December 18, 1995, p. 18.

101.   Carolyn King, "EPA Orders 71 Miners to Dig Through 117 Years of Records," *Wall Street Journal*, July 29, 1997.

102.   D. F. Oliveria, "Mindless Demand Validates Paranoia," *Spokane Spokesman-Review*, June 22, 1997.

103.   Ibid.

104.   Senate Judiciary Committee, *Superfund Improvement Act of 1985*, June 7, 1985 (Washington: Government Printing Office, 1985), p. 300.

105.   Ibid., p. 255.

106.   Cindy Skrzycki, "EPA Moves to Clean Up Liability Issues in Waste Disposal," *Washington Post*, August 22, 1997.

107.   *Ex parte Grossman*, 267 U.S. 87, 108-9 (1925).

108.   Richard Epstein, *Simple Rules for a Complex World* (Cambridge: Harvard University Press, 1995), p. 72.

109.   Even prior to the wave of legislation and activist federal agencies beginning in the 1920s and 1930s, the common law had deteriorated from its original orientation towards protecting individuals and their property and requiring compensation for injuries. As Professor Bruce Benson observed in his path-breaking book, *The Enterprise of Law:* "The common law system we have inherited was largely shaped, not by some desire to organized society in the 'public interest,' but by the self-interested goals of kings, their bureaucrats and powerful groups in England." Bruce L. Benson, *The Enterprise of Law* (San Francisco: Pacific Research Institute, 1990), p. 76.

110.   "Amicus Brief of the National Association of Criminal Defense Lawyers, Wlademar Ratzlaf and Loretta Ratzlaf v. U.S., Supreme Court, October Term 1993," no. 92-1196, pp. 29-30.

111.   The habit of bragging about convictions sometimes gets the best of federal agencies; the Associated Press revealed in 1997 tha the 125 convictions of violators of the Wild Free-Roaming Horse and Burro Act that the Interior Department's Bureau of Land Management (BLM) claimed over a ten-year period was a slight exaggeration—the actual number of convictions was 3. A BLM spokesman explained that the agency "defines convictions" differently than do others, such as counting as a conviction any case in which the Justice Department refused to prosecute an alleged violator. Martha Mendoza, "Federal Claims about Horse Abuse Convictions Shown to be False," Associated Press, August 7, 1997.

112.   Roberto Suro, "Law Enforcement Ethics: A New Code for Agents," *Washington Post*, August 21, 1997.

113.   *Brogan v. U.S.*, 1998 U.S. Lexis 648, January 26, 1998.

114.   Elkan Abramowitz, "'Brogan v. United States' and the 'Exculpatory No' Doctrine," *New York Law Journal*, November 4, 1997.

115.   Giles Birch, "False Statements to Federal Agents: Induced Lies and the Exculpatory No," *University of Chicago Law Review*, vol. 57, Fall 1990, p. 1273.

116.   "Brief of National Association of Criminal Defense Lawyers, Amicus Curiae, Supreme Court case: James Brogan v. U.S.," No. 96-1579, August 21, 1997.

117.   *Brogan v. U.S.*, 1998 U.S. Lexis 648, January 26, 1998.

118.   Ibid.

119.   David Wise, "Big Lies and Little Green Men," *New York Times,* August 8, 1997.

120.   To argue that an agreement that lowers trade barriers around the world is a step towards One World Government misses the key point: the GATT agreement will reduce the power of governments over their citizens around the world. Anything that tends to decrease politicians' arbitrary power over trade will tend to increase individual freedom. The ineptly named World Trade Organization, by countervailing some of the arbitrary power of governments over trade, is a tiny step in the right direction. James Bovard, "Two Cheers for GATT," National Center for Policy Analysis, November 24, 1994.

121.   Rep. Don Young, "The Globalization of United States Domestic Land Use Policy," Lincoln Heritage Institute, 1997.

122.   Matthew Wald, "Thousands Have Thyroid Cancer from Atomic Tests," *New York Times,* August 2, 1997.

123.   Matthew Wald, "U.S. Alerted Photo Film Makers, Not Public, About Bomb Fallout," *New York Times,* September 30, 1997.

124.   Jim Wolf, "Pentagon Planned 1960s Cuban 'Terror Campaign,'" Reuters, November 19, 1997.

125.   Paul M. Weyrich, "Who Do Americans Trust?" Washington Times, May 21, 1997.

126.   Dana Todd, "In Defense of the Outrageous Government Conduct Defense in the Federal Courts," *Kentucky Law Journal,* vol. 84, winter 1995-1996, p. 432.

127.   Don Terry, " Shabazz Cases: Informer Says U.S. Paid Him," *New York Times,* March 24, 1995.

128.   "Campaign '96: Transcript of the Vice-Presidential Debate," *Washington Post,* October 10, 1996.

129.   "Finance Release on Chair's Opening Statement at Committee Hearings on IRS Treatment of Taxpayers," *Tax Notes Today,* September 24, 1997.

130.   "Excerpts from Testimony before the Senate Finance Committee Oversight Hearing," *Tax Notes Today,* April 28, 1998.

131.   "IRS Releases Report on Collection Seizure Actions," *Tax Notes Today,* July 14, 1998.

132.   "American Institute of Certified Public Accountants' Comments on Taxpayer Advocate's Report," *Tax Notes Today,* March 20, 1997.

133.   George Guttman, "Evaluating the IRS: The Senate Finance Hearings in Retrospect," *Tax Notes Today,* October 6, 1997.

134.   Cheryl Thompson, "D.C. Police Zero in on Petty Crime," *Washington Post,* May 5, 1997.

135.   David Vise, "D.C. to Resume Warning Drivers to Renew Licenses," *Washington Post,* July 8, 1998.

136.   "Three-Pointer," American Civil Liberties Union press release, January 9, 1998 (quoting an article from the *San Jose Mercury News,* December 27, 1997).

137.   Quoted in *Morrison v. Olson,* 487 U.S. 654 (1988).

138.   Rory Little, "Who Should Regulate the Ethics of Federal Prosecutors?" *Fordham Law Review,* vol. 65, October 1996, p. 355.

139.   "Prepared Statement by Frederick Krebs, American Corporate Counsel Association, before the House Judiciary Committee, on H.R. 3386, the Ethical Standards for Federal Prosecutors Act," Federal News Service, September 12, 1996.

140.   Bennett Gershman, "Prosecuting Prosecutors," *New York Law Journal,* December 20, 1996.

141.   Jim McGee and Brian Duffy, "Truth and Consequences," *U.S. News & World Report,* July 1, 1996, p. 28.

142.   Grossly unjust incentive systems are, unfortunately, not a novelty in the federal statute book. Perhaps the most brazen conflict of interest occurred in the Fugitive Slave Act of 1850. This act was passed to placate southern congressmen worried about their valuable property hot-footing it into free states north of the Mason-Dixon line. Congress created a special class of federal court officials to pursue alleged runaway slaves. As author Jeffrey

Hummel noted, "All the slaveholder needed to do was present an affidavit. The alleged fugitive enjoyed no right to a jury trial or even to testify. Furthermore, commissioners had financial incentive to rule against the fugitive. They receive a $10 fee from the government for deciding that a black was an escaped slave, but only $5 for not." The law, which helped changed northern opinion on slavery, generated great anxiety: "Free blacks were the northern group in greatest jeopardy. They had no legal recourse if a Southerner claimed they were escaped slaves. The law consequently fostered an unsavory class of professional slave catchers, who could make huge profits by legally kidnapping free blacks in the North and selling them into slavery in the South." Jeffrey Rogers Hummel, *Emancipating Slaves, Enslaving Free Men* (Chicago: Open Court, 1996), p. 94.

143. Rep. Henry Hyde, "Civil Asset Forfeiture Reform Act of 1993—A Briefing Paper," June 1993, p. 10.

144. *U.S. v. All Assets of Statewide Auto Parts, Inc.,* 971 F. 2d 905 (1992).

145. *U.S. v. $277,000 U.S. Currency and One Dodge Ram Charger,* 69 F. 3d 1491 (1995).

146. "Rubin Allows Forfeiture Fund Use for Local Police Salaries," *Money Laundering Alert,* June 1996.

147. Editorial, "Rico Reform Needed," *Arizona Republic,* March 26, 1994.

148. Lisa Brennan, "Verniero, Civil Suit Target Bissell Forfeiture Abuses," *New Jersey Law Journal,* July 7, 1997.

149. House Committee on Ways and Means, *Abuses and Mismanagement in U.S. Customs Service Commercial Operations,* February 8, 1990 (Washington: Government Printing Office, 1990), p. 7.

150. Eric Blumenson and Eva Nilsen, "Policing for Profit: The Drug War's Hidden Economic Agenda," *University of Chicago Law Review,* vol. 65, winter 1998, p. 58.

151. *San Diego Gas & Electric Co. v. City of San Diego,* 450 U.S. 621 (1981).

152. Gregory M. Stein, "Regulatory Takings and Ripeness in the Federal Courts," *Vanderbilt Law Review,* vol. 48, January 1995, p. 1.

153. Michael Berger and Gideon Kanner, "The Need for Takings Law Reform: A View from the Trenches," *Santa Clara Law Review,* vol. 38, no. 3, 1998, p. 839.

154. Peggy Reigle, "Ocie Mills' Motto: Never Give Up!" *Land Rights Letter,* May 1993.

155. Interview with lawyer James Moody, August 5, 1998.

156. Senate Committee on Labor and Human Resources Committee, *Affirmative Action and the Office of Federal Contract Compliance,* June 15, 1995 (Washington: Government Printing Office, 1995), p. 46.

157. Interview with three lawyers who wished to remain anonymous, April 1996.

158. "Prepared Statement of Daniel Yager, Vice President and General Counsel, Labor Policy Association," Senate Committee on Labor and Human Resources, Hearing on National Labor Relations Board, September 17, 1996.

159. Reed Larson, "Union Bosses Lose a Friend at the NLRB," *Wall Street Journal,* July 9, 1998.

160. Paul M. Bator, "What is Wrong with the Supreme Court?" *University of Pittsburgh Law Review,* vol. 51, Spring 1990, p. 673.

161. Ibid.

162. "Prepared Statement of Gerald B. Lefcourt, President, National Association of Criminal Defense Lawyers Before the House Appropriations Committee, Subcommittee on Commerce, Justice and State, and the Judiciary," Federal News Service, April 1, 1998.

163. Arnold Burns, "What By-the-Book Prosecutors Can Get Away With," *Wall Street Journal,* March 23, 1998.

164. W. Gardner and Michael Greenberger, "Judicial Review of Administration Action and Responsible Government," *Georgetown Law Journal,* vol. 63, no. 2, p. 29.

165. William Simon, *A Time For Truth* (New York: Reader's Digest Press, 1978), p. 204.

166. "Full Text: Unofficial Transcript of Finance Hearings on IRS Abuses," *Tax Notes Today,* October 2, 1997.

167. Tom Herman, "Tax Report," *Wall Street Journal,* October 15, 1997.

168. A.V. Dicey, *Lectures on the Relation Between Law and Public Opinion in England During the Nineteenth Century* (1905; reprint, London: Macmillan, 1952), p. 206.

169. John Taylor, *Tyranny Unmasked,* p. 257.

170. David Schoenbrod, *Power Without Responsibility* (New Haven: Yale University Press, 1993).

171. Kenneth C. Davis, *Administrative Law Treatise,* vol. 2, (San Diego: K.C. Davis Pub. Co., 1979), p. 220.

172. *Mississippi v. Johnson,* 71 U.S. 475 (1866).

173. *Pollock v. Farmers' Loan & Trust Co.,* 157 U.S. 429, (1895).

174. "Contract Services for Drug Dependent Federal Offenders Act Amendments of 1981," *Public Papers of the Presidents,* January 14, 1983, p. 47.

175. Associated Press, "Gov't Group: U.S. Needs 'Food Czar'," August 20, 1998.

176. Peter Brimelow and Leslie Spencer, "Food and Drugs and Politics," *Forbes,* November 22, 1993, p. 115.

177. Ibid.

178. Ibid.

179. Editorial, "Tough Guys at FDA," *Washington Times,* September 12, 1991.

180. Robert M. Goldberg, "What the FDA Doesn't Want You to Know," *Wall Street Journal,* May 4, 1998.

181. Henry Miller, "FDA Oversteps Bounds With Vague, New Rule," *Baltimore Sun,* July 15, 1998.

182. Oliver Perry Colvin, "A Constitutional Challenge to Rule 10b-5," *Insights,* May 1992, p. 19.

183. John F. Olson, John H. Sturc, and Gerald T. Lins, "Recent Insider Trading Developments: The Search for Clarity," *Northwestern University Law Review,* vol. 85, spring 1991, p. 715.

184. Paul Beckett, "Courts Frown on Absence of Clear Rules From SEC," *Wall Street Journal,* April 14, 1998.

185. Ibid.

186. "U.S. v. Krizek: DC Circuit Remands Liability Determination in FCA Case," *Government Contract Litigation Reporter,* June 5, 1997.

187. Interview with lawyer Monika Krizek, April 12, 1996.

188. *U.S. v. Krizek,* 859 F. Supp. 5, 10 (1994).

189. *U.S. v. Krizek,* 859 F. Supp. 5, 14 (1994).

190. *U.S. v. Krizek,* 859 F. Supp. 5, 8 (1994).

191. *U.S. v. Krizek,* 859 F. Supp. 5, 14 (1994).

192. Jody Robinson, "I'm a Doctor, Not a Paper Pusher," *Wall Street Journal,* April 1, 1998.

193. "James Keightley Testimony before Restructuring Commission," *Tax Notes Today,* November 8, 1996.

194. Alan Brinkley, Nelson Polsby, and Kathleen Sullivan, *New Federalist Papers* (New York: W. W. Norton, 1996), p. 131.

195. Robert Goodin, *Reasons for Welfare* (Princeton: Princeton University Press, 1988), p. 321.

196. Benjamin Constant, *Political Writings* (Cambridge: Cambridge University Press, 1988), pp. 290-91.

197. Richard Morin and Dan Balz, "Americans Losing Trust in Each Other and Institutions," *Washington Post,* January 28, 1996.

198. H. L. Mencken, *A New Dictionary of Quotations* (1942; reprint, New York: Alfred Knopf, 1984), p. 657.

199. Quoted in Damian Halstad, "The Tao of Litigation," *Journal of the Legal Profession,* vol. 19, 1995, p. 116.

200. John Roberts, "T.H. Green," in *Conceptions of Liberty,* p. 255.

201. Dawn Margolis, "10 Things Your Doctor May Not Know," *American Health,* November 1994, p. 84.

202. Jacob Sullum, "No Relief in Sight," *Reason,* January 1997, p. 22.

203. John Machacek, "Report Says Americans Getting Inadequate End-of-Life Care," Gannett News Service, June 4, 1997.

204. Erick Damian Kelly, "Enforcing Zoning and Land-Use Controls," American Planning Association Planning Advisory Service Report no. 409, 1988, p. 15.

205. Interview with Ike Sugg, January 17, 1997.

206. Transcript, "U.S. Senate Committee on Finance Holds Hearing on the IRS," Federal Document Clearing House, September 25, 1997.

207. "AICPA Says Financial Status Audit Techniques Undermine Taxpayers' Rights," *Tax Notes Today,* April 25, 1996.

208. Editorial, "Ethics in Annapolis? Don't Ask," *Washington Post,* April 1, 1998.

209. Steve Twomey, "If the Question Is Ethics, The Answer Is 'Later,'" *Washington Post,* March 23, 1998.

210. Bill Dedman, "Study Criticizes Illinois's Rules For Legislators," *New York Times,* March 30, 1998.

211. Waldo Browne, ed., *Leviathan in Crisis* (New York: Viking, 1946), p. 195.

212. *A Dictionary of Economic Quotations,* Simon James, ed. (Totowa, NJ: Barnes & Noble, 1981), p. 99.

213. Charlotte Twight, "Evolution of Federal Income Tax Withholding," *Cato Journal,* vol. 14, winter 1995.

214. For information on the deterioration of the dollar's purchasing power, see the website of the U.S. Bureau of Labor Statistics at http://stats/bls/gov/cpihomc.htm.

215. Bruce Bartlett, "How Inflation Hikes the Capital Gains Bite," *Washington Times,* March 31, 1997.

216. Quoted in Benjamin Constant, *Political Writings,* p. 116.

217. Ibid., p. 116

218. *The State of the Union Messages of the Presidents, 1790-1966,* vol. 2 (New York: Chelsea House, 1966), p. 1167.

219. Elizabeth MacDonald, "Breakdown at the IRS," *Worth,* March 1995.

220. Cited in Lawrence J. Haas, "Troubled Tax Man," *National Journal,* June 30, 1990, p. 1601.

221. Department of Justice, Bureau of Justice Statistics, *Sourcebook of Criminal Justice Statistics 1995,* p. 388, table 3.176.

222. Jonathan Tolman, "The Dry Facts About 'Wetlands,'" *Wall Street Journal,* August 25, 1993.

223. Department of Justice, Bureau of Justice Statistics, *Sourcebook of Criminal Justice Statistics 1995,* p. 349, table 3.119.

224. Office of the U.S. Trade Representative, *U.S. Proposal for Uruguay Round Market Access Negotiations [CONFIDENTIAL],* March, 1990, p. 416.

225. Gary Clyde Hufbauer and Kimberly Ann Elliot, *Measuring the Costs of Protection in the United States* (Washington: Institute for International Economics, 1994), p. 3.

226. Thomas Hobbes, *Leviathan* (London: Penguin, 1974), p. 388.

227. Hannah Arendt, *Totalitarianism* (New York: Harcourt, Brace, and World, 1951), p. 92.

228. Sidney and Beatrice Webb, *Soviet Communism: A New Civilization?,* vol. 2 (New York: Charles Scribner's Sons, 1936), pp. 1051.

229. Friedrich Hayek, *The Constitution of Liberty* (1960; reprint, Chicago: Henry Regnery, 1972), p. 137.

230. Burt Neuborne, "Blues for the Left Hand," *University of Chicago Law Review,* vol. 62, winter 1995, p. 429.

231. Dirk Johnson, "Volunteer: Now, That's an Order," *New York Times,* September 13, 1998.

232. "Remarks by President Clinton at the President's Summit for America's Future," Federal News Service, April 28, 1997.

233. Benson, *The Enterprise of Law,* p. 171.

CHAPTER 6

1. Ambrose Bierce, *The Devil's Dictionary* (New York: Dover, 1993), p. 97.
2. Arthur Lionel Smith, "English Political Philosophy in the Seventeenth and Eighteenth Centuries," in *Cambridge Modern History,* vol. 6 (Cambridge: Cambridge University Press, 1909), p. 800.
3. Quoted in Gordon Woods, *The Radicalism of the American Revolution* (New York: Random House, 1993), p. 237.
4. For examples of current abuses, see Scott Gartner, "Strip Searches of Students: What Johnny Really Learned at School and How Local School Boards can Help Solve the Problem," *Southern California Law Review,* vol. 70, March 1997, p. 921.
5. *Kawananakoa v. Polyblank,* 205 U.S. 349, 353 (1907).
6. For instance, see *Anthony McIlvain Ostheimer, et al., v. Sheila Lindquist, John Doe, Jane Roe, Internal Revenue Service,* 1990 U.S. Dist. LEXIS 2212, February 16, 1990.
7. Kenneth Davis, *Administrative Law Treatise,* vol. 3 (San Diego: K.C. Davis Pub. Co., 1979), p. 509.
8. *Chisholm v. Georgia,* 2 U.S. 419, 466 (1793).
9. Cited in Davis, *Administrative Law Treatise,* vol. 3, p. 437.
10. *Kennecott Copper Corp. v. State Tax Commission,* 327 U.S. 573, 580 (1945).
11. Nestor Davidson, "Constitutional Mass Torts: Sovereign Immunity and the Human Radiation Experiments," *Columbia Law Review,* vol. 96, June 1996, p. 1203.
12. Jeremy Travis, "Rethinking Sovereign Immunity After Bivens," *New York University Law Review,* vol. 57, June 1982, p. 607.
13. "Deals and Suits," *Legal Times,* April 14, 1997, p. 17. (*Federal Express Corp. v. U.S. Postal Service.*)
14. Michele Kayal, "Ruling Chips Away at Postal Service Immunity," *Journal of Commerce,* January 22, 1998.
15. "Postal Service Loses Court Battle," Associated Press, August 1, 1998.
16. Linda Greenhouse, "Court Upholds Antitrust Immunity of Local Governments," *New York Times,* April 2, 1991.
17. "TVA Seeks Reno Investigation," *Electricity Daily,* April 18, 1997.
18. Adam Thierer, "The TVA vs. Free Speech," *Washington Times,* May 3, 1997.
19. Editorial, "Badge of Immunity," *Columbus Dispatch,* June 27, 1997.
20. Michael J. Berens, "1991 Case Still Up in The Air," *Columbus Dispatch,* June 22, 1997.
21. Michael J. Berens, "Some Claims are a Horse of a Different Color," *Columbus Dispatch,* June 23, 1997.
22. Lucy Soto, "Sovereign Immunity Bills Face Tough Road," *Atlanta Journal and Constitution,* March 1, 1996.
23. Toni Locy, "D.C. Police Accused Of Coverup; Officers Allegedly Lied About Fatal Shooting," *Washington Post,* July 3, 1997.
24. Editorial, "Drop the '48-Hour Rule'," *New York Times,* July 16, 1998.
25. Rad Sallee, Jo Ann Zuniga, and S.K. Bardwell, "Cops May Have Had Right to Shoot," *Houston Chronicle,* July 17, 1998.
26. James Bovard, "No Accountability at the FBI," *Wall Street Journal,* January 10, 1995. Louis J. Freeh, letter to editor, *Wall Street Journal,* January 26, 1995; and James Bovard, letter to editor, *Wall Street Journal,* February 27, 1995. For an excellent analysis of the government's action and cover-up, see Alan Bock, *Ambush At Ruby Ridge: How Government Agents Set Randy Weaver Up and Took His Family Down* (Irvine, Cal.: Dickens Press, 1995).
27. Department of Justice, "Report Regarding Internal Investigation of Shootings at Ruby Ridge, Idaho During Arrest of Randy Weaver," 1994. (This report was never released by the Justice Department; *Legal Times* acquired the report and put it on the Internet in mid-1995.)
28. Jerry Seper, "Ruby Ridge Charges Brought," *Washington Times,* August 22, 1997.

29. John Wiley, "FBI Agent Indicted for Ruby Ridge," Associated Press, August 22, 1997.

30. Department of Justice, "Report Regarding Internal Investigation of Shootings at Ruby Ridge, Idaho During Arrest of Randy Weaver," 1994.

31. George Lardner, "U.S. Argues Idaho Can't Prosecute FBI Sniper," *Washington Post,* March 14, 1998.

32. *State of Idaho vs. Lon Horiuchi,* Case no. CR 97-097-N-EJL, May 14, 1998.

33. Interviews with restaurant co-owners John Colaprete and Ted Bonk, various dates, 1997. Interviews with Jewish Mother counsel Robert Haddad, April 1997. Also, "First Amended Complaint and Demand for Jury Trial," *Mom's Inc. v. Judith Weber et al.,* civil action no. 2:96CV246, U.S. District Court for the Eastern District of Virginia, Norfolk Division, April 9, 1997.

34. Interviews with Stuart Gerson and Robert Haddad, April 10, 1997.

35. Ronald Smothers, "The Fall of Newark," *New York Times,* July 14, 1997.

36. John Collis, *Educational Malpractice* (Charlottesville, VA: Michie Co., 1990), p. xvii.

37. Collis, *Educational Malpractice,* p. 455.

38. House Committee on Ways and Means, *Abuses and Mismanagement in U.S. Customs Service Commercial Operations,* February 8, 1990 (Washington: Government Printing Office, 1990), p. 39.

39. James Bovard, "Customs Service's Chain Saw Massacre," *Wall Street Journal,* March 27, 1992.

40. *Winstar v. United States,* 25 Cl. Ct. 541 (1992).

41. Brief for the Petitioner (U.S. government), U.S. v. Winstar, Supreme Court case no. 95-865, March 1, 1996.

42. Ibid.

43. *U.S. v. Winstar,* 518 U.S. 839 (1996).

44. Jerry Knight, "Judge Rules Against U.S. in S&L Damages Case," *Washington Post,* December 23, 1997.

45. Angela Martin, "The Discretionary Function Exemption Returns Sovereign Immunity to the Throne," *Creighton Law Review,* vol. 28, December 1994, p. 247.

46. Davis, *Administrative Law Treatise,* vol. 3, p. 469.

47. Martin Schwartz, "Bivens Revisited: Slip, Sliding Away," *New York Law Journal,* November 21, 1989, p. 3.

48. Ibid.

49. Ibid.

50. Stuart Taylor, "High Court Bars Suits by Those in the Military," *New York Times,* June 26, 1987.

51. *Bivens v. Six Unknown Named Agents of Federal Bureau of Narcotics,* 403 U.S. 388 (1971).

52. Ibid.

53. Perry M. Rosen, "The Bivens Constitutional Tort: An Unfulfilled Promise," *North Carolina Law Review,* vol. 67, January 1989, pp. 337 and 343.

54. Sandra Bandes, "Reinventing Bivens: The Self-Executing Constitution," *Southern California Law Review,* vol. 68, January 1995, p. 289.

55. Quoted in William R. Hartl, "Sovereign Immunity: An Outdated Doctrine Faces Demise in a Changing Judicial Arena," *North Dakota Law Review,* vol. 69, 1993, p. 401.

56. Janelle Greenberg, "Our Grand Maxim of State, 'The King Can Do No Wrong,'" *History of Political Thought,* vol. 12, summer 1991, p. 226.

57. "East Germany is Expelling Critics, *New York Times,* September 24, 1977, p. 1.

58. Stephen Pelletiere, *The Iran-Iraq War: Chaos in a Vacuum* (New York: Praeger, 1992), p. 41.

59. Edgar O'Balance, *The Gulf War* (London: Brassley's Defense Publishers, 1988), p. 79.

60. Quoted in Walter McDougall, "Back to Bedrock: The Eight Traditions of American Statecraft," *Foreign Affairs,* March/April 1997, p. 134.

61. Quoted in Editorial, "Humbled, and Proud of It," *Washington Times,* April 16, 1995.

62.	Quoted in John Berlau, "War Planners Carried Out Strategy of Lies, Deception," *Insight,* June 9, 1997, p. 14.

63.	H.R. McMaster, *Dereliction of Duty* (New York: HarperCollins, 1997), p. 309.

64.	"McNamara Defends his Failure to Resign," *Memphis Commercial Appeal,* April 18, 1995.

65.	"In Retrospect," MacNeil/Lehrer Newshour, April 17, 1995, Transcript no. 5207.

66.	Anthony Lewis, "Guilt for Vietnam," *New York Times,* May 30, 1994.

67.	Samuel T. Dickens, "Robert McNamara's War," *Washington Times,* April 24, 1995.

68.	Editorial, "Tough Cops, Thin Skin," *New York Times,* November 22, 1997.

69.	David Kocieniewski, "In Brutality Case, Penalty Was Lost Vacation," *New York Times,* April 23, 1998.

70.	Deborah Sontag and Dan Barry, "Challenge to Authority: Disrespect as Catalyst for Brutality," *New York Times,* November 19, 1997.

71.	Dan Barry and Deborah Sontag, "Safir Has Dismissed 106 Officers, 8 for Brutality," *New York Times,* October 6, 1997.

72.	Roberto Suro and Cheryl Thompson, "Group Says Police Abuses Persist Because of Lack of Prosecution," *Washington Post,* July 8, 1998.

73.	*Interstate Transit Lines v. Commissioner,* 319 U.S. 590, 593 (1943).

74.	*U.S. v. Carlton,* 512 U.S. 26, 33 (1994).

75.	*Congressional Record,* August 5, 1994, p. H4993.

76.	Marilyn Werber, "Pennsylvanian Congressmen Speak Out Against Steel Imports," *American Metal Market,* February 18, 1988.

77.	*Congressional Record,* October 10, 1985, p. H8647.

78.	Helen Dewar, "Chafee Pushes Handgun Confiscation," *Washington Post,* June 2, 1992.

79.	*Congressional Record,* February 13, 1997, p. H 585.

80.	*U.S. v. Lopez,* 514 U.S. 549, 602 (1995).

81.	Frederick S. Calhoun, "A Brief History of Federal Firearms Enforcement," in *U.S. Department of the Treasury, Bureau of Alcohol, Tobacco, and Firearms Investigation of Vernon Wayne Howell also known as David Koresh* (Washington: Government Printing Office, 1993), p. g-7.

82.	Robert J. Cottrol, "The Gun Control Debate: The Overlooked Civil Rights Dimension," paper presented at American Shooting Sports Council conference, October 18, 1997, Washington.

83.	See Jay Simkin and Aaron Zelman, *Gun Control: Gateway to Tyranny* (Milwaukee: Jews for the Preservation of Firearms, 1994).

84.	Stephen Holmes, *Passions and Constraint: On the Theory of Liberal Democracy* (Chicago: University of Chicago Press, 1995), p. 38.

85.	John Locke, *Two Treatises of Government* (New York: Cambridge University Press, 1960), p. 437.

86.	John Lott, *More Guns, Less Crime: Understanding Crime and Gun Control Laws* (Chicago: University of Chicago Press, 1998), p. 159.

87.	Locke, *Two Treatises of Government,* p. 320.

88.	John Trenchard and Thomas Gordon, *Cato's Letters; or Essays on Liberty, Civil and Religious, and Other Important Subjects,* vol. 2 (1733; reprinted, New York: Russell and Russell, 1969), p. 249. This quote is from an essay dated January 20, 1721.

89.	John Phillip Reid, *The Concept of Liberty in the Age of the American Revolution* (Chicago: University of Chicago Press, 1988), p. 53.

90.	Nicholas Kittrie and Eldon Wedlock, eds., *The Tree of Liberty: A Documentary History of Rebellion and Political Crime in America,* vol. 1 (Baltimore: Johns Hopkins University, 1998), p. 50.

91.	Quoted in Jack Rakove, "James Madison and the Bill of Rights: A Broader Context," *Presidential Studies Quarterly,* vol. 23, Fall 1992, p. 669.

92.	Reid, *The Concept of Liberty,* p. 97.

93. Benedict de Spinoza, *A Theologico-Political Treatise and A Political Treatise* (New York: Dover, 1951), p. 206.

94. Quoted in Arthur Lionel Smith, "English Political Philosophy in the Seventeenth and Eighteenth Centuries," in *Cambridge Modern History*, vol. 6, p. 802.

95. Quoted in Hans Kelsen, *What is Justice?* (Berkeley: University of California, 1971), p. 23.

96. William Tucker, *The Excluded Americans* (Washington: Regnery Gateway, 1990), pp. 152-166, 253 et seq.

97. Randy Kennedy, "Many Tenants Are Struggling to Pay Rent," *New York Times*, September 8, 1997.

98. Peter Salins, "Untangling New York's Housing Web," *New York Times*, October 27, 1996.

99. G. Edward Schuh, "The Costs of PIK," unpublished essay, University of Minnesota, April 1983.

100. "The Nixon Tapes Unleashed—Manipulative Master Politician," *Seattle Times*, November 9, 1997.

101. See James Bovard, "This Farm Program is Just Plain Nuts," *Wall Street Journal*, August 30, 1995, and James Bovard, "Trade Nuttiness," *Wall Street Journal*, December 13, 1990.

102. Donald Pevsner, "It's Time to Stop Poking Along at 55," *New York Times*, September 29, 1991.

103. Letter from Jim Baxter of the National Motorists Association to author, May 7, 1998.

104. Charles Lave and Patrick Elias, "Resource Allocation in Public Policy: the Effects of the 65-mph Speed Limit," *Economic Inquiry*, July 1997, p. 614.

105. George Will, "Why Speed Doesn't Always Kill," *Washington Post*, November 6, 1997.

106. Dan Beyers, "Montgomery to Review Record on Expulsions," *Washington Post*, June 17, 1997.

107. Fred Barnes, "Bauer Power," *Weekly Standard*, December 22, 1997.

108. Rich Karlgaard, "Slouching toward Phoenix; Dark Ages II Conference," *Reason*, April 1997, p. 37.

109. Doug Bandow, "Demagogic Politics," Copley News Service, October 14, 1997.

110. Department of Justice, "Almost 19,000 State, Local Law Officers Fight Drugs Full Time," U.S. Newswire, May 7, 1992.

111. Bruce Benson and David Rasmussen, "Illicit Drugs and Crime," Independence Institute, 1996.

112. Department of Justice, "Almost a Third of All Convicted State Felons were Sentenced for Drug Trafficking or Possession," press release, January 12, 1997.

113. Stuart Taylor, Jr., "How a Racist Drug War Swells Crime," *Legal Times*, February 22, 1993.

114. Interview with U.S. Sentencing Commission official who wished to remain anonymous, May 23, 1997.

115. For examples of cases of disparities between drug offenders and violent criminals, see James Bovard, "Time Out for Justice," *Playboy*, December 1997, p. 54.

116. Robert D. Hershey, Jr., "Obeying the Tax Laws: Small Business Burden," *New York Times*, January 30, 1994.

117. "Testimony of James Woehlke for the New York State Society of Certified Public Accountants before the U.S. Senate Finance Committee, September 23, 1997," *Tax Notes Today*, September 24, 1997.

118. "Tax Notes," *Wall Street Journal*, March 29, 1995.

119. Steven Duke and Albert Gross, *America's Longest War* (New York: Putnam, 1993), p. 178.

120. Bertrand de Jouvenel, *Sovereignty* (Chicago: University of Chicago Press, 1957), p. 37.

121. House Post Office and Civil Service Committee, *Implementation of New First-Class Mail Delivery Standards*, September 27, 1990 (Washington, D.C.: Government Printing Office, 1990), p. 1.

122. The Postal Service investigated 17 companies for possible violations of its monopoly in 1993. Interview with Postal Service spokesman Lou Eberhard, September 29, 1993.

123. Chester Finn, "Why America Has The World's Dimmest Bright Kids," *Wall Street Journal,* February 25, 1998.

124. For further information on this topic, see Sheldon Richman, *Separating School and State* (Fairfax, VA: Future of Freedom Foundation, 1994).

125. David Field, "Facing Up to a Midlife Crisis," *Washington Times,* June 23, 1996.

126. Eric Peters, "Fuel Tax Fakery by Design," *Washington Times,* December 30, 1997.

127. Gabriel Roth, "How to Solve Our Highway Problems," *Consumers' Research,* June 1997, p. 10.

128. Alice Reid, "Area's Gridlock Still 2nd Worst in Nation," *Washington Post,* October 22, 1997.

129. Gabriel Roth, Letter to the Editor, *Weekly Standard,* May 11, 1998.

130. Jim Keary, "D.C. Closes Few Robbery, Burglary, Theft Cases," *Washington Times,* October 20, 1997.

131. Hamil Harris and Vanessa Williams, "D.C. Council Targets Prostitution," *Washington Post,* July 8, 1998.

132. Don Kates and Gary Kleck, *The Great American Gun Debate* (San Francisco: Pacific Research Institute, 1997), p. 181.

133. Editorial, "The 'Social Work' Military." *Orange County Register,* August 5, 1997.

134. Editorial, "Stay on Alert," *Wall Street Journal,* January 20, 1998; see also, Melanie Kirkpatrick, "What's Blocking Missile Defense? A Defunct Treaty," *Wall Street Journal,* August 3, 1998.

135. Barry Meier, "States and Cities Impose New Laws on Young Smokers," *New York Times,* December 7, 1997.

136. Richard Berman, "Anti-Smoking: The Outer Limits," *Washington Times,* October 28, 1996.

137. Stanley Benn, "The Uses of 'Sovereignty,'" in Anthony Quinton, editor, *Political Philosophy* (Oxford: Oxford University, 1967), p. 67.

138. Stephen Holmes, *Passions & Constraint: On the Theory of Liberal Democracy* (Chicago: University of Chicago, 1995), p. 103 and 104.

139. Sir Robert Filmer, *Patriarcha and Other Political Works* (Oxford: Basil Blackwell 1949), p. 320.

140. Thomas Hobbes, *Leviathan* (London: Penguin, 1974), p. 230.

141. William Archibald Dunning, *A History of Political Theories from Rousseau to Spencer* (New York: Macmillan, 1936 (first published in 1920), p. 21.

142. Bertrand de Jouvenel, *On Power: The Natural History of its Growth* (Indianapolis: Liberty Fund Press, 1993), p. 41 and 43.

143. Edward Corwin, *The "Higher Law" Background of American Constitutional Law* (Ithaca: Cornell University, 1955), p. 79.

144. Jean Bethke Elshtain, "Sovereign God, Sovereign State, Sovereign Self," *Notre Dame Law Review,* 1991, vol. 66, p. 1373.

145. Chisholm v. Georgia, 2 U.S. 419, 471-72 (1793).

146. Nixon v. Sirica, 487 F.2d 700, 711, October 12, 1973.

147. Gordon Wood, *The Radicalism of the American Revolution* (New York: Random House, 1993), p. 165-66.

148. Locke, *Two Treatises of Government,* p. 467.

149. Ibid., p. 432.

150. John Taylor, *Tyranny Unmasked* (1822; reprint, Indianapolis: Liberty Fund, 1992), p. 134.

151. Richard Perry, ed., *Sources of Our Liberties: Documentary Origins of Individual Liberties in the U.S. Constitution* (New York: American Bar Foundation, 1959), p. 383.

152. Interview with Joyce Lee Malcolm, August 5, 1998.

153. Interview with Joyce Lee Malcolm, August 5, 1998.

154. Quoted in Stephen Holmes, *Passions & Constraint: On the Theory of Liberal Democracy* (Chicago: University of Chicago, 1995), p. 132.

155. Robert J. Cottrol and Raymond T. Diamond, "The Second Amendment: Toward an Afro-Americanist Reconsideration," *Georgetown Law Journal,* vol. 80, December 1991, p. 309.

156. For an excellent book on the potential of nonviolence, see Gene Sharp, *The Politics of Nonviolent Action* (Boston: Porter Sargent, 1973). For an excellent survey of the historical development of nonviolent resistance, see Bryan Caplan, "The Literature of Nonviolent Resistance and Civilian-Based Defense," *Humane Studies Review,* vol. 9, no. 1, Summer 1994.

157. Etienne de la Boetie, Murray Rothbard, ed., *The Discourse of Voluntary Servitude* (New York: Free Life Editions, 1975), p. 50.

158. Thomas Babington Macaulay, "Nares's Memoirs of Lord Burghley," in *Critical and Miscellaneous Essays,* vol. 2, (Philadelphia: Carey & Hart, 1842), p. 115

159. Locke, *Two Treatises of Government,* p. 460.

160. Joyce Lee Malcolm, *To Keep and Bear Arms: The Origins of an Anglo-American Right* (Cambridge: Harvard University Press, 1994). For a superb analysis of the thinking of the Founding Fathers, see Stephen Halbrook, *That Every Man Be Armed: The Evolution of a Constitutional Right* (1984; reprint, Oakland, CA: Independent Institute, 1994).

161. Hannah Arendt, *Between Past and Future* (New York: Penguin, 1968), p. 165.

CHAPTER 7

1. Tacitus, *Complete Works of Tacitus* (New York: Modern Library, 1942), p. 115. (This quote is from *The Annals* 3.25, referring to A.D. 20-22.)

2. Robert Conquest, *The Harvest of Sorrow* (New York: Oxford University Press, 1986), p. 92.

3. Quoted in Donald VanDeVeer, *Paternalistic Intervention* (Princeton: Princeton University Press, 1986), p. 24.

4. Ibid., p. 3.

5. Quoted in Anthony Flew, *The Politics of Procrustes: Contradictions of Enforced Equality* (Buffalo: Prometheus Books, 1981), p. 91.

6. Tom G. Palmer, "The Literature of Liberty," ed. David Boaz, *The Libertarian Reader* (New York: Free Press, 1997), p. 443.

7. B.C. Forbes, "Thoughts on the Business Life," *Forbes,* May 16, 1988.

8. *The Public Papers and Addresses of Franklin D. Roosevelt, 1936* (New York: Random House, 1938), p. 235.

9. As Kant wrote: "An act of generosity is permissible only if it does not violate anybody's right; if it does, it is morally wrong." Donald VanDeVeer, *Paternalistic Intervention,* p. 95.

10. "Government, Rights, Mood," Public Opinion Online, March 8, 1996.

11. Baron de Montesquieu, *The Spirit of the Laws* (New York: Hafner, 1949), p. 26.

12. Office of Sen. William Roth, "Committee to Take Unprecedented Look at the IRS," Congressional Press Releases, Federal Document Clearing House, September 11, 1997.

13. Quoted in Isaiah Berlin, *Four Essays on Liberty* (New York: Oxford University Press, 1969), p. 137.

14. Conquest, *Harvest of Sorrow,* p. 19-20.

15. Martin Anderson, *The Federal Bulldozer* (Cambridge: MIT Press, 1964).

16. Harold Laski, *Liberty in the Modern State* (1930; reprinted, Clifton, NJ: Augustus Kelley Publishers, 1972), p. 145

17. Ludwig von Mises, *Socialism* (1922; reprint, Indianapolis: Liberty Fund Press, 1981).

18. *Hoffman Homes, Inc. v. Administrator, United States Environmental Protection Agency,* 1992 U.S. App. LEXIS 7329, April 20, 1992.

19. The phrase "welfare receptacle" is from VanDeVeer, *Paternalistic Intervention,* p. 424— but it is used in this sentence in a way that he might disagree with.

20. Hans Kelsen, *What is Justice?* (Berkeley: University of California Press, 1971), p. 3.

21. Blandine Kriegel, *The State and the Rule of Law* (Princeton: Princeton University Press, 1995), p. 140.

22. "Prepared Statement of Dennis Schindel, Assistant Inspector General for Audit, Office of Inspector General, Department of the Treasury before the House Ways and Means Committee, Subcommittee on Trade," Federal News Service, April 30, 1998. For further discussion of this curious policy, see James Bovard, "Good Enough for Government Work," *American Spectator,* September 1998.

23. Poll conducted for the Council for Excellence in Government, "Public Opinion Online," accession no. 0236536, 1995.

24. Keith Halpern, "Citizens to Government: Stop Holding Me Back," *New Democrat,* July-August, 1995, p. 4. (This poll result must be taken in light of the fact, discussed in the Democracy chapter, that people sharply underestimate the amount of taxes that they themselves are paying. With a more accurate recognition of their own tax burden, significantly more people would feel like the current government was giving them a bad deal).

25. Ibid.

26. "Transcript of Clinton Remarks at Luncheon for Sen. Boxer," U.S. Newswire, June 23, 1997.

27. Michael Sandel, *Democracy's Discontent: America in Search of a Public Philosophy* (Cambridge: Harvard University Press, 1996), p. 333-334.

28. Ibid., p. 279. Despite the Supreme Court ruling a half century ago that children cannot be forced to pledge allegiance, school systems around the country continue "cultivating virtue" by commanding such pledges. A 1997 Connecticut lawsuit detailed the plight of one high school student who was repeatedly sent to the principal's office and prevented from joining the National Honor society as penalties for refusing to stand and recite the pledge each day. Nat Hentoff, "Pledging Allegiance to the Constitution," *Washington Post,* August 23, 1997.

29. Quoted in Melvyn Krauss, *How Nations Grow Rich* (New York: Oxford University Press, 1997), p. 85.

30. See Doug Bandow and Ian Vasquez, eds., *Perpetuating Poverty* (Washington: Cato Institute, 1994).

31. Bruce Bartlett, "Fantasies about Foreign Aid," *Washington Times,* July 14, 1997.

32. Ibid.

33. George Ayittey, "African Thugs Keep Their Continent Poor," *Wall Street Journal,* January 2, 1998.

34. Ibid.

35. For a masterful analysis of the history of bureaucratic failure and inherent incompetence of bureaucracies, see Gordon Tullock, *The Politics of Bureaucracy* (Washington: Public Affairs Press, 1965).

36. Cindy Skrzycki, "When It Comes to Bike Lights, Not Everyone is Beaming," *Washington Post,* July 19, 1996.

37. "Up in Smoke," CBS News Transcripts, March 27, 1994.

38. Lois Romano, "The Reliable Source," *Washington Post,* May 26, 1994.

39. Ibid. This statement was excerpted from Dawson's testimony to the House Subcommittee on Commerce, Trade and Hazardous Materials, March 29, 1996.

40. Quoted in *Consumer Product Safety Commission Monitor,* published by Consumer Alert, November 11, 1996.

41. Sharon Walsh, "Drive-By Warning," *Washington Post,* October 29, 1993.

42. Sally Beatty and John Simons, "FTC Eyes Liquor Ads' Kid-Appeal, Forces Companies to Yank Ads," *Wall Street Journal,* August 7, 1998.

43. Robert Higgs, "Tobacco's Show Trial," *Liberty,* September 1997, pp. 43-45.

44. Robert Goldberg, "The Kessler Legacy at FDA," Institute for Policy Innovation, January 1997. (The quote is originally from a 1992 article by Kessler in the *New England Journal of Medicine*.)

45. Editorial, "A Dangerous FDA," *Orange County Register*, August 30, 1991.

46. Quoted in Doug Bandow, "The FDA Can be Dangerous to Your Health," *Fortune*, November 11, 1996, p. 56.

47. Arthur Allen Leff, "Unconscionability and the Code: The Emperor's New Clause," *University of Pennsylvania Law Review*, 1967, vol. 115, p. 557.

48. A. V. Dicey, *Lectures on the Relation Between Law and Public Opinion in England During the Nineteenth Century* (1905; reprint, London: Macmillan, 1952), p. 262.

49. Editorial, "Medicare Showstopper," *Wall Street Journal*, August 22, 1997.

50. Ibid.

51. Amy Goldstein, "U.S. Will Pay To Reduce Doctor Glut," *Washington Post*, August 24 1997.

52. Steve Twomey, "A Doting Uncle One 'Victim' Didn't Need," *Washington Post*, October 22, 1997.

53. James Bovard, "FEMA Money! Come and Get It! Reinventing Disaster," *American Spectator*, September, 1996.

54. National Research Council, *Youth Employment and Training Programs* (Washington: National Academy Press, 1985), p. 177.

55. General Accounting Office, "Multiple Employment Training Programs: Most Federal Agencies Do Not Know if Their Programs Are Working Effectively," April 8, 1994. For further details on the history of failed federal training programs, see James Bovard, "Clinton's Summer Jobs Sham," *Wall Street Journal*, March 5, 1993.

56. George Orwell, *The Orwell Reader* (New York: Harcourt, Brace, Jovanovich, 1956), p. 366.

57. Ruth W. Grant, *Hypocrisy and Integrity* (Chicago: University of Chicago Press, 1997), p. 2.

58. William Graham Sumner, *Protectionism* (New York: Henry Holt & Co., 1888), p. 31.

59. Henry George, *Protection or Free Trade* (1886; reprint, New York: Robert Schalkenbach Foundation, 1966), p. 35.

60. Joseph, M. Jones, *Tariff Retaliation* (Philadelphia: University of Pennsylvania Press, 1934), p. 12.

61. Jagdish Bhagwati, *A Stream of Windows: Unsettling Reflections on Trade, Immigration, and Democracy* (Cambridge: MIT Press, 1998).

62. Dave Larsons, "The Cost of Import Protection in the United States," U.S. Treasury Department, 1979; cited in Michael Finger, H. Keith Hall, and Douglas Nelson, "The Political Economy of Administrative Protectionism," *American Economic Review*, June 1982, p. 453.

63. David Tarr and Morris Morkre, "Aggregate Cost to the United States of Tariffs and Quotas on Imports," Federal Trade Commission, 1984.

64. Martin Wolf, "Why Voluntary Export Restraints? An Historical Analysis," *World Economy*, September 1989, p. 284.

65. Rob Quartel, "The Jones Act? Gimme a Break," *Journal of Commerce*, October 8, 1991.

66. The General Accounting Office issued a comprehensive report on government assets and liabilities in 1998—and curiously left Social Security obligations out of the liabilities. A *New York Times* article noted, "A footnote in a draft portion of the report released Monday notes that after 2029, the Social Security trust fund will be 'totally exhausted' and 'current tax income will be sufficient to pay approximately 75 percent of the benefits due.' But that is not really a liability, the administration's accounting experts explained Monday, because technically the government owes the money to itself, not the pensioners, and because Congress is free to change the amount paid Social Security recipients. After thinking about the political implications of that statement, however, more politically sensitive administration officials called reporters late Monday to stress that the government did not really have plans to cut back on Social Security payments. 'It's an accounting device,' one official said.

'That's all it is.'" David Sanger, "Glitches Galore Pop Up in Full Audit of Government," *New York Times,* March 31, 1998.

67. Martha Derthick, *Policymaking for Social Security* (Washington: Brookings Institution, 1979), p. 232.

68. Two classic books on this topic are Dillard Stokes, *Social Security—Fact and Fancy* (Chicago: Henry Regnery, 1956) and Abraham Ellis, *The Social Security Fraud* (1971; reprint, Irvington-on-Hudson, NY: Foundation for Economic Education, 1996).

69. "Outgoing Social Security Head Assails 'Myths' of System and Says It Favors the Poor," *New York Times* December 2, 1979.

70. Pat Wechsler, "Will Social Security Be There for You?" *Newsday,* January 14, 1990.

71. Michael McKee, "Success Led to Program Problems," *Cleveland Plain Dealer,* January 11, 1997.

72. Martin Feldstein, "Economics: His Defense," *New York Times,* October 5, 1980.

73. Jake Hansen, "Medicare's Dire Outlook," *Washington Times,* June 3, 1995.

74. James Glassman, "No-Account Government," *Washington Post,* April 21, 1998.

75. Editorial, "What the GAO Found—or Didn't Find," *Washington Times,* April 3, 1998.

76. Editorial, "What the GAO Found—or Didn't Find," *Washington Times,* April 3, 1998.

77. "First Government Audit Completed," Associated Press, March 30, 1998.

78. House Commerce Committee, *Survey of Federal Agencies on Costs of Federal Regulations,* House Report 97-H-272-1, January 1997.

79. Ibid.

80. Eric Foner, Review of *Democracy's Discontent* by Michael Sandel, *Nation,* May 6, 1996.

81. Michael Lerner, *The Politics of Meaning* (New York: Addison-Wesley, 1996), p. 97.

82. William Wong, "America May be Ripe for Idea of 'Communitarianism,'" *Austin American-Statesman,* June 10, 1996.

83. David Kopel and Christopher Little, "Communitarians, Neorepublicans, and Guns: Assessing the Case for Firearms Prohibition," *Maryland Law Review,* vol. 56, March 1997, p. 438.

84. Amitai Etzioni, *The New Golden Rule: Community and Morality in a Democratic Society* (New York: Basic Books, 1996), p. 39. Etzioni warned: "American society in the 1980s was slipping in [the direction of anarchy]; although it stayed within the communitarian pattern, it was not quite far from its edge." Ibid., p. 46.

85. Sandel, *Democracy's Discontent,* p. 323.

86. Quoted in Irving Kristol, *Two Cheers for Capitalism* (New York: Basic Books, 1978), p. 179. Dworkin also declared: "We must take care not to use the Equal Protection Clause to cheat ourselves of equality." Ronald Dworkin, *Taking Rights Seriously* (Cambridge: Harvard University Press, 1977), p. 239.

87. Quoted in Ward E. Y. Elliot, *The Rise of Guardian Democracy* (Cambridge: Harvard University Press, 1974), p. 29.

88. Tamar Lewin, "Uneven School-Financing Systems Under Fire Nationwide," *New York Times,* April 8, 1998.

89. Amity Shlaes, "Vermont Levels Its Schools," *Wall Street Journal,* April 22, 1998.

90. Al Gore, *Earth in the Balance* (New York: Houghton Mifflin, 1992), p. 277.

91. As author Eugene Meyer observed, "If rights and duties are made directly dependent one upon the other, they cease to be rights or duties. Losing their moral autonomy, rights become privileges dispensed to the individual by society or the state, and duties become obedience extorted by power as a payment for privileges. Meyer, *In Defense of Freedom* (Chicago: Henry Regnery, 1962), p. 72.

92. Dan Balz, "Wanted: Policies on a Shoestring," *Washington Post,* November 9, 1997.

93. Herbert Spencer, *The Man versus the State* (1884; reprint, Baltimore, MD: Penguin, 1969), pp. 134-35.

94. According to the Organization for Economic Co-operation and Development (OECD), government policies in the leading 24 industrial countries inflated the price of food for

consumers in those countries by $95 billion during 1996; in addition, taxpayers provided $166 billion in subsidies to agriculture in the same year. Government research has contributed to some breakthroughs in agricultural productivity, but politicians have worked overtime to insure that citizens do not reap benefits from their tax-financed research. Organization for Economic Co-operation and Development, *Agricultural Policies in OECD Countries: Measurement of Support and Background Information 1997* (Paris: Organization for Economic Co-Operation and Development, 1997), pp. 31-32.

95. Alan Riding, "Communism and Crimes: French Bristle at Best-Seller," *New York Times,* November 21, 1997.

96. R. J. Rummel, *Death by Government* (New Brunswick, NJ: Transaction, 1994), p. 9.

97. Gerald W. Scully, "Murder by the State," National Center for Policy Analysis report No. 211, September 1997.

98. James Bovard, "Big Government's Big Lobby," *American Spectator,* February 1998.

99. Interview with Lee Herring, November 19, 1997.

100. Gottfried Haberler, "Schumpeter's Capitalism, Socialism and Democracy after 40 years," in Arnold Heertje, ed., *Schumpeter's Vision* (New York: Praeger, 1981), p. 88.

101. "On average, government expenditures in 1995 consumed only 20% of GDP in the five economies with the most rapid real economic growth rates during 1980-95: Hong Kong, Singapore, South Korea, Taiwan and Thailand. In these countries, the size of government in 1995 was virtually the same as in 1975." James Gwartney, "Less Government, More Growth," *Wall Street Journal,* April 10, 1998.

102. Ibid.

103. Tiffany Danitz and Jennifer Hickey, "Regulation Kills," *Washington Times,* September 22, 1997.

104. Ludwig von Mises, *Bureaucracy* (New Rochelle, NY: Arlington House, 1969), p. 68.

105. "Playboy Interview: Scott Adams," *Playboy,* May 1998, p. 151.

106. Henry David Thoreau, *The Portable Thoreau* (New York: Viking, 1964), p. 325.

107. Ibid., p. 325.

108. Ralph Waldo Emerson, *Essays* (New York: Thomas Crowell, 1951), p. 55.

109. Julian Simon, *The Ultimate Resource* (Princeton: Princeton University, 1981).

110. Aleksandr Solzhenitsyn, *The Gulag Archipelago* (New York: Harper & Row, 1973), pp. 392-4.

111. Friedrich Hayek, *Law, Legislation and Liberty,* vol. 1., *Rules & Order* (Chicago: University of Chicago Press, 1973), p. 56.

112. *Philosophical Writings of Pierce,* ed. by Justus Buchler (New York: Dover, 1955), p. 271.

113. William James, *Essays in Pragmatism* (New York: Hafner, 1948), p. 147.

114. Friedrich Nietzsche, *Thus Spoke Zarathustra* (Baltimore: Penguin, 1969), p. 137.

115. John Stuart Mill, *Utilitarianism, Liberty, and Representative Government* (New York: E.P. Dutton, 1951), p. 94.

116. Ibid., p 95.

117. Sumner, *Protectionism,* p. 62.

CHAPTER 8

1. Ruth W. Grant, *John Locke's Liberalism* (Chicago: University of Chicago Press, 1987), p. 203. For another excellent analysis of the contemporary relevance of Locke's writing, see A. John Simmons, *On The Edge of Anarchy: Locke, Consent, and the Limits of Society* (Princeton: Princeton University Press, 1993).

2. Quoted in Thomas B. McAffee, "The Federal System as Bill of Rights: Original Misunderstandings, Modern Misreadings," *Villanova Law Review,* vol. 43 (1998), p. 117.

3. A. V. Dicey, *Introduction to the Study of the Law of the Constitution* (1885; reprint, Indianapolis: Liberty Fund Press, 1982), p. 110 and 120. Dicey also specified that the Rule

of Law in Britain meant that "the constitution is pervaded by the rule of law on the ground that the general principles of the constitution . . . are with us the result of judicial decisions determining the rights of private persons in particular cases brought before the Courts. . . ." Ibid., p. 115.

4. For a good analysis of the limits of the Rule of Law, see Ronald Hamowy, "Hayek's Concept of Freedom: A Critique," *New Individualist Review,* vol. 1, April 1961, p. 28.

5. Rodolphe J.A. de Seife, "The King is Dead, Long Live the King!" *Hofstra Law Review,* vol. 24, summer 1996, p. 1021.

6. *National Party Platforms,* vol. 1, 1840-1956 (Urbana: University of Illinois Press, 1978), p. 66.

7. *Compania General de Tabacos de Filipinas v. Collector,* 275 U.S. 87, 100 (1927).

8. Quoted in James W. Ely, Jr., *The Guardian of Every Other Right* (New York: Oxford University Press, 1992), p. 28.

9. James Glassman, "The Surplus: Cheer and Fear," *Washington Post,* October 13, 1998.

10. See Guy Gugliotta, "Redoubled Effort Targets Derelict Public Housing," *Washington Post,* May 31, 1996.

11. Friedrich Hayek, *Choice in Currency: a Way to Stop Inflation* (London: Institute of Economic Affairs, 1976).

12. Quoted in George Kennan, *Memoirs,* vol. 2 (Boston: Little, Brown, 1972), p. 173.

13. See for instance, Robert Pear, "U.S. Revises Plan to Aid Opposition in Nicaragua Vote," *New York Times,* September 22, 1989.

14. See Marvin Olasky, *The Tragedy of American Compassion* (Washington: Regnery Gateway, 1992).

15. Richard Epstein, *Takings: Private Property and the Power of Eminent Domain* (Cambridge: Harvard University Press, 1985), p. 321.

16. Bertrand de Jouvenal, *The Ethics of Redistribution* (1950; reprint, Indianapolis: Liberty Fund Press, 1989), p. 73.

17. Lysander Spooner, *The Lysander Spooner Reader* (San Francisco: Fox & Wilkes, 1992), p. 23.

18. Hamil R. Harris and Vanessa Williams, "D.C. Council Targets Prostitution; Emergency Law Gives Police Wider Power to Make Arrests," *Washington Post,* July 8, 1998.

19. See Dana Mack, *The Assault on Parenthood: How Our Culture Undermines the Family* (New York: Simon & Schuster, 1997).

20. Rick Weiss, "Study Faults the Way NIH Sets Budget Priorities; Political Pressure to Combat 'Pet' Diseases Cited as Influence on Funding Decisions," *Washington Post,* July 9, 1998.

21. Benjamin Constant, *Political Writings* (Cambridge: Cambridge University Press, 1988), p. 176.

CHAPTER 9

1. Thomas Hobbes, *Leviathan* (London: Penguin, 1974), p. 317.

2. H. L. Mencken, *Treatise on Right and Wrong* (New York: Knopf, 1934), p. 317.

3. Paul Johnson, *Modern Times* (New York: Harper & Row, 1983), p. 284.

4. As Hannah Arendt observed of the Third Reich, "Nothing proved easier to destroy than the privacy and private morality of people who thought of nothing but safeguarding their private lives." Arendt, *Totalitarianism,* (New York, Harcourt, Brace, and World, 1951) p. 36.

5. Gordon Wood, *The Radicalism of the American Revolution* (New York: Random House, 1993), pp. 165-66.

INDEX